Black Soldiers in the Rhodesian Army

During Zimbabwe's war of liberation (1965–80), fought between Zimbabwean nationalists and the minority-white Rhodesian settler-colonial regime, thousands of black soldiers volunteered for and served in the Rhodesian Army. This seeming paradox has often been noted by scholars and military researchers, yet little has been heard from black Rhodesian veterans themselves. Drawing from original interviews with black Rhodesian veterans and extensive archival research, M. T. Howard tackles the question of why so many black soldiers fought steadfastly and effectively for the Rhodesian Army, demonstrating that they felt loyalty to their comrades and regiments and not the Smith regime. Howard also shows that units in which black soldiers served – particularly the Rhodesian African Rifles – were fundamental to the Rhodesian counter-insurgency campaign. Highlighting the pivotal role black Rhodesian veterans played during both the war and the tumultuous early years of independence, this is a crucial contribution to the study of Zimbabwean decolonisation.

M. T. Howard is a historian and journalist from East Sussex and holds a master's and a doctorate from the University of Oxford, where he won the Terence Ranger Prize. He also received the Society for Military History's 2021 Coffman Prize honourable mention. His work has been published in journals including the *Journal of Military History*, the *Journal of Southern African Studies*, and the *Journal of Cold War Studies*.

African Studies Series

The African Studies series, founded in 1968, is a prestigious series of monographs, general surveys, and textbooks on Africa covering history, political science, anthropology, economics, and ecological and environmental issues. The series seeks to publish work by senior scholars as well as the best new research.

Editorial Board:
David Anderson, *The University of Warwick*
Carolyn Brown, *Rutgers University, New Jersey*
Christopher Clapham, *University of Cambridge*
Richard L. Roberts, *Stanford University, California*
Leonardo A. Villalón, *University of Florida*

Other titles in the series are listed at the back of the book.

Black Soldiers in the Rhodesian Army

Colonialism, Professionalism, and Race

M. T. Howard
University of Oxford

Shaftesbury Road, Cambridge CB2 8EA, United Kingdom

One Liberty Plaza, 20th Floor, New York, NY 10006, USA

477 Williamstown Road, Port Melbourne, VIC 3207, Australia

314–321, 3rd Floor, Plot 3, Splendor Forum, Jasola District Centre,
New Delhi – 110025, India

103 Penang Road, #05–06/07, Visioncrest Commercial, Singapore 238467

Cambridge University Press is part of Cambridge University Press & Assessment, a department of the University of Cambridge.

We share the University's mission to contribute to society through the pursuit of education, learning and research at the highest international levels of excellence.

www.cambridge.org
Information on this title: www.cambridge.org/9781009348447

DOI: 10.1017/9781009348423

© M. T. Howard 2024

This publication is in copyright. Subject to statutory exception and to the provisions of relevant collective licensing agreements, no reproduction of any part may take place without the written permission of Cambridge University Press & Assessment.

First published 2024

A catalogue record for this publication is available from the British Library.

A Cataloging-in-Publication data record for this book is available from the Library of Congress

ISBN 978-1-009-34844-7 Hardback

Cambridge University Press & Assessment has no responsibility for the persistence or accuracy of URLs for external or third-party internet websites referred to in this publication and does not guarantee that any content on such websites is, or will remain, accurate or appropriate.

This book is dedicated to my mother, Serena, an immigrant who was abandoned and left to raise three children without an income. During this time, our youngest sister, Tamzin, lost a prolonged battle with cancer. Despite these adversities, my sister Chantelle and I received a good upbringing, a testament to our mother's fortitude and bravery. It is also dedicated to Graham Warren, who selflessly and steadfastly parented us too.

The stars are dead. The animals will not look.
We are left alone with our day, and the time is short, and
History to the defeated
May say Alas but cannot help nor pardon.

W. H. Auden, *Spain 1937*.
Reproduction by kind permission of Curtis Brown, New York

Contents

List of Figures	page ix
Preface	xi
Acknowledgements	xvi

1 Introduction: The Loyalties of Colonial Soldiers   1
- Book Outline   2
- A History Misunderstood, Marginalised, and Distorted   6
- The Motivations and Loyalties of Colonial Troops   17
- Chapter Outline   49

2 The Creation of Black Rhodesian Soldiers' Regimental Loyalties   51
- The Early History of Black Troops in Rhodesia   51

3 'The Rhodesian Army Was the Best in Everything': The Professionalism of Black Rhodesian Soldiers   86
- Military Socialisation   87
- The Importance of the 'Professional' Ethos   101
- Conclusion   109

4 Racism and Soldierly Loyalty During the War   110
- Structural Racism in the Rhodesian Army   111
- The Increasing Military Importance of Black Soldiers   119
- The Integration of the Rhodesian Army   123
- 'No Second-Class Officers': The First Black Officers in Rhodesia   128
- Race and Professionalism within the RAR   134
- Conclusion   142

5 The Impact of the War upon Soldierly Loyalties   143
- The Absence of 'Disloyalty' among Black Rhodesian Troops   145
- Black Soldiers' Faith in Their Military Prowess   151
- Rhodesian Air Power Informing Black Soldiers' Perceptions of Combat   164
- Black Rhodesian Soldiers' Conception of the War's Morality   174
- Solidarities Generated by Guerrilla Targeting of Black Soldiers and Their Families   182
- Conclusion   188

viii   Contents

6 'They Just Follow the Government of the Day': The
  Politics of 'Apolitical' Black Rhodesian Soldiers   189
  Regional and Class Backgrounds As Influencing the Politics of Black
  Soldiers   190
  The Army's Policing of Politics among Black Soldiers   192
  Vested in the State: The Politics of 'Apolitical' Soldiers 197
  Contrasting Loyalties   205
  Conclusion   209

7 A New 'Government of the Day' Dawns: The Loyalties
  of 'Formers' in Zimbabwe, 1980–1981   211
  Loyalties in the Moment of Transition   213
  'That's Why They Were Loving RAR': A Marriage of Convenience 219
  Postcolonial Enforcers: The Old RAR Fight for Mugabe's Government 226
  Postlude: 'Formers' in the ZNA and 'Nostalgia' for Rhodesia 240
  Conclusion   248

Conclusion: The Loyalties of Professionals   249

Bibliography   260
Index   281

Figures*

1.1	RAR troops post-Entumbane clearing captured weapons	page 2
2.1	The RAR in Burma during World War II	57
2.2	WOII Pisayi and his Military Medal citation for gallantry in Malaya, 1957	60
2.3	Composite image of the RAR band, regimental march, and regimental Colour	75
3.1	RAR soldier with FN FAL rifle	103
4.1	Lt Tumbare presented with Lt Col. Rule's sword, 1977	129
4.2	Newly commissioned officer receiving a prize from Maj. Gen. John Hickman	132
5.1	1RAR Fireforce pre-deployment preparations	168
5.2	Composite image of A Coy 1RAR on Fireforce duty, 1978	170
7.1	A Coy, 1RAR convoy of Mine Protected Combat Vehicles (MPCVs), 1981	230
7.2	The Beer Hall at Entumbane, referred to by the RAR as 'The Alamo'	231
7.3	RAR troops with captured Chinese-origin 75mm recoilless rifles, and with mounted 106 RCLs	232
7.4	Soldiers from 3 Pl A Coy 1RAR pictured in 1981	233
7.5	RAR soldiers with a captured T34 at Brady Airfield in 1981	237
7.6	An RAR WOII poses with a T-54/55 from E Sqn RhAC in 1981	238
7.7	A former RAR soldier pictured as a captain of the ZNA Paragroup	242

---

* The author and publishers acknowledge the following sources of copyright material and are grateful for the permissions granted. While every effort has been made, it has not always been possible to identify the sources of all the material used, or to trace all copyright holders. If any omissions are brought to our notice, we will be happy to include the appropriate acknowledgements on reprinting and in the next update to the digital edition, as applicable.

Preface

Here I provide an extremely short overview of Zimbabwe's colonial past and the events leading up to, and of, its war of liberation (1965–79). It is not exhaustive or authoritative, for the history and historiography of this period remain highly contested, but it is simply intended to serve as a broad sketch for readers unfamiliar with the complex history and provide context for later discussion. Those versed in the history may wish to proceed to Chapter 1.

Zimbabwe's antecedent was the settler colony of Rhodesia, established in 1890 by the arch-imperialist Cecil Rhodes' British South Africa Company (BSAC).[1] Rhodesian settlers and administrators divided the heterogeneous African population of the country into two supposed ethnic categories: 'Shona' and 'Matabele', a gross simplification based upon the main languages spoken.[2]

Rhodesia was, as per David Fieldhouse's typology of settler colonialism, a 'mixed' settler colony, where 'settlers had encountered a resilient and sizeable indigenous population'.[3] Two early wars occurred: in 1893 between the settlers and the Ndebele kingdom, and in 1896 when Shona-speaking peoples in the east joined a swift and lethal uprising by Ndebele-speaking peoples. The white settler population was 'literally decimated',[4] its losses 'greater than the proportion of casualties suffered by white colonists in the Algerian national rising or the Mau Mau war in

---

[1] Rhodesia was initially named Zambesia. It was testament to Cecil Rhodes' rapacious sub-imperialism and propensity for extreme violence that he became 'the only European capitalist to have an African colony actually named for him' (Freund, *Making of Contemporary Africa*, p. 102).

[2] Dorman, *Understanding Zimbabwe*, p. 18; Ranger, *Revolt in Southern Rhodesia*, p. 4. Many people have both 'Shona' and 'Ndebele' ancestry. See Lindgren, 'Internal Dynamics of Ethnicity'.

[3] Fieldhouse, *Colonial Empires*, as cited in Veracini, *Settler Colonialism*, p. 5. In contrast, the 'plantation' colonies were dependent upon slavery and bondage (e.g. European colonial rule in the Caribbean from the fifteenth century to the nineteenth), and the 'pure settlement' colonies were where 'white settlers had eradicated and/or marginalised the indigenous population' (e.g. Australia, Canada).

[4] McLaughlin, *Ragtime Soldiers*, p. 73.

Kenya'.[5] But for British reinforcements – the last British troops sent to Rhodesia until 1979 – the settlers would have been defeated.

Thereafter settler authorities foregrounded internal security, reflecting the vulnerability of Rhodesia's white population, which was always tiny. It only exceeded 5 per cent of the total Rhodesian population for 'nine years from 1955 to 1964, peaking in 1961 at 5.7 per cent' – or 277,000 – and thereafter falling until the end of settler rule in 1980.[6]

Settlers speculatively based Rhodesia's early economy on gold, hoping to repeat the Witwatersrand rush. However, it came to be dominated by farming, particularly cash export crops. Land assumed paramount importance.

In 1923, BSAC rule was ended and the settlers obtained self-government as Southern Rhodesia. Although formally part of the British Empire, Southern Rhodesia was not administered from London and its government had near-total internal autonomy. Westminster never once used its constitutionally enshrined veto over Southern Rhodesian legislation pertaining to the rights of the African population.

By the onset of World War II, settlers 'had dramatically transformed the land and authority over it, creating a racially based division between freehold "European" land and the "communal" reserves'.[7] Segregationist policies were implemented and Southern Rhodesian authorities passed a great array of legislation 'to ensure an expanding supply of labour and to divide the economy into non-competing racial groups'.[8] The Land Apportionment Act of 1930 segregated the land, giving whites exclusive use of more than half of it – which included most of the best-watered and most fertile areas – and largely restricting blacks to poorer-quality and remote 'Native Reserves' and 'Native Purchase Areas'. It was implemented fully in the 1940s and 1950s, leading to large-scale evictions.[9] In 1953, British fears of the rise of the National Party in South Africa and its potential influence on Rhodesian whites prompted London to integrate Southern Rhodesia, Northern Rhodesia (Zambia), and Nyasaland (Malawi) into the Federation of Rhodesia and Nyasaland, an ersatz Dominion dominated by white political interests.

African nationalism was well established in Rhodesia by this time, particularly in the country's new industrial urban and suburban areas.[10] The Southern Rhodesian government banned all nationalist parties and

---

[5] Gann, *History of Southern Rhodesia*, pp. 9–10, as quoted in Ranger, *Revolt in Southern Rhodesia*, p. 225. See also Selous, *Sunshine and Storm in Rhodesia*, p. 250.
[6] Brownell, *Collapse of Rhodesia*, p. 5.   [7] Alexander, *Unsettled Land*, p. 39.
[8] Arrighi, 'Political Economy of Rhodesia', p. 41.
[9] Ndlovu-Gatsheni, 'Mapping Cultural and Colonial Encounters', pp. 66–7.
[10] See Scarnecchia, *Urban Roots of Democracy*.

in 1960 enacted the notorious Law and Order (Maintenance) Act, which facilitated repression on an enormous scale. Federal Chief Justice Robert Tredgold described it as removing 'the last vestige of doubt about whether Rhodesia is a police state'.[11]

The rise of African nationalism, and the consequent British policy of decolonisation signalled by Harold Macmillan's 1960 'Wind of Change' speech, rendered the Federation unviable, and it was dissolved in 1963, with Zambia and Malawi achieving their independence the next year. Southern Rhodesia's white political right coalesced around the Rhodesian Front (RF) party, founded in explicit opposition to majority rule. In its first electoral campaign of 1962, it won thirty-five out of sixty-five seats, thereafter remaining in power until 1979. Ian Smith, a boorish squire with hard-right political views, extensive links to South Africa, and storied World War II service with the Royal Air Force (RAF), took the leadership of the party in 1964, becoming the country's first Rhodesian-born prime minister.

Intent on resisting decolonisation, Smith made the infamous Unilateral Declaration of Independence (UDI) in 1965, illegally seceding from Britain. Smith's rebellion against the Crown created an unrecognised, renegade state thereafter widely known as Rhodesia, which declared itself a republic in 1970. It acquired pariah status, becoming the first recipient of mandatory economic sanctions in the history of the United Nations.[12] African nationalists concluded that 'the only way to attain majority rule in Rhodesia was through an armed struggle'.[13] This was expected by the Rhodesian government, which had commenced preparations in the mid-1950s for an internal counter-insurgency (COIN) campaign.[14]

The war for Zimbabwe commenced around this time.[15] There were two main nationalist parties, the Zimbabwe African People's Union (ZAPU) and the Zimbabwe African National Union (ZANU). The

---

[11] Harold-Barry, 'One Country, Two Nations', pp. 254–5.
[12] See Minter and Schmidt, 'When Sanctions Worked'. Rhodesia became perhaps the world's strangest case study in demonstrating the success of state-sponsored import substitution, for its economy boomed during the early UDI period. Although this growth did not last once capital inputs deteriorated and replacements could not be purchased on the open world market, the Rhodesian GDP grew 'on average an impressive 8.6 per cent annually in real terms between 1968 and 1974' (Anglin, 'Zimbabwe', p. 671).
[13] Tungamirai, 'Recruitment to ZANLA', p. 36.   [14] Melson, *Fighting for Time*, p. 19.
[15] In Zimbabwe, the war is commonly referred to as the war of liberation, which is also the term most frequently used in the scholarly literature and succinctly conveys that the conflict was fought to end the oppressive, racist, settler-colonial control of the state. I thus use this term throughout this book. However, no real consensus has been reached on the name of the war. For those aligned with ZANU, the conflict has been referred to as the Second Chimurenga, rendering it a successor to the anti-colonial uprising of 1896–7. Rhodesians named the conflict the Bush War.

former, founded in 1961, was led by Nkomo and its army was supported primarily by the Soviet Union and the Frontline States.[16]

In 1963, ZANU split from ZAPU owing to disagreements over strategy, among other things, and was led by nationalists who favoured a more militant strategy to deliver independence. It primarily drew patronage from the Frontline States and China.

The armed wing of ZAPU, named the Zimbabwe People's Revolutionary Army (ZIPRA) in 1971, was primarily based in Zambia. The Zimbabwe African National Liberation Army (ZANLA), which was formed by ZANU, largely operated from Mozambique after the early 1970s.

The availability of sanctuary in neighbouring countries was of paramount strategic importance to ZANLA and ZIPRA, as they could not hold territory within Rhodesia until the very end of the war. Mozambique and Zambia provided bases for training, organisation, and preparation for assaults into Rhodesia.[17]

Until the mid-1970s, the war was fought at a low intensity, and instances of fighting were infrequent. Inexperienced and inadequately trained guerrillas from the liberation movements suffered numerous heavy defeats against the Rhodesian Security Forces (RSF). Subsequently there was a lull in guerrilla activity as ZAPU reappraised its strategy, alongside a period of internecine factional struggle.[18]

In 1972, ZANLA launched an assault on a farmstead in Centenary, opening an eastern front, which is the moment many Rhodesians considered the war to have commenced in earnest.[19] Mozambique's independence in 1975 altered the dynamic of the conflict significantly, its 1,200-kilometre border fully permeable to ZANLA cadres based there. A contemporaneous South African and Frontline State–led 'détente' mandated a temporary lull in fighting that allowed ZANLA in particular time to consolidate its forces following its own internal conflict.[20] After the failure of negotiations, the war reignited and escalated.

Fighting escalated most rapidly after 1977, by which time the liberation movements had grown enormously in military strength.[21] The RSF

---

[16] The Frontline States were southern African countries – Tanzania and Zambia predominant among them – which opposed white-minority rule in South Africa and Rhodesia and offered support to liberation movements.
[17] Dabengwa, 'ZIPRA in Zimbabwe's War of National Liberation', p. 25.
[18] Mtisi, Nyakudya, and Barnes, 'War in Rhodesia', pp. 141–4.
[19] Abbott and Botham, *Modern African Wars*, p. 12; Moorcraft, *A Short Thousand Years*, p. 29.
[20] Tungamirai, 'Recruitment to ZANLA', p. 42; Cilliers, *Counterinsurgency in Rhodesia*, p. 23; Tendi, 'Transnationalism, Contingency and Loyalty'.
[21] Mtisi, Nyakudya, and Barnes, 'War in Rhodesia', pp. 141–2.

'could not expand fast enough to match the growth of ZANLA and ZIPRA, and were soon outnumbered except at times of total mobilization'.[22] As early as 1977, the highest command echelon of the Rhodesian war effort assessed that the war was being lost, and in March 1979, Rhodesian intelligence told the government that it assessed the trained strength of ZANLA as 21,000, and ZIPRA 20,000,[23] numbers far superior to the Rhodesian Army's 6,000 regular soldiers[24] and 15,000 reservists.[25] Although the regular Rhodesian Army was an effective and formidable fighting force, it was in danger of being overrun.

A mid-1979 Rhodesian Army briefing stated that, given its soldiers were outnumbered one to three, 'in classical COIN terms, this is a no-win [war] or rather, a sure lose equation'.[26] Two thousand people were being killed or injured per month, and by the middle of 1979, '95 per cent of Rhodesia was under martial law'.[27] After previous false dawns, including the Kissinger-mandated Geneva talks of 1976, Smith and his RF hardliners were finally compelled to accept binding negotiations. This was in no small part due to pressure from RSF commander Lt Gen. Walls and intelligence chief Ken Flower.

In December 1979, active hostilities ended, with the Lancaster House Agreement brokered by Britain prompting a ceasefire. The outcome of the war was an ambiguous stalemate wherein the RSF, ZANLA, and ZIPRA were all undefeated in military terms, and all retained the capacity to revert to arms.[28] Led since 1977 by Robert Mugabe, ZANU swept to a conclusive victory in the February 1980 election. Two months later, crowds filled Rufaro Stadium to celebrate independence.

---

[22] Wood, 'Countering the Chimurenga', p. 199.
[23] Flower, *Serving Secretly*, pp. 175, 221.
[24] Rupiya, 'Demobilization and Integration', p. 31.
[25] Moorcraft and McLaughlin, *Rhodesian War*, p. 57.
[26] Cilliers, *Counterinsurgency in Rhodesia*, pp. 239–40.
[27] Moorcraft, 'Rhodesia's War of Independence'.
[28] Kriger, *Guerrilla Veterans in Post-war Zimbabwe*, p. 4.

Acknowledgements

I am immensely grateful to Jocelyn Alexander. Her insight, kindness, patience, and commitment to my research and well-being have been incredible. I consider myself highly fortunate to have had such a wonderful mentor.

This research work would not have been practicable without the assistance and advice provided by TM, one of my key interviewees, and Verity Mundy in Zimbabwe. I owe both a debt of gratitude.

Sincere thanks is expressed to all of my interviewees in Zimbabwe, whom I have not named in order to protect their safety. It was a huge privilege to spend time with these veterans, who shared their memories and stories with me candidly and warmly.

Cornelius Thomas and his staff at the Cory Library for Historical Research at Rhodes University in Makhanda, South Africa, provided much kind assistance. I would also like to thank Maria Marsh and Laheba Alam at Cambridge University Press, the book's excellent copy editor Ami Naramor, the historian Lennart Bolliger, my great friend Lucas Zimmer, and Elizabeth Winkler at Curtis Brown who kindly helped acquire permission to use Auden's verse in the epigraph.

Permissions to use some of the photographs in this book were generously provided by two former RAR officers, John Wynne Hopkins and Mike Matthews. Despite wartime photographs of the RAR being rare, they did not request payment. I have made a donation to the Royal Commonwealth Ex-Services League in lieu.

Lastly, but most importantly, I thank my wife, Esther, and our lovely children, Zebadiah and Boaz. M. T. Howard can be contacted at mtjhoward@outlook.com.

1 Introduction
The Loyalties of Colonial Soldiers

From 1964 through to the 1979 ceasefire, Zimbabwean nationalists fought a war of liberation against the white-minority Rhodesian government. It was, in the main, a counter-insurgency (COIN) war with few large battles. The Rhodesian Army was one of the most prominent actors throughout the war. Its regular forces were dominated by black soldiers, a fact that many have found paradoxical.

Zimbabwe's independence settlement left three undefeated armies in situ in 1980, two from the liberation forces – the Zimbabwe African National Liberation Army (ZANLA) and the Zimbabwe People's Revolutionary Army (ZIPRA) – and their antagonist, the Rhodesian Army. Robert Mugabe's new government commenced a tense process of integrating these former antagonists into one Zimbabwe National Army (ZNA).

In November 1980, serious inter-factional fighting, including the use of heavy weapons, broke out between members of ZANLA and ZIPRA, who had been housed in nearby camps in the suburbs of Bulawayo pending integration. In February 1981, the fighting reignited in fiercer form, and was widely perceived at the time as posing the danger of civil war.[1] Although the death toll was suppressed by the government, it was widely claimed that hundreds were killed.[2]

During both incidents, Prime Minister Robert Mugabe ordered the Rhodesian African Rifles (RAR), a colonial regiment in which all soldiers were black and almost all officers were white, to stop the fighting, suppress mutinous forces, and restore order. The RAR had spent the previous fifteen years fighting the liberation forces, during which time Mugabe's party had labelled them as sell-outs. Mugabe himself had repeatedly threatened them with post-war reprisals (see Figure 1.1).

To utilise the RAR was thus seemingly a strange choice for the new government, and a dramatic intervention. As one newspaper headline summed up the situation: 'Mugabe sets old enemy on rebels.'[3] It was

---

[1] See, for instance, Lelyveld, 'Zimbabwe Quells Mutiny', p. 3; Borrell, 'Civil War Averted', p. 6.
[2] White, 'Battle of Bulawayo'.   [3] Borrell, 'Mugabe Sets Old Enemy on Rebels', p. 1.

Figure 1.1 RAR troops post-Entumbane clearing captured weapons (Photograph courtesy of John Wynne Hopkins)

striking too that these ex-colonial soldiers agreed to fight for a government led by their wartime enemy. Luise White has argued that their intervention 'saved the new state'.[4]

Yet the 'old enemies' of the RAR did not perceive their loyalty to Mugabe's new government as strange. In explaining their actions to me, they held that they had long conceived of themselves as 'professional' soldiers. In their view, this conception of professionalism mandated that they act in an 'apolitical' manner, and so they were duty-bound to fight loyally for the 'government of the day'. Drawing upon oral history interviews with black Rhodesian veterans, I argue that these concepts are fundamental to understanding why these soldiers fought loyally for the Rhodesian Army during Zimbabwe's liberation war.

Book Outline

This book is a history of RAR veterans as well as black soldiers who served in other Rhodesian units. Although most of my interviewees were combat troops, I also interviewed veterans who had roles in the support services as

---

[4] White, 'Battle of Bulawayo', p. 631.

clerks, drivers, teachers, and signallers. However, the RAR features prominently in this book as it was the regiment in which most black soldiers served and was one of the most important Rhodesian units of the war. Although the RAR is little known today, during the colonial era, it was a famous, prestigious infantry unit with an enviable reputation earned during service overseas in Burma during World War II and, later, the Malayan Emergency.

A detailed history of the RAR is provided in Chapter 2; however, a brief historical sketch is provided here for context. The RAR was raised in 1940 as an *askari* ('soldier' in Swahili) regiment (black soldiers commanded by white officers); such units had existed in colonial Africa from the late nineteenth century and were commonplace in British colonies. During World War II, colonial regiments in British Africa ballooned in size and played important roles, notably in the Burma campaign. After the war, these units, much reduced in size, provided internal security and external 'imperial policing'.

All other *askari* regiments – perhaps the most famous being the King's African Rifles (KAR) which raised battalions in Kenya, Tanzania, and Uganda – were disbanded, merged, or amalgamated into the national armies of newly independent African nations as decolonisation occurred in the early-to-mid 1960s. The RAR was exceptional in this regard, disbanding only in 1981. Its soldiers were the last *askaris*.

The RAR's longevity was on account of the war fought by the Rhodesian government against Zimbabwean nationalists. Unlike most other *askari* regiments, the RAR played a major role during a war of decolonisation.[5] The scope of this book spans the RAR's last imperial involvement, when it fought in the British COIN war in Malaya as part of the East Africa Command, returning in 1958, through to its role in post-independence Zimbabwe, culminating in its amalgamation into the new ZNA in late 1981. This focus allows an exploration of how the loyalties of black soldiers were honed during an era of decolonisation, alongside why these loyalties remained resilient, and were indeed strengthened, during the liberation war, in which they played a prominent role in fighting against their nationalist kin.

For these soldiers, 'professionalism' not only incorporated technical military proficiencies, but also emphasised loyalty to their comrades and unit. Instilled through elaborate processes of military socialisation and

---

[5] The obvious exception is Kenya's Mau Mau conflict, in which units of the KAR fought. Kenya was also a settler colony; that it and Rhodesia (the only British settler colonies in Africa) saw protracted and bloody wars of decolonisation was no coincidence, as discussed later in this chapter.

rigorous training, 'professionalism' was an all-encompassing ethos to which they were strictly required to adhere.

'Professionalism' was undergirded by the 'regimental loyalties' of these soldiers, in which their allegiance was vested in their regiment and the army, rather than any political faction. Service in the RAR was frequently a family trade, with soldiers following in the footsteps of their fathers and grandfathers. Vivid institutional memory – reinforced through tradition and pageantry – and widespread intergenerational loyalty created a powerful regimental culture.

Inherent to these 'professional' ideals was a normative conception that soldiers were 'apolitical', which meant that their primary allegiance was to the army, irrespective of their personal political preferences. These bonds of loyalty remained strong throughout the war, despite placing these soldiers in direct opposition to the nationalist movements whose strongholds were the very same rural areas from which most black Rhodesian troops hailed.

The bedrock of 'professionalism' was most obviously wartime military efficacy and this formed an important component of these soldiers' loyalty. 'Professionalism' was honed during the long COIN war in Rhodesia, during which RAR troops were heavily involved in airborne and heliborne infantry operations.

Black Rhodesian troops, all of whom were volunteers, were of significant military importance. They came to dominate the regular Rhodesian Army, comprising 50 per cent of its strength by 1967, 65 per cent by 1976, and more than 80 per cent by 1979.[6] They were also highly skilled, well trained, and experienced, renowned as 'probably the best trained black troops in Africa'.[7] Rhodesian Army studies determined that the RAR was 'by every possible measure' its most effective unit in the field.[8] The RAR was not only the largest,[9] but also the 'longest-serving unit of the regular army',[10] making it the senior and most prestigious regiment in Rhodesia.[11]

While the fighting efficacy of black troops has been noted in accounts of the war, there is little research on how their loyalty actually manifested. In

---

[6] Stapleton, *African Police and Soldiers*, p. 178; Horne, *From the Barrel of a Gun*, p. 214; Moorcraft and McLaughlin, *Rhodesian War*, p. 51; Downie, *Frontline Rhodesia*; Preston, 'Stalemate', p. 75; Evans, *Fighting against Chimurenga*, p. 10; International Institute for Strategic Studies, *Strategic Survey*, pp. 26–39.
[7] Burns, 'Rhodesia Fearful'. [8] White, *Fighting and Writing*, p. 128.
[9] Rupiya, 'Demobilization and Integration'; Kriger, *Guerrilla Veterans*, pp. 41, 109; Anti-Apartheid Movement, *Fireforce Exposed*, p. 5. 1RAR alone comprised more than 1,200 troops, and 2RAR 1,000 (Wood, *War Diaries*, p. 344).
[10] McLaughlin, 'Victims As Defenders', p. 264.
[11] Roberts, 'Towards a History of Rhodesia's Armed Forces', pp. 103–10.

1995, Ngwabi Bhebe and Terence Ranger noted that 'further historical work on the Rhodesian forces' was required, particularly on 'the Blacks who fought in the Rhodesian forces'.[12] This book builds upon the small literature on black Rhodesian soldiers, which has principally focused on why these troops were motived to enlist in the first instance.

The first account of the RAR appeared in 1970, but offered little insight into black soldiers' lives, for it was written in exile by Christopher Owen, a white ex-RAR officer who resigned in protest at the white settler government's Unilateral Declaration of Independence (UDI) in 1965. Thereafter he wrote a short monograph chronicling the RAR's formation and World War II campaign in Burma, in which he commented that 'I had set myself a mammoth task. No history of the RAR had previously been published, and what information there was was both scanty and piecemeal.'[13] His book comprised just seventy-one pages.

Subsequently, two scholars have published work on black Rhodesian soldiers, with a focus on explaining 'the apparent paradox of the African volunteer serviceman' in Rhodesia.[14] In 1978, Peter McLaughlin, an academic at the University of Rhodesia (after 1980 the University of Zimbabwe), was the first scholar to devote serious attention to black Rhodesian soldiers as part of his wider work on the Rhodesian military.[15] Later, his 1991 journal article, 'Victims As Defenders: African Troops in the Rhodesian Defence System 1890–1980', was the first scholarly piece specifically devoted to black Rhodesian soldiers, and it utilised the official colonial archive.[16] It was, however, empirically thin when covering the post–World War II period, reflecting the great difficulty in researching this topic. The lack of sources that plagued Owen also troubled McLaughlin. A full 128 citations were used to write the history of African soldiers from 1890 through to the end of World War II, but the section covering the post–World War II period to 1980 cited not a single source.

A sea change occurred with two monographs published by Canadian historian Timothy Stapleton: *No Insignificant Part: The Rhodesia Native Regiment and the East Africa Campaign of the First World War* (2006) and *African Police and Soldiers in Colonial Zimbabwe 1923–1980* (2011). The former reconstructs the regimental history of the Rhodesia Native Regiment (RNR), using accounts written by its white officers preserved in the National Archives of Zimbabwe (NAZ). The latter is a sweeping account, drawing upon the NAZ and other official sources, local and foreign press reports, and oral history interviews with police and army veterans.

---

[12] Bhebe and Ranger, 'Introduction', p. 16.   [13] Owen, *Rhodesian African Rifles*, p. 70.
[14] McLaughlin, 'Victims As Defenders', p. 243.   [15] McLaughlin, 'Thin White Line'.
[16] McLaughlin, 'Victims As Defenders'.

Stapleton analyses the lives of black police and soldiers throughout this period thematically, focusing on key aspects including day-to-day life in camp, policemen and soldiers' perspectives of their service, and opportunities for 'education and upward mobility'. Aside from Stapleton and McLaughlin, very little scholarship has been produced on black Rhodesian soldiers, in contrast to the wide-ranging literature on the wars of those who fought for ZANU and, to a lesser extent, ZAPU.[17]

I return to Stapleton's *African Police and Soldiers* momentarily to situate it as part of a wider literature on colonial troops in Africa. Firstly I discuss how many accounts of black Rhodesian soldiers have marginalised or obscured their role and the nature of their loyalties.

A History Misunderstood, Marginalised, and Distorted

Most narratives of black Rhodesian soldiers have obscured and misrepresented their loyalties and military function. This, in part, reflects the lack of a credible alternative. In contrast to other wars of decolonisation, an authoritative history of Zimbabwe's war remains to be written.[18] The systematic destruction or removal of official Rhodesian archives at the war's conclusion has posed significant challenges for scholars, as discussed later in this chapter. Furthermore, systematic wartime Rhodesian censorship and propaganda impaired accurate contemporary reporting.[19] Journalists were heavily restricted, making it difficult to establish the credibility of information, and many accounts drew heavily upon the Rhodesian government's narrative for lack of alternative.[20]

---

[17] See, for example, Nhongo-Simbanegavi, *For Better or Worse?*; Kriger, *Zimbabwe's Guerrilla War*; Bhebe and Ranger, *Soldiers in Zimbabwe's Liberation War* and *Society in Zimbabwe's Liberation War*; Sibanda, *Zimbabwe African People's Union*; Lan, *Guns and Rain*; Bhebe, *ZAPU and ZANU Guerrilla Warfare*; Alexander and McGregor, 'War Stories'; Mhanda, *Dzino*; Martin and Johnson, *Struggle for Zimbabwe*; Frederikse, *None but Ourselves*; Mutambara, *The Rebel in Me*.

[18] Compare to the vast number of scholarly monographs on other Cold War-era conflicts: R. B. Smith's *An International History of the Vietnam War* extends to three volumes; J. A. Marcum's history of the Angolan Revolution comprises two volumes, *The Anatomy of an Explosion* and *Exile Politics and Guerrilla Warfare*. See also Horne, *Savage War of Peace*; Nzongola-Ntalaja, *The Congo*; Short, *Communist Insurrection in Malaya*; and Feifer, *Great Gamble*. The two histories of Zimbabwe's war generally cited remain Moorcroft and McLaughlin, *Rhodesian War*, written by two scholars who were Rhodesian reservist servicemen during the conflict and who draw much of their account from unpublished and un-cited Rhodesian sources, and Martin and Johnson, *Struggle for Zimbabwe*, which has been considered as partial towards ZANU's perspective (particularly at the expense of ZAPU), and features a foreword written by Robert Mugabe.

[19] Evans, 'Wretched of the Empire', pp. 180, 186–7; Godwin and Hancock, *'Rhodesians Never Die'*, pp. 311–12. See also pp. 39, 74–5, 115–16, 170, 182.

[20] Burns, 'In Rhodesia', p. 4.

A History Misunderstood, Marginalised, and Distorted 7

The small amount of scholarship published during or soon after the war was also largely characterised by poor accuracy for, as McLaughlin argued in 1978, 'researchers are reduced to relying largely on official communiques, hearsay and intelligent guesswork'.[21] For instance, Cynthia Enloe, a renowned scholar of military affairs, used black Rhodesian soldiers as a case study in her book *Ethnic Soldiers*, but makes several notable errors, asserting that 'in 1976 it was announced that ... some blacks would be allowed to become non-commissioned officers [NCOs] in their own regiments', despite the fact that black soldiers had been NCOs since the formation of the RNR in 1916.[22] Likewise, she claimed that 'paratroopers, an elite unit in many militaries, likewise remain an all-white institution in Rhodesia',[23] which is incorrect given that the RAR provided half of the airborne Fireforce companies, discussed later, and that many African soldiers boasted more than forty combat parachute jumps, placing them firmly among the most experienced combat paratroopers in the history of warfare.[24]

During the war, journalists critical of the Rhodesian government tended also to make misleading assertions about black soldiers because they simply inverted the story told in Rhodesian propaganda. The academic and novelist David Caute – a fellow of All Souls College, Oxford – authored a widely cited account of the war, *Under the Skin: The Death of White Rhodesia*, which falls into this trap. Caute trumpets his prolonged period of research in Rhodesia, but his discussion of black soldiers is error-strewn. For instance, he falsely claimed that 'the 3,000 black troops of the RAR were regarded essentially as support units' in an effort to counter Rhodesian claims that they signalled black support for the war against the liberation movements.[25] As was obvious to any casual observer of the war, the RAR were in fact front-line infantry troops.

Caute also claimed that the Selous Scouts was 'a unit just like any other', though, as discussed later, it was in fact a highly unusual unit, and gained much infamy for this reason.[26] Caute further diminishes the role of black troops by depicting RAR recruits as 'famished peasants, desperate refugees from the shanty-towns, and a few genuine uncle Toms [who] come in search of $(R)47 a month'.[27] As we shall see, none of these claims (including the rate of pay) are accurate, while the 'uncle Tom' jibe implies racial servility and moral failing.[28]

Under the Skin highlights how many powerful Rhodesian whites were racist and hypocritical and casually embraced extreme forms of violence

---

[21] McLaughlin, 'Thin White Line', p. 186. [22] Enloe, *Ethnic Soldiers*, p. 81.
[23] Ibid., p. 125.
[24] Stapleton, *African Police and Soldiers*, p. 206; Downie, *Frontline Rhodesia*.
[25] Caute, *Under the Skin*, p. 187. [26] Ibid., p. 106. [27] Ibid., p. 190.
[28] See, for instance, Martin and Turner, 'Why African-Americans Loathe "Uncle Tom"'.

to perpetuate a colonial lifestyle. But Caute's discussion of black soldiers resorts to a crude inversion of Rhodesian propaganda that lacks evidence and serves to denigrate their military effectiveness and to cast them as motived by desperation, greed, or a traitorous alliance with white settlers. Caute's book demonstrates that even accounts of the war researched at length failed to get to grips with the nature of black soldiers' military service and loyalties.

I have highlighted the errors in these texts by Enloe and Caute because they show how even noted scholars erred significantly in their depiction of black soldiers owing to the prevalence of Rhodesian narratives. They also indicate how some chroniclers of the war allowed their political beliefs to fundamentally inform their writing. Enloe and Caute's accounts – along with others with similar flaws – have subsequently been widely cited. This has led to an unwitting reproduction of images and narratives of black Rhodesian troops that are grossly distorted or are simply untrue.

Outside of the scholarly literature, the predominant narratives of the war have come to be bisected between two schools which I identify as 'Patriotic History' and 'neo-Rhodesian'. These renderings have long dominated the popular literature and public discourse of the war: Patriotic History for a ZANU(PF)-derived nationalist discourse, and neo-Rhodesian literature sympathetic to minority rule. These discursive polar opposites reflect the 'myths and simplistic narratives which have come to dominate "official" Zimbabwean histories of the war, in which "whites" are positioned against "blacks"'.[29] In this regard, they reflect writing on other wars of decolonisation, such as the 'Manichean perspective that has framed the great bulk of writing on the Algerian War and the French Army'.[30]

Before discussing neo-Rhodesian narratives, I turn to Patriotic History, which is a form of victor's history that has come to prominence in Zimbabwe since the post-1998 economic and political crisis. Inherent to this discourse is a political reimagining of wartime history that portrays it as won solely by ZANU(PF), reduces it to a simplistic binary racial narrative, and castigates all those associated with the colonial state as sell-outs.

Patriotic History primarily takes the form of media, performance, speeches, and memorial practices, in contrast to the largely textual narratives sympathetic to the Rhodesian perspective (discussed below). It silences and demonises black soldiers for the political purpose of legitimising continued ZANU(PF) rule. It deliberately simplifies or ignores the

---

[29] Dorman, *Understanding Zimbabwe*, p. 17.
[30] Alexander, Evans, and Keiger, 'The "War without a Name"', p. 2.

nature of black Rhodesian troops' loyalties, for its reductionist spin on liberation war history cannot parse their nuanced form of allegiance.

Wartime history is frequently contentious. The military historian Samuel Hynes cautions us to be wary of how wars are mythologised in retrospect, condensed into a comprehensive, oversimplified, and biased narrative – one which often deems them a 'good war' or a 'bad war'.[31] Post-war myths can become intractable and are often tied up in the politics of the present. For instance, in 2002, Polish and Russian scholars created a working group to reassess twentieth-century Russo-Polish history, pockmarked by conflict, and even among these learned peers, 'the gap in perceptions was so wide that, when they published a book under the title *White Spots, Black Spots*, they decided to let a Polish and Russian historian give separate treatment to each delicate event'.[32] In Ireland, the salient political divide for almost all of the past 100 years was not that of left and right, but that between two parties representing factional allegiance during the country's post-independence civil war.[33] It is not uncommon for post-war regimes to craft distorted historical narratives for political advantage.

In much of southern Africa, independence was achieved only through prolonged liberation struggle, and the post-independence politics of these countries have been drawn along wartime lines. The post-independence version of history that has been framed and endorsed by ruling parties has often been no less partial than the colonial hagiography and settler myth it replaced.[34] For such states founded through victory in conflict, wartime myths provide ruling parties with a deep well of lore; a foundational, binding narrative of the nation. These retellings often extol military sacrifices and achievements. As the historian Ronald Krebs noted, 'it is no accident that the symbols and rituals surrounding festivals of national independence and unification have traditionally been interwoven with martial imagery'.[35] Such folklore advances a narrative of victors' virtue, the losers condemned to perpetual pillory, thus constituting an ongoing basis for claiming legitimacy.

Former liberation movements in southern Africa realised the value of controlling the historical narrative during their transition to power,[36] and many subsequently sought to 'instrumentalise and appropriate national history for their own means' as part of a strategy to legitimise increasingly autocratic rule and corruption, or to marginalise new political enemies.[37] Examples include what Metsola refers to as the 'liberationist dichotomy

---

[31] Hynes, *Soldiers' Tale*, p. xiii.   [32] Barber, 'Russia Is Once Again Rewriting History'.
[33] See Dolan, *Commemorating the Irish Civil War*.
[34] Ndlovu-Gatsheni, 'Death of the Subject'.   [35] Krebs, *Fighting for Rights*, p. 17.
[36] Werbner, *Memory and the Postcolony*, p. 2.   [37] Schubert, '2002, Year Zero', p. 835.

[as] the basis of SWAPO's legitimacy',[38] manifested in the militaristic and triumphalist memorialisation of Namibia's war of independence in Windhoek;[39] and the People's Movement for the Liberation of Angola's (MPLA) propagation of a 'master narrative' wherein it portrays itself 'as the winner of the liberation struggle and the "natural representative" of the Angolan people as a whole' to the detriment of its political rivals.[40]

Zimbabwe's history has been instrumentalised in this fashion. After winning power in 1980, Mugabe's government became increasingly reliant upon a highly partial narrative in which its supposed military achievements underwrote its authority. As White argued, 'the political world of the 1970s' became 'the founding moment of the nation', with the ZANU(PF) government deriving its legitimacy from the war.[41] This tendency to rely on wartime narratives was greatly increased with the onset of Zimbabwe's economic crisis in the late 1990s.[42]

Precipitous economic decline and social unrest meant that Mugabe's capacity to appeal to the delivery of development as a basis for legitimacy became far more difficult, and ZANU(PF) faced a major new opposition party, the Movement for Democratic Change (MDC), that was a serious rival for power.[43] This questioning of ZANU(PF)'s competence posed an existential threat to its dominance of post-independence politics.[44] Its response was to look inwards and to revert to and ratchet up rhetoric which 'emerged from the hegemonic and authoritarian circumstances of the nationalist liberation struggle'.[45]

Terence Ranger labelled this post-2000 narrative 'Patriotic History'.[46] Its loci are cultural nationalism and wartime patriotism, which provide a 'usable past' in service of a partisan ZANU(PF) agenda.[47] As Miles Tendi has argued, it rendered all Zimbabweans either 'patriots' or 'sell-outs', with the pejorative affixed to ZANU(PF)'s opponents, who were 'automatically typecast as "sell-outs", "puppets", "un-African" and "pro-colonial"'.[48]

---

[38] Metsola, 'The Struggle Continues?', p. 608.
[39] Kössler, 'Facing a Fragmented Past', pp. 369–72.
[40] Schubert, '2002, Year Zero'. Elsewhere see the Kenya African National Union's (KANU) instrumental usage of the 'ritual and spectacle of [Kenya's] anniversary celebrations to advertise and perpetuate their ideologies' through the 'inscription of monuments into Nairobi's landscape' – see Larsen, 'Notions of Nation', pp. 277–8.
[41] White, *Assassination of Herbert Chitepo*, p. 94.
[42] See Raftopoulos, *Becoming Zimbabwe*, pp. 201–32, for a detailed summary.
[43] Ndlovu-Gatsheni, 'The Post-colonial State', pp. 104–7.
[44] Sachikonye, 'Whither Zimbabwe?'
[45] Scarnecchia, 'The "Fascist Cycle" in Zimbabwe', p. 222.
[46] Ranger, 'Nationalist Historiography'.
[47] Ndlovu-Gatsheni and Willems, 'Making Sense of Cultural Nationalism', p. 946. See also Scarnecchia, *Urban Roots of Democracy*; Kriger, 'Patriotic Memories'.
[48] Tendi, 'Patriotic History', p. 380.

Counter-narratives were deemed illegitimate or disloyal, while the party's narratives of liberation, authority, and legitimacy were sacrosanct. Inherent to Patriotic History discourse is a manipulation and simplification of the country's history.[49] The liberation struggle is cast as a binary conflict between black and white. Those black soldiers who served in the Rhodesian Army were automatically deemed sell-outs or stooges deprived of agency.[50] As the historian Gerald Mazarire noted, many scholars writing today grew up 'in a context where the popular depiction of the war branded all African soldiers of the Rhodesian army as "sell outs" ... Some prejudices against the so-called "sell-outs" persist to this day'.[51]

In contrast to the members of the liberation armies, who have exercised important political influence under the banner of 'war veterans', those who served in the Rhodesian Army have been denied the status of 'veteran'.[52] One consequence of this 'memory politics' is that the histories of those who fought against the nationalist forces are rendered voiceless, even invisible. Not only does the mere existence of black troops who fought for the colonial power become heretical, but their history cannot be accommodated in the all-encompassing nationalist narratives.

In these circumstances, it is unsurprising that 'there is a general stigma attached to colonial military service', and that no books have been written by black Rhodesian veterans.[53] Some of my interviewees worried telling their stories might attract trouble from the authorities, both for them and for myself. Upon seeing my mobile phone, MSW told me that 'you must be very careful in Zimbabwe. They bug'. GMH told me 'even talking with you [now could be cause for being deemed a "sell-out"] ... There is no freedom of speech here in Zimbabwe'.[54]

Patriotic History thus has few uses for black soldiers of the Rhodesian Army. They are either absent or sell-outs. This depiction leaves no room for an exploration of the nature of their loyalties or indeed the military roles they played not only before but after independence.

The distortion of the role and loyalties of black Rhodesian soldiers was also a tactic used by the Rhodesian government, which had long sought to marginalise their contribution. Stapleton noted that Rhodesian government historians in the 1960s and 1970s, when compiling a history of the Rhodesian contribution to World War I, interviewed white veterans of the World War I-era RNR, but none of its black veterans.[55] This is

---

[49] Munochiveyi, 'We Do Not Want to Be Ruled by Foreigners', p. 69.
[50] ZANU(PF), 'Traitors Do Much Damage to National Goals'.
[51] Mazarire, 'Rescuing Zimbabwe's "Other" Liberation Archives', p. 95.
[52] Ndlovu-Gatsheni, 'Death of the Subject', p. 10; Kriger, 'War Veterans' and 'Zimbabwe'.
[53] Stapleton, *African Police and Soldiers*, p. 15.   [54] Interviews with MSW and JMH.
[55] Stapleton, *No Insignificant Part*, p. 8.

remarkable given that the vast majority of the *askari* regiment's personnel were black.

Texts about Zimbabwe's war published by ex-Rhodesian authors after 1980 largely continued this trend. As Zoe Flood argued:

> Despite the importance of black soldiers to the Rhodesian Army, acknowledged by both former white soldiers and the Rhodesian Government at the time, they are a largely neglected group ... Whilst a range of literature by white writers, mostly memoirs or semi-official regimental histories largely published in South Africa, does focus on the Rhodesian experience of the war, black soldiers are generally marginalised.[56]

This literature has subsequently only grown in volume, with at least two dozen such monographs published.[57] Owing to the lack of available official records (discussed later) and a 'standard' account of the war, 'these memoirs substitute for an operational history'.[58] Their sheer volume has also in effect afforded them a de facto authority, as they are cheaply and readily accessible via online bookstores.[59]

These texts have sustained an influential set of views on the history of the Rhodesian Army which, a handful of exceptions aside, largely omit the contributions and histories of black troops. As Mazarire argued, the story of the Rhodesian Army has been 'biased towards white soldiers and white participants in the Rhodesian war' and reiterated their perspectives.[60]

The predominant narrative of these texts has been described as 'neo-Rhodesian' to describe how white ex-Rhodesians living abroad revisited and revised wartime discourse in order to criticise Mugabe's government, particularly following the onset of serious political, social, and economic crises in Zimbabwe after 1998.[61] Many of these neo-Rhodesian texts rehash wartime Rhodesian propaganda when discussing black soldiers. This messaging emphasised the high number of black personnel in the security forces and argued this was indicative of the support of the wider black population.[62] For instance, in 1977, the Rhodesian government

---

[56] Flood, *Brothers-in-Arms?*, pp. 3–4.
[57] Examples include, inter alia, Crouks, *The Bush War in Rhodesia*; Pringle, *Dingo Firestorm*; Parker, *Assignment Selous Scouts*; Wessels, *Handful of Hard Men*; Balaam, *Bush War Operator*; O'Brien, *Bandit Mentality*; Bax, *Three Sips of Gin*; Bird, *Special Branch War*; French, *Shadows of a Forgotten Past*; Ballinger, *Walk against the Stream*.
[58] White, 'Animals, Prey, and Enemies', p. 9.
[59] On this point see White, *Assassination of Herbert Chitepo*, in particular chapters 4 and 5, which illustrate these white constructions of the Rhodesian nation.
[60] Mazarire, 'Rescuing Zimbabwe's "Other" Liberation Archives', p. 98.
[61] Primorac, 'Rhodesians Never Die?', p. 204. The discourse has clear antecedents too – see Chennells, 'Rhodesian Discourse'.
[62] See Maxey, *Fight for Zimbabwe*, pp. 33–4; Grundy, *Soldiers without Politics*, p. 17; Whitaker, *The 'New Model' Armies of Africa?*, p. 193.

A History Misunderstood, Marginalised, and Distorted 13

supported the publication of a book entitled *Contact: A Tribute to Those Who Serve Rhodesia*. Its straightforward hagiography espoused this narrative, with the president of Rhodesia writing in its foreword that 'Africans and Europeans were "serving side by side against a common enemy"' in the form of 'communism' and that the Rhodesian Army was a non-racist institution.[63] Rhodesian narratives sought to portray the loyalty of black soldiers as supportive of the minority-rule regime, which, as we shall see, was manifestly not the case. This elision of black soldiers can also be seen as a perpetuation of the racist attitudes held by some white Rhodesian servicemen, who stereotyped black soldiers as incompetent.[64]

However, a few texts by white ex-Rhodesian veterans do not marginalise or ignore the contribution of black soldiers during the war. These have been authored by veterans of the RAR (or other units in which black and white troops served together). This is perhaps unsurprising, as the black veterans I interviewed emphasised that white RAR officers, and other white soldiers with whom they routinely served, did not speak or act in a racist manner – in contrast to white troops from other units, as discussed in Chapter 4. Yet these texts nonetheless distort black soldiers' loyalties by excluding their voices and by adhering to Rhodesian narratives when discussing their loyalties. Here I provide three examples.

In 2007, a history of the RAR, *Masodja: The History of the Rhodesian African Rifles and Its Forerunner the Rhodesia Native Regiment*,[65] was published by the Rhodesian Army Association, which Stapleton noted is an 'all-white veterans' organisation based outside Zimbabwe'.[66] One of a series of books on Rhodesian Army regiments written by Alexandre Binda and published by 30° South Publishers of Johannesburg, it comprises a series of detailed operational histories. In this respect it is a highly informative and very valuable text, as the author draws extensively from the closed-access Rhodesian Army Archive (RAA, discussed later) and other operational materials.

Although *Masodja* very briefly discusses how white officers witnessed no incidents of disloyalty from black soldiers during the war, it does not discuss their loyalties in any further detail.[67] The book cites RAA documents, secondary texts, and Rhodesian Army documents provided by white veterans; the only black voices cited are accounts reproduced verbatim from issues of *Nwoho*, and an account of Entumbane in the last chapter written by an anonymous black veteran in 1999.[68]

---

[63] Lowry, 'The Impact of Anti-communism', p. 187.
[64] White, 'Heading for the Gun', p. 237. A similar phenomenon of marginalising and damning has been observed by Andrew Wiest of Army of the Republic of Vietnam (ARVN) soldiers during the Vietnam War; see Wiest, *Vietnam's Forgotten Army*, p. 5.
[65] Binda, *Masodja*.   [66] Stapleton, *African Police and Soldiers*, p. 14.   [67] Ibid., p. 12.
[68] See, for example, ibid., pp. 296–7.

In 2015 and 2019, ex-RAR officers published a pair of books entitled *Chibaya Moyo: The Rhodesian African Rifles: An Anthology 1939–1980* and *Chibaya Moyo 2* ('Chibaya Moyo', the motto of B Company 2RAR during the war, means strike or stab to the heart).[69] Both state that they are not an attempt at a 'researched history', but rather are an 'anthology of anecdotes', almost all contributed by white veterans. As with many such semi-official texts, the contributors and readership alike largely comprise white Rhodesian veterans now living elsewhere in the Anglosphere.

In the first *Chibaya Moyo*, 178 of the 179 vignettes are from white authors (the only black voice is a *Nwoho* reprint). The 178 accounts include not only white ex-RAR officers, but also white soldiers from other units who were only briefly attached to the RAR, or who fleetingly encountered them on operations, or the wives or children of white ex-RAR officers. That the recollections of white persons who had a small impact upon the regiment are featured, whereas those of black soldiers are not, indicates both whose history is being recorded and the intended audience.

The second *Chibaya Moyo* volume contains contributions from two black veterans living in South Africa, Tinarwo Manema and Carl Chabata, whose contributions together account for three of the total 206 vignettes. They are, unfortunately, rather brief, at three paperback pages each. They comprise a statement of motivation for joining the RAR, short summaries of their wartime deployments, and some reminiscences of their comrades, with a further four pages from Chabata on his time in the Selous Scouts. There is no discussion of their loyalties.

Contributors to *Chibaya Moyo* express a great love and respect for the black soldiers with whom they served with. Two chapters of the first book are dedicated to lauding the courage, professionalism, and steadfastness of black soldiers.[70] It is clear that the authors and contributors to these texts hold black veterans in the highest esteem. This makes their almost total exclusion as contributors somewhat incongruous. While some contributors to these – and other – texts have proffered logistical issues or concerns for the security of black veterans in Zimbabwe as the reasons for their omission, these obstacles are by no means insurmountable.

The *Masodja* and *Chibaya Moyo* texts are not unique in this regard. In 1998, J. R. T. Wood published a detailed history of D Company, 1RAR's experience on an operation across the north-eastern border into Mozambique to attack a ZANLA camp in 1976. The article is an excellent operational account. However, its sole primary sources are the

---

[69] Telfer and Fulton, *Chibaya Moyo* and *Chibaya Moyo 2*.
[70] Telfer and Fulton, *Chibaya Moyo*, pp. 393–465.

recollections and documents provided by a white ex-officer, David Padbury.[71] The detail is impressive, but the fact that a peer-reviewed piece on the combat experiences of the RAR neglects to hear from *any* black voices is striking, particularly given that many more black RAR veterans were alive in the late 1990s than are now, and that they were in fairly close proximity to the South Africa–based author, himself also a Rhodesian Army veteran. This is a fundamental weakness of the article, for beyond lauding black troops as 'tough African soldiers' and 'battle-hardened professionals' who fought bravely, displaying 'hardiness and effectiveness', Wood says little else of them. Although lauded, black soldiers' perspectives are not present.

Furthermore, all white officers are mentioned by their full name, and a small description is given of their role and sometimes their background, even if they were of tangential importance to the operation. Contrastingly, only one black soldier is referred to by his full name – John Selete, who was Padbury's batman (an officer's servant in the British tradition) – and two others referred to as 'Sergeant Saul' and 'PWO [Platoon Warrant Officer] Barnard', with all others referred to as 'an MAG gunner', 'a rifleman', or 'an RAR soldier'. It is striking that the author recalled the full names of the white officers but not even a single name of most of the black soldiers involved in the operation. This echoes what Michael West referred to as the 'depersonalization of the colonized', in which Rhodesian authorities sought to diminish the social status of blacks through the 'denial of individuality'.[72] It also reflects a lingering 'depersonalization' prevalent among some white Rhodesian veterans, for it was only in 1958 that 'African Westernised elites and security force personnel' in Rhodesia could officially 'have more than one name'.[73]

Why, then, have the voices of black veterans not been included in these accounts of the RAR? In part, the answer may be found in how they frequently portray black soldiers' loyalty to the Rhodesian Army solely as a product of the merits of Rhodesia; a predominant colonial-era narrative, as noted earlier in this chapter. This narrative has similarities with white farmers' portrayal of farm workers, which present life on the farms as an 'idealised view of race and labour relations' in which 'labourers had no problems, issues or worries and are presented as happy, industrious workers who were always content under their benevolent, white employer'.[74]

---

[71] Wood, 'Counter-punching on the Mudzi'.
[72] West, *Rise of an African Middle Class*, pp. 27–8.
[73] Stapleton, *African Police and Soldiers*, p. 161.
[74] Pilossof, 'Unbearable Whiteness of Being', pp. 629–30.

Such portrayals of entirely positive, hierarchical relations between white and black were a common trope in Rhodesian society (as they are in neo-Rhodesian literature) and were rarely disrupted by allowing unmediated black voices to appear. The *Masodja* and *Chibaya Moyo* texts, while acclaiming and honouring black Rhodesian troops, similarly marginalise the voices of black soldiers and account for their loyalties largely through reductive and idealised terms.

This point should not be taken to imply that relationships between black and white soldiers in the RAR and other comparable regiments were not strong – as this book will show, black veterans recall very strong bonds of loyalty and affection with their white comrades, and the enduring warmth of these relationships was readily apparent during research interviews. Instead, this point should be understood as highlighting how reasons posited retrospectively by some white veterans for the steadfast loyalties of black Rhodesian troops are overly simplistic, lack nuance, and – above all – largely reflect only white perspectives.

Criticism of the marginalisation of black Rhodesian soldiers in these texts should not, however, be understood to imply that the authors have overtly sought to disparage or disrespect black veterans. During the course of my research, I met with many white veterans who had served with black soldiers in the RAR and other units. These white veterans – some of whom were contributors to the aforementioned texts – uniformly evinced a sincere, deep admiration and respect for the black soldiers they served alongside. It was apparent during my fieldwork that the bonds between black and white veterans remained undimmed by the passage of nearly four decades since the war's conclusion.

It was also very clear that members of the RAR Association care very deeply for black veterans and have undertaken a considerable – and unheralded – amount of fundraising and voluntary work to provide welfare support for those in need. I have seen first-hand how vital and appreciated this assistance is among black veterans who otherwise subsist on meagre, devalued government pensions.

Furthermore, it should be noted that neo-Rhodesian views are far from uniformly held among white veterans. None of the white ex-RAR veterans I met in Zimbabwe espoused the neo-Rhodesian version of history. During my research in Zimbabwe, I was generously assisted in contacting several potential interviewees by a group of white ex-officers of the RAR Association. They were enthusiastic that the history of black soldiers should be recorded and recognised.

The Motivations and Loyalties of Colonial Troops

Stapleton's *African Police and Soldiers* is part of a wider school of literature that has emerged during the past three decades. In general, little has been published on African colonial soldiers, despite the fact that more than 1 million served in the armies of the European powers during World War II alone,[75] and hundreds of thousands more thereafter in conflicts of decolonisation.

The historian Richard Reid argued that this neglect was a consequence of the 'decidedly Eurocentric' approach of many military historians.[76] It also stemmed from the tendency among authors interested in or sympathetic to nationalism during the era of decolonisation to view colonial 'collaborators' through a moral prism.[77]

As McLaughlin argued, 'historians of Africa have fallen into the same trap as Western Europeans who felt and feel compelled to explain their "Quislings" and "Collabos" as if they were a malignant disease or aberration rather than flesh-and-blood humans adjusting to changing political, social and economic conditions with limited foresight at their disposal'.[78] Michelle Moyd, writing on the *askaris* of the Schutztruppe (German colonial soldiers in east Africa), noted that:

Nationalist historians prioritised research on East African resistance to colonial authority and virtually ignored the histories of African agents of colonialism like the askari, who were so obviously situated on the wrong side of history. While their emphasis on creating a usable past is certainly understandable, it has also meant that historians who came after them tended to view the German colonial period in East Africa through the prisms of African independence and the Cold War. Neither of these perspectives left much room for studying colonial agents like the askari beyond stereotypes.[79]

An emergent 'new school' – in which Moyd is eminent – has sought to move past these reductive framings.[80] According to Charles Thomas and Roy Doron, it has 'played a key role in revitalizing African military history' by placing increased emphasis upon the 'social histories of the colonial forces'.[81] Soldiers chronicled by this 'new school' include the Schutztruppe

---

[75] Killingray and Plaut, *Fighting for Britain*, p. 8.   [76] Reid, *Warfare*, p. x.
[77] For a summary of such overtly nationalist literature on colonial soldiers in general, see Parsons, 'African Participation in the British Empire', pp. 258–60, and Cooper, 'Conflict and Connection'. For Tanzania, see Moyd, *Violent Intermediaries*, pp. 9–10; for Kenya, see Anderson, 'Making the Loyalist Bargain', p. 70; for Zimbabwe, see Stapleton, *African Police and Soldiers*, pp. 11–14; for Namibia, see Bolliger, 'Chiefs, Terror, and Propaganda', p. 126.
[78] McLaughlin, 'Victims As Defenders', pp. 241–3.
[79] Moyd, *Violent Intermediaries*, p. 9.   [80] Bolliger, *Apartheid's African Soldiers*, pp. 5–7.
[81] Thomas and Doron, 'Out of Africa', pp. 12–13. A contemporaneous emergent school is that of 'the rise of indigenous military history', which looks at the service of indigenous

of German East Africa, the KAR, the Tirailleurs Sénégalais and other African soldiers in France's colonial army, Malawian soldiers in the KAR and other regiments, the *harkis* of French Algeria, the Katangese Gendarmes, and black soldiers in apartheid South Africa.[82]

This 'new school' has sought to explain the heterogeneous motivations of African colonial soldiers, such as Timothy Parsons, who argued that 'colonial military service must be examined in its social context ... the willingness of Africans to serve in the colonial army was determined by a variety of social and economic factors that changed over time'.[83] Parsons showed that recruits were typically not those from the 'martial races' of colonial officers' imaginations, but rather those already integrated into the colonial labour network. This social and economic context was crucial: 'African societies were most "martial" when taxation and land shortages forced them to seek paid employment, and educational limitations and racial discrimination in hiring limited their options to unpaid wage labour.'[84] Contrary to earlier nationalist-inspired discourses that inferred immoral or treacherous motivations among these supposed 'collaborators' or 'mercenaries', African colonial soldiers' motivations differed little to other soldiers around the world throughout modern history.

Other scholars have also affirmed that soldiers' motivations varied widely and depended upon the historical context, such as in Kenya and Nigeria.[85] Moyd developed this point. 'African soldiers' loyalties had far more to do with their own understandings of social hierarchies and relationships of mutual obligation than with any abstract loyalties to European causes or governments.'[86]

A similar argument has been made of black soldiers in Rhodesia. McLaughlin argued of black Rhodesian troops that 'the military life appeals to many people, and Africans are surely no exception'.[87]

---

soldiers across 'the major Anglo-settler societies' (defined as Australia, New Zealand, Canada, the United States, and South Africa), whose writers have emphasised 'the valiant efforts of Indigenous service personnel and their diverse motivations to serve, in conjunction with the often exploitative government approaches to Indigenous recruitment'. See Riseman, 'Rise of Indigenous Military History', p. 901.

[82] For example, see Moyd, *Violent Intermediaries*. German East Africa comprised present-day Tanzania, Rwanda, and Burundi; Parsons, *African Rank-and-File*. The KAR were recruited from Kenya, Malawi, Uganda, and Somaliland; Echenberg, *Colonial Conscripts*; Woodfork, *Senegalese Soldiers*; Ginio, *The French Army and Its African Soldiers*; Lovering, *Authority and Identity*; Crapanzano, *Harkis*; Kennes and Larmer, *Katangese Gendarmes*; Grundy, *Soldiers without Politics*.

[83] Parsons, *African Rank-and-File*, p. 1.   [84] Ibid., p. 9.

[85] Anderson, 'Making the Loyalist Bargain', p. 51; Ukpabi, 'Changing Role of the Military in Nigeria', p. 63.

[86] Moyd, *Violent Intermediaries*, pp. 12–13.

[87] McLaughlin, 'Victims As Defenders', p. 263.

Stapleton contended that 'it is obvious from many personal accounts that material incentives were certainly important but hardly ever the only factor' and 'when looking at individual cases it is difficult to find any awestruck fools, greedy mercenaries, or clever manipulators of the colonial system'.[88] Motivations were 'heterogeneous' and multiple,[89] including, inter alia, the status of the uniform, adventure, the stability of a government job, opportunities for education, social mobility, provision for dependents, the availability of a pension, and sometimes patriotism.[90]

Stapleton's work has provided an understanding of the motivations to enlist among black soldiers in Rhodesia. But the act of enlistment was only part of the story, as he recognised:

> It is clear that the reasons why people initially volunteered were different than the reasons why they remained [in the RAR, with many joining] to gain stable employment and [who] then discovered other elements of the ... army experience, often less tangible ones like pride and discipline, which kept them in uniform.[91]

Given the his interest in both police and soldiers, and the sweeping temporal range of 1923 to 1980, Stapleton understandably devotes little attention in *African Police and Soldiers* to these 'less tangible' elements. In this book, I build upon Stapleton's formidable work and argue that these elements were highly important in explaining soldierly loyalty. They comprised two distinct factors.

Foremost was these soldiers' 'professionalism'. Inherent to this ethos was their soldierly prowess, honed through continuous training and operational experience, which was also co-constitutive of a deep, emotive sense of mutual obligation between fellow soldiers, as per the work of the military sociologist Anthony King, discussed later. Furthermore, these soldiers were socialised into a distinctive 'military culture', which created a powerful, emotive 'regimental loyalty' which incorporated 'traditions' to cultivate an accentuated sense of in-group belonging and homogeneity that bound them to their regiment, and thereafter the wider army. The 'professionalism' and 'regimental loyalties' of these troops ensured that they remained steadfast during combat and in the face of the surge in popularity of the nationalist challenge to white settler-colonial rule.

The aforementioned 'new school' has addressed the motivations of African soldiers to enlist. However, it has not devoted substantial

---

[88] Stapleton, *African Police and Soldiers*, pp. 29–33, 43.
[89] McLaughlin, 'Legacy of Conquest', p. 132, as cited in Stapleton, *No Insignificant Part*, p. 41.
[90] Stapleton, *African Police and Soldiers*, chapter 2, particularly pp. 43–4. [91] Ibid.

attention to the actual production and nature of the loyalties of these troops. Aside from Stapleton, two scholars have recently published work that argues for the salience of the cleavage between soldiers' initial motivations for enlisting and their actual loyalties once in service. Lennart Bolliger, who interviewed black veterans of apartheid South Africa's external military units, noted that 'the reasons for joining [the] security forces were not always the same as the reasons for remaining in them'.[92]

Kaushik Roy, in his article on colonial soldiers in the Indian Army during World War II, also advanced a bifurcated understanding of soldierly loyalty, in which he divided 'the factors that influenced the soldiers' behaviour roughly into external and internal categories ... while societal factors are important in shaping pre-combat motivation, the organisational apparatus of the army to a great extent shaped the in-combat motivation'.[93] These scholars both stress the importance of institutional 'military culture' in forging loyalties that sustain troops during war.

Stapleton, Bolliger, and Roy all highlight a crucial aspect of the soldiery loyalties of colonial troops: they were not only largely distinct from the initial motivation to enlist, but were also forged within the military milieu, within and by military institutions. It is no coincidence that these three scholars made use of the oral testimony of colonial veterans, for this cleavage is not readily apparent from documentary sources. Indeed it has evaded other authors of the 'new school', who have written about African colonial veterans who have long passed away. This book contributes to this body of work by using oral histories to show that black Rhodesian soldiers' loyalties were forged in the particular context of a small regular army which emphasised 'professionalism' and 'regimental loyalty'. These bonds, I argue, account for their distinctive and steadfast loyalties, and also explain why the Zimbabwean government retained these troops after independence.

I discuss the loyalties of soldiers drawn from marginalised communities in more depth shortly. I first advance a typology of soldierly loyalty based on a wider reading of military history.

Soldierly Loyalty and Professionalism

In the scholarly military literature, a long-standing argument stresses that armies demand total loyalty from their soldiers and require of them great acts of self-sacrifice, including willingly putting their lives at risk. The battlefield is often dangerous, and commonplace among soldiers are 'fear

---

[92] Bolliger, *Apartheid's African Soldiers*, pp. 104–9.
[93] Roy, 'Military Loyalty in the Colonial Context', p. 500.

of wounds, fear of death, fear of putting into danger the lives of those for whose well-being one is responsible'.[94] Soldiers must be relied upon to carry out their mission in spite of this. As King has pointed out, 'it is a striking and extraordinary fact that, despite the evident attractions of desertion, soldiers have often preferred to fight and die together'.[95]

In much of the analysis of this 'togetherness', the cheek-by-jowl existence of soldiers has frequently been depicted as akin to familial bonds. Such groups of soldiers are often referred to as the 'primary group'. As Hynes argued, wartime loyalties are pledged 'not to an army or a nation or a cause, but to a battalion, a company, a platoon. For a man adrift in alien space, his unit becomes the focus of his love and loyalty, like a family, and his feelings for it may be as strong, as complex, as family feelings are'.[96]

Soldiers have long enunciated such feelings in their correspondence. For instance, during World War I, in a letter to his subordinates, the commander of the US Army's 38th Infantry Battalion wrote, 'from the depths of a heart that knows soldierly affection, soldierly love, soldierly loyalty and soldierly devotion, I wish to commend you ... for your wonderful valor and amazing devotion to your Colonel'.[97] These affective loyalties have been seen as imperative to the ability of a unit to fight for a sustained period. Very much in this vein, in the aftermath of World War II, a scholarly literature on what motivated soldierly loyalty blossomed, foremost of which was Shils and Janowitz's seminal work which made the revolutionary argument that, contrary to prior understanding, the 'extraordinary tenacity' of German soldiers during World War II was not attributable to ideological motivation, but explained by the strength of 'primary groups' such as a soldier's fire team or platoon.[98]

A subsequent literature has foregrounded the link between the deep connections forged between troops at war and loyalty. As the sociologist of warfare and violence Siniša Malešević argued:

[E]mpirical research on the performance of soldiers in combat has persuasively demonstrated that very few of them are motivated by their loyalty to their nation, state, ethnic group or to abstract ideological principles such as socialism, liberalism or religious commitment. Instead, the primary motive was a feeling of solidarity with other soldiers in their platoon.[99]

Malešević defines this solidarity within primary groups as occurring on a *micro level*, as distinct from the *macro-level* factors of patriotism, ideology, or creed. Micro-level bonds achieve their primacy during wartime.

---

[94] Keegan, *Face of Battle*, p. 18.   [95] King, *Combat Soldier*, p. 13.
[96] Hynes, *Soldiers' Tale*, p. 10.   [97] Harris, *Rock of the Marne*, p. 325.
[98] Shils and Janowitz, 'Cohesion and Disintegration'.
[99] Malešević, *Sociology of War and Violence*, p. 187.

As Malešević argued, 'the battlefield context changes people's perceptions of social reality: a great majority of soldiers substitute macro-level ideological motivation for the micro-level solidarity of a small-group bond'.[100] Other scholars have referred to micro-level solidarities by different terms which nonetheless depict the same substantive meaning.[101]

In the aftermath of World War II, as militaries were reformed in various ways, these micro-level bonds became intertwined with an idea of 'professionalism'. The scholarly military literature historically tended to define military 'professionalism' as the technical-managerial capabilities of the officer corps.[102] For instance, Samuel Huntington famously delineated officers, who can be 'professionals', from soldiers, who cannot, arguing that the former engage in a 'higher calling', whereas the latter only enlisted for "monetary gain".[103] This approach was borne both of its time, when Western armies were still reliant on large numbers of conscripts instead of regulars (those for whom soldiering is their full-time occupation, and often a career, within a permanent force), and of a scholarly approach oriented around the civil-military relations of elites, which supposed that officers' 'professional' identities guaranteed their political impartiality and, furthermore, distinguished them from enlisted troops.

In contrast to Huntington, King has argued not only for the primacy of affective micro-level bonds, but for the importance of the specific form they take among regulars, as the 'cohesion typical of the mass citizen army has been superseded by a new kind of solidarity among the all-professional volunteer forces'.[104] King contends that the micro-level bonds present among regulars are qualitatively distinct to those of the mass-conscript or semi-professional armies that came before them. Professional soldiers, he claims, are not only the most militarily efficacious members of their armed forces, which may also include large part-time, reservist, or conscripted elements, but they possess particular micro-level solidarities that render them beholden to one another. This 'professional ethos' King defines in terms of a fastidious approach to military competencies, including skills such as marksmanship or battlefield

---

[100] Ibid., p. 223.
[101] See, for instance, Siebold, 'Essence of Military Group Cohesion', pp. 288–9. Guy Siebold criticised King's conception of soldierly cohesion and in turn was subject to a sharp rejoinder from King in an illuminating debate. See King, 'Existence of Group Cohesion in the Armed Forces'.
[102] See, for instance, Gates, '"New" Military Professionalism'.
[103] Huntington, *The Soldier and the State*, p. 8.   [104] King, *Combat Soldier*, p. 22.

tactics. The importance of this ethos is not solely that it makes individual soldiers proficient fighters:

Professionalism – substantially engendered through training – does not merely improve the practical performance of soldiers. It fundamentally alters the social relations between them; it transforms the nature of the associations between them. Professionalism generates a solidarity whose distinctiveness is often overlooked.[105]

I utilise this definition of 'professionalism' throughout this book to refer to soldiers' micro-level loyalties, for its tenets capture the nature of the solidarities between members of the RAR and, as I will show, my interviewees frequently referred to their 'professionalism'. This 'professional' ethos and its emphasis upon training were vitally important to the small regular component of the Rhodesian Army. This is unsurprising, for it was a facsimile of the British Army, which as King noted was itself 'one of the first western forces to professionalize and, indeed, it was the first all-volunteer military to be engaged in combat operations after the Second World War'.[106]

This is not to claim that the RAR was identical to a British regiment, or to any of King's other Western case studies, but instead to illustrate the pertinence of his 'professional' model in this context. Military proficiencies, such as marksmanship, tracking, and, later in the war, parachuting, were among the key 'professional' skills of RAR soldiers. Proficiency in these skills generated King's distinctive form of solidarity among black soldiers, in which they adhered to the goals of the 'primary group' not merely because of their high level of training in martial proficiencies, but also because this kinship was founded upon the reciprocal demand made of all RAR soldiers to strive for the highest standards of soldierly performance.

The ethos of 'professionalism' encompassed more than technical soldierly skills. Since the advent of all-volunteer regular armies, the professional soldier 'is almost by definition a social isolate, for his values and norms, his sense of commitment, his socialization and his self-realization seem to distinguish him from other members of society'.[107] Such forms of isolation, however, take historically specific forms that produce a particular normative conception of the role of the soldier. In the case of black Rhodesian soldiers, the narrative of 'professionalism' was used not simply to indicate their intergroup norms, skills, and training, but to negotiate the institutional racism inherent to the Rhodesian Army (as Chapter 4 discusses). In this manner, it was invoked by both black and white soldiers during their racial integration in the late 1970s, when the systematic racism of Rhodesia was trumped by 'professional' dynamics

[105] Ibid., p. 338.   [106] Ibid., p. 346.
[107] Harries-Jenkins and Van Doorn, 'Armed Forces and the Social Order', p. 17.

premised upon merit, such as gradations of rank. The RAR soldiers also used the 'professional' narrative to distance themselves from other factions of the security forces who were not 'professional', such as the Security Force Auxiliaries.

This concords with King's depiction of 'professionalism' as also functioning as a form of 'status honour' in which 'members of the group judge themselves and others and enforce appropriate conduct to each other'.[108] As I will argue, for black soldiers, this 'status honour' inherent to their 'professional' conduct legitimised their wartime role in a way not afforded to other combatants, such as guerrilla fighters, who they portrayed as preying on non-military targets, particularly civilians.

In tandem with the emphasis upon 'professionalism' as formulated in these contexts, new forms of what Malešević termed *macro-level* solidarities also became salient among black soldiers. These differed from the canonical scholarly military literature's understandings of macro-level solidarities, which implicitly incorporate a Western normative conception foregrounding patriotism, ideology, and sometimes religion. This extant literature's understandings of the loyalties of soldiers – from the World War II Soviet *krasnoarmiich* through to American troops at war post–9/11 – are almost wholly rooted in instances where soldiers have fought on behalf of their own country rather than for a settler or colonial power. A different approach is required in a colonial context. As Malešević argued:

Rather than being a cause or a direct product of war, the ostensible macro-level solidarity and group homogeneity exhibited in times of violent conflicts originate outside of these conflicts. In other words, instead of being an automatic social response, homogenisation is a complex process that requires a great deal of long-term institutional work. In-group solidarity is not something that 'just happens' and naturally occurs in times of war.[109]

This argument is a critique of arguments that suppose war is itself constitutive of macro-level solidarities, but it also opens a pathway to a fascinating alternative perspective on the macro-level solidarities of black Rhodesian troops, one that doesn't presuppose a patriotic or political loyalty vested in the Rhodesian settler-colonial regime, but instead asks how macro-level loyalties were created within the unique environment of a black regular regiment that served in a minority-rule state.

Indeed, while patriotic or imperial-patriotic motivations did exist among some colonial soldiers, they were relatively rare.[110] In Roy's

---

[108] King, *Combat Soldier*, p. 363.   [109] Malešević, *Sociology of War and Violence*, p. 179.
[110] See Grundy, *Soldiers without Politics*, p. 57 for South Africa; McLaughlin, 'Victims As Defenders', p. 263; Stapleton, *African Police and Soldiers*, pp. 26–9, for Rhodesia.

work on Indian troops during World War II, he argued that 'patriotism was probably not an important factor', and instead 'the organisational apparatus of the army to a great extent shaped the in-combat motivation' of Indian colonial troops.[111] Likewise, Bolliger, who interviewed many black veterans of apartheid South Africa's external units, argued that these soldiers were not united 'by a supposed national identity', and instead idiosyncratic 'military cultures' played an important role in how soldiers of these units 'operated during the war'.[112]

Similarly, I argue that black Rhodesian soldiers derived their sense of what Malešević terms 'group homogeneity' and 'in-group solidarity' from the military culture of the Rhodesian Army, most importantly the RAR. As noted, the Rhodesian Army overtly mimicked the British system, and particularly the pageantry and symbolic power of the British regimental system, which had proven effective in garnering loyalty among troops across anglophone colonial Africa.[113] As I shall show, conspicuously 'invented traditions' were shaped to create a sense of collective identity and purpose. This 'in-group solidarity' was felt primarily towards the army, and only thereafter to the 'state'. Some of my interviewees rendered the state in the abstract as a 'willed-for' entity that mirrored the RAR in being meritocratic and competent, instead of the state as it existed – that is, captured by the RF.

The soldierly loyalties of black Rhodesian soldiers were quite different from those of black soldiers in apartheid's external units, as depicted in Bolliger's work. In one respect, this is somewhat surprising, as many South African personnel served on attachment to the Rhodesian Security Forces (RSF) during the war for the express purpose of acquiring an understanding of COIN conflict in order to improve South Africa's own capabilities,[114] and South Africa made a concerted effort to recruit former Rhodesian officers into its army after 1980 in order to administer its own COIN units.[115] Indeed, Kevin O'Brien has argued that 'the centrality of the Rhodesian example' was 'reflected in the South African forces by the mid-1980s', and in particular 'the RAR would reflect on 32 Battalion and its counter-guerrilla operations in Angola'.[116] Yet the production and nature of their loyalties differed radically.

The key reason for this difference was that, as Bolliger argued, the 'military cultures' of apartheid South Africa's external units were 'highly

[111] Roy, 'Military Loyalty in the Colonial Context', pp. 499–500.
[112] Bolliger, *Apartheid's Black Soldiers*, pp. 6, 120.
[113] Killingray and Plaut, *Fighting for Britain*, p. 136.
[114] Ellert, *Rhodesian Front War*, p. 93; Bolliger, 'Apartheid's Transnational Soldiers'.
[115] O'Brien, 'Special Forces for Counter Revolutionary Warfare', pp. 84–92.
[116] O'Brien, *South African Intelligence Services*, p. 58.

heterogeneous and divided... often characterised by extreme brutality and violence, of which [black soldiers were] both targets and perpetrators'.[117] For instance, although many of these troops may have nominally been 'volunteers', their enlistment was often a desperate last resort. The Angolan soldiers of 32 Battalion, many of whom were ex–National Front for the Liberation of Angola (FNLA) troops already buffeted by the winds of the shifting transnational dynamics of a regional conflict nexus, faced a Hobson's choice: soldier or starve.[118] As I will show in Chapter 2, black soldiers in the Rhodesian Army were not only all volunteers, but were recruited in a fundamentally different manner; my interviewees often emphasised 'traditions' of familial and regional service, the social mobility offered by enlistment, or the opportunity for adventure.

In addition, the loyalties of 32 Battalion soldiers were not created through lengthy processes of military socialisation, nor through an institutional effort to create 'in-group homogeneity', as was the case with the RAR. Instead, they were enforced by 'the violent enforcement of discipline among black troops',[119] which often took shocking and extreme forms, including regular and widespread use of the '*sjambok* (a heavy leather whip)'.[120] As I will argue, this violence was inimical to the 'professional' ethos of the Rhodesian Army, which emphasised a juridical form of military discipline in the British mould that black RAR soldiers understood as 'fair'. In contrast, 32 Battalion's white officers possessed practically untrammelled authority. In this truly extreme military culture, deserters were simply executed and there was little accountability for officers, with one veteran describing soldiering in 32 Battalion as 'a life in slavery and bondage'.[121] The relationships between white officers and black soldiers in the RAR, while still characterised by racism, were nonetheless premised upon a perception by black soldiers of a shared notion of 'professionalism' that emphasised respect and reciprocal obligation.

These differences can also be seen among those who served in the South African paramilitary unit Koevoet. They experienced a hyperviolent, ill-disciplined culture that ritualised brutality both internally, for the purposes of discipline akin to 32 Battalion, and externally, through the widespread use of bounties for 'confirmed kills' and wanton violence levied against civilians.[122] Black soldiers of the Rhodesian Army

---

[117] Bolliger, *Apartheid's African Soldiers*, p. 329.
[118] Ibid., pp. 112, 135–7. Other 32 Battalion recruits had not been members of the FNLA, but had volunteered to join as their circumstances as refugees, migrant labourers, or ex-guerrillas made soldiering a relatively attractive proposition (ibid., pp. 141–7).
[119] Bolliger, *Apartheid's Black Soldiers*, p. 92. [120] Ibid., pp. 92, 101.
[121] Ibid., pp. 106–8.
[122] Ibid., p. 104; Bolliger, *Apartheid's African Soldiers*, pp. 168–9, 173.

emphasised their 'professional' norms and held that these precluded the mistreatment of civilians. Indeed, they frequently invoked their 'professional' status as encompassing the protection of civilians. In this sense, they were similar to soldiers of the South West Africa Territorial Force (SWATF) – an army that recruited Namibian soldiers but was funded and officered by the apartheid regime and that resembled more closely a well-trained conventional army. Unlike veterans of 32 Battalion or Koevoet, its veterans did not emphasise the prevalence of 'physical punishment' but rather 'spoke of the importance and the professionalism of their military training', and emphasised that 'that the soldiers of SWATF "were not trained to kill innocent people [but] to take care of and to protect people"'.[123] A comparison to Bolliger's work illustrates that, while the armies of the settler-colonial powers shared commonalities, there were manifest differences in the ways the loyalties of black soldiers were produced and the form they took.

In sum, this section has argued for the importance of reinterpreting the loyalties of black Rhodesian soldiers as distinct from their initial motivations for enlisting. 'Professional' micro-level solidarities served to create not only proficient troops, but troops possessed of a distinctive bond of mutual obligation to one another which stressed a high level of performance. These bonds were reinforced by powerful solidarities in the form of the RAR's 'military culture' that served to create 'in-group homogenisation' among black soldiers. As we have seen, the differences among black soldiers' understandings of loyalty in southern Africa's settler-colonial armies were large. The differences were even greater between soldiers and other forms of paramilitary combatants who fought on the side of (settler-)colonial powers during wars of decolonisation.

Soldiers As Distinct from Other Colonial-Allied Combatants

The loyalties particular to regular soldiers distinguished them from other types of combatants allied to settler or colonial regimes that often played a significant coercive role during wars of decolonisation. It is important to understand this distinction, for it not only clarifies not the distinctive military role of soldiers, but also illustrates how their loyalties were fundamentally different to those of other types of colonial combatants, which had important implications at the moment of independence.

The high-water mark of colonial soldiering was World War II. More than 1 million African troops enlisted in the hitherto small armies of the colonial powers. That widespread inequity, and the increased

[123] Ibid., pp. 168–9, 175, 177, 180.

dependence of European empires upon African servicemen during World War II, would likely change the status quo in the aftermath of the war was widely observed. Orwell's 1939 observations of the Tirailleurs Sénégalais are revealing in this respect:

> But there is one thought which every white man ... thinks when he sees a black army marching past. 'How much longer can we go on kidding these people? How long before they turn their guns in the other direction?'[124]

As nationalist movements across Africa gained mass support and challenged imperial rule, they were heavily suppressed by colonial authorities. This was most pronounced in Africa's settler colonies. Every white settler regime resorted to violence to preserve itself, and nationalist movements took up arms in response. As Reid argued, the 'presence of sizeable and politically powerful European settler communities' complicated processes of decolonisation. In Algeria, in Kenya, and in southern Africa settler regimes introduced 'new grievances and patterns of conflict ... as did especially obstinate metropolitan regimes, as in the case of the Portuguese colonies'.[125] To fight nationalist forces, settler-colonial regimes recruited thousands of paramilitary combatants, rather than greatly expanding the number of regular soldiers who were expensive to train and sustain.

This phenomenon has recently been the subject of a groundbreaking historical enquiry. Those who 'were willing to remain loyal to the colonial regime in the face of the nationalist challenge' during the 'wars of liberation and decolonization fought in Africa and Asia' after 1945 have been termed 'loyalists' by the historians Anderson and Branch.[126] During these wars of decolonisation:

> European colonial powers held the dominant position in these asymmetric wars, and they often used local auxiliaries to turn insurgency into civil war – immensely destructive for all the indigenous forces draw in on both sides, but effectively limiting the level of military commitment required from the metropole.[127]

Anderson and Branch's invocation of the term 'loyalist' is explicitly intended as a neutral way to reference combatants who fought for the colonial powers, shorn of the pejorative connotations of terminology such as 'collaborator'. Their 'loyalist' framework is broad by design, incorporating auxiliaries, paramilitaries, policemen, and militia, as well as soldiers. During wars of decolonisation, David M. Anderson and Daniel Branch argue, membership in any of these forces 'became politically toxic.

---

[124] Orwell, 'Marrakech', as quoted in Grundy, *Soldiers without Politics*, p. 45.
[125] Reid, *Warfare*, p. 159.   [126] Anderson and Branch, 'Allies at the End of Empire', p. 2.
[127] Ibid., p. 3.

Loyalty to empire was now denigrated as betrayal, its adherents castigated as "self-seeking scoundrels" and the "running dogs of imperialism"'.[128] While all those in the employ of the state became prime targets for guerrilla violence in insurgencies, members of the security forces were especially so, for military reasons, but also for reasons of political symbolism, indicative of how quickly the concept of loyalty to the colonial state had become taboo.

The first widespread use of the term 'loyalist' in this context was its application to and embrace by Kenyan opponents of Mau Mau during the 1950s.[129] Rendering colonial security force members as 'loyalists' should not be taken to imply that they subscribed to the political ideologies of the colonists, nor that they wished to perpetuate imperial or settler-colonial rule. For instance, in 1971:

> Bethwell Alan Ogot was the first of Kenya's historians to probe the question of what defined loyalism in these difficult years of insurrection. Ogot identified several types of loyalist, each with differing motivation, but he did not think that any of them were genuine supporters of British colonialism.[130]

Branch developed this argument, arguing that 'loyalism' was a phenomenon that cut across class lines, inspired by heterogeneous motivations ranging from economic opportunism through to an imperial patriotism personified by the Crown, and 'was not solely imposed by colonial masters, but also an intellectual position embedded in local culture and social relations'.[131]

These forms of loyalty were very different from the solidarities of soldiers outlined in the previous section, particularly as regards the ideas of 'professionalism' that animated micro-level solidarities within regular armies. A marked distinction existed within colonial security forces between regular soldiers and 'auxiliaries'. They fought in the same wars, but their roles and, I argue, their loyalties, were quite different.

As Anderson and Branch noted, auxiliaries were *irregular* forces employed on a wide scale by the 'declining imperial powers [who] were either unable or unwilling to commit sizeable numbers of regular troops'.[132] Sybille Scheipers described auxiliaries as 'military forces that support the military efforts of regular armed forces of a state. They are hence distinct from regular armies'. Scheipers also noted that 'they did not undergo a process of regularisation' in contradistinction to regular colonial forces 'such as the tirailleurs, Gurkhas, KAR, and Malay

---

[128] Ibid., p. 7. [129] Branch, 'The Enemy Within'.
[130] Anderson, 'Making the Loyalist Bargain', p. 51.
[131] Branch, 'The Enemy Within', p. 293.
[132] Anderson and Branch, 'Allies at the End of Empire', p. 4.

Regiment',[133] a list to which the RAR can be appended. That auxiliaries 'did not undergo a process of regularisation' had significant implications for the nature of their loyalties.

Regular colonial units required considerable investment in both time and resources: for instance, RAR soldiers received six months of basic training, yet were deemed by their commanders to require a 'further two years under good NCOs and officers' before they were considered fully trained.[134] In RAR soldiers' accounts, this produced fundamentally different loyalties to auxiliaries. Soldiering was their métier, not merely a job but a way of life. As argued earlier, their micro-level loyalties were premised upon a 'professional' ethos and were rooted in the 'military culture' of the army as an institution, rather than in 'local culture' or social or political divisions. In other words, soldiers' macro-level solidarities were vested in their regiment and the army while, in contrast, locally recruited and deployed auxiliary forces often abused their power to pursue personal gain or settle pre-war scores, or to advance the interests of a particular political or ethnic faction. Regular soldiers claimed legitimacy – and were at times afforded it even by their adversaries – because the targets of their violence were military in nature.

Auxiliaries played a fundamentally different role to that of professional soldiers. Cynthia Enloe argued that they were 'inherently less "professional"' than regular soldiers.[135] Scheipers, drawing upon case studies of auxiliaries from Vietnam, Malaya, Algeria, and Oman, argued that auxiliaries were generally poorly trained, inadequately equipped, ill trusted by their command hierarchies, and militarily ineffective. Auxiliaries were 'a departure from the earlier trend towards the increasing regularisation of colonial troops. They were deliberately set apart from regular armed forces and often stayed outside of the regular military command structures'.[136] Their primary value to the imperial power was political,[137] as their familiarity with local language, culture, and terrain provided useful information to regular forces, and their massed presence offered a propaganda boost in rural areas.

Their utility in combat against a military opponent was minimal: auxiliaries were largely used to deny insurgents access to the civilian population, as their continuous static presence deterred insurgent infiltration of rural settlements. This meant that their violence was mostly directed at civilians. Their ubiquity and presence as the public face of the imperial forces often made them loathed and rendered them prime targets: many

---

[133] Scheipers, 'Irregular Auxiliaries', pp. 15, 25.
[134] Downie, *Frontline Rhodesia*, 5m:00s–5m:30s. [135] Enloe, *Ethnic Soldiers*, p. 222.
[136] Scheipers, 'Irregular Auxiliaries', p. 15.
[137] See also Kalyvas, *Logic of Violence*, p. 107.

auxiliary units suffered horrific casualties. In Angola, the Portuguese raised local militias 30,000 strong by 1974. They were poorly equipped, with 'only a small percentage [having] access to proper firearms', and 'were considered "expendable", frequently being deployed for the interception and pursuit of enemy groups, coups de main, and other "risky" missions'.[138] In Rhodesia, the use of auxiliaries came relatively late in the war, was militarily disastrous, and cost civilians dearly, as we shall see.

The case studies within Anderson and Branch's edited edition on 'loyalists' foreground auxiliary forces rather than soldiers,[139] an apposite approach given the important – and somewhat novel – role of auxiliaries in these wars. This emphasis builds upon the approach of earlier scholars, such as Karl Hack, who argued that the effectiveness of the British COIN effort in Malaya was reliant upon 'deployment of Home Guard or local militias on a massive scale'.[140]

The spotlighting of auxiliaries is also present in the literature on civil wars, of which the seminal text, Stathis Kalyvas' *The Logic of Violence in Civil War*, questions 'individual motivations for joining progovernment militias', noting that they were complex, heterogeneous, and changeable over time.[141] Despite the monograph's broad sweep, Kalyvas does not query the loyalties of regular military forces. Given that regular soldiers played a significant military role in many of the case studies Kalyvas draws from, this is a puzzling and significant omission.[142]

Although there were some commonalities between soldiers and 'auxiliaries', given the large differences between them as I have outlined, I do not use the term 'loyalist' to refer to black Rhodesian soldiers, so as to

---

[138] Oliveira, 'Saved by the Civil War', pp. 130–1.
[139] With the notable exception of Pedro Oliveira's article on African soldiers in Angola, discussed in detail later.
[140] Hack, 'Everyone Lived in Fear', p. 691. See also Ucko, 'Malayan Emergency', pp. 19, 22, 34.
[141] Kalyvas, *Logic of Violence*, pp. 97–100, 107–9.
[142] Ibid. Kalyvas provides a definition of militias that highlights their political rather than military nature, and utilises historical comparisons to outline their characteristics and usage across several regions and time periods. Yet he also includes the example of 'Algerian men who joined the French *Army*' in the midst of his many examples of loyalists joining *militia* (both emphases mine) and gives no explanation or context as to the reason for lumping auxiliaries and regular soldiers together. This may be a result of the frequent misuse of the term *harki*, which has rendered it slightly ambiguous. While the harkis were auxiliaries (*supplétifs*) that augmented regular forces, the delineation between auxiliaries, regular soldiers, and others (such as civil servants) allied to the French has lapsed with time (Crapanzano, *Harkis*, pp. 29, 70). In the decades following the war, *harki* 'became the blanket term for all pro-French Algerians'; this ambiguity can cloud understanding, given that in 1962, the number of harki auxiliaries was 58,000, yet there were also 20,000 Algerians serving as regulars in the French Army, alongside 40,000 conscripts and 15,000 police (Evans, 'Reprisal Violence', p. 92).

avoid confusion with auxiliaries, and the general association of the term 'loyalist' with the Mau Mau conflict in Kenya. I do, however, build upon aspects of the colonial 'loyalist' approach for, as Anderson and Branch noted, their case studies have 'a resonance that carries forward into other examples of exit from less conventional imperialist settings in the Cold War era', for which they cite apartheid South Africa's units of externally recruited African soldiers as an example.[143] Likewise, black soldiers in the Portuguese Armed Forces and the Rhodesian Army are also examples of 'less conventional' settings.

These three instances were highly interconnected. The 'White Redoubt' powers of apartheid South Africa, Rhodesia, and the Portuguese government all perceived the wave of African decolonisation in the early 1960s as posing an existential threat to their settler populations.[144] In response, the 'White Redoubt' often coordinated their COIN efforts and provided mutual support in an attempt to preserve minority rule across southern Africa.[145]

As Crawford Young argued, 'a striking paradox of the terminal colonial state is that, in the large majority of countries where decolonization was managed by negotiation, internal security was maintained with strikingly small military forces', but the opposite was the case in settler-colonies, where liberation movements had to fight for their independence.[146] Not only did the white settler states arm themselves to the teeth, but they were willing to use this force liberally. As the political scientist Kenneth Grundy asserted, 'constraints that inhibit a more powerful metropolitan power's employment of force are virtually absent in the case of a settler regime. For settlers, the issue is not whether to fight opponents but how'.[147]

The 'how' involved large-scale and complex COIN operations, which necessitated not only auxiliaries or militia, but also increasing numbers of well-trained regular soldiers. The perpetual shortage of white recruits was an enduring strategic issue in Rhodesia, colonial Angola and Mozambique,

---

[143] Anderson and Branch, 'Allies at the End of Empire', p. 8.

[144] Portugal, 'both the weakest and the most obdurate of the European imperial powers', oversaw a large African empire which it deemed provinces of a singular 'pluricontinental' state. While Portuguese resistance to decolonisation was driven primarily by metropolitan politics, there were also large communities of influential settlers in both Angola (more than 300,000 in 1974) and Mozambique (more than 180,000). See MacQueen, 'Portugal', pp. 163–70.

[145] See several recent works by Filipe de Meneses and Robert McNamara: 'Last Throw of the Dice', 'Origins of Exercise ALCORA', and *White Redoubt*.

[146] Young, 'End of the Post-colonial State in Africa?', pp. 28–9.

[147] Grundy, *Soldiers without Politics*, p. 273.

and South Africa,[148] and was exacerbated as these conflicts intensified and the military demand for soldiers increased.[149]

Consequently, settler authorities abandoned their historic reluctance – premised upon fears of disloyalty – to arm black troops and rapidly increased their number. The Portuguese Army expanded the number of African troops from 9,000 (18 per cent of the total) to 61,800 (41 per cent) between 1961 and 1974.[150] Likewise, in Rhodesia, where the settler government had long insisted on maintaining a one-to-one ratio of black and white regular soldiers as we shall see, the recruitment of black soldiers rapidly increased in tandem with the intensification of the war, and by 1979, black troops outnumbered whites in the regular army by more than four to one.

These colonial soldiers became the vanguard of the settler forces during the latter stages of these wars.[151] Their loyalties functioned in particular ways and were distinct to those of auxiliaries. Colonial soldiers were often involved in protracted and dangerous combat, which placed particular demands upon their loyalties and, in some historical instances, caused them to break. Historically, colonial armies have attempted to forestall this by maintaining a 'social contract' with their soldiers, which I now turn to, alongside a wider literature that addresses loyalties in other regular armies comprised of soldiers drawn from marginalised groups.

The Loyalties of Colonial or Marginalised Soldiers As a Social Contract

The soldierly loyalties of African colonial troops were not usually premised upon the abstract political ideas or patriotism that has been observed as comprising macro-level solidarities in other armies, and were vested in the army itself rather than the state. This made them contingent upon a continually negotiated 'social contract' with the army. The loyalties of soldiers could only be created and perpetuated when their basic needs were met, for loyalty alone could not sustain troops through difficult

---

[148] South Africa's use of black soldiers differed from Portugal's and Rhodesia's as it had a much larger and longer-established white population, which provided the bulk of its military forces in line with the Boer commando tradition – as late as 1977, regular troops constituted only 7 per cent of the South African military, with reservists and part-timers making up the rest (Grundy, *Soldiers without Politics*, p. 102). Black soldiers were admitted to the Permanent Force only after 1975 and by January 1980, there were only 490 black soldiers – 2 per cent of total troop numbers (ibid., pp. 199–200, 210).

[149] For Portugal, see Wheeler, 'African Elements in Portugal's Armies', pp. 239–40; Coelho, 'African Troops in the Portuguese Colonial Army', pp. 135–7. For South Africa, see Bolliger, *Apartheid's African Soldiers*, p. 55.

[150] Coelho, 'African Troops in the Portuguese Colonial Army', p. 136.

[151] Grundy, *Soldiers without Politics*, p. 280.

periods of fighting if they had nothing to eat, were not paid, or were abused by their officers. Likewise, soldiers had to have faith that their commanders would look out for their interests and protect them from needless danger, and that the sacrifices of their service would result in fairer treatment by the authorities. Colonial troops had long framed their soldiering in such a manner. For instance, the regimental song of the Natal Native Horse, raised in 1906, concluded:

> Oh what more can be done
> To earn the recognition of our King
> Than to give our life for King and country;
> Oh may we receive loyalty's fair reward –
> The faith and confidence of our rulers.[152]

As will be shown later, RAR soldiers also deemed that their service would result in more equitable treatment from the army.

In this manner, soldierly loyalties were not merely bonds of obedience, but were a form of mutual obligation between the troops and the army they served, and if one party ceased to meet these obligations, it would lapse. Soldiers expected the army to meet the promises made to them upon enlistment and during service. Breaking the expected conditions of service voided this 'social contract' and meant that soldiers would not re-enlist, and it sometimes resulted in disobedience and mutiny. For instance, to return to Roy, Indian Army troops remained remarkably loyal during World War II, despite many inimical factors. However, their loyalties faltered in peacetime when the drawdown of the colonial army jeopardised their future.[153]

Timothy Lovering writes of similar concerns among colonial Malawian soldiers, for whom dissent 'was most often a reflection of a belief that a "contract" between the Government and the soldier had not been fulfilled, or a reflection of a desire for fuller inclusion in the military system, rather than a rejection of the military authorities'.[154] As argued later, black Rhodesian soldiers expectations of this 'contract' being met were of key concern to Rhodesian authorities, who instituted a series of reforms during the war in areas such as pay, so as to ensure that black troops' loyalties were not corroded.

This 'social contract' was continually negotiated. As colonial soldiers' loyalties were vested, at the macro level, in the army rather than the state, the army's treatment of them was fundamentally important. During the wars of decolonisation in southern Africa, soldiers in the Portuguese colonial army

---

[152] Thompson, 'Loyalty's Fair Reward', p. 656.
[153] Roy, 'Military Loyalty in the Colonial Context', p. 527.
[154] Lovering, *Authority and Identity*, p. 301.

and apartheid South Africa's external units secured markedly improved status, pay, and conditions of service as settler-colonial authorities became more reliant upon them.[155] The importance of this 'social contract' has also been demonstrated in other contexts where marginalised soldiers have enlisted in the army of state that has repressed their political or ethnic group.

A small literature exists on such soldiers. Foremost is Alon Peled's *A Question of Loyalty: Military Manpower in Multi-ethnic States*, which looks at three case studies: Israel, apartheid South Africa, and post-independence Singapore. Peled's titular 'question' refers to how elites in such societies have perennially raised what he terms the 'Trojan Horse dilemma': 'if allowed into the military, will young ethnic soldiers become Trojan horses, or will they serve loyally?'.[156] Peled argues that there is a 'causal relationship' between how professional a military force is and how equitably it treats troops from disadvantaged groups.[157] For Peled, the history of regular military forces demonstrates that a 'professional' approach that emphasises the fair treatment of soldiers and a gradual approach to integration engenders loyalty: 'whenever and wherever they were given a chance, ethnic soldiers have served their countries loyally, including on the battlefield'.[158]

Peled argues that even in the most discriminatory societies, the regular army can still be a (relatively) equitable institution. This exceptionalism is the product of its adherence to 'professional' norms, which generate loyalty among soldiers (i.e. his use of this term is very similar to what I have termed micro-level loyalties). For Peled, these loyalties are powerful enough to supersede other factors that would ordinarily be expected to be corrosive to soldierly loyalty, such as the stigma of 'collaborating' in the colonial army, or a soldier's fear of their family being persecuted as a result of their service. Peled's argument is rooted in a rather mercenary martial logic: he advises hypothetical officers serving in the military of such a state to 'sell' the ethnic integration of their forces to sceptical politicians by emphasising its 'combat performance rewards' rather than aspects of 'social justice'.[159] His argument supports the notion that, in such contexts, the army as an institution can form an enduring 'social contract' with its soldiers, which facilitates the creation of a macro-level bond of loyalty between soldiers and the army itself, rather than the state. So long as the army abides by its professional norms and treats these soldiers fairly, these bonds of loyalty will endure.[160]

---

[155] See, for instance, Coelho, 'African Troops in the Portuguese Colonial Army', p. 136; Bolliger, *Apartheid's African Soldiers*, pp. 49–50, 82.
[156] Peled, *Question of Loyalty*, pp. 2, 172.   [157] Ibid., p. 10.   [158] Ibid., p. 173.
[159] Ibid.
[160] Aside from this 'professional' argument, Peled does not explicitly discuss how soldierly loyalties are formed nor how they are manifested. Such ambiguity is also found in several other scholarly texts published on troops recruited from minority, marginalised,

Peled's case studies also highlight a further, important aspect of macro-level loyalties. It is clear that the loyalties of troops drawn from marginalised communities are not borne of a macro-level political or ideological affinity for the regime, be it colonial, settler-colonial, or otherwise oppressive (as I will argue, the men of the RAR did not support the Smith regime, or minority rule, whatsoever). Nor do the loyalties of marginalised soldiers signal uncritical endorsement of discrimination or oppression. Instead, these loyalties were often a strategy of acquiring improved rights, both individually and collectively, through military sacrifice.

Understanding of the loyalties of minority soldiers was bolstered by the 2008 publication of Rhoda Kanaaneh's *Surrounded: Palestinian Soldiers in the Israeli Military*, which uses interviews conducted with seventy-two members, or veterans of, the Israeli security forces.[161] For marginalised Palestinians, enlisting in the military, despite being 'unpopular and rare', offers one of the only viable routes to acquire citizenship and 'lies at the extreme of a continuum of Palestinian strategies that range from collaboration and informing all the way to armed struggle against the state'.[162]

Palestinian soldiers who enlist to pursue this route of social mobility, and their families, are stigmatised in a manner comparable to how black Rhodesian soldiers were, suffering attacks in their home areas and sometimes being housed elsewhere in response.[163] Arab soldiers in the Israeli Defense Forces (IDF) are often concentrated in the lowest ranks and have few opportunities for promotion beyond a 'glass ceiling', a source of great frustration.[164] Yet this discrimination is juxtaposed with the *relative* meritocracy available within the IDF: as one 'Arab soldier ... who complained of the ethnic limitations he faced within the Israeli military [stated,] "As bad as it is in there, I only wish we would be treated the same way outside the military"'.[165] This further supports the notion that, so long as an army adheres to the tenets of 'professionalism' and fulfils the

---

overseas, or suppressed communities. See, for example, Enloe, *Ethnic Soldiers*; Krebs, *Fighting for Rights*; Ware, *Military Migrants*; Johnson, *True to Their Salt*.

[161] The number of actual soldiers Kanaaneh interviewed is ambiguous – while she states that 'between 2000 and 2005', she interviewed 'seventy-two' members of the security forces (pp. 70, 113), her interviewees were not solely drawn from the IDF, but also from the police and border guards. She argues that the distinctions between these groups are immaterial, insisting from a functionalist perspective that the loyalties and everyday experiences of soldiers, policemen, and border guards are similar, and that she thus often uses 'the term soldiers to refer to what were, in fact, policemen, Border Guards, and members of the military of varying rank' (p. 114), a point with which I do not agree, given my argument that soldierly loyalties are exceptional. While references to 'soldiers' within Kanaaneh's text are often to members of other services, I have only used quotes from her book in which she specifically refers to soldiers in the IDF. Kanaaneh, *Surrounded*, pp. 70, 113–15.

[162] Ibid., pp. 6–7.   [163] Ibid., pp. 18, 24.   [164] Ibid., pp. 70–1.   [165] Ibid., p. 97.

obligations of its 'social contract', soldiers drawn from marginalised communities will remain loyal.

Elsewhere, the macro-level loyalties of marginalised soldiers to the state is often ambivalent. As Roger Reese argued when writing of Soviet soldiers who fought for the Red Army despite their contempt for Stalinism, macro-level loyalties oft described as 'patriotic' in fact span an array of emotive attachments towards the army and the state:

> In the larger picture of people at war and their manifestation and internalization of patriotism it is very possible for people to fight for a country whose leadership they do not like, or whose policies negatively affect them personally. The Neisei in the United States for example, dispossessed and disenfranchised, were recruited out of internment camps and formed the all-volunteer 442nd Regimental Combat Team, which became the most decorated unit of its size in the United States Army in World War II. The Tuskegee airmen, the men of the 761st Tank Battalion and the 777th Artillery Battalion, and all the other African-American men and women who served the United States armed forces were in no way endorsing the segregation and discrimination of Jim Crow society ... In fact, people can fight for their country with the hope that their efforts will, in the post war years, change the social and political order.[166]

Reese's insights here are striking, and his notion of 'patriotism' as a spectrum which can incorporate a rejection of a regime in power, and a belief among soldiers that their service will reform the discriminatory practices of the state, is useful in thinking about soldiers who come from marginalised groups.

Similarly, in 1979, a black sergeant in the South African Army stated that 'now, after fighting, we have a right to claim our share in (this country), alongside the white man'.[167] In 1987, the first Druze general in the IDF also advocated that military loyalty could influence how the state treated the marginalised:

> [T]he young Druze have to realise that our future progress depends on our [military] progress [i.e. performance in combat units, and as specialists and officers]. We must not fail. If we fail, doors will be closed. If we succeed more doors will be opened ... We must not forget that Israel is a young country, and if we Druze look around the world at other peoples in our situation we can see that they did not reach every position of authority overnight. It took time.[168]

One of Kanaaneh's Palestinian interviewees expressed a similar sentiment. Commenting on how 'recently some Druze have reached very high ranks, ranks we could not dream of before', he argued that 'it is not unrealistic that in ten, fifteen, or twenty years there will be real

---

[166] Reese, 'Motivations to Serve', pp. 266–8.
[167] Grundy, *Soldiers without Politics*, p. 222.   [168] Peled, *Question of Loyalty*, pp. 162–3.

decision makers in this state who are Arab'.[169] Colonial and marginalised soldiers have forged macro-level loyalty to the army, rather than the state, as the army is perceived as a reasonably fair institution which offers a path to social mobility that would otherwise be closed. This dynamic recalls the regimental song of the Natal Native Horse, sung more than a century ago, in which its soldiers expressed their wish to 'receive loyalty's fair reward'.[170] As I will show later, my interviewees perceived the Rhodesian Army's (glacial) reforms of the late 1970s as indicative that their service could produce change.

Furthermore, this 'patriotic' spectrum has been observed as incorporating nuanced loyalties on part of colonial soldiers that distinguish between the state and the government of the day. In their own renderings of their service to the state, soldiers from oppressed groups have often portrayed their soldiering as inherently apolitical, a term I define in this book as making a distinction between the state's institutions and the policies of the incumbent regime. These narratives, prevalent among colonial or marginalised troops, are crafted to depoliticise their service and exculpate them from moral judgement, while simultaneously recognising that the state they serve has been fundamentally compromised by the political interests of the regime, and expressing hope that this will change in the future. For instance, some of Kanaaneh's interviewees in the IDF advanced a 'motivation of defending the state, the law', rather than the interests of settlers.[171] Black Rhodesian soldiers also argued fulsomely that they served the government of the day and that they were apolitical soldiers whose allegiance was not to the settler state or the Smith regime.

In summary, it is important to recognise that the factors which motivated colonial soldiers to enlist were typically not the same as the loyalties that sustained them during wartime. I have divided these loyalties into micro-level ('professional') and macro-level ('regimental loyalties') solidarities. 'Professional' loyalties, as set out by King, not only incorporate high levels of soldierly proficiency, but also denote the powerful mutual obligations that exist among regular troops, which create a distinctive solidarity.

At the macro level, it is important to understand the loyalties of colonial soldiers as shaped by the particular 'military culture' of the army, which serves to create 'in-group solidarity' among members of a regiment. It is to the army that colonial soldiers' wider loyalties were pledged, which were not simply bonds of obedience, as the 'social contract' inherent to

---

[169] Kanaaneh, *Surrounded*, p. 19. [170] Thompson, 'Loyalty's Fair Reward', p. 656.
[171] Kanaaneh, *Surrounded*, pp. 19–20.

this loyalty was continually negotiated. These loyalties rendered soldiers fundamentally distinct from other kinds of paramilitary combatants who allied with colonial authorities. As Kanaaneh argued, contrary to the view that soldiers' loyalties 'are often regarded as primordial', they are in fact 'contingent and shifting', and can be vested in a seemingly paradoxical manner.[172] These other cases of colonial and marginalised soldiers further understanding of the strategies such troops used to negotiate their circumstances, and how they understood their own loyalties and told stories about them.

Much of this literature on colonial soldiers or soldiers from marginalised groups can only, however, speculate as to the specific ways in which such loyalties were forged at the micro and macro levels. Aside from a handful of notable examples such as the work of Bolliger and Kanaaneh, the emergent literature has not had sufficient evidence, and specifically oral historical sources, to explore the views of rank-and-file soldiers themselves. Such sources are rare and difficult to access. In the next section, I set out my own methodological approach to these questions.

Methodological Challenges and Approaches

The task of researching black Rhodesian veterans was complex. Many colonial-era documents have been destroyed or stolen, although a fragmentary form of the colonial archive remains. However, this book foregrounds the views of black veterans, making an oral history approach particularly suitable. In the latter part of this chapter, I discuss the process I undertook in making contact with these veterans and how I established a research relationship with them.

In Zimbabwe, historians have struggled to access much of the colonial archive relevant to the war, as Rhodesian officials coordinated the mass destruction of official records as the war came to its end, including the entirety of the archives of the Special Branch and the Central Statistical Office, and 'Rhodesian army and policy files [which were] either burnt in a great holocaust of documents or smuggled to South Africa'.[173] These acts of censorship mirrored British de facto policy during the era of decolonisation, which was to undertake the organised removal or destruction, often on an industrial scale, of records deemed politically sensitive.[174]

[172] Ibid., pp. 15–16.
[173] Pandya, *Mao Tse-tung and Chimurenga*, p. 10; Moorcraft and McLaughlin, *Rhodesian War*, p. 183; Bhebe and Ranger, 'Introduction', p. 3.
[174] Banton, 'Destroy?'.

I have been told that the motive for the removal of the Rhodesian archive to South Africa was the same 'lack of trust in the new Zimbabwean regime' that saw many items of RAR regimental property moved to Durban in 1981.[175] Some of the smuggled Rhodesian material has periodically and belatedly surfaced. In the early 2000s, the Rhodesian Army Association, 'an all-white veterans' organisation based outside Zimbabwe',[176] acquired at least some of the smuggled Rhodesian Army files.

This archive was transported from South Africa to Britain and for a brief time was made available to scholars as the 'Rhodesian Army Archive' (RAA) within the now-defunct British Empire and Commonwealth Museum in Bristol, which closed to the public in 2008.[177] The archive was not thought comprehensive: 'the dearth of, for example, personnel records suggests that many documents were destroyed prior to the 1980 elections'.[178]

I have been informed that the RAA is now once again in the private possession of Rhodesian Army Association veterans. Its illicit custodians allow only their preferred researchers access to it; such texts include Charles Melson's recently published *Fighting for Time*.[179] The holders of the RAA have refused to return it to its rightful owner, the NAZ. Thus the records sit in limbo. At least one academic library has refused the deposit of the stolen RAA, and its intransigent holders remain unwilling to return it.[180]

During my research, foreign scholars were not allowed to access the NAZ without acquiring a research permit, the granting of which had become near impossible. In lieu of access to this archive, I carried out research at the Cory Library for Historical Research at Rhodes University in South Africa, which houses a vast collection of Rhodesian Government Cabinet papers held in Ian Smith's own archive, dating from 1962 to 1978. This archive – often referred to as the 'Smith Papers' – afforded me great insight into the government and army's changing policies towards black soldiers in the army, demonstrating the increasing Rhodesian dependence upon black soldiers and how the settler authorities

---

[175] See Binda, *Masodja*, pp. 398–9. [176] Stapleton, *African Police and Soldiers*, p. 14.
[177] Banton, 'Destroy?', p. 323. [178] Flood, *Brothers-in-Arms?*, p. 7.
[179] Melson, *Fighting for Time*.
[180] I am grateful to Yagil Henkin for allowing me to see his photographs of parts of this archive that he took before it was closed. However, I have utilised only two RAA documents in this book, as those excerpts comprise only top-level Rhodesian discussions of national military strategy at the end of the war. I have also used secondary citations from other texts that had access to the RAA. It is highly likely that more relevant material pertaining to the RAR exists in the RAA, but no other academics I contacted who had accessed the RAA could furnish me with copies.

implemented policies and slow reforms to maintain their 'social contract' obligations to black soldiers.[181] I also accessed papers belonging to Ken Flower, held at the Bodleian Library in Oxford, which provide insight into the discussions among Rhodesian securocrats and politicians.

During my research, I also acquired access to four copies of the RAR's journal, *Nwoho: The Rhodesian African Rifles Regimental Magazine*, published between 1976 and 1978. These are invaluable, for they contain first-hand accounts written by black soldiers during the war. These accounts are short, unvarnished descriptions of life in the wartime RAR, and some are startling for their candid discussion of wartime violence. Stapleton drew upon some of these accounts too, and argued that 'these statements reveal the typical bravado of young men', and that although they 'were published as propaganda, it seems reasonable that, given the wartime context, they accurately reflected soldiers' opinions. If white Rhodesians made these statements, their veracity would not be questioned'.[182]

Having spent hundreds of hours with black Rhodesian veterans, I agree with Stapleton's assessment that these accounts accurately reflect some RAR soldiers' opinions. However, I disagree with his depiction of them as propaganda. *Nwoho* was clearly modelled on the regimental journals long published by British regiments, and is strikingly similar in tone, style, and presentation. Its contents are a mixture of accounts of regimental life, sporting successes, heartfelt tributes to lost comrades, crude masculine jokes, regimental history, accounts of previous wars, gallows humour, detailed accounts of operations, and relentless teasing of other soldiers and subunits. *Nwoho* was clearly not intended for a wide distribution beyond members of the regiment and its veterans, and I argue that it should therefore not be considered mere propaganda.

However, *Nwoho* was also obviously not impartial. It clearly reflected the views of the white RAR officers who edited it. It is highly likely that contributions would have been solicited only from keen soldiers possessed of high morale, whereas the accounts of dissenting or demoralised troops would not have been included. *Nwoho*, while portraying the RAR's particular perspective, also reflected the 'official mind' of the army, as it was subject to the military censor, sometimes to the chagrin of its contributors. For instance, a white RAR company commander lamented that

---

[181] The Smith Papers contained plentiful documents on organisational and administrative matters relating to the Rhodesian Army and were of great use to me. However, it was clear that the Smith Papers had been thoroughly pruned of potentially controversial or sensitive material prior to deposit at Rhodes University, a similar process that many researchers think occurred with the RAA.

[182] Stapleton, *African Police and Soldiers*, p. 201.

his contribution to a previous issue had been excised owing to the 'censor's scrutiny'.[183] Thus, while *Nwoho* was not simply propaganda, it was clearly biased to the official views of white army officers, and it cannot be considered representative of the views of all black soldiers. Nonetheless, it provides an unparalleled contemporary insight into key aspects of black soldiers' lives in their own words and provides rich – and sometimes surprisingly candid – detail as to their wartime experiences that would otherwise be unavailable.

While useful, the archival sources were not as plentiful as I wished and, *Nwoho* aside, did not allow insight into the views of rank-and-file black soldiers. Others researching the loyalties of black soldiers who fought for settler-colonial regimes have faced similar problems. Writing in 1976 on African soldiers in Portugal's colonial armies, Douglas Wheeler argued that 'distressingly little is known about African morale, esprit de corps, promotion, discipline, and racial attitudes and conflicts among groups'.[184] Bolliger likewise argued, more than forty years later, we still know little about the 'tens of thousands of Africans [who] fought in the security forces of the settler and colonial regimes', despite 'their significant impact on southern Africa's military and political history'.[185] This has largely been the result of a lack of access to relevant evidence. For instance, Grundy wrote an excellent book on black soldiers in the apartheid-era South African Army, but he readily acknowledged that his data was limited to documentary sources and elite interviews.[186] Works on other contexts have also, out of necessity, tended to rely on documentary sources.[187]

However, in accounts of the end of colonialism, historians have frequently turned to methods that look beyond the official record in order to tell a fuller story.[188] Oral histories, in particular, have long provided 'an essential corrective' to official records produced by racist states and societies,[189] and scholars of the transnational conflicts of liberation in southern Africa have also found oral histories fruitful where little or no written records are available.[190]

---

[183] 'C Company (Chamuka Inyama) Notes', *Nwoho* (October 1977), p. 45.
[184] Wheeler, 'African Elements in Portugal's Armies', p. 242.
[185] Bolliger, *Apartheid's African Soldiers*, pp. 1–2.
[186] Grundy, *Soldiers without Politics*, p. 23.
[187] See, for instance, Gortzak, 'Using Indigenous Forces'; Peled, *A Question of Loyalty*; McLaughlin, 'Victims As Defenders'. An exception is Crapanzano's *Harkis*, an ethnography of Algerian colonial veterans and their children, in which the author interviewed former auxiliaries, some of whom had previously served in the French Army during World War II or the First Indochina War.
[188] See Stockwell, 'Decolonisation'; Thomas and Doron, 'Out of Africa', pp. 5–8.
[189] Thompson, *Voice of the Past*, p. 81. [190] White and Larmer, 'Introduction'.

Bolliger's book is a watershed moment, as it looks at the histories of black soldiers through 'their own accounts – a new methodological approach to the study of African soldiers of colonial and settler armies'.[191] For historians writing on the history of wars and soldiers, 'allowing the combatants to speak for themselves' is imperative, particularly if we are to seek out 'the voice of the common man', rather than solely those of senior commanders.[192] The individual narratives of soldiers 'work at a level below the big words and the brave sentiments, down on the surface of the earth where men fight. They don't glorify war, or aestheticize it, or make it literary or heroic; they speak in their own voices, in their own plain language'.[193] Paul Thompson, the doyen of oral history, argued that oral history has 'been particularly important in illuminating ordinary experience' of the military rank and file.[194]

Oral history is thus a powerful method for exploring the history of black Rhodesian soldiers, and especially their own views on their loyalties. Yet it must also be recognised that oral histories have their own biases. As the social anthropologist Elizabeth Tonkin argued, oral testimonies suffer from the same weaknesses of fallibility and inaccuracy as textual sources, and are 'not intrinsically more or less likely to be accurate than a written document'.[195] The context of the interview and the positionality of the teller and researcher are important factors.

My interviewees were soldiers who were treated relatively well by the Rhodesian government. It is therefore perhaps unsurprising that they look more favourably upon the Rhodesian era than many civilians. Nonetheless, these recollections should not be mistaken for approval of minority rule. As Luisa Passerini, who chronicled the Italian working class under Fascism, argued, 'acceptance of the social order should not be confused with approval of the regime', and cautioned historians not to repeat the mistakes of predecessors who had failed to be mindful of the subjectivity of their interviewees.[196]

Other scholars have stressed the context of the interview. For instance, Tonkin argued that all oral histories are, fundamentally, both socially constructed and conditioned by the boundaries of acceptable discourse: 'the product of canons of appropriateness and rhetorical stereotypes'.[197] In other words, my interviewees' testimonies sought to justify their military service in a manner acceptable in the political and social context of almost forty years after independence. Their narratives cannot be divorced from the prevailing political wind in Zimbabwe, in which the

---

[191] Bolliger, *Apartheid's African Soldiers*, p. 325.   [192] Keegan, *Face of Battle*, p. 32.
[193] Hynes, *Soldiers' Tale*, p. 30.   [194] Thompson, *Voice of the Past*, pp. 15, 69.
[195] Tonkin, *Narrating Our Pasts*, p. 160.
[196] Passerini, *Fascism in Popular Memory*, p. 6.   [197] Tonkin, *Narrating Our Pasts*, p. 45.

ZANU(PF) government has largely portrayed service in the Rhodesian Army as a form of heinous 'collaboration' since the onset of the country's post-2000 'crisis', as discussed later.

Aside from the meta-story of my interviewees' recollections, the accuracy of recalled events is also fallible. It is commonplace for the memories of veterans to vary enormously, and they diverge even amongst members of the same unit who collectively experienced the same events. As Bao Ninh wrote of North Vietnamese Army veterans:

> We had shared all the vicissitudes, the defeats and victories, the happiness and suffering, the losses and gains. But each of us had been crushed by the war in a different way. Each of us carried in his heart a separate war which in many ways was totally different, despite our common cause. We had different memories of people we'd known and of the war itself.[198]

Such fragmented recollections are not uncommon, particularly in retrospect. Stephen Davis, in his history of Umkhonto we Sizwe, noted how the accounts of struggle participants were often 'frustratingly contradictory' and that it is difficult to arrive at any '"comprehensive truth" of the armed struggle'.[199] The solution, Davis argued, is not 'to attempt to cobble together some patchwork account that achieves a probable accuracy', but rather to interpret how these memories are interwoven with prevailing historical winds, predominant narratives, and the personal circumstances of the storytellers themselves.

While acknowledging the malleable nature of personal testimony, we must also be wary not to throw the baby out with the bathwater and remember that even though memories are modulated by circumstances, they are nonetheless recollections of real events and are frequently very accurate. Furthermore, they are often the only source available.[200] As Thompson argued, historians should interpret oral testimony:

> Neither with blind faith, nor with arrogant scepticism, but with an understanding of the subtle processes through which all of us perceive, and remember, the world around us and our own part in it. It is only in such a sensitive spirit that we can hope to learn the most from what is told to us.[201]

Adopting such an understanding, I attempted to ground my interviewees' recollections not only in their own meta-story, but also in my own understanding of the history of the war and the military context, situated in a deep reading of the secondary literature, Rhodesian archives, and interviews already conducted with other veterans. By adopting this

---

[198] Ninh, *Sorrow of War*, p. 232.   [199] Davis, *The ANC's War against Apartheid*, p. 2.
[200] Passerini, *Fascism in Popular Memory*, p. 8.
[201] Thompson, *Voice of the Past*, p. 116.

approach, I sought to emulate Passerini, who utilised non-oral sources to 'follow up on what had been said' during interviews, in order to facilitate a process of 'supporting or refuting the oral evidence'.[202]

Interview Practicalities

Approaching military veterans and finding further interviewees through snowballing have often posed significant practical difficulties.[203] As Zoe Flood noted in 2005, black Rhodesian veterans 'are not only tremendously difficult to locate, due to the time lapse since the end of the war, but they are understandably reluctant to claim an association with the Smith regime, particularly given the current climate of political intimidation in Zimbabwe'.[204] My own research commenced a decade later, and these difficulties had only increased.

The fear of reprisals from those aligned with ZANU(PF) persists among some veterans, although in a less intense form than in the recent past, as discussed shortly. This fear, alongside the enduring stigma surrounding association with the colonial state, has had a chilling effect on this aspect of the history of Zimbabwe's liberation war. As Mazarire argued:

> Oral archives of Zimbabwe's war still remain lopsided because researchers are yet to transcend the stereotypes invented about this war defining heroes and collaborators. For this reason also, researchers have been unable to win the confidence and access information from those long considered to be on the 'wrong' side of the war.[205]

The difficulty of making contact with interviewees and establishing confidence initially hindered my ability to carry out oral history research. In late 2015, I sent tentative enquiries to the email addresses displayed on the website of the UK-based RAR Regimental Association, stating the nature of my research and asking how I could meet with black RAR veterans in Zimbabwe. This was met with a mixture of silence and refusal.

I was told by a member of the Association that its members did not want 'another bloody Marxist like Terry Ranger' writing a history of 'their regiment' and that its members deemed all researchers and academics axiomatically biased against them.[206] This was a clear echo of the colonial-era contempt for scholarship among many of the Rhodesian elite,

---

[202] Passerini, *Fascism in Popular Memory*, p. 9.
[203] Liebenberg, 'Evolving Experiences', p. 58; Moore, 'In-Depth Interviewing', pp. 117, 127.
[204] Flood, *Brothers-in-Arms?*, p. 8.
[205] Mazarire, 'Rescuing Zimbabwe's "Other" Liberation Archives', p. 10.
[206] The noted historian Terence Ranger wrote many well-regarded books on Zimbabwe. Once a lecturer at the University of Rhodesia, he was deported by the Rhodesian government in 1963 for his support of Zimbabwean nationalism.

who disdainfully referred to the University of Rhodesia as the 'Kremlin on the Hill'. As noted earlier in this chapter and in Chapter 2, some white Rhodesian veterans have utilised their control of archival documents in an attempt to influence a favourable historical narrative.

It seems, however, that my initial enquiry email was circulated among RAR Association members, as shortly afterwards a sympathetic individual emailed me to say that while the Association would 'not lift a finger' to help me, they would pass me the details of an RAR veteran in Zimbabwe, but only if the veteran and his UK-based daughter consented, which they subsequently did.

Thereafter I made contact with TM in late 2015, and he kindly agreed to be interviewed for my fieldwork when I visited Zimbabwe. I am indebted to TM, a kind, scholarly man who vouched for me among other veterans. This trust was a highly important factor in other veterans granting interviews to me, and in this respect, I learned the lessons of the military anthropologist Dirk Kruijt, who noted the importance of 'interviewing on the basis of shared confidence … generated by the introduction via a dependable intermediary that the researcher is reliable'.[207] This bolstered my credibility with potential interviewees immensely.

My second vital intermediary was Verity Mundy, introduced to me by a mutual friend in Bulawayo during 2017. From the outset, Verity's deep commitment to the welfare of these forgotten veterans was evident. She generously provided me with assistance in contacting and meeting veterans and with essential practical guidance as to how to arrange interviews and contact more veterans.

In a turn of events, during this period of fieldwork in Zimbabwe, I also met several members of the RAR Association in person. In a reversal of my initial experience with some other members, those I met in Zimbabwe were friendly, interested in my research, and generous with their time, providing me with introductions to several interviewees.

I interviewed the greatest number of veterans in Matabeleland. This did not reflect a bias towards isiNbebele speakers: most of these veterans had not grown up in the region, but had been posted to the RAR depot at Llewellin Barracks or one of the other military sites clustered around Bulawayo during their career, and had settled in their surrounds upon retirement. I also interviewed black veterans in Harare, Gweru, Masvingo, and Mutare, both from the RAR and other regiments. In total I interviewed fifty-four former Rhodesian soldiers. Additional participants were happy to discuss their service with me but did not wish to be

---

[207] Kruijt, 'Research on Latin America's Soldiers', p. 158.

formally interviewed; others did not wish their interview to be recorded or have notes taken. From these 'non-interviews', I have only drawn context.

I met many interviewees through snowball sampling. Many preferred to meet me away from where they lived owing to the suspicion that meeting with a white foreigner would create within their neighbourhoods. During interviews, many recalled comrades they had served with who were 'now late', and the number of veterans dwindles every year. The World Bank Group put life expectancy in Zimbabwe at sixty-two in 2020; in the early 2000s, it was as low as forty-three. Some of the veterans I interviewed have since passed away.

I interviewed just four women, all the wives of soldiers. This reflects the fact that black soldiers in the Rhodesian Army were exclusively male, mirroring contemporary trends where 'up to the 1970s, even during periods of war, women played a minor role' in armies that adhered to Western norms and 'almost without exception, they served in nursing and administrative roles'.[208] I had hoped to interview more wives of soldiers, but unfortunately this was not often possible, as my interviewees generally travelled alone to meet me, again to avoid arousing suspicion.

Given my reliance upon snowballing to locate interviewees, selection bias was a pitfall I was conscious of from the outset. This is, however, an intrinsic drawback of researching veterans who have been retired for decades, as the military historian Brenda Moore noted in her own work on World War II–era US Air Force veterans,[209] as many have moved around the country or lost contact with former comrades. Snowballing was the only possible way of conducting this research given that the sole organisation in possession of a comprehensive list of the names and contact details of Rhodesian Army veterans is the Zimbabwean government, which was unlikely to assist in this research.

As Mazarire has argued, winning the confidence of black veterans of the Rhodesian army has long been difficult for researchers. My interviewees explained their willingness to speak to me about their service for three reasons: first that their story has been ignored, grossly misrepresented, or simply silenced, which has frustrated and saddened them, with some commenting that as a result they have concealed their time as a soldier even from their own grandchildren. I got the sense during many interviews that speaking of their past was cathartic for veterans. Many were pleased a foreigner had taken an interest in their history and were keen to contribute their memories. Several mentioned that they hoped it would serve as a corrective to the reductive and polarised narratives that all too frequently dominate such discussions.

[208] King, *Combat Soldier*, p. 383.   [209] Moore, 'In-Depth Interviewing', p. 126.

Secondly, some explained that the passage of time has dimmed the controversy surrounding black participation in the Rhodesian Army a little, and that while their service may still be contentious, compared to a decade ago, the stigma is less intense, given that many of those who were participants in the war or lived through it have now passed away. Most of my interviewees still opted to be anonymous to stay on the safe side, and stated that this was a habit of sensible precaution, rather than stemming from a feeling that their ex-Rhodesian Army status posed imminent danger. Others were happy for their full names to be used. However, I have anonymised all of my interviewees so as to err on the side of caution.

Thirdly, many stated that their own diminishing numbers and advancing age posed a risk that their side of the story could well be lost for good if it was not recorded. Roy experienced this when he attempted to interview colonial Indian Army veterans in 2002, but could find only a handful, most of whom by then 'were in their late eighties' and 'seemed to remember little. At best they could say they served in Burma or Italy'.[210] This desire to have one's military service recorded in history concords with the observation made by Kruijt, who noted that military veterans often articulated a sincere desire for an authoritative account of their lives and wartime deeds to be recorded for posterity.[211]

During preparation for fieldwork, I formulated a lengthy consent procedure that I rigidly adhered to at the commencement of each interview. Given my own positionality as a foreigner from a wealthy country, I took particular care to ensure that my interviewees were giving truly informed consent. I elaborated in considerable detail why I was conducting this research and how the data would be used. I made clear that I was a researcher and that my work was solely for academic purposes; that I had no contacts with either non-governmental or governmental organisations; and that taking part in this research would not result in any assistance, financial or otherwise.

This was of particular moral importance to me, for organisations of dubious integrity have made promises to these veterans in the past but not delivered on them. Furthermore, many veterans were also curious as to the size of the potential readership and keen that greater awareness be made for their wartime histories and post-war plight. I responded that much academic work takes years to be published, and its readership is often small and specialised, but that I hoped academic articles and a monograph would result, reaching a wider readership in time.

---

[210] Roy, 'Military Loyalty in the Colonial Context', p. 502.
[211] Kruijt, 'Research on Latin America's Soldiers', pp. 167–9.

I do not speak any of Zimbabwe's languages aside from English. However, all of my interviewees spoke good English, meaning that translation was not necessary, with just two exceptions. One RAR veteran, MC, preferred to listen to my questions in English and then respond in chiShona through his son. MS, the wife of a veteran, preferred to both hear questions and give answers in chiShona – translation was carried out by her friend DC, himself a veteran.

Chapter Outline

Chapter 2 outlines the history of black troops in Rhodesia and in the Rhodesian Army, and argues that the RAR created in-group homogenisation through mimicking the regimental structure and pageantry of British colonial regiments. Invented traditions were important in establishing the regiment and the army as a focal point of soldiers' macro-level loyalties, in shaping its military culture, forming what I term the 'regimental loyalties' of black Rhodesian soldiers. I argue that in the early 1960s, the recruiting practices of the RAR and the focus of its training changed in response to the new government's preparation for an internal COIN war, which had particular implications for black soldiers' 'professionalism'.

In Chapter 3, I argue that the ethos of 'professionalism' was of key importance to the micro-level solidarities of black Rhodesian soldiers, and, drawing upon King, that their soldierly identities and 'professionalism' were co-constitutive. 'Professionalism' was forged through an intensive process of 'military socialisation' and reinforced through continuous training. 'Professional' soldiers were members of a distinctive military culture, which generated profound loyalties.

These loyalties were to an army that was systematically racist. As I argue in Chapter 4, this racism was pervasive, particularly in the higher levels of the army and government. It was only military necessity that influenced RF politicians and senior army officers to expand the number of black soldiers in the army and to improve their conditions of service in order to maintain the 'social contract'. As black soldiers became vital to the Rhodesian war effort, a clear desire not to violate the government's end of this contract is evidenced by the archive, and a slow process of reform occurred towards the end of the war, including the commissioning of black officers. The tenets of the 'professional' ethos were widely invoked to traverse the barriers of systematic racism, and within the particular military culture of the RAR, relationships between black and white troops were premised upon bonds of mutual respect, comradeship, and shared sacrifice.

Chapter 5 argues that the impact of the war and combat was to cement these soldiers' loyalties and that the push and pull causal factors scholars have observed as underpinning desertion in other conflicts were largely not applicable to them. The RAR soldiers experienced a long war, and their own experiences of combat almost exclusively comprised battlefield success. Although this was partly explained by their high level of training and military proficiency, it also reflected the decisive military advantages, notably airpower, possessed by the RSF. Black soldiers' faith in their military prowess informed their perception that they would not lose the war. I argue that this experience of combat success, and a sense that they were winning the war, were important factors in their enduring loyalty. Furthermore, RAR soldiers came to perceive as their wartime role as moral and contrasted their self-portrayal as protectors of civilians with the guerrillas, who they asserted used violence towards rural people. This heightened in-group solidarity was further bolstered by widespread guerrilla targeting of off-duty soldiers and their families as the war intensified.

Black soldiers' conception of their own role as apolitical soldiers who fought for the government of the day instead of a political faction is the focus of Chapter 6. I argue that this apolitical ethos was fundamental to these troops' conception of their service, and that it was also informed by the Rhodesian government's vigorous policing of the politics of black soldiers. As the war intensified, and loyalty to the army became contentious, black soldiers articulated this conception of themselves as apolitical in order to portray their allegiance as not to the settler regime. This was also a subtle form of politicking in and of itself, designed to assure their post-independence safety and status – a strategy that was quite successful.

Chapter 7 highlights the importance of these soldiers' apolitical status and their professional and regimental loyalties during Zimbabwe's difficult first two years of independence, and how their actions during post-independence conflict assured their integration into the ZNA. It then reflects upon how black Rhodesian veterans' memories have been influenced by a form of nostalgia in the context of Zimbabwe's post-2000 crisis.

2 The Creation of Black Rhodesian Soldiers' Regimental Loyalties

This chapter builds upon the framework set out in Chapter 1 and contends that the RAR created a particular military culture in which its troops developed powerful bonds of soldierly loyalty to their regiment. This loyalty was created through the Rhodesian Army mimicking the invented traditions of British colonial regiments, which were historically successful in creating in-group solidarity among troops.

By the onset of the war for Zimbabwe in 1964, soldiers of the RAR were bound together by an influential set of regimental traditions and their martial potency had been greatly enhanced by operational experience. The structure and ethos of the RAR underwent significant changes at the tail end of the Federation and after the RF's rise to power. In particular, a new emphasis upon the COIN doctrine learned during the Malayan Emergency indicated a shift in the RAR's role towards being deployed on COIN tasks within Rhodesia.

Firstly, this chapter provides a brief sketch of the history of black servicemen in Rhodesia, outlining how they were crucial to the settler-colonial state from the outset. It also shows how early colonial conflicts fundamentally informed settler conceptions of black soldiers for decades.

The Early History of Black Troops in Rhodesia

Rhodesia's origins were found in Cecil Rhodes' Pioneer Column of 1890. Comprised of military men and civilian colonists, it executed an armed incursion eastwards from Bechuanaland (Botswana) in 1890, 'expecting to fight its way into the country of the Ndebele and Shona. An invasion force of latter-day conquistadores in search of land and gold'.[1]

Black troops played an important role during Rhodesia's genesis as they would throughout its existence. The Pioneer Column was accompanied by 'armed African mercenaries from the Cape Colony, and local African

---

[1] Saunders and Smith, 'Southern Africa', p. 611; Good, 'Settler Colonialism in Rhodesia', p. 11.

allies', along with thirty-six of Chief Khama's mounted scouts from Bechuanaland.[2] The Column did not engage in combat as it had expected. On the way to its terminal destination of Harare Kopje,[3] a cantonment was established, named Fort Victoria (Masvingo), which became an enduring source of African police, auxiliaries, and, later, soldiers.[4]

The BSAC's 1889 charter – which gave the company authority over the settler colony – granted it permission to raise a police force, which was in effect a colonial gendarmerie. Initially a confusing array of units existed – including a volunteer cavalry unit with attached artillery – until 1896, when the British South Africa Police (BSAP) was created.[5] Its raison d'être was the two major wars of Rhodesia's first decade.

As per David Fieldhouse's typology of settler colonialism, Rhodesia was a 'mixed' settler colony, where 'settlers had encountered a resilient and sizeable indigenous population'.[6] The bellicosity of the BSAC resulted in the First Matabele War of 1893, fought between the settlers and the Ndebele kingdom. The advanced weaponry available to the BSAC carried the day, and white settlers gained control over swathes of the Ndebele kingdom's lands and livestock.[7]

Black troops allied to the Rhodesians were present in large numbers during the 1893 war, fighting 'alongside the settler forces, either directly under their control as auxiliaries or as independently formed units, under their own leadership and organisation, which operated as allies. The columns of settler volunteers from Victoria and Salisbury were both accompanied by detachments of "200 picked Mashona all armed with guns, under white men"'.[8]

Following the 1893 war, the BSAC created two separate paramilitary police forces; in 1894, black policemen were recruited in Mashonaland as part of the Native Department, and by 1895, the Matabeleland Native Police 'consisted mostly of Ndebele warriors ... trained in Western-style military drill and musketry'.[9]

On 29 December 1895, Cecil Rhodes' right-hand man, Leander Jameson, launched his eponymous Raid on the Transvaal to try and

---

[2] Stapleton, *African Police and Soldiers*, p. 7.
[3] Harare Kopje was founded on 12 September 1890, becoming Salisbury during the Rhodesian era and renamed Harare in 1981. See Samkange, *Origins of Rhodesia*, pp. 234–5.
[4] Stapleton, *No Insignificant Part*, p. 10.
[5] Roberts, 'Towards a History of Rhodesia's Armed Forces', pp. 103–4.
[6] Fieldhouse, *Colonial Empires*, as cited in Veracini, *Settler Colonialism*, p. 5. Contrastingly, the 'plantation' colonies were dependent upon slavery and bondage (e.g. European colonial rule in the Caribbean from the fifteenth century to the nineteenth), and the 'pure settlement' colonies were where 'white settlers had eradicated and/or marginalised the indigenous population' (e.g. Australia, Canada).
[7] Ranger, *Revolt*, p. 102; Rotberg, *Founder*, pp. 448, 552.
[8] McLaughlin, *Victims As Defenders*, p. 241. See also Stapleton, *No Insignificant Part*, p. 14.
[9] Stapleton, *African Police and Soldiers*, p. 3.

seize control of the Witwatersrand gold reserves. In doing so Jameson committed the bulk of the BSAC's military forces, leaving 'only 48 white police' in Matabeleland.[10]

Unsurprisingly, the grossly mistreated Ndebele, marshalled by key leaders from the precolonial state, rebelled against BSAC rule on 20 March 1896, with some chiefs in Mashonaland following suit three months later. The rising was swift and lethal.[11] Lasting until 1897, this war was Rhodesia's second major conflict, termed variously 'The First Chimurenga' (revolutionary struggle) by nationalists and 'The Second Matabele War' by settlers. But for British reinforcements (the last British troops sent to Rhodesia on active service until 1979) the settlers would have been defeated. During the uprising, the white settler population was 'literally decimated',[12] its losses 'greater than the proportion of casualties suffered by white colonists in the Algerian national rising or the Mau Mau war in Kenya'.[13]

These losses sowed the seeds for a pervasive white monomania over the use of black soldiers, planting 'a fear of black perfidy – and of arming black men – deep into the settler psyche',[14] as a slight majority of the Matabeleland Native Police had defected and joined the insurrection.[15] The settlers' sense of betrayal was acute, as the police had been 'raised and trained by the Whites themselves',[16] and by putting 'their firearms and training to use against the colonial forces',[17] these defectors offered the rebels a chance of matching the military might of the settlers.

This settler narrative of betrayal ignored the fact that a significant number of the Matabeleland Native Police did not defect and many fought on behalf of the Rhodesians.[18] Furthermore, many other black police and auxiliaries fought for the Rhodesian settlers.[19] Of particular importance were those from Victoria (Masvingo) – home of Fort Victoria, the first cantonment established in Rhodesia by the Pioneer Column – whose

collaboration linked to their position had a vital effect on the 1896–7 risings. By their collaboration they safeguarded the Victoria District and surrounding areas.

---

[10] Ranger, *Revolt*, p. 125. [11] Ibid., p. 127. [12] McLaughlin, *Ragtime Soldiers*, p. 73.
[13] Gann, *History of Southern Rhodesia*, pp. 9–10, as quoted in Ranger, *Revolt*, p. 225. See also Selous, *Sunshine and Storm*, p. 250.
[14] Alexander, 'Loyalty and Liberation', p. 169.
[15] Selous described a force of 330 members, 126 of whom he deemed 'loyal', 172 'rebels', and 32 'doubtful' (*Sunshine and Storm*, p. 282).
[16] McLaughlin, 'Victims As Defenders', pp. 244–5.
[17] Stapleton, *African Police and Soldiers*, pp. 3–4.
[18] Selous described a force of 330 members, of whom 126 he deemed 'loyal', 172 'rebels', and 32 'doubtful'. Selous, *Sunshine and Storm*, p. 282.
[19] McLaughlin, 'Victims As Defenders', p. 241.

This enabled the Company to coordinate striking forces that weakened and eventually destroyed the rebel Shona polities of Belingwe, Gwelo and Selukwe, which were fighting on independently of the main Ndebele forces that surrendered at the Matopos indabas.[20]

Settlers at the time recognised the emergence of Fort Victoria as a source of black troops; in the aftermath of the 1896–7 war, all black Rhodesian constables were summarily dismissed and replaced by extraterritorial recruits, 'with the exception of the Victoria District where most were local Karanga Shona'.[21] As discussed later in this chapter, Victoria continued to be an important source of black Rhodesian military recruits throughout the colonial period, particularly for the RAR.

Following the 1896–7 war, 'most of Southern Rhodesia's white settlers would always deeply distrust armed blacks working for the colonial state ... it became illegal for Africans to possess firearms and there was a rigorous disarmament campaign'.[22] Bearing arms acquired a cachet in colonial society, embodying visceral power and the status of state-sanctioned authority.

The war also 'profoundly affected white thinking' on the 'recruitment of African troops', for settler officials feared 'that the arming and training of African troops in European-style tactics would create a "Trojan horse" which could form the core of future local or nation-wide insurgencies'.[23] It was largely for this reason that, prior to 1940, Rhodesia did not possess a standing army as – given the small white population – this would have necessitated black soldiers.

Rhodesian security during this period was the responsibility of the British South African Police (BSAP), which, to paraphrase the quip aphoristically attributed to Voltaire on the Holy Roman Empire, was neither British, nor South African, nor solely a police force. It resembled more a colonial gendarmerie 'charged with the dual duty of external defence and the maintenance of internal security'.[24] Members of the BSAP fought in South Africa during the Boer War; one early commissioner remarked that its men 'were more soldiers than policemen'.[25]

A small core of black BSAP members were engaged in a paramilitary role and have often been considered Rhodesia's first black troops. Recruited in 1898, they were 'given military training and held in

---

[20] Beach, 'Politics of Collaboration', p. 2.
[21] Stapleton, 'Extra-territorial African Police and Soldiers', p. 101.
[22] Stapleton, *African Police and Soldiers*, p. 7.
[23] McLaughlin, 'Victims As Defenders', p. 244.
[24] Gann, 'Development of Southern Rhodesia's Military System'; Roberts, 'Towards a History of Rhodesia's Armed Forces'.
[25] Stapleton, *African Police and Soldiers*, p. 4.

Salisbury, where, despite their [later] amalgamation into other organisations, they retained a certain separateness'.[26] The BSAP's Force Orders of 16 February 1906 deemed the Reserve Company 'part of the military force which might conceivably be called upon to protect white settlers against natives'.[27] These black troops 'took part in the military action [against German forces] in the Caprivi Strip in 1914 and then formed the nucleus of the Rhodesia Native Regiment (RNR) raised in 1916'.[28]

The RNR was raised comparatively late in World War I, and only after sources of white recruits were exhausted.[29] This reluctance was rooted in enduring white hostility and paranoia stemming from the 1896–7 war. However, military necessity overcame white paranoia, and a total of 2,360 black soldiers served in the RNR, which fought in the east African theatre.[30] The organisational structure of the RNR mirrored colonial society: 'a small group of Europeans was at the top and a mass of Africans was at the bottom'.[31] The pay, accommodation, and benefits given to black soldiers were meagre. Nonetheless, they performed well and several earned prestigious imperial gallantry awards.[32]

The RNR also received frequent praise from the top brass and the imperial war office. This respect and appreciation did not extend to Rhodesia's political leaders, however, who frequently omitted or overlooked the service of the RNR while highlighting the contributions of white officers and soldiers.[33] At the culmination of the war, the RNR returned home and was demobilised with great haste, partly as imperial war funding ceased,[34] and partly owing to settler hostility towards black soldiers.

After the RNR's disbandment, Rhodesia reverted to the BSAP, fulfilling its security needs. Although the 1926 Defence Act instituted a system of conscription and reservist service, this excluded the black population entirely.[35] Nonetheless, a continuity of service was preserved: demobilised RNR veterans formed the kernel of the BSAP's Askari Platoon.[36]

---

[26] Roberts, 'Towards a History of Rhodesia's Armed Forces'.
[27] Gibbs, Phillips, and Russell, *Blue and Old Gold*, p. 132, as quoted in Stapleton, 'Extra-territorial African Police and Soldiers', p. 101.
[28] Roberts, 'Towards a History of Rhodesia's Armed Forces'. See also Horrocks, 'Introduction', in Owen, *Rhodesian African Rifles*.
[29] Stapleton, *No Insignificant Part*, pp. 19–20.
[30] McLaughlin, 'Victims As Defenders', pp. 256–7.
[31] Stapleton, *No Insignificant Part*, p. 42. [32] Ibid., pp. 90–1, 116, 133–4.
[33] Ibid., p. 121.
[34] Ibid., p. 136. The KAR in east Africa was trimmed by sixteen battalions for similar reasons (Page, *King's African Rifles*, p. 51).
[35] McLaughlin, 'Victims As Defenders', p. 258.
[36] Which would itself morph into the paramilitary Police Support Unit that saw significant combat during the 1964–79 war and that still functions in this role for the ZRP. See Stapleton, 'Extra-territorial African Police and Soldiers', pp. 102–3.

In the same manner as their Reserve Company forebears, the members of this Platoon served as 'an emergency quick reaction force', and were exceptional as they were 'permitted to carry firearms on a regular basis'.[37] The Askari Platoon supplied the NCOs for the RAR when it was formed in 1940.[38] Thus, as Ray Roberts noted, by the start of Zimbabwe's war of liberation in 1964 the RAR had a 'direct line of descent and continuity back into the nineteenth century'.[39]

Raised in 1940 to fight as part of the British effort in World War II, the RAR formed Rhodesia's only contribution of an entire infantry battalion.[40] White paranoia had not dissipated with the passage of time, and 'a clear generation after the event, the ghosts of settlers killed by mutinous black servicemen in 1896–97 were once more mobilised in arguments against placing trust in African soldiery', although the government once more overruled these objections on military grounds.[41] Unlike in South Africa, where racist policies restricted black soldiers to non-combat roles, the RAR was an infantry battalion serving as part of the 22nd East African Brigade alongside other British colonial troops.[42] As with their RNR forebears, 'Africans were discriminated against within the services even though they were accorded more status than the bulk of blacks. Their pay was markedly inferior to that of white servicemen; there were no Africans commissioned; and in the early days of the war African soldiers were subjected to corporal punishment while European soldiers were not.'[43] After intensive training in Rhodesia, east Africa, and Ceylon (Sri Lanka), the RAR deployed to Burma (Myanmar) to fight against the Japanese from 1944 to 1945 (see Figure 2.1).

The RAR soldiers experienced intense combat. Just as the members of the RNR had before them, the men of the RAR won plaudits for their combat performance. In April 1945, the RAR 'overcame well-prepared

---

[37] Ibid., p. 102.
[38] Roberts, 'Towards a History of Rhodesia's Armed Forces'; Owen, *Rhodesian African Rifles*, p. x.
[39] Roberts, 'Towards a History of Rhodesia's Armed Forces'.
[40] During this period, two battalions of the Rhodesian Air Askari Corps were also raised. These troops acted as guards and sentries, protecting the aerodromes, landing strips, and training facilities that had quickly been constructed when Rhodesia was chosen as a major site of the Empire Air Training Scheme and some 10,000 aircrew underwent instruction in the country. Unfortunately, details of the Air Askari Corps are few, and it seems that records of its service have been forgotten or destroyed. See Kay, 'Geopolitics of Dependent Development in Central Africa', p. 399; McLaughlin, 'Thin White Line', p. 176.
[41] McLaughlin, 'Victims As Defenders', p. 259.
[42] Editorial Notes, 'Rhodesian African Rifles', pp. 51–2.
[43] McLaughlin, 'Victims As Defenders', p. 264.

The Early History of Black Troops in Rhodesia

An Askari dugout.

THE RAR AT WAR IN BURMA

Figure 2.1 The RAR in Burma during World War II (*Nwoho*, April 1978)

hilltop Japanese defensive positions around Tanlwe Chaung'.[44] A white officer later recalled of this attack:

> The way our fellows [the RAR] charged their way along these paths, yelling, makes a lump come to my throat when I think of it even now. It was sheer suicide for the leading group and the whole force faced machine guns up the sides of the slopes above them, on the sides of the features ahead of them, and even in the trees above them, with snipers behind who let them pass before opening fire. For sheer cold-blooded bravery, I can't believe it has ever been beaten in any other theatre of war; and this went on for three weeks solid.[45]

Despite this praise and sacrifice – thirty-two RAR soldiers were killed and sixty-seven were wounded in combat – the service of black soldiers was once more marginalised in accounts of the war by the white Rhodesian authorities.

A popular Rhodesian myth held that the colony contributed the highest proportion of manpower among all the countries of the British Empire, a claim the RF used later. Yet this was based solely upon the white population and ignored black soldiers, an aspect of the 'white Rhodesian tendency to visualize "Rhodesians" as White, with Africans having some indeterminate status in national self-images'.[46]

Upon its soldiers' return home, the RAR was due to be disbanded as the RNR had been before it, owing to yet another outcry of 'European complaints about creating a permanent armed African unit'. Once again, however, military exigency prevailed, and an official defence review in 1946 mandated the creation of a permanent military,[47] of which 'the RAR formed the regular army's core'.[48]

Now a regular unit, the RAR was briefly charged with guarding air stations and providing military labour, an undemanding role discarded in the early 1950s. Rhodesia's army was to be professionalised so as to enable it to contribute to conflicts of decolonisation in the crumbling empire.[49] African colonial troops were deployed on COIN duties abroad, particularly those regiments, such as the RAR, that had fought overseas during World War II,[50] and to reinforce imperial bases in east Africa and the Middle East.[51]

---

[44] Stapleton, *African Police and Soldiers*, p. 188. See Binda, *Masodja*, pp. 41–7, for a detailed account of the RAR during World War II.
[45] Stapleton, *African Police and Soldiers*, p. 190.
[46] McLaughlin, 'Thin White Line', pp. 175–6.
[47] Stapleton, *African Police and Soldiers*, p. 9.
[48] McLaughlin, 'Victims As Defenders', p. 264.
[49] Bhebe and Ranger, 'Introduction', p. 15.
[50] These deployments were hardly the 'Imperial African Army' long mooted by British officers and seriously re-proposed after World War II. See Killingray, 'Idea of a British Imperial African Army'.
[51] Percox, *Circumstances Short of Global War*, p. 35.

The RAR's first such deployment was to garrison the Suez Canal in 1952. With the creation of the Central African Federation in 1953, the enlarged Federal armed forces were dominated by white officers from Southern Rhodesia. The desire of the settler government to ingratiate itself with London and secure dominion status 'led to Salisbury taking an active role in Britain's military activities during the 1950s'.[52] This had important implications for black Rhodesian soldiers, who were to become familiar with COIN warfare, which required sophisticated training and high standards of soldierly proficiency. Nationalist insurgencies flared throughout the decaying empire: the British Army fought irregulars in ten countries between 1944 and 1952,[53] and by the early 1950s, 'a clear model of British counterinsurgency had emerged'[54] which drew formative lessons from the first four years of the Malayan Emergency (1948–60).

African colonial regiments, including the RAR (1956–8), were widely deployed in Malaya.[55] The RAR received instruction in the British COIN doctrine developed in Malaya, and put it into practice during its lengthy two-year deployment. This knowledge transfer through training, and the operational experience acquired, were of later significance. This established loyalties within the RAR based on a key claim to military skills and proficiency, which were then passed on to a younger generation through the RAR's enduring military culture.

As GMH, an RAR soldier who fought in Malaya and later in Zimbabwe's liberation war, told me, 'RAR was very good because they've got experience from Malaya ... That's why RAR was very good in the jungle; they were very good hunting these guerrillas.'[56] PM told me his generation of Malayan veterans shared the tactics, training, and procedures learned during this tour with the later generations of RAR recruits that they moulded as instructors and non-commissioned officers (NCOs).[57] The RAR soldiers developed the skills later deployed in Zimbabwe's liberation war. These included conducting long-range patrols, reconnoitring areas for guerrilla presence, operating in inhospitable terrain for prolonged periods of time without revealing their position, ambushing, and honing tracking skills that allowed the movements of guerrillas through the jungle to be traced by detecting their 'spoor', such as footprints or discarded foodstuffs (see Figure 2.2).

The Malayan experience also proved the basis for the wider Rhodesian COIN doctrine. Many of the Rhodesian Army's most important officers during the war for Zimbabwe, such as Lt Gen. Walls, Lt Col. Reid-Daly,

---

[52] Stapleton, *African Police and Soldiers*, p. 9.   [53] Jones, 'British Army', pp. 265–6.
[54] Popplewell, 'Lacking Intelligence', p. 348.
[55] Nissimi, 'Illusions of World Power in Kenya', p. 828.   [56] Interview with GMH.
[57] Interview with PM.

Figure 2.2 WOII Pisayi and his Military Medal citation for gallantry in Malaya, 1957. London Gazette citation with accompanying official photograph (Crown Copyright, 1957)

and Lt Col. Brian Robinson, served there and were sometimes referred to as the 'Malayan clique'.[58] They witnessed first-hand the efficacy of aerial capabilities in fighting guerrilla forces, and Rhodesian forces 'became the first Commonwealth troops to be trained in jungle dropping techniques and helicopter operations'.[59] These lessons were ingrained and the Rhodesian government explicitly drew upon the Malayan experience when deeming helicopters 'an established and indispensable requirement' in 1967.[60] Malayan operations also informed the later Rhodesian doctrinal emphasis upon tracking.[61]

GMH recalled that his training left him unafraid of the challenges of the war in Malaya: 'When we heard the news about fighting the war, we weren't scared about fighting the war. We wanted to go and fight the

---

[58] Cilliers, *Counter-Insurgency in Rhodesia*, p. 76; Evans, *Fighting against Chimurenga*, p. 8.
[59] Anti-Apartheid Movement, *Fireforce Exposed*, p. 13.
[60] Ian Smith Papers, Cory Library for Historical Research, Rhodes University, Makhanda, South Africa [hereafter CL] Rhodesian Cabinet [hereafter R.C.] (S) (67) 12, 'R.R.A.F.: Requirements for Additional Helicopters', 20 January 1967, p. 1.
[61] Melson, *Fighting for Time*, p. 37.

war.' His description of life on operations in Malaya mixed the thrill of soldiering and the danger and difficulty of operating in the jungle:

[W]e went to the deep jungle ... When we go to the jungle, we got big beards, big moustaches. Three to four months in the jungle; it's no joke. Malaysia has got big trees, and the rain – it's raining all the time ... mosquitos, *eish!* We enjoyed it, to stay in the jungle, it was nice ... And then your finger is always on the trigger ... We didn't like to stay in the camp, we wanted to stay in the bush.[62]

GMH's Malaya stories also demonstrated the military skills he had acquired as a section commander during the war. He described how his section came across a large deer that had seemingly gotten its leg caught, which they were tempted to shoot for meat.

However, GMH anticipated a trap and said, '"No, don't shoot that deer. I think there's something going on here. When we shoot, they will hear the gun." So I took my looking glass and looked, looked – I saw the sentry, their sentry. "Ah!"' Having identified the enemy position, GMH's platoon and a platoon of nearby Gurkhas planned an assault: 'And then we attacked the camp; after that, we go back to here, then soldiers skinned that deer and then they make a *braai*! [*laughs*]. That was very nice. I think it was, we were nearly to come out from the bush then come back home. Yeah, I think that was our last operation ... I enjoyed [the deployment to Malaya].' Thereafter the RAR returned to Rhodesia.

In sum, the early experiences of the RAR veterans of being deployed abroad to fight in a COIN campaign created a cadre of experienced black soldiers whose knowledge and training played an important role in establishing a powerful military culture among future generations of RAR recruits. The RAR quickly became practiced in cutting-edge COIN techniques. With the end of the Federation, the RAR was quickly repurposed towards internal COIN duties, which had important implications for its make-up.

The Basis for Expanded Recruitment into the Rhodesian African Rifles

With one eye on an anticipated COIN war at home, in the early 1960s, the Rhodesian government expanded the number of black soldiers in the Rhodesian Army and sought to remove alien soldiers from neighbouring countries from the ranks. While practices of regional and familial recruitment were important in the RAR, and as I will show, were stoked by the army, it is important to note that the military culture of the RAR explicitly stressed that soldiers' loyalties were premised upon a regimental identity,

[62] Interview with GMH.

not ethnic or regional allegiance. The RAR's regimental identity was itself a conspicuously invented tradition which functioned to create in-group solidarity among soldiers, and it was to the RAR first and then to the wider army that their macro-level loyalties were pledged.

Colonial armies in Africa often emphasised traditions of recruitment. One manifestation was regional, wherein volunteering for the colonial forces was commonplace in a certain area and became self-perpetuating as recruiting efforts targeted these areas and encouraged peers of serving soldiers to enlist.[63] This often went hand in hand with an ethnic identity supposed by colonial officers.

Another manifestation was patriarchal, such as with the Sudanese *askari* serving in the Schutztruppe in German East Africa, whose keen martial loyalty was vested in 'the patron who assumed responsibility for their honour, their working conditions, and their families'.[64] Another tradition was recruitment within families, both horizontally among siblings and vertically across generations.[65] Soldiering became the *métier* of men from military families, and the regiment an important source of employment and status, to which loyalties were accordingly pledged. Colonial regiments in the British Empire often saw the children of serving soldiers as a reliable source of loyal recruits and incubated them as such through the free education often offered within military cantonments, and by providing incentives for them to attest.[66]

Shortly after the RAR returned from Malaya, both regional and familial traditions of recruitment, which already existed to an extent, were deliberately encouraged by the Rhodesian authorities as part of an attempt to lessen the army's reliance upon what it termed 'aliens' – that is, recruits from Northern Rhodesia (Zambia), Nyasaland (Malawi), and Portuguese East Africa (Mozambique). With the anticipated end of the Federation and its joint military enterprise, the newly elected RF government sought to reduce the number of aliens within Southern Rhodesia.

Aliens had been an important source of RAR and police manpower prior to 1960. This was not itself a practice premised upon 'the "Austrian" model of imperial control, based on the stationing of troops from one part of the empire in another',[67] but stemmed from the long-standing integration of what Stapleton termed 'extra-territorial' men into a regional labour market.[68]

---

[63] See, for instance, Lovering, *Authority and Identity*, pp. 88–90.
[64] Bührer, 'Muslim *Askaris*', pp. 74–6.   [65] Oliveira, 'Saved by the Civil War', p. 137.
[66] As Roy notes, these dynamics were commonplace among both the British colonial Indian Army and the empire's African colonial armies. Roy, 'Military Loyalty in the Colonial Context', p. 506.
[67] McLaughlin, 'Victims As Defenders', p. 246.
[68] Stapleton, *No Insignificant Part*, pp. 40–1; McLaughlin, 'Victims As Defenders', p. 255.

These men volunteered to soldier as it was no more hazardous or unpleasant than alternative occupations such as mining.[69] Extraterritorial soldiers constituted 60–70 per cent of the manpower of the RNR during World War I, 45 per cent of the RAR during World War II, and 25 per cent of the RAR by the early 1950s.[70]

As Stapleton noted, although enlistment records during and after World War II are 'vague or non-existent', this precipitous decline of 'extra-territorial recruits' 'would seem to indicate that military service was becoming a less attractive form of wage labour for migrant workers. It could also mean that more local men were becoming incorporated into the capitalist economy, perhaps in lower paying jobs, and thus began to see the army as an attractive employment option'.[71]

The Smith Papers show that the decline of extraterritorial recruits was also deliberately hastened by the Rhodesian Army after the breakup of the Federation. The Rhodesian government made a concerted effort to remove what it deemed 'foreign labour' from the workforce, partly in order to ease black unemployment in Rhodesia, and partly for what it termed the 'security aspect'. A Cabinet committee on 'Foreign Labour and Unemployment' recommended to public and private employers that African foreign workers with less than ten years' service be repatriated and replaced with 'locally recruited labour'.[72] This particularly applied to workers from Zambia and Malawi,[73] who formed the majority of foreign workers, and was implemented across all sectors of the economy. Unlike some government departments and private employers, the Rhodesian Army implemented these directives fulsomely.

As a result, by 1961, 79 per cent of black members of the security forces were already from Southern Rhodesia, the rest hailing largely from Nyasaland and Northern Rhodesia. By 1965, 98.5 per cent of black soldiers were from Southern Rhodesia. Major Sandy Maclean (later a senior general in the Rhodesian Army and ZNA) wrote that this was the result of a 'firm policy in the engagement of Africans. The forces do

---

[69] This pattern of recruitment was similar to that seen across other groups and locations, such as the KAR in Kenya and elsewhere in east Africa. See Parsons, *African Rank-and-File*, p. 9.
[70] Stapleton, *African Police and Soldiers*, p. 29. These recruits were largely from Nyasaland (Malawi), Northern Rhodesia (Zambia), and Mozambique. See also Stapleton, 'Extra-territorial African Police and Soldiers', p. 108.
[71] Stapleton, *African Police and Soldiers*, p. 29.
[72] CL, R.C. (S) (66) 83, 'Foreign Labour and Unemployment', 4 March 1966, p. 7.
[73] The post-Federation Rhodesian government referred to workers from Zambia and Malawi as 'non-indigenous Africans', a quintessentially Rhodesian oxymoron, and one laced with irony given that half those Rhodesian ministers who signed the UDI were themselves recent immigrants.

not recruit aliens except where an indigenous African with the necessary specialist qualifications cannot be found'.[74]

By January 1966, of the 1,617 black soldiers in the Rhodesian Army, just 174 were aliens,[75] and by the end of that year, a mere thirty-six aliens remained.[76] Thus the precipitous fall in the number of extraterritorial soldiers was not only a product of decreasing incentives for men from Zambia and Malawi to migrate to Rhodesia and enlist in the army, but also the consequence of deliberate Rhodesian policy.

This resulted in a shortfall of soldiers and a recruitment drive. The overall number of black troops from within Rhodesia in the military increased by 46 per cent between 1961 and 1965.[77] MN, from Buhera in Manicaland, told me that when he joined the army in 1964, 'it was just after the Federation, people from Northern Rhodesia had gone, people from Nyasaland had gone, so it was just Rhodesian people', meaning a larger number of vacancies than normal.[78]

There was a regional element to this expanded recruitment. As Stapleton argued, 'many of the locals who replaced [extraterritorial recruits] were from Gutu-Masvingo', reflecting a longer-term pattern.[79] As an Anti-Apartheid Movement report documented: 'a disproportionate number of African volunteers have always tended to be drawn from certain parts of the country with a tradition of army and police service – notably from among members of the Karanga tribal group, located mainly in the Fort Victoria [Masvingo], Gutu and Chibi districts and numbering about 500,000 people'.[80]

While these regions were an important source of military recruits – and had been since Rhodesia's earliest conflicts in the 1890s – some scholars and writers have exaggerated their importance, suggesting that the vast majority of RAR soldiers were Karanga and drawn from the areas around Gutu in Masvingo Province.[81]

None of these claims cite primary sources. It is likely that this narrative of the dominance of Karanga recruits was afforded credence by the frequency with which it was invoked by generalist scholars and writers who required a simple and familiar explanation as to why black soldiers

---

[74] CL, R.C. (S) (66) 83, 'Foreign Labour and Unemployment', 4 March 1966, Annex II.
[75] CL, R.C. (S) (66) 44, 'Rhodesian Army and Royal Air Force: Review of Pay and Conditions of Service', 3 February 1966, p. 1.
[76] CL, R.C. (S) (67) 26, 'Foreign Labour and Unemployment', 3 February 1967, Appendix A.
[77] CL, R.C. (S) (66) 83, 'Foreign Labour and Unemployment', 4 March 1966, Annex II.
[78] Interview with MN.
[79] Stapleton, 'Extra-territorial African Police and Soldiers', p. 109.
[80] Anti-Apartheid Movement, *Fireforce Exposed*, p. 41.
[81] See, for instance, Wilkinson, 'Insurgency in Rhodesia', p. 14; Moorcraft, *Short Thousand Years*, p. 170; Godwin, *Mukiwa*, p. 283, as quoted in Stapleton, *African Police and Soldiers*, p. 43.

fought for Rhodesia. In doing so, they perpetuated colonial 'martial race' and ethnic stereotypes. In other contexts, the supposedly 'martial' attributes of soldiers from particular regions have likewise been demonstrated as false, their preponderance instead largely accounted for by socio-economic factors.[82]

Similarly, other scholars, such as Cynthia Enloe, have argued that Karanga were recruited in order to 'foster an esprit de corps among African soldiers'.[83] This was untrue, and reflects the prevalence of Rhodesian narratives, which later percolated into some scholarly understandings. As Stapleton contended, since the Rhodesian Army's recruitment patterns 'contradicted widely held settler views on ethnicity, the Karanga were rarely portrayed as a martial tribe' by settlers, in contrast to the supposedly 'martial' Ndebele.[84]

This reflected long-held settler myths dating back to the 1893 war. Scholars have long argued that the Rhodesian settler conception of the Ndebele as warriors and the Shona as meek was rooted in a settler-colonial distortion of history that Rhodes and the BSAC perpetuated so as to justify annexing Ndebele (and later Shona) territory.[85] Even during the liberation war some white officers still anticipated Ndebele dominance of the army owing to their supposed martiality.

As TM, who joined the army in 1958 and was from Rusape in Manicaland Province, told me:

Although the RAR was based in Bulawayo, which is Matabeleland, the young Matabele boys did not show any enthusiasm in joining the army. So as a result, all the recruitment drives were directed towards Mashonaland, especially in Victoria Province [Masvingo Province since 1982]. It was the common thing for a young boy to emulate what his seniors, his brothers, had done. Joining the army was sort of 'the in thing' for a young boy when he grows up ... You would often end up with siblings in the army. When they were doing recruiting it was [routine] to get many from Masvingo. Although the common question used to be that historically the Matabeles had been known to be good warriors and good fighters, for this conventional army we found that not many were willing to join.[86]

---

[82] Jeffery, 'Irish Military Tradition and the British Empire'; Maley and Hawkins, 'Southern Military Tradition', pp. 211–12.
[83] Enloe, *Ethnic Soldiers*, p. 81.
[84] Stapleton, *African Police and Soldiers*, p. 43. When the RNR was raised in 1916, it was initially intended to be called the 'Matabele Regiment' (Stapleton, *No Insignificant Part*, pp. 20–2). The Rhodesian commandant general at the time argued that the Ndebele 'are by instinct a warlike race, easily trained and far less expensive to raise and maintain after they are raised' (McLaughlin, 'Victims As Defenders', p. 249).
[85] See, for instance, Beach, 'Ndebele Raiders and Shona Power', pp. 633–4, 650.
[86] Interview with TM.

Not only was Karanga recruitment not as prevalent as these claims imply, it was also not due to an ethnic or martial quality. The disproportionate number of recruits from Victoria/Masvingo was rather a combination of history, economics, and an army-promoted 'tradition' of service.

RAR veterans told a complex story of recruitment. I asked WR, who hailed from Shurugwi in Midlands Province, if a majority of RAR troops came from Masvingo Province, and he told me, 'no, I think countrywide', although 'quite a few did come from Masvingo'.[87] WM, from Gutu in Masvingo, told me that he thought '50 per cent were from Masvingo and then 50 per cent from other provinces'.[88] In the early 1950s, in fact only 22 per cent of RAR recruits were from Masvingo, and it seems unlikely that they would have so rapidly come to constitute more than a bare majority during the war.[89]

Even though the numbers of recruits from Masvingo were not as high as has been claimed, they still formed a high proportion of RAR soldiers, given Masvingo's relatively small population of approximately 500,000. The reasons are partly historical. The Fort Victoria cantonment was Rhodesia's first settler town, established by the Pioneer Column in 1890 as noted earlier, and Victoria Province continuously supplied recruits for the RSF thereafter.

It is also likely that, as Stapleton argues, this history of military service was influenced by the fact that young men from Masvingo had long faced a dearth of local employment opportunities, as the area was 'one of the least productive agricultural zones of the country', making enlistment more attractive than it might have been elsewhere.[90] Likewise, in 1976, a journalist from *The Times* argued that 'the Karanga suffer from land shortage' to explain why they 'predominate[d] among Rhodesia's black troops' and why they 'predominate[d]' in ZANLA too.[91]

A tradition of military recruitment within Masvingo was instrumentally stoked by the Rhodesian Army, which deliberately recruited from the area. This was a successful recruitment strategy, and by encouraging a high concentration of soldiers, the army established soldiering as a socially acceptable metier in this area. The scholarly literature has long asserted that veterans make particularly effective recruiters, and those areas where they live in large number see markedly higher numbers of enlistees.[92] My interviewees from the region, including WM, PM, GM, GN, JM, and MSW, told me that their decision to enlist was heavily

---

[87] Interview with WR.   [88] Interview with WM.
[89] Stapleton, *African Police and Soldiers*, p. 43.   [90] Ibid.
[91] Knipe, 'Is Mr Smith Trying to Split the African Tribes?', p. 12.
[92] Maley and Hawkins, 'Southern Military Tradition', p. 211.

influenced by the high number of locals they knew who were soldiers or veterans.[93]

While Masvingo was an important recruitment catchment area, for reasons of history, economics, and the Rhodesian Army's creation of a local tradition of service, it is important to highlight that recruitment was not contingent upon Karanga identity in particular, and no special privileges were awarded to Karanga soldiers. The army's practices of recruitment did not confer an ethnic character on the RAR.[94] In correspondence with the Rhodesian Cabinet, the army stated that it placed great emphasis upon attempts 'to remove tribal discrimination as far as possible'.[95] *The Times* reported in 1976 that 'according to white officers in the RAR', the high number of Karanga soldiers 'has created no problems with non-Karanga troops'.[96] In 1977, the *Herald*, covering the 'passing out' of 400 RAR recruits, interviewed the officer in charge of training, who 'said "half the men were Ndebele and the other half Shona"'. He ruled out the possibility of tribal differences, saying the men were loyal to the army'.[97]

All of my interviewees emphasised that discrimination between different African ethnolinguistic groups did not exist in the Rhodesian Army, and that preferential treatment was not accorded to one group. They often contrasted this with how such factors were used in the 1980s by the Mugabe government against Ndebele-speaking soldiers.

HZ, who was from Gutu and joined the RAR in 1967, told me, 'in 1RAR we used to speak English, Shona and Ndebele. And we were very friendly to each other. You didn't mind where you come from, whatever race you are. Shona and Ndebele used to get on very well'. He noted that there existed a significant minority of Ndebele soldiers, and that they often did well during promotion boards, as well as achieving coveted postings such as clerking and administrative posts.

HZ contrasted this context with the post-1980 stoking of ethnic tensions by ZANU(PF), telling me 'there were lots of Ndebeles during our time' in the Rhodesian Army, 'but it is only now people seem to be against each other'.[98] As argued later, many of my interviewees lamented what

---

[93] Interviews with WM, PM, GM, GN, JM, and MSW.
[94] Indeed, given that the literature has widely asserted Karanga were also prominent among ZANLA's recruits, it is quite possible that Stapleton's observation that the region's fewer employment opportunities generated higher numbers of RAR recruits also meant it generated more recruits for ZANLA too.
[95] R.C. (S) (76) 111, 'Schools for the Sons of Chiefs and Senior African Members of the Uniformed Forces and Civil Service', 3 September 1976.
[96] Knipe, 'Is Mr Smith Trying to Split the African Tribes?', p. 12.
[97] Reynolds, 'Army Crash Course for Africans', p. 1.   [98] Interview with HZ.

they perceived as the deliberate stoking of 'tribalism' after 1980 by officers in the ZNA, which marginalised Ndebele soldiers.

RAR soldiers stressed in their accounts the unit's ethnic mix and easy coexistence. GN and MSW, both from Masvingo, told me that Ndebele recruits comprised some 15–20 per cent of the training intake at the time of their recruitment.[99] MS, who was from Gwanda in Matabeleland South, married an RAR soldier from Masvingo, in 1964, who she had met after he had been posted to the area.

She told me that, in contrast to the period after 1980, this posed no difficulties and was 'all plain sailing', apart from the fact that she had to learn chiShona when her husband was later posted to Masvingo, which she found challenging.[100] Although some soldiers could speak both chiShona and isiNdebele, most did not prior to enlisting. As MC, the wife of a soldier and herself a teacher in the army schools provided for the children of soldiers, told me:

> It was quite a good experience to meet people from different regions and different provinces. And working together. You see, the army had got so much discipline, so everything went on well, working with people with discipline and everything... We had a special interest, because some of the children had come from Bulawayo, who speak Ndebele, some from [areas where other languages were spoken], we'd learn the different languages from the children; it was quite interesting. So we know quite a bit of everything... The main languages we taught in were English and then Shona. The Ndebeles, when time for Shona comes, they would go to the Ndebele teacher. All languages were taught.[101]

BM, who joined the RAR in 1968 from Mberengwa in Midlands Province, told me that he was fluent in English and Shona, but also that he knew 'Ndebele very well', having learnt it in the RAR after enlisting 'because in the army we used to be speaking three languages – English, Shona, Ndebele'.[102] As DSN told me, it was not uncommon for commanders to ensure that sticks deployed on operations contained both Shona and Ndebele speakers, particularly during his time in the Psychological Operations Unit, which collected information from civilians.[103]

Just as regional traditions of recruitment have been misinterpreted by some, the familial tradition of service in the RAR has often also been misunderstood in some of the literature, although this is not to downplay its importance as a recruitment factor. As Stapleton argued, 'family relationships were extremely important' in facilitating patterns of recruitment, with many soldiers following in the footsteps of their fathers and

---

[99] Interview with GN. [100] Interview with MS. [101] Interview with MC.
[102] Interview with BM. [103] Interview with DSN.

grandfathers, and the military authorities particularly encouraged applications from kinsfolk.[104]

For instance, in 1979, the most senior African soldier in the army, WOI(RSM) Manunure of 1RAR, was 'one of eight brothers who joined the army or police'.[105] My interviewees from Masvingo noted that the regional and familial tradition there often went hand in hand, perhaps unsurprisingly given the aforementioned important role that veterans play in encouraging military recruitment. As WM told me, 'there were cousins, there were fathers in the army ... there were many'. MSW told me most of his male relatives had fought in either Burma or Malaya.[106] PM told me, 'a relative, my *sekuru* – my [matrilineal] uncle, he was in the army. So I joined'.[107] BM told me his brother was already in the army, and also several of his friends and other young men of the same age he knew of in Mberengwa, an area adjacent to Masvingo.[108]

As with the supposed Karanga 'dominance' of the RAR, some white Rhodesians exaggerated this family tradition. Cohen interviewed a white Rhodesian Army deserter in 1978 who said that 'the black Rhodesian army is very patriarchal in that a man will probably join the army to follow his father's footsteps; there's a lot of pride involved'.[109] In 1975, the *Rhodesia Herald*, the mouthpiece of the regime, stated: 'The vast majority of RAR troops are drawn from Rhodesia's East Victoria region. Recruiting is kept within the family as much as possible, and most of the soldiers are from the Vakaranga tribe, part of the Mashona, and are related to each other in some way.'[110] In fact, the family tradition was not only found in Masvingo, but applied to soldiers recruited from throughout the country, as my interviewees outlined. For instance, DSN was from Bulawayo, and his father was a colour sergeant who had served in both Burma and Malaya and retired in 1967, the same year he himself enlisted.[111] CD was also from Bulawayo, and his relatives had served in Malaya and Burma too.[112] Moreover, familial ties were far from the only basis for recruitment.[113] A history of family service was an important inducement, but it was merely one motivation to enlist among many. As McLaughlin noted, 'it would be exaggerated to speak of a "military caste" in black society in Rhodesia, but family links were very important nonetheless'.[114]

---

[104] Stapleton, *African Police and Soldiers*, pp. 33, 37–9.
[105] Burns, 'How Blacks View Their Larger Role in Rhodesia's Army'.
[106] Interviews with WM and MSW.   [107] Interview with PM.   [108] Interview with BM.
[109] Cohen, 'War in Rhodesia', p. 484.
[110] As quoted in Maxey, *Fight for Zimbabwe*, p. 34.   [111] Interview with DSN.
[112] Interview with CD.   [113] Stapleton, *African Police and Soldiers*, p. 37.
[114] McLaughlin, 'Victims As Defenders', p. 270.

My interviewees' life histories demonstrate that some recruits had no previous family connection to the army. SJM told me, 'I didn't know anybody in the army, but when I was in school, we used to talk about the army,' owing to having seen soldiers in rural areas 'when they were doing their exercises, especially the 1RAR; they used to go to rural areas for their operations ... we saw them there, we liked to see them, so that's why I just decided to go and join the army.' He joined the Rhodesian Army Services Corps, and his friend joined the Military Police.[115] GMH, from Ntabazinduna in Matabeleland North, told me:

> There was one friend of mine, we were together at school, and then he left school and joined the army. So when we meet we talk and [he recommended the RAR and] that's why I chose the army ... He said to me, 'When you join the army, you'll see the world.' So I was very, very interested [to] see the world. He said, 'Don't be afraid with the war. You may go to the war, but don't get upset about that.'[116]

DT, from Bulawayo, told me that after leaving school, he was working for 'Shackleton & Co.; there I was doing a safe job selling fruit'. He applied to join the army as he was looking for a challenge and to improve himself by learning new skills.[117] MK joined for the training opportunities, as he 'wanted to learn the job, you know [the Rhodesian Army Corps of] Engineers they are electricians, they are bricklayers, they are carpenters and so forth'. He became a bricklayer.[118]

A commonality among my interviewees' stories of recruitment is the existence of a relationship to a white person. Many had long-standing positive relationships with local farmers, clergymen, or officials. For instance, BM told me how:

> Ah we, I can say myself, the time I was born and the time I was grown up, I was no stranger to the European people. I used to like Europeans ... myself I was looked after by Europeans [in school and church] ... all the time I was young ... I've grown up like a European chap and them they were liking me very well. Missionaries, anybody who were doing government jobs, to the D[istrict] C[ommissioner] ... they were my friends. Plus I learned how to start shooting with the air gun, with the Europeans which were my friends here [from then] until today. That's why I liked them. To come and join the army I've written a letter [with a white friend, who asked him,] 'You want to join the army or you want to do what?' I said, 'I want to be a policeman or an army chap. Only two ways.' He wrote me a letter to come to RAR, a European chap. Then I was successful, which is good.[119]

---

[115] Interview with SJM. [116] Interview with GMH. [117] Interview with DT.
[118] Interview with MK. [119] Interview with BM.

Other enlistees simply said that they fancied the status of being a soldier. HZ told me, 'since when I was still at school, I wanted the army or I wanted the police. I was eager to just to have a rifle in my hands!'.[120] WM had been influenced by British war comics, such as *Commando War Stories in Pictures*, which he read as a boy: 'I was reading a lot of comics and all the like. I wanted the adventure, which I achieved because I ended up a parachutist!'[121] For others it was a chance encounter: JC met RAR soldiers returning from Malaya when he was working on the railways in Bulawayo and decided that he would like to be a soldier too.[122]

These varied forms of recruitment had effects on the nature of solidarities within the RAR, and family traditions were important in this regard. For instance, CD was inspired by the service of his grandfather with the RAR in Burma and Malaya, alongside that of several other members of his family. During his own service, his grandfather:

> told me of the hardships [that he had endured during World War II], I believe the terrain was a tough one. He would say the terrain and rubber trees, it was quite heavy. He would say, 'You think you have had it rough, you guys – we had it rougher than you! You guys, now everything, you are given everything good but now you complain!' He would never want us to complain, you know, he was kind of a strict and laughing disciplinarian, he didn't want us to go anywhere out of fault; he always kept us on check. 'Everything is now good for you guys, yet you complain!' Then you start to put more effort [in], because if my grandfather had it rough and he is saying 'this [combat in the liberation war] is nothing', then I think that in itself also made things easier for us.[123]

Likewise, PM told me that in enlisting he had followed in the footsteps of his father, who 'went as far as Burma' with the RAR in World War II. His father kept tabs on his son's career: 'he always kept questioning to the instructors – saying, "How is he? Is he all that and that?"'[124] Soldiers whose family had served felt a keen sense of responsibility to match the standards that had been set before them.

This familial dynamic was also described by Pat Lawless, a white RAR officer, who interpreted it in terms of his own obligations to black soldiers. He recalled that after the RAR took over Methuen Barracks near Bulawayo in 1954, it became a tradition that retiring soldiers be offered accommodation there. During 1978, Lawless greeted a group of these aged veterans, of whom one responded: 'I am retired Lance Corporal Taureyi, and my grandson Corporal Jack is one of your section commanders.' For Lawless, 'in the RAR there was always this recognition of an additional human factor – of having to "account" to men such as these

---

[120] Interview with HZ. [121] Interview with WM. [122] Interview with JC.
[123] Interview with CD. [124] Interview with PM.

old veterans for your actions and decisions that provided just that little added inspiration'.[125] In this manner, the RAR was constructed as an extended regimental family by white officers as well as among generations of black RAR soldiers. In a personification of this sentiment, one of my interviewees, who during the war served in the north-eastern area of the country which the army designated 'Operation Hurricane',[126] named his firstborn son Hurricane.[127]

In conclusion, my interviewees remembered no preferential treatment for particular ethnolinguistic groups within the Rhodesian Army. The predominance of Masvingo as a recruitment area did not feed into a privileged status for Karanga soldiers, but was instead a consequence of historical recruitment patterns, a regional dearth of employment opportunities, and the Rhodesian Army's focusing its recruitment efforts there. Familial traditions of service were important, serving as incentives to enlist among black soldiers, and in some cases, creating an additional source of loyalty among troops who sought to emulate the combat performance of their elder relatives. They were, however, not decisive, and motivations to enlist were myriad. The RAR did not forge its soldiers' loyalties along lines of ethnic or regional affiliation, and nor was there a black Rhodesian military caste. Instead, as we shall see, the army forged black soldiers' loyalties to the regiment itself.

Regimental Traditions and Loyalties in a New Army
As noted, Malešević highlighted the importance of group homogeneity and in-group solidarity within military regiments, and I refer hereafter to these solidarities among black Rhodesian soldiers as their 'regimental loyalties'. As the regiment and the wider army served as their main interaction with the state, instead of feeling a sense of patriotic or ideological alignment with the Rhodesian government, soldiers would instead feel macro-level loyalty to the regiment and army.

An important manner in which these regimental loyalties were created was through the RAR's traditions, and I now turn to how they were deliberately forged. As Ray Roberts argued, the supposed 'long Rhodesian military tradition' was in fact somewhat mythic, given the lack of a regular army prior to World War II.[128] Nonetheless it played a powerful and elaborate role in soldiers' lives, taking the form of marches, parades, songs, the regimental band, and oral histories of service in Burma, Egypt, and Malaya as discussed earlier.

---

[125] Telfer and Fulton, *Chibaya Moyo*, pp. 132–3.
[126] Cilliers, *Counter-Insurgency in Rhodesia*, p. 14.
[127] Interviewee anonymised by author. [128] Bhebe and Ranger, 'Introduction', p. 14.

After becoming a regular regiment, white RAR officers invested much effort into crafting a regimental identity. This was not exceptional: as Terence Ranger argued, British colonial administrators had long created martial 'neo-traditions' which emphasised the 'admittance of Africans into the European military tradition', one 'in which Europeans commanded and Africans accepted commands, but both within a shared framework of pride and loyalty'.[129] Great symbolic importance was placed upon parading soldiers in public, an elaborate display of martial pageantry and ritual intended to bolster the prestige of the colonial regime, demonstrate the potency of the armed forces, and impress upon 'the governed a healthy respect for the rulers' as S. C. Ukpabi argued of the army in colonial Nigeria.[130]

The RAR's regimental structure was a facsimile of the British regimental model, which deliberately created regimental 'tribes' within its own army that remain to this day. As Frank Ledwidge contended, 'more than any other British institution, the British army – with its regiments and their rituals and nuances of dress, behaviour and even language – is a tribal organization. Loyalty to regiment is lifelong.'[131] As Reid noted, African colonial units followed suit and 'acquired the regimental "traditions" and ethos, symbols and insignia, associated with their European counterparts'.[132]

The RAR's traditions were conspicuously 'invented',[133] but that made them no more artificial than those of many army 'traditions' the world over, which often boast of deep, organic, and historic roots, yet upon closer inspection are frequently revealed to have been confected from assorted anecdotes and infused with a healthy dollop of artistic licence.[134] The provenance of these traditions is of tangential importance compared to the message they convey. Clifford Geertz's dictum that culture is

---

[129] Ranger, 'Invention of Tradition in Colonial Africa', pp. 221, 224.
[130] Ukpabi, 'Changing Role of the Military in Nigeria', p. 66.
[131] Ledwidge, *Losing Small Wars*, p. 138.   [132] Reid, *Warfare*, p. 150.
[133] It is perhaps more apt to speak of these RAR traditions as 'mimicked inventions', given the regiment was created in 1940 – long after the initial creation of Ranger's 'neo-traditions' in the late nineteenth and early twentieth centuries. Thus its organisational tenets were derived not only from the RNR's but also copied from other African colonial regiments, given the preponderance of colonial military service throughout the British Empire, and particularly India and Kenya, among early white RAR officers.
[134] For instance, Britain's most prestigious gallantry medal, the Victoria Cross (awarded for valour 'in the presence of the enemy') was long mooted to have been cast from the metal of Russian cannons captured during the Crimean War at the battle of Sevastopol. A recent paper has found that 'there is no corroboration for this belief beyond an entry in *The Times* in 1857', although 'it is likely that many Victoria Crosses were indeed sourced from captured ordnance, but probably using Chinese guns. Some may even have been cast from entirely unprovenanced metal'. See Marriott, 'Manufactured Tradition?'.

simply the 'stories we tell ourselves about ourselves' is no less applicable to military culture.[135] These 'traditions' served to create an exclusive, durable soldierly identity adopted by black troops, which also ascribed the role a modern status.

As Zoe Flood noted, white ex-RAR officers 'perceived the regiment, or a sub-unit within the regiment, as the focal point of black soldiers" loyalty, bolstered by 'its traditions, the Colours, and being "on parade"'.[136] My interviewees, such as HZ, described to me how RAR soldiers took fastidious care over the smartness of their public appearance. He told me with pride how he wore 'very, very smart stick [drill] boots' polished and buffed to a mirror shine, with an immaculately ironed formal uniform. This 'smart' standard of appearance required much time and effort to maintain; a form of discipline innate to the process of 'military socialisation', but which also served to distinguish professional soldiers in the eyes of civilians and embody their status. As HZ told me, when he was attired as such, 'people saw us and said: "Ah, these people are very smart, beefy", and so on!'[137]

Parades were not just a visual spectacle of impeccably turned-out soldiers. They were also accompanied by martial music played by army bands. Formal military bands have been integral to armies since at least the Ottoman Empire. Roland Bannister argued that they were an important part of the British colonial military modus operandi, a 'powerful and widespread agent of colonisation', and that martial music was 'characterised by precision and obedience to authority', a sonic incarnation of soldierly virtues.[138] Its effect upon creating and sustaining regimental loyalties, while long chronicled by scholars, has in recent decades been neglected.[139]

It is no accident that every major military in the world today retains a corps of musicians and that colonial armies, perpetually short of money, managed to find the resources to field them. This was the case in Rhodesia, where military bands were always raised side by side with soldiers. In tandem with the RNR, the Corps of Drums was formed, which was disbanded alongside it at the end of World War I.[140] In 1940, this Corps was reformed with the RAR, and thereafter became a dazzling regimental band, featuring brass, woodwind, and drum sections. The RAR Band regularly featured at 'public ceremonies and events', and also served as a potent recruiting tool (see Figure 2.3).[141] As WM remembered, 'at times the battalion would send out a military band into the districts, play them some music and do army demonstrations.

---

[135] Geertz, *Interpretation of Cultures*, p. 448.   [136] Flood, *Brothers-in-Arms?*, p. 24.
[137] Interview with HZ.   [138] Bannister, 'How Are We to Write Our Music History?', p. 2.
[139] See, for instance, Hart, 'British Regimental Marches'.
[140] 'History of the Regimental Band', *Nwoho*, October 1977, p. 37.
[141] Stapleton, *African Police and Soldiers*, pp. 45–6.

Figure 2.3 Composite image of the RAR band, regimental march, and regimental Colour. *Nwoho*'s heading page for the lyrics of 'Sweet Banana' featuring an RAR soldier carrying out the drill command present arms, the RAR band in Bulawayo during 1977, bandmaster Warrant Officer I E. Kampion in Malaya (dated '1956–1958'), the RAR regimental Colour in Bulawayo, 1977. All images from *Nwoho* issues April 1976 and October 1977.

That's when people would come and join', and the band was an important part of the RAR's identity.[142]

Parades were also an opportunity for the regiment itself to be put on display, its history signified by its Colours. In the British tradition, these are flags that were, prior to the era of modern warfare, carried into battle to rally troops, and over which much blood was shed capturing and defending.[143] They retain an immense symbolic importance and much fanfare was accorded the award of Queen's Colours to the RAR by the Queen Mother in July 1953.[144] Not only was the RAR the only regiment in Rhodesia that received Queen's Colours,[145] but the RAR was a light infantry regiment,

[142] Interview with WM. [143] Keegan, *Face of Battle*, p. 184.
[144] Binda, *Masodja*, pp. 109–13; Stapleton, *African Police and Soldiers*, pp. 26–8, 47.
[145] 'Passing of Former Chief of RAR', *Nwoho* (October 1976), p. 53.

which for arcane reasons of tradition do not normally carry colours,[146] making the RAR's possession of them prestigious and distinctive. On the RAR's colours were inscribed its battle honours, and those of the RNR, which served to reinforce the historical achievements of black soldiers and to inspire each new intake of soldiers to emulate their forefathers. As WM told me, colours were an important embodiment of the regiment's history.[147]

Other routine aspects of RAR soldiers' day-to-day lives were shaped to buttress this regimental identity. In the British tradition, the historical achievements of a regiment, and references to its contemporary mettle, are routinely referenced at the most quotidian level, inscribed upon, for instance, soldiers' uniforms, and in the names of subunits, buildings, and barracks.[148] The RAR's 'invented traditions' mimicked this: its regimental badge, worn on the headwear and belts of all members, was 'a Matabele shield upon which is laid a stabbing assegai and a Mashona spear, crossed, under a vertical knobkerrie',[149] symbolising the African precolonial history of soldiering.[150] Its regimental day, an annual festival, was Tanlwe Chaung Day, named after its famous World War II victory over the Japanese.

Companies adopted vernacular names, such as 2RAR's B Company, *Chibaya Moyo* (strike or stab to the heart), C Company, *Chamuka Inyama* (whatever comes), and D Company, *Shumba Mupedza Hondo* (the lions end the war), that sought to encapsulate their combat attitude and prowess. The RAR had a regimental song, 'Sweet Banana', first sung in 1942 and inspired by the bananas RAR soldiers came across in Natal when escorting Italian prisoners of war.[151] It was often sung on the march and was played by the band on ceremonial occasions. Its lyrics were a paean to the constituent parts of the regiment and its pride in how it had fought during past conflicts. When one recalls that in many instances RAR soldiers served for more than twenty years, the battles sung about were very much lived memories for many of those in the ranks, and this tapestry of African soldiers' past heroics served to inspire newer recruits.

The RAR was also held in high esteem by many members of the white public. As McLaughlin argued, 'the very strong, positive attitude displayed towards African soldiers by whites may have attracted more' recruits, and the 'RAR was the recipient of extravagant praise and was given an elite status not enjoyed by other Africans' outside the army.[152]

---

[146] Wood, *War Diaries of Andre Dennison*, p. 14. Light infantry regiments, also known as rifle regiments, did not traditionally carry colours as their soldiers were historically lightly armed skirmishers and thus did not fight in formation.
[147] Interview with WM.   [148] Kirke, 'Seeing through the Stereotype', p. 23.
[149] Owen, *Rhodesian African Rifles*, p. 9.   [150] Owen, *Rhodesian African Rifles*, p. 9.
[151] The song enjoyed some commercial success in Rhodesia. See also Binda, *Masodja*, p. 41.
[152] McLaughlin, 'Victims As Defenders', p. 263.

As Christopher Owen, a former RAR officer, noted in 1970: 'Within a few short months of its inception, an extraordinary surge of feeling for the new regiment began to grip the general public. White Rhodesians took the Battalion to their hearts, and any parade always attracted an enthusiastic audience. It was soon apparent that the regiment was regarded with widespread pride and affection.'[153]

Public displays of this status, such as parades celebrating the award of the 'Freedom of the City', or public anniversaries, served to reinforce the notion of the RAR and the wider army as a legitimate, competent, and prestigious military force. This attracted new recruits and consolidated the loyalties of serving soldiers. Importantly, these regimental loyalties were enduring: their historicity afforded them a legitimacy that predated the liberation war. As I argue in Chapter 6, this narrative of RAR men being soldiers that served loyally in the traditions of their forefathers was one my interviewees drew on when discussing their apolitical stance.

Here I have outlined how traditions functioned to create a powerful regimental loyalty among black soldiers. By establishing a historical link to the deeds and heroics of their predecessors, and imbuing the very fabric and material of the regiment's physical presence with iconography, solidarities to the regiment were cemented. Before discussing how the most powerful form of soldierly loyalty, the micro-level bonds between soldiers, were forged in Chapter 3, I turn to discuss how the army 'professionalised' after the end of the Federation, which had important implications for the role of the RAR and its professional ethos.

Black Soldiers in the Post-Federation Rhodesian Army

The Rhodesian Army underwent rapid change after 1962 and was essentially bisected between its small permanent component of regular troops, of which the RAR were a key part, and its larger number of part-time troops, who were not professional and were much less efficacious. The small regular army was itself de facto split between the RAR and the white units, principally the Rhodesian Light Infantry (RLI), which reflected the enduring mistrust of black soldiers by army and government elites, and had important implications for the RAR's own distinctive military culture, and black soldiers' loyalties in the midst of a racist system, as we shall see. The literature has not provided an accurate understanding of the complex structure of the Rhodesian Army, which has distorted understanding of just how vital black soldiers were to the Rhodesian war effort.

The RAR returned from Malaya in 1958 to immense political turbulence. The ascendency of the far-right RF to power in Salisbury in 1962

---

[153] Owen, *Rhodesian African Rifles*, p. 4.

and the end of the Federation in 1963 prompted a marked change in the army, which intensified preparations for internal COIN operations. By the onset of the war, the Rhodesian Army was 'well suited to counter-insurgency', and 'some 50 per cent of all regular training' was in COIN.[154]

In the early 1960s, Southern Rhodesian officers, who were dominant in the Federal Army, created white-only regular army units, largely financed by Zambian copper revenues.[155] Their purpose was transparent. Federal Prime Minister Welensky 'admitted that the reason for the new units was not external threat but internal "Communist subversion"'.[156] It was no coincidence that at the dissolution of the Federation, (formerly Southern) Rhodesia received the lion's share of these units' assets and almost all their personnel.[157]

In 1961, the RLI, a commando infantry battalion, was formed. It was 'intimately connected with the maintenance of White supremacy in Rhodesia' as it was intended not only to relieve white reservists, but to 'be available should the African units prove disloyal or unreliable in a political crisis'.[158] The RLI and its special forces counterpart, the Rhodesian Special Air Service (RhSAS), were the 'only two units not to be racially integrated' prior to independence.[159] Officers in the Rhodesian Army thought these new formations would 'help "to strike the balance between the European [i.e. Territorial] and African units"'.[160] Patently, this 'balance' was one in which white soldiers would function as the regime's Praetorian guard.

As late as 1963 there were calls from influential voices, including senior RF politicians and some of the RSF top brass, for the RAR to be completely disbanded. However, other white voices had long argued not only for keeping the RAR, but for expanding it. These included Southern Rhodesian RAR officers who, during the dissolution of the Federal armed forces, requested a second RAR battalion be created.[161] Welensky 'suggested raising 10 RAR battalions' in the late 1960s.[162]

As Stapleton argued, for the first decade of the war, debates raged within the government and military as to whether to recruit more black soldiers, and as late as 1975, some white Rhodesian officers doubted 'the

---

[154] Beckett, 'Rhodesian Army', p. 176.
[155] Whitaker, 'New Model' Armies of Africa?, p. 155.
[156] Stapleton, African Police and Soldiers, p. 207.
[157] Bhebe and Ranger, 'Introduction', p. 15.
[158] McLaughlin, 'Thin White Line', p. 177.
[159] Abbott and Botham, Modern African Wars, p. 17.
[160] McLaughlin, 'Victims As Defenders', p. 265.
[161] White, Fighting and Writing, pp. 10–11.
[162] Wood, 'Countering the Chimurenga', p. 192.

loyalty of African troops', despite there being no grounds for doing so.[163] The RF government, insistent upon retaining a 'balance' in the army, continually rejected calls to raise more black soldiers.[164] Even as the war escalated in the 1970s, 'right-wing politicians refused to accept black soldiers in numbers exceeding those of whites',[165] which meant that 2RAR was not raised until 1975, as the RF 'did not want the African troops to outnumber the European troops'.[166] As a white ex-RAR officer told Stewart, 'regrettably, the Rhodesian Front did not trust the African soldier'.[167]

Although many white settlers remained hostile to the recruitment of black soldiers, it was clear to a succession of RF defence ministers, just as it had been to the settler government during World War I and World War II, that Rhodesia's white male population of military age, which hovered at approximately 65,000 throughout the war,[168] was not large enough to provide a standing army without destroying the economy.[169] Furthermore, only a third of the soldiers drawn from this already shallow pool would serve on the front line, given that in modern warfare, a large proportion of an army comprises non-teeth-arm troops, such as logisticians, signallers, chefs, armourers, medics, and pay clerks.[170]

Compounding this finite potential number of white troops, the RF's designs upon a white army were also corroded by the simple fact that not many white Rhodesians were keen to soldier, with high numbers emigrating and going AWOL as the war escalated. Although these shortages were most noticeable from 1973 onwards, when annual white emigration averaged 13,070 per year (or 4.9 per cent of the white population), they were also evident from the earliest days of the war.[171] For instance, in January 1966, the RLI was already short of 26 officers and 137 men, whereas the RAR was fully manned, a trend that continued throughout the conflict.[172]

---

[163] Stapleton, *African Police and Soldiers*, pp. 176–9.
[164] CL, R.C. (S) (66) 87, 'Extension of National Service', 7 March 1966.
[165] Petter-Bowyer, *Winds of Destruction*, p. 301, as quoted in Stapleton, *African Police and Soldiers*, p. 179.
[166] Flood, *Brothers-in-Arms?*, p. 10.   [167] Stewart, 'Rhodesian African Rifles', p. 68.
[168] Stedman, 'End of the Zimbabwean Civil War', p. 130.
[169] No country at war can mobilise more than a fraction of its population. Even during World War II, the UK, USSR, and Germany mobilised no more than 23 per cent of their workforces (Harrison, 'Resource Mobilization for World War II').
[170] For instance, the US Army's combat forces have consistently comprised approximately 30 per cent of its deployed strength during its campaigns in Korea, Vietnam, and the 1991 and 2003 Iraq Wars (McGrath, *Other End of the Spear*, p. 66). At the peak of the US Army's commitment to the Vietnam War in 1968, 'fewer than 80,000' out of a total of 543,000 were 'combat troops that could be put into battle' (Sevy, *American Experience in Vietnam*, p. 92).
[171] Brownell, *Collapse of Rhodesia*, p. 75.
[172] CL, R.C. (S) (66) 44, 'Rhodesian Army and Royal Rhodesian Air Force: Review of Pay and Conditions of Service', 3 February 1966, pp. 1–2.

80   The Creation of Regimental Loyalties

The RF government increasingly turned to conscription. This had initially been implemented in a limited manner for whites, and the small ethnic groups defined by the Rhodesians as 'Coloured, Asian and Eurasian' (CAE), by the Defence Act of 1955. As the war intensified, the Rhodesians ratcheted up the frequency and duration of conscription and expanded the eligibility criteria. This dependence upon conscripts produced an army formed of two distinct parts: regulars and reservists.

A small number of full-time, professional troops formed the regular soldiers of the Rhodesian Army and primarily comprised the infantry battalions of the RAR and the RLI, alongside personnel in units such as the Rhodesian Corps of Signals and Corps of Engineers. In January 1966, there were 3,199 regulars,[173] which had grown to approximately 4,300 by December 1973,[174] and perhaps 5,000–5,500 by the end of the war, of which, as stated in Chapter 1, more than 80 per cent were black. Despite being few in number, the regulars were by far the best trained and possessed vast combat experience. They were used in the most challenging missions. These regular forces were augmented by two companies of National Servicemen (NS), in which white conscripts served as full-time infantrymen for a year.[175]

Owing to the RF's insistence on a 'balanced' regular army, de facto segregation existed between black and white soldiers. This was not all-encompassing: there were many joint operations between the RAR and RLI, and in units such as signals detachments and headquarters, black and white soldiers routinely served side by side, even prior to the army reforms that formalised widespread integration in the late 1970s, as discussed later.[176] However, by design, the regular army's fighting force was de facto segregated between the RAR and the RLI.

---

[173] These regulars comprised 1,590 black soldiers, of whom 903 were RAR; 1,338 white enlisted soldiers and 271 officers (ibid.).

[174] 'Just over' 2,000 black soldiers and 2,255 white officers and soldiers (CL, R.C. (S) (73) 162, 'National Service: Territorial Training: Priorities in the Organisation and Utilisation of Defence Manpower', 7 December 1973, p. 1).

[175] In military terms, these NS companies fulfilled much the same role as the regulars, with some serving in the RLI, for instance. The duration of NS, originally four and a half months, increased throughout the war, doubling to nine months in 1966, increasing to one year in 1973 (CL, R.C. (S) (75) 52, 'National Service: Proposed Amalgamation of the Territorial Force and Reserve', 18 April 1975), and eventually doubling once more, to eighteen months by the end of the 1970s, alongside which the age limit was increased to apply to those up to thirty-four (Cohen, 'War in Rhodesia', p. 483; White, *Unpopular Sovereignty*, p. 179). Approximately 2,000 NS were called up each year, of which at any one time 750 were undergoing training and 1,250 were serving on operations (CL, R.C. (S) (73) 98, 'National Servicemen: Pay and Allowances', 8 August 1973, p. 1).

[176] For instance, in 1975, newly passed out RAR soldiers awaiting posting to their units 'had been conducting integrated operations with 1RLI in the Hurricane area' (Wood, *War Diaries of Andre Dennison*, p. 17).

Only in the mid-1970s did integrated units first appear in the form of small regiments of special forces. The Grey's Scouts were dragoons (mounted infantry) that carried out infantry tasks across terrain that vehicles found difficult to traverse. As DSN, an RAR soldier who became a Grey's Scouts officer in 1978, told me, most 'black soldiers in Grey's were not active [as combat troops]. Their main task was to clean the horses and feed them. Clean them – the stables, feed horses and so forth', with others working as farriers, whereas only a small number served as dragoons in combat.[177]

The other unit was the notorious Selous Scouts. It undertook a hybrid military and intelligence role and was largely comprised of hundreds of 'turned' former guerrillas (i.e. not regular soldiers) who were used to infiltrate guerrilla units and rural areas. Their wartime mystique and their appearance in many neo-Rhodesian accounts have given them a reputation that exceeds their military significance. Something of a law unto themselves, the Selous Scouts were in many ways not a regular army unit at all,[178] and the regiment was loathed by many in both the army and the Central Intelligence Organisation (CIO).[179] A handful of African soldiers were recruited from the RAR when the unit was being created, to the chagrin of RAR officers, who swiftly put a stop to this practice. These ex-RAR soldiers largely functioned as NCOs and, later, as officers; however, their numbers were always small and, even after recruitment of RAR soldiers, likely did not exceed 100.[180]

[177] Grey's Scouts used their horses to cover large distances across difficult terrain. See Binda, *Equus Men*.
[178] For instance, BSAP Special Branch and CIO personnel were embedded in the Selous Scouts from the outset, and Major Jeremy Strong, its founding second in command, was of the 'opinion the Selous Scouts was not a military unit but a Special Branch unit' (Baxter, *Selous Scouts*, pp. 40–2).
[179] The Selous Scouts were afforded considerable autonomy, answering only to Lt Gen. Walls, with the regular army having no authority over it. This caused considerable friction and rivalry with the CIO and other elements of the RSF (ibid., pp. 85–6). Lt Col. Reid-Daly, its founder and commanding officer (CO), discovered a bugging device in his telephone in 1979, placed on the orders of the army commander, reflecting the internal rivalry and factionalism prevalent with the RSF at the end of the war. Allegations of Selous Scout involvement in illegal poaching and the sale of captured weapons were widespread.
[180] Interview with SM, former 'African RSM' of the Selous Scouts. The exact size of the Selous Scouts, nor its number of regular black soldiers, is not known, as its records seem to have been destroyed (see Chapter 2). At its formation, it had only a handful of ex-RAR troops (Baxter, *Selous Scouts*, p. 33). Reid-Daly wrote that the regiment was 500 strong during the war (Reid-Daly and Stiff, *Selous Scouts*, p. 98). Conventional soldiers in the Selous Scouts troops were, after 1976, involved in some large-scale 'external' raids (see Chapter 4), but it seems that white TF servicemen, rather than black soldiers, provided the bulk of these troops (Baxter, *Selous Scouts*, pp. 74–5); Melson put the number of white TF in the 'assault group' at 100 along with a '14-man reconnaissance troop and mortar troop' (Melson, *Fighting for Time*, p. 170). Melson, quoting Reid-Daly

82   The Creation of Regimental Loyalties

Many black soldiers also served in important non-infantry roles. A 1967 army report noted: 'most of the Army's communications network is manned by African signallers. African drivers, cooks, clerks, medical orderlies and engineers also play a most important part in the order of battle'.[181] However, the greatest number of black soldiers were always within the RAR: in 1966, more than 55 per cent served in the RAR, and a 1977 study of 500 black regular soldiers noted that two-thirds served in the RAR as infantrymen.[182] As argued earlier, the regular army was utterly dependent upon black soldiers, and by June 1979, the army commander declared that 'he was expecting the security forces to be 95% African by the end of the year'.[183]

The second part of the Rhodesian Army was its reservists, known as the Territorial Force (TF),[184] whose number formed two-thirds of the paper strength of the Rhodesian Army.[185] These were civilians who, after completing their National Service year of full-time conscription, had a further four years of part-time service liability, during which they were called up annually for short periods of operational service. The TF soldiers were increasingly mobilised for lengthy periods as the war intensified, and many were mobilised for several months a year, which corroded white morale and prompted increased rates of emigration.[186]

After 1976, members of the TF could be placed on 'continuous call-up', which resulted in high rates of white desertion.[187] While the paper

and another secondary text, wrote that there were '516 attested [i.e. Rhodesian Army] Selous Scouts and 800 "turned" guerrillas', which with white TF troops 'made up a total of 1,500' in the regiment (ibid.). Luise White wrote that the maximum size of the Selous Scouts was 1,800, although she provided no source for this and no breakdown of membership by background (e.g. 'turned' guerrilla, ex-RAR, white national serviceman, Rhodesian Army regular) (White, *Fighting and Writing*, p. 77).

[181] Stapleton, *African Police and Soldiers*, p. 178.
[182] CL, R.C. (S) (66) 44, 'Rhodesian Army and Royal Rhodesian Air Force: Review of Pay and Conditions of Service', 3 February 1966, pp. 1–2; Mutangadura, *Study*, p. 17.
[183] Anti-Apartheid Movement, *Fireforce Exposed*, p. 40.
[184] Prior to 1975, those soldiers who had completed their TF liability of four years were then placed in the Reserve and had a reduced call-up and training liability, but could still be called up by the government on an emergency basis. As the war intensified, the line between TF and Reserve became increasingly blurred and the Reserve were formally merged into the TF in 1975 (CL, R.C. (S) (75) 52, 'National Service: Proposed Amalgamation of the Territorial Force and Reserve', 18 April 1975).
[185] CL, R.C. (S) (67) 132, 'Financial Provision for Defence Purposes', 23 June 1967, Annex A.
[186] For instance, a December 1973 memo by the minister of defence warned of the 'consequences for the economy' of the increasingly frequent and lengthy TF and Reserve call-ups, with many part-timers having been called up for three months of that year, and that white emigration rates had soared as a result. CL, R.C. (S) (73) 162, 'National Service: Territorial Training: Priorities in the Organisation and Utilisation of Defence Manpower', 7 December 1973, p. 1.
[187] White, *Unpopular Sovereignty*, p. 179.

strength of the TF troops was large, only a small fraction could be called up concurrently. For instance, although 8,500 TF were called up throughout 1973, only 2,000 were on active service at any one time.[188] TF companies were also chronically undermanned. In 1977, the Rhodesian government's War Council was told that the army was forty-eight companies strong in total, but that twenty-six of these were drawn from the TF, which 'were well below strength and represented only 11 full companies of 100 each', with 58 per cent of white TF units described as 'well below strength'.[189]

There was also a vast qualitative difference between the regulars and the reservists. The TF troops received much less training than regulars, and what little they received was of poor quality, owing to a shortage of regular instructors.[190] As a result, the quality of TF NCOs and officers was generally deemed to be poor.[191] Predictably, TF troops were nowhere near as operationally effective as regular forces. A 1973 memorandum from the Rhodesian minister of defence noted that TF units were 'less proficient ... because of their infrequent and periodic involvement in military skills'.[192] Chris Cocks, an RLI soldier, remarked that 'as regulars we had little respect for the territorials'.[193]

Part-time soldiers were never as effective as the professionals and their performance frequently came in for criticism. For this reason, TF soldiers were not used in the same manner as regular soldiers, and they were generally deployed in the border control role, undertaking routine patrolling in order to detect the presence of guerrillas in the hinterlands.[194] Upon encountering guerrilla forces, the TF would often call in regular units from the RAR or RLI to engage them. Thus the TF's mission was focused on routine reconnaissance rather than combat, and TF soldiers played little role in 'Fireforce' or other combat operations, in marked contrast to regular troops.[195] For instance, discussing Fireforce operations, in 1975 the Rhodesian senior command overseeing the war effort called 'for the employment of only "well-trained troops" such as the RLI or RAR to ensure success'.[196]

---

[188] CL, R.C. (S) (73) 98, 'National Servicemen: Pay and Allowances', 8 August 1973, p. 4.
[189] Papers of Ken Flower, Bodleian Library [hereafter PKF], War Council (S) (77) 7, OCC/1/1, 'OCC Memorandum on Sterile Zones and Food Control', 16 February 1977, p. 3.
[190] Moorcraft and McLaughlin, *Rhodesian War*, pp. 56–8.
[191] For NCOs, see Whitaker, *'New Model' Armies of Africa?*, pp. 171–2; for officers, see Cohen, 'War in Rhodesia', p. 484.
[192] CL, R.C. (S) (73) 162, 'National Service: Territorial Training: Priorities in the Organisation and Utilisation of Defence Manpower', 7 December 1973, Annex A, p. 2.
[193] Cocks, *Fireforce*, p. 76.
[194] R.C. (S) (75) 52, 'National Service: Proposed Amalgamation of the Territorial Force and Reserve', p. 2.
[195] Melson, *Fighting for Time*, p. 140.   [196] Ibid., p. 110.

It is therefore apt to speak of two Rhodesian armies. One was a vast reservist force, comprising largely conscripted whites, which undertook routine duties for short periods of time and suffered from chronic manpower problems.[197] The other was the regular Rhodesian Army, whose soldiers were the army's most 'critical commodity'.[198] They carried out the war's main combat tasks and the Rhodesian Army was more than 80 per cent black by the end of the war.

Given this gulf in capability between regular and TF soldiers, a distinction should be made between them when detailing the strength of the Rhodesian Army. Accounts of the war have not always done so. For instance, articles by generalist scholars of warfare have greatly exaggerated the regular army's strength at the end of the war, providing estimates ranging from 10,800,[199] to 14,000,[200] and even 20,000.[201] These inflated figures are likely the result of scholars simply tallying the number of regular and TF soldiers. Given that we know that, by the end of the war, the RAR was 4,100 strong, these figures imply that black soldiers were a minority in the regular army.[202] This was not the case, as argued earlier in this chapter, and credible, specialist scholars have provided more realistic estimates of the strength of the Rhodesian Army, which give an approximate size of 5,000–5,500 regular soldiers by the end of the war.[203] Furthermore, after late 1977, the RAR Depot commenced training more black soldiers than the RAR battalions could absorb. These extra RAR troops were integrated with white troops, some in the TF battalions, and others in the independent companies. They may have numbered two battalions in strength (approximately 1,250 soldiers) at the war's conclusion.[204]

---

[197] Cilliers, *Counter-Insurgency in Rhodesia*, p. 2. [198] Ibid., p. 43.
[199] Gregory, 'Zimbabwe Election', p. 2
[200] Mills, 'BMATT and Military Integration in Southern Africa'.
[201] Jackson, 'Civil War Roots of Military Domination in Zimbabwe', p. 380.
[202] Rupiya, 'Demobilization and Integration'.
[203] For instance, Mills and Wilson asserted that the Rhodesian Army comprised '3,400 regulars' (Mills and Wilson, 'Who Dares Loses?', p. 22). Cilliers asserted that in 1979, the Rhodesian Army lamented that it only had 3,900 'well trained troops' – that is, regulars (*Counter-Insurgency in Rhodesia*, p. 239). Wood said 'the Rhodesian Army had 5,000 regulars' ('Countering the Chimurenga', p. 189). The International Institute for Strategic Studies cited 6,000 regulars and 14,000 TF (*The Military Balance*, 79, 1 (1979), p. 56). Rupiya also cited 6,000 by the end of the war ('Demobilisation and Integration', p. 31). Evans stated 8,500 (*Fighting against Chimurenga*, p. 14).
[204] Interview with anonymous white ex-RAR officer, Bulawayo, 2017. Without access to the RAA, it is difficult to know their number. Some of the army's independent companies, formerly of the Rhodesia Regiment, were rebadged as RAR independent companies, which provided the nucleus for the formation of 3RAR in November 1979 (Binda, *Masodja*, pp. 365–6). See 'RAR Masodja in the Rhodesia Regiment 1977–80', https://johnwynnehopkins.wordpress.com/2020/05/02/rar-masodja-in-the-rhodesia-regiment-1977-80 [Accessed June 2020].

In sum, black soldiers were utterly vital to the Rhodesian Army's efficacy and increasingly dominated the crucially important regular army, particularly as the war intensified. This is important in understanding the RAR's solidarities and loyalties, which foregrounded its 'professional' skills and martial status. As we shall see, the RAR's predominance within the regular army meant it experienced a considerable period of wartime operations and much combat.

Conclusion

This chapter has shown that the make-up of the RAR changed dramatically at the end of the Federal period as a result of the government's drive to remove 'aliens'. This had a knock-on effect of consolidating RAR recruitment, and the Masvingo catchment area became important, although not dominant, in supplying recruits. Likewise, soldiering became a metier prevalent within certain families, although in contrast to much received opinion, recruitment to the RAR was not dependent upon either ethno-regional or familial identity, and soldiers from all over the country joined the army for myriad reasons.

Furthermore, as the Rhodesian Army intended that the loyalties of its soldiers were pledged to the regiment above all else, and were not to be premised upon regional or ethnic allegiance, it placed great emphasis upon the creation of a durable identity to which 'regimental loyalty' was pledged. This was forged through the invocation of the regiment's history, which emphasised its past service in Burma, Egypt, and Malaya, and the creation of an elaborate set of powerful, albeit invented traditions, including the RAR's own songs, band, mascot, and colours.

Scholars have previously simply conflated different elements the Rhodesian Army's manpower when judging its combat strength and drawn false equivalence between regulars and reservists. There was an important and pronounced qualitative distinction between the regulars and the TF, which means that the RAR's dominance of the regular army was much more militarily significant than has hitherto been recognised. As the war escalated, the RAR formed a large majority of the regular army, and was thus at the forefront of much of the conflict's military operations and combat. In tandem with the end of the Federation, the RAR underwent a metamorphosis into a regiment that was trained in COIN warfare as part of a Rhodesian militarisation effort that increasingly emphasised professionalism, as Chapter 3 argues.

3 'The Rhodesian Army Was the Best in Everything'
The Professionalism of Black Rhodesian Soldiers

Once the RAR was an established, regular force, new forms of micro-level solidarities particular to regular soldiers took root which fundamentally differentiated these soldiers from other combatants. Unlike the military culture of apartheid South Africa's army in which black soldiers served, the military culture of the Rhodesian Army did not deviate markedly from Western norms.[1] The professionalism of the Rhodesian Army, modelled upon British practice, was institutionalised and embedded during the RAR's transformation to a regular army.

In the words of the Rhodesian minister of defence, prior to UDI, the Rhodesian Army functioned 'largely as an adjunct to Commonwealth forces'.[2] Its doctrine, practices, traditions, and ethos were derived from Britain, and during the Federal period, it was routine for British officers to serve in Rhodesian regiments.[3] Thus a literature that has studied the British practice of creating soldierly cohesion and loyalty is also of much use in analysing the Rhodesian Army. Incorporating the arguments of military sociologists, particularly the work of Anthony King, and historians, I contend that these intense micro-level bonds of loyalty were forged through a dual-pronged approach.

In this process, firstly a soldierly identity is shaped, which requires the individual to wholly sublimate his personal desires and needs to those of the unit. Secondly, soldiers are drilled and exercised to conform to an ideal of professionalism, which involves achieving high levels of performance in individual military skills and competencies, such as marksmanship and map-reading, through to collective proficiency in drills that combine fire and manoeuvre, and the coordinated use of fire support from mortars or heavy weapons. As King argues in his seminal text *The Combat Soldier*, soldierly identity and professionalism become co-constitutive: the individual willingly submits to the goals of the group not merely because he feels a strong affective bond for his comrades, but also because he knows that this kinship is founded

---

[1] Bolliger, *Apartheid's African Soldiers*, p. 329.
[2] CL, R.C. (S) (67) 100, 'Financial Provision for Defence Purposes', 11 May 1967.
[3] Telfer and Fulton, *Chibaya Moyo 2*, p. 84.

upon a demand made of all soldiers in the unit to strive for the highest standards of soldierly performance. For King, '[P]rofessionalism – engendered through training – does not merely improve the practical performance of soldiers: it fundamentally alters the social relations between them; it transforms the nature of the associations between them. Professionalism generates a solidarity whose distinctiveness is often overlooked.'[4]

All soldiers are expected to reciprocate, and thus a virtuous cycle of performance excellence is perpetuated which symbiotically binds the survival of the unit and the survival of the individual during combat. This dynamic was evident among my interviewees, who powerfully evoked the strength of those soldierly bonds.

Military Socialisation

The institutional nature of an army was best encapsulated by Erving Goffman, who chose it as one of his archetypes of a 'total institution', defined as those he deemed possessed of an 'encompassing or total character' and which require the total subordination of their subjects.[5] The structure and customs of the total institution are instrumentally geared to performing a strategic mission, to which all other needs are subsumed. Unlike in the civilian sphere, in a total institution, 'all aspects of life are conducted in the same place and under the same single authority', with a strong collective ethos and approach, rigidly formal adherence to set timings, the ritualization of communal meal times and out-of-hours socialising, conformity to set standards of behaviour and dress, mandatory commitment to an overall strategic goal, and a bisected hierarchy between a 'large managed group' (i.e. soldiers) and a small group of managers (officers).[6] Goffman used the British Army extensively as an example of the total institution, and thus the archetype readily applies to the Rhodesian Army which mimicked this process, as did many British African colonial units.[7]

For an army, the purpose of total institution organisational precepts is to foster and propagate a culture and ethos that serves its strategic goal: combat performance. As the military sociologists David Segal and Mady Segal maintained, the key lesson of twentieth-century warfare is that 'strong affective ties in military units have been shown to be essential for effectiveness'.[8] Thus the imperative for commanders is to create as strong a bond as possible between soldiers. As King argued: 'Military institutions depend on a level of social cohesion that is matched in few other

---

[4] King, *Combat Soldier*, p. 338.   [5] Goffman, *Asylums*, pp. 4–12.   [6] Ibid.
[7] Ranger, 'Invention of Tradition in Colonial Africa', p. 225.
[8] Segal and Segal, 'Change in Military Organization', p. 153.

social groups. In combat, the armed forces are able to sustain themselves only so long as individual members commit themselves to collective goals even at the cost of personal injury or death.'[9]

Clearly, it is imperative for commanders to create bonds of loyalty. After World War II, many military scientists attempted to discover the most effective way to inspire loyalty. The 'extraordinary tenacity of the German Army' during World War II was frequently – and mistakenly – attributed to the political-ideological beliefs of its soldiers. The military sociologists Edward Shils and Morris Janowitz convincingly posited that political factors were actually of marginal motivational importance.[10] They illustrated this point with an eye-opening anecdote: 'A German sergeant, captured toward the end [of World War II] was asked by his interrogators about the political opinions of his men. In reply, he laughed and said, "When you ask such a question, I realize well that you have no idea of what makes a soldier fight."'[11]

Rather than being inspired by abstract political ideals, German soldiers were most effective in combat when serving in small 'primary groups' that offered them 'affection and esteem' and whose members implicitly trusted each other to carry out their duties. The German Army's backbone was its NCOs, many of whom joined prior to the Nazification of the army and were 'neither very interested in politics nor very aggressive, but were thoroughly trained, solid men who were doing their job out of a deeply-rooted sense of duty to the soldierly profession'.[12] This description could also be readily applied to black Rhodesian soldiers. CD described how his strong connection to the Rhodesian Army was motivated largely by its commitment to high soldierly standards: 'The Rhodesian Army was the best. It was the best in everything. The standards, you know? Everything: they were just excellent, above excellence, I think.'[13] The roots of this excellence were found in how the Rhodesian Army inculcated a professional ethos among its civilian recruits.

Civilians were far from being guaranteed acceptance into the RAR. Although recruits were generally young, 65 per cent had already been in wage employment prior to enlisting, and there existed 'very high physical standards for enlistment', including a competitive twenty-kilometre run.[14] The army retained this stringent selection criteria throughout the war. It could afford to be highly selective, as it attracted high numbers of volunteers, meaning there were 'always more potential recruits' than it had the capacity to train.[15] For instance, the RAR's two intakes of 1976

[9] King, 'Word of Command', p. 493.
[10] Shils and Janowitz, 'Cohesion and Disintegration', p. 281.   [11] Ibid., p. 284.
[12] Ibid., p. 299.   [13] Interview with CD.
[14] Stapleton, *African Police and Soldiers*, p. 31.   [15] Downie, *Frontline Rhodesia*, 4m:55s.

accepted only 520 recruits from 1,607 applicants to proceed to basic training.[16] This meant that those accepted as recruits were possessed of not only the aptitude to become a professional soldier, but also a deep well of motivation. Armies have long recognised that volunteers willing to endure the rigors of soldiering generally make the best troops; as the old British military adage, dating from the eighteenth century and widely circulated during World War II, asserts, 'one volunteer is worth ten pressed men'.[17] The Rhodesian Army's stringent selection criteria meant that those who were accepted were the most likely to be loyal, and those not disposed to soldiering on through arduous conditions were filtered out.

Life in a professional army is inherently removed from and intentionally unrelatable to civilian life.[18] Amos Nhlanhla recalled of his early days in the RAR: 'we were taught how to become experienced soldiers and the civilian habits were vanishing'.[19] As per Goffman's archetype, the total institution of the army is perpetuated through a process of assimilation during which raw recruits are inducted into a military culture that motivates and inspires soldiers to willingly carry out arduous and difficult duties. Military sociologists have used the term 'military culture' to define the social environment of the military unit – particularly its norms and values – and how it is constructed and perpetuated over time.[20] This culture is given historical meaning and imbued with an emotive potency by the regimental ethos and traditions as depicted in Chapter 2, which impose 'powerful normative demands' upon soldiers.[21]

Socialisation into a unit's military culture is achieved, in the first instance, through a demanding and gruelling period of basic training, generally three to six months in duration, that is perceived as a rite of passage. Recruits are treated harshly and regularly demeaned, earning the status of a soldier only after performing satisfactorily during military exercises, aptitude tests, and physical trials. Only once recruits have 'passed out' of basic training, symbolised by a spectacular parade put on for family and friends and accompanied by a military band, are they considered fully fledged soldiers.[22]

---

[16] Stapleton, *African Police and Soldiers*, p. 30. See also Lohman and MacPherson, *Rhodesia*, p. 32; Godwin and Hancock, *'Rhodesians Never Die'd*, p. 159.
[17] Simpson and Speake, *Oxford Dictionary of Proverbs*; Imperial War Museum, World War I Poster, 'One Volunteer Is Worth Ten Pressed Men', Art. IWM PST 6064.
[18] See, for example, Gill, 'Creating Citizens, Making Men', p. 533.
[19] '1RAR Notes, A (The Champion) Company', *Nwoho* (October 1977), p. 18.
[20] Soeters, Winslow, and Weibull, 'Military Culture', pp. 238–40.
[21] Kellett, *Combat Motivation*, p. 112.
[22] See, for example, King, *Combat Soldier*, p. 72; Soeters et al., 'Military Culture', pp. 249–51.

As BM attested, Rhodesian Army basic training was challenging, and two of his fellow recruits 'ran away [left the army] because the training was too tough'.[23] DSN recalled that of his intake of twelve recruits, four left as 'it was tough, yeah, especially for them because they were from the reserve, you know? They didn't know what soldiering is and so forth, so they thought they were being mistreated ... Harassed'.[24]

DSN's statement offers a crucial insight, as his palpable disdain for those recruits who did not meet the standards expected of a soldier is demonstrative of how training also functioned as a secondary filter of those who had passed the initial recruitment phase. Recruits who could not meet the highly demanding standards were released. As MSW, who joined the RAR in 1969, told me, of his training intake of forty-three, only twenty-three made it through.[25] As in any professional army, there was no room for dissent or protest and young volunteers had to submit to the utter remoulding of their identities into soldiers.

For those who endured its rigors, basic training was challenging but rewarding, a period of metamorphosis between civilian and soldier. BM recalled:

Ah, the training was tough, yes, but those six months they give us a lot of work and [made us] 'switched on' [military slang for being alert and responsive to orders]. We are asleep but we end up switched on, haha! I enjoyed [training]. Especially the corporals who were training us [as instructors] – they were very tough, but they were giv[ing] us some good training: drill [military marching], weapons, tactics, everything, map reading, everything. Ah, I was enjoying a lot; that's why I passed out. Because I enjoyed those six months.[26]

Similarly, PM came to enjoy the instilled discipline:

[W]hat was tough was the drill. They started with foot drill [marching]. When you completed foot drill, then weapon – with rifle drill ... and then after that they take you to the course for tactics. Map reading and organising how to do all this and that ... the reason why I liked [training and the army], I was under grip of instructions – all enforced that I cannot do this and this and this. That whatever you must do is instruction, that you must do your instruction of your commander.[27]

GMH told me that although 'the training was not easy, it was very hard', it was also 'good because it keeps you strong'.[28] HZ commented that the difficulty of training also depended upon one's background: 'It was tough

---

[23] Interview with BM.
[24] Interview with DSN. 'The reserve' is a reference to poor, rural areas of marginal agricultural productivity where the Rhodesian government forced most of the black population to reside.
[25] Interview with MSW. [26] Interview with BM. [27] Interview with PM.
[28] Interview with GMH.

for somebody who was not yet used to that. But as time went on it became okay for me.'[29] Likewise, WM stated that in contrast to others: '[T]he training itself was not hard on me because I was the best recruit! I was presented with a wristwatch – I broke the history of the RAR. I was the first one to be awarded a wristwatch by the commanding officer because I was the all-round best recruit.'[30]

Of course, training was not solely about instilling loyalty. Practical military skills were vital too. GN, a long-standing instructor at the RAR depot, recalled the life-and-death pressure he felt to ensure his charges were trained to the highest possible level:

Since I was the instructor . . . I used to say to the last word making sure this person I was teaching understood all that I'd taught. If he failed to understand, he is going to be killed in the action. So I wasn't very pleased when someone was killed in the action . . . I was not pleased to hear that message. I used to ask myself, 'What went wrong? Where did I fail?' Because that person came through my hands, I bring him to be a soldier, now why he got killed? That is the main point I used to pass to those I used to train.[31]

GN's sombre warning is also indicative of a further facet of the make-up of African recruits. Those who enlisted did so knowing they would likely be involved in dangerous combat, particularly after the war escalated. HZ told me:

The day I joined the army when we were interviewed by the CO – Colonel Godwin by that time – he said a box [coffin] of the first killed soldier from Chinhoyi was arriving. He said, 'You two young boys, you want to join the army? Do you see that aeroplane? It's coming to drop [the coffin].' He had been shot and killed, so his body was coming back. We said, 'We don't mind if we get killed.' There [were] three of us that same day, and he [the colonel] laughed [in appreciation of their bravado].

I told HZ that I presumed he went into the army as a recruit with no illusions as to the danger. He responded, 'no, no, we didn't mind the danger that would come'.[32] During wartime, soldiers such as HZ were attracted to what they perceived as the adventure of combat, a motivation highly conducive to them committing to the rigors of training and becoming loyal soldiers.

GMH told me:

If you've got experience in tactics for the war and you're very interested in the [conduct of] war, it's not [hard to fight effectively during combat situations] . . . if you get trained like a person who is at school who didn't listen to the teacher, you

[29] Interview with HZ. [30] Interview with WM. [31] Interview with GN.
[32] Interview with HZ.

cannot pass – the army is just the same. But if you listen to your instructors, [you will be fine].[33]

Other recruits struggled during basic training, but not on account of the physical or mental rigors.

A small minority of recruits were well educated and already possessed a civilian profession, generally as teachers or medical professionals. They found the rigid discipline and obedience demanded by the army patronising. DC, a teacher in civilian life, joined the Rhodesian Army Education Corps 'as a qualified artisan', meaning he was instantly promoted to sergeant and given pay incentives. TM recalled how 'having eight years of education – Standard VI – you were considered the best material for the Education Corps. After writing an examination, I was successful and selected to train as an educational instructor'.[34] However, those recruited as teachers still had to undergo the same six months of gruelling formative training as every other recruit. DC commented that his level of education rendered him somewhat anomalous, and this afforded him a particular insight into the qualities he thought made a good infantry soldier. He deemed those who possessed less education as more suitable for adopting a soldierly identity:

> But you see, what I discovered was these people who were not educated they were also good soldiers. Because soldier basically means a disciplinarian. You have got to have discipline. You tell a soldier to dig there, he mustn't ask why. He must just dig [*laughs*]! So they were more disciplined than the educated people. And like that, they were preferred [as] soldiers and they operated effectively, especially during the war. Because when you are in a war ... and you're advancing towards the enemy ... these soldiers when they are not well educated they just go to the enemy and they are not allowed to turn or look at the commander, they only follow the instruction, you see? So they were much better soldiers [than well-educated recruits], anyway, despite being uneducated. And physically they were good. Physically, I like the way they operated. But when it came to trying to get them to read their map, map-reading, you know these things – they had quite a few problems, when it comes to reading and all that. But in the bush they were good.[35]

These are, of course, rather derogatory comments, indicative of a certain class snobbery among better-educated soldiers. Those who joined as qualified professionals, such as TM and DC, were older and better educated than not only most of their peers, but also some of their instructors and officers. This could cause friction, as the teachers sometimes struggled with being expected to instantly adhere to commands without hesitation or question, a vital part of the formation of a soldierly identity. DC recalled:

> And there the question of discipline was [*he laughs*], because when you are a bit educated, you sort of select reasonable commands and unreasonable commands!

[33] Interview with GMH.   [34] Interview with TM.   [35] Interview with DC.

And, oh, we had a bit of problems. If the problem did not come from me, it would maybe come from another [fellow recruit to the Education Corps] teacher there [*laughs again*]. 'Ah, no, that is rubbish,' telling the instructor – you know, it was not very good. But as time went we coped with the situation; we completed our six months well.[36]

Despite these frustrations, both DC and TM completed training (almost a decade apart from one another) and were both rapidly promoted to the rank of Warrant Officer II – indeed TM became the youngest, at twenty-three, to hold this rank in the entire army.

Basic training comprises only the first phase of military socialisation. The second occurs when the newly minted soldier has passed out of basic training and joins his peers in his battalion, living, eating, working, and socialising in close proximity.

Downie commented of RAR recruits that during basic training, they 'absorb little more than the rudiments of their new profession. It takes a further two years under good NCOs and officers before they can be regarded as fully trained'.[37] This 'secondary socialisation produces an extreme in-group bias' within the total institution of the army,[38] the 'product of personal bonds forged in exclusive informal interactions'.[39] Through continuous training, exercising, and active service, bonds of fierce loyalty are created. During combat, these feelings are most pronounced amongst members of the same section (small combat groups generally of fewer than ten soldiers) or a fire team (typically half a section, known as a 'stick' in the Rhodesian Army).[40]

In the British regimental system, individuals are socialised to feel loyalty towards several vertically integrated groups. A soldier is loyal to not only his immediate section, but also his platoon (comprised of three sections), company (three to five platoons), and battalion (three to five companies). Akin to Russian dolls, these hierarchical stages of the chain of command form 'a nesting series of different sized groups' between which loyalty is shuttled:

> Thus an infantry soldier would express his identity as a member of his platoon and feel loyalty to it in competition with other platoons of the same company. However, where his company is in competition with other companies, these attitudes and feelings would be transferred to the company, rather than the platoon, and this process is continued up to levels beyond the unit (and down to those below the platoon).[41]

---

[36] Interview with DC.   [37] Downie, *Frontline Rhodesia*.
[38] Castro, 'Anthropological Methods and the Study of the Military', pp. 10–11.
[39] King, 'Word of Command', p. 494.   [40] Keegan, *Face of Battle*, p. 53.
[41] Kirke, 'Seeing through the Stereotype', p. 22.

Such intra-unit rivalries were also prevalent in the Rhodesian Army, which often hosted inter-company competitions,[42] of which sporting fixtures – particularly football – were a key aspect.[43] Individual companies could accrue great prestige by being crowned 'champion company' in intra-battalion military skills competitions 'designed to promote esprit de corps and a competitive spirit', and many pages of the regimental journal *Nwoho* were dedicated to the latest scores and results, along with much intra-regimental joshing.[44]

CD recalled how even within one platoon there could be fierce inter-section rivalry:

We were sort of a clique, really; we stuck together. We are like brothers, you see. My section, like, say, another guy from [another section] he beats up any one of our guys, it's all chaos! We would go on, we would definitely go on to them and destroy our own guys – but not with guns! Fists, boots, whatever. We were kind of, you don't touch my brothers. These are my brothers; you don't touch them. Anyone touches them or says, say he goes to town, a nightclub in town, he is beaten up, he comes back beaten up. We would go there. This is how we were. We would definitely go there all of us and then we would definitely do something very bad there, then we will run away, that's how. So we were sort of, we kind of stuck together, say, even if we are going for R&R we would go together ... as our section [and the other sections in the platoon would] also stick together.[45]

CD's depiction of brotherly loyalty outlines how, just as with the World War II soldiers of the Wehrmacht, the intense bonds formed among subunit members impelled soldiers to sublimate their individual will to the needs of the collective.

Bonds created by military socialisation ensure loyalty to the mission of the unit and to one's comrades. However, they are not always alone sufficient to guarantee conformity to the rules and regulations of the army. Given the strict discipline and restrictions upon personal freedom innate to life in such a total institution, this is unsurprising. Indiscipline and acts of petty rebellion are rife in even the best armies. Consequently, all professional armies implement a system of military discipline that is notably harsh.

Soldiers are subject to the vertically hierarchical chain of command, characterised by some academics as more coercive than its civilian counterparts, whose (legal) orders cannot be refused or disputed.[46] Military law applies to soldiers on account of their special responsibilities and privileges. Disobedience, when it comes to obeying orders and mission

---

[42] See, for instance, Wood, *War Diaries of Andre Dennison*, p. 118.
[43] I. Dube, 'Tanlwe Chaung Week Soccer Scene 1977', *Nwoho* (October 1977), p. 25.
[44] 'The Champion Company Competition', *Nwoho* (October 1977), pp. 26–7.
[45] Interview with CD.   [46] Soeters et al., 'Military Culture', p. 242.

performance, is a cardinal form of disloyalty, in a way that other commonplace infringements – such as being late to return from leave, using cannabis, or engaging with sex workers – were not, for these transgressions did not have a large or potentially deleterious impact upon military efficacy, and as such were dealt with more leniently by the military hierarchy. Most disciplinary issues stem from this type of conduct, which is not in and of itself inimical to the strategic goal of the army.

These minor transgressions are often dealt with 'in house' by the errant soldier's NCOs or platoon commander, generally by the awarding of extra duties or cancellation of leave. Informal in-house discipline occurs widely, typically involving the use of violence by NCOs as a de facto form of corporal punishment, which is routine, even if officially prohibited.

In some instances, particularly during wartime, these minor infractions are even tacitly condoned, and I refer to such acts as 'permissible indiscipline'. For instance, like soldiers since time immemorial, during the war, RAR troops frequently used their disposable income to engage the services of sex workers. The officer commanding (OC) of A Company, 2RAR noted with humour the militarily deleterious effects this could have: 'the bad news about the R&R/training period was the horrific V[enereal] D[isease] rate, the syphilitic sirens of Mucheke [Township] having once again succeeded where ZANU has hitherto failed'.[47] Although brothels were declared out of bounds to soldiers, these minor infractions were not deemed worthy of punishment. In a comparable manner, in the Wehrmacht during World War II:

> Private personal transgressions of 'civil' ethics were regarded as of slight importance, since they were outside the limits of the 'manly comradeship' of the military primary group. Drunkenness and having women in the barracks were crimes which the officers overlooked … soldiers could reassure themselves about their manliness without disrupting the disciplinary structure of the Wehrmacht. This combination of practices lowered the probability of tensions in officer-man relationships.[48]

Alcohol loomed also large in this permissible indiscipline. Some behaviours – behaving drunkenly and raucously in town while on leave – were more or less tacitly condoned by the army as a way to let off steam, even if they would typically involve bad conduct and soldiers getting in trouble with the civilian authorities and military police.

Fighting with civilians was not only commonplace, but almost de rigueur. Sometimes this even extended to fighting with the police. The commander of A Company 2RAR wrote in his diary how, prior to going

---

[47] Wood, *War Diaries of Andre Dennison*, p. 118.
[48] Shils and Janowitz, 'Cohesion and Disintegration', p. 298.

on operations, 'the morning of our departure was immortalised by a police identification parade where a bevy of stuffed-up policemen walked the poker-faced ranks of A Company trying to identify those who had stuffed them up in the Mucheke Township, outside Fort Victoria, the night before. Their quest was unsuccessful and the police brass left the showgrounds breathing fire, brimstone and vengeance'.[49]

Russell Fulton, a white ex-RAR officer, has written of two separate instances where, his platoon having a brief stopover in Bulawayo prior to redeployment, he was implored by his soldiers 'to go to Bulawayo to "have some pints" with them' and readily accepted, reasoning 'how could I refuse these beautiful, proud men?'. Fulton wrote of enjoying lengthy and raucous drinking sessions with his soldiers which, in both instances, ended up in fights with nightclub bouncers, and one of his soldiers being arrested for defending their officer during the fracas.

In both incidents, the RAR hierarchy firmly sided with their soldiers irrespective of their guilt, and told Fulton to do whatever necessary to secure their release. Fulton managed to have one soldier released from Bulawayo's central police station through 'sycophantic praise' of the BSAP and telling the senior officer that Private 'Sibanda was an outstanding soldier who had been cited for gallantry (a slight but deliberate embellishment for effect) and that he was only acting on instinct but really meant no harm'. In the second instance, the matter reached court martial, where Fulton acted as Private Kananda's advocate, going 'to some length to expound upon the gallantry in action of Private Kananda', and submitted as evidence Kananda's citation for bravery in the field. Fulton's defence was successful and only a fine was levied as punishment, which Fulton paid from his own pocket as 'Kananda had stood up for me and I would never allow him to be penalised for doing so ... It was tantamount to me condoning an act "unbecoming" but ... the welfare of my men was my only consideration back in the day, it would be fair to say that I knew my *masodja* better than I did my own family.'[50]

Such instances are not atypical of soldiers on leave in any army. In the RAR, they were a way for the in-group of soldiers to assert their hypermasculine potency in dishing out violence and for troops to reaffirm their fierce loyalty to one another. Despite both bouncers requiring stitches, Fulton justified this behaviour as largely harmless, caused by operational stress after lengthily deployments in the field, and in the context of

---

[49] Wood, *War Diaries of Andre Dennison*, p. 28.
[50] Telfer and Fulton, *Chibaya Moyo*, pp. 138–41; Telfer and Fulton, *Chibaya Moyo 2*, pp. 459–51.

Military Socialisation

promised periods of R&R suddenly being cut short and occasioning a drinking spree in town.

The pent-up adrenaline, angst and aggression that built up like a pressure cooker without release; the result was inevitable... Good luck to anyone who fell afoul of the *sodja* whose fuse blew because it was what it was. The actions of this good man [Kananda] are revealed in this anecdote to simply highlight to the loyalty of our wonderful, loyal men who would compromise everything to ensure the welfare of their *Ishe* [officer]. We lived a privileged life in the company of outstanding men. *Tinorwira kukna!* We fight to win!

Here Fulton is deeming these actions as a form of permissible indiscipline, the sort which the army hierarchy not only perceives as inevitable, but also often renders trivial, often humorous. Punishment, if carried out in house, is done with a smirk by subunit authorities, who often wistfully refer to such behaviour not only as understandable on the part of soldiers sticking up for one another, but also as a form of transgression they themselves were guilty of in the past.

An errant soldier guilty of permissible indiscipline would likely have his punishment reduced if his officers vouched for his conduct and pleaded for mitigation. For instance, Major Dennison wrote how he left operational command for several days 'to defend an A Company "old boy" Cpl Madewe, who was court-martialled for possessing dagga [cannabis]'.[51]

While these cases are clearly instances of indiscipline, they were in fact tacitly condoned by army officers, for they did not compromise intra-unit loyalty (indeed they seemed to bolster it), nor did they impact the military mission. The tacit permissibility of these acts (albeit a permissibility not wholly devoid of sanction) also delineates them from wholly impermissible acts. In this manner, minor rule breaking was somewhat tolerated in order to avert more serious breaches, such as going AWOL. As MSW told me, soldiers who were tempted to go AWOL most often did not act on the desire, as they knew not only that the punishment would be severe, but also that the army would 'really chase you and find you'.[52] Likewise, JM said 'the army did not like a soldier to be attacked by malaria. The discipline. He'd be charged, because we give you medicine tablets every Wednesday, four times a month, so you did not use the medicine tablets; that's why you're malaria diseased now'.[53]

Serious offences – which I term 'impermissible indiscipline' – render the soldier subject to punishment by the commanding officer of his regiment, who can impose punishments of up to a month in military

---

[51] Wood, *War Diaries of Andre Dennison*, p. 175.   [52] Interview with MSW.
[53] Interview with JM.

detention. The most serious offences were dealt with by military courts, known as courts martial. In the Rhodesian Army, errant soldiers were sent to 'detention barracks', a form of military prison, to undergo a tortuous and turbocharged form of basic training under the eye of 'sadistic' wardens, with a typical day commencing at 0600 and involving continuous menial and tedious tasks, such as drilling and forced manual labour, concluding at 2100.[54]

DC was heavily involved with the administration of military law, particularly in Mashonaland West, where 'during the war, I was appointed sometimes as a prosecutor. We had *rascal* soldiers who went about stealing from people and we had to [*clicks fingers*] court-martial them and discharge them'. DC commented on the senselessness of the thefts committed by soldiers, who would 'steal even very small things, and you'd think, "Are you going to leave your job for this petty crime?"' The motivation of the guilty soldiers puzzled DC, but he speculated that perhaps the power soldiers enjoyed – many of whom were from humble backgrounds and possessed little education – presented too great a temptation. Certainly, many of the crimes that made it to courts martial did not demonstrate a great deal of planning or forethought. For instance, during A Company, 2RAR's two weeks of R&R in August 1977, 'four soldiers succeeded in getting themselves put away for four months with labour for robbing a bus'.[55] DC recounted how soldiers would be punished for theft: 'first, six months [in the] detention barracks then discharge with ignominy'.

Of course, the motivations of these troops were likely more complex, and also demonstrated that the total institution was not always successful in moulding behaviour. DC noted that such serious offences were rare, but when they did occur, they were 'of theft, rape, desertion. These – ah, these were serious cases'. These crimes were not only morally wrong, but they also tarnished the reputation of the army in the eyes of civilians, which had a strategic resonance in the COIN context. For DC, this was an important aspect to his role as prosecutor, and he thought 'it was a good system, because if you are a soldier, you are there to protect the people, not to steal from them'.[56]

In general, my interviewees spoke approvingly of the military discipline system. JM, an RAR pay clerk, was falsely accused of siphoning off soldiers' pay by an army chef, himself a thief looking to cover his own tracks: the matter reached a court martial and JM was absolved of

---

[54] Interview with SJM; Cocks, *Fireforce*, p. 139.
[55] Wood, *War Diaries of Andre Dennison*, p. 131.   [56] Interview with DC.

wrongdoing, much to his satisfaction.[57] Likewise, BM was in favour of the strict sentences a court martial handed down to two deserters, roaring with approval that 'they were squashed [for] doing rubbish!'[58] While the coercive side of military authority underwrites the system of discipline, its role is intended to function as a deterrent and its importance should not be overemphasised. As Ian Beckett noted, 'there is little evidence of disciplinary problems among black personnel' in the Rhodesian Army.[59] In the normal course of events, coercive measures were used rarely, as soldiers' loyalties assured that they acted in a disciplined fashion.

Lastly in my discussion of military socialisation, the total institution of the army also cultivated the loyalties of black soldiers by quite literally becoming their family home through offering free housing for their families. As 'most African regulars' lived in or near barracks, this also served to inculcate the familial military tradition among the children of soldiers, as discussed in Chapter 2.[60] Furthermore, the army offered free education for soldiers' children. MC, the wife of a long-serving soldier, told me living in the barracks 'was good for us at that time and we enjoyed [living there], because we were so healthy; we are getting what we want to eat, we get what we want and houses'.[61] MZ, the wife of another RAR soldier, told me that living in barracks had upsides and downsides:

> The good side was you don't pay rent, water, so many things. It was good. It wasn't like these days. We could get ration, you get firewood, those who were at high ranks like WOII – from WOII you had electrical stoves, a nice house – six roomed houses, and so on, with your own accommodation, your own house, you do whatever you want. So it is unlike here [today in Zimbabwe where], you pay rates, you pay water, you pay a lot of things – ZESA [electricity bills], ahh![62]

However, for MZ, the drawbacks were the social aspect of living in a tight-knit, small community: 'you need to be careful for yourself; you don't have to talk too much [i.e. spreading rumours or gossiping] ... it's like a boarding school. So you have to be careful with your life and your marriage if you want to stay in there quietly!'.[63] MZ joined various clubs and recreational schemes set up for the wives in the barracks as they were stranded there – 'you can't go out; you can't go to the rural areas' – owing to the threat from the guerrillas. She remarked that she enjoyed these clubs, which were typically organised around activities such as sewing and knitting, but affirmed with laughter that she found the range of activities on offer quite sexist.

---

[57] Interview with JM. [58] Interview with BM. [59] Beckett, 'Rhodesian Army', p. 174.
[60] Anti-Apartheid Movement, *Fireforce Exposed*, p. 41. [61] Interview with MC.
[62] Interview with MZ. [63] Ibid.

MC likewise attended similar clubs, organised around 'sewing and gardening', which 'provided something to do'. Both MZ and MC noted that these clubs also tended to be organised and run by the white officers' wives, replicating the power dynamic of the regiment itself, discussed in Chapter 4, much to their dismay. MC noted that 'some of [the white women] were good – it's not all of them [who were racist]. The problem was the system – the system was not very good'.[64]

MS, the wife of an RAR soldier from Masvingo, met her husband in Bulawayo when he was serving at the Llewellin barracks. After they were married, she followed him throughout the country on his various postings, from Bulawayo to Gweru, and finally Masvingo Province. This last move proved a little bit difficult for her as she hailed from Gwanda and spoke Ndebele and Sotho, but not Shona, which she had to learn from scratch as an adult. This, however, did not pose 'any difficulties [and it was] plain sailing' as she had a supportive community to welcome her.[65] Like MC and MZ, MS recalled that 'life in the camp was very comfortable. We were getting a lot of free things – freebies like rations, free water, free lighting, accommodation'.

Not only was living in barracks a big saving in terms of utility bills and school fees, but, as GM told me, the fact that 'the children lived with their mother in barracks' and went to 'school as normal, no problem' while he was away on operations meant that he did not fear for their safety at all, which provided enormous peace of mind.[66] HZ did not have children of his own as he was 'very young by then', but he sent his younger brothers, who lived in the military cantonment with him, to school on his army salary, and they were ferried to and from school by army drivers.[67] Conversely, for the women and children remaining in barracks, these times were troubling. MC recalled that when her husband was away on operations, she feared for his safety: 'we were really scared, we were worried, but we had to rely on God'.[68]

Created through material provision and institutional efforts to foster community, the attachment of the families of soldiers to the military lifestyle was another embodiment of the total institution which, in turn, bound troops to the army. It is also another reason as to why there were so few defections during the war, as these men and their families lived, ate, socialised, learned in, and worked for the same total institution, which cared for their welfare as well as shielding them from the very real possibility of violence from guerrilla forces in the rural areas as the war escalated.

---

[64] Interview with MC. [65] Interview with MS. [66] Interview with GM.
[67] Interview with HZ. [68] Interview with MC.

In sum, this section has argued that the creation of a soldierly identity was key to instilling discipline and mutual belief among troops. These soldiers lived in a total institution, separate from wider society both physically in terms of their barracks and cantonments, and in an abstract sense as social isolates whose loyalties were pledged to their comrades and unit. Another important aspect of this soldierly identity was its reliance upon another key plank of black soldiers' loyalties: the ethos of professionalism.

The Importance of the 'Professional' Ethos

After the huge mobilisation of soldiers during World War II, a 'long-term trend' emerged where military forces became 'smaller, fully professional, and more fully alerted and self-contained ... the direction was away from a mobilization force to a military force "in being"'.[69] Colonial armies were no exception. For instance, the sizeable French Army in Africa underwent a programme of reform designed to create a well-trained force, epitomised by the creation of African paratroopers, whose service in these 'prestigious combat units' was publicly feted 'as an example of the professionalization of African soldiers'.[70] The Rhodesian Army underwent similar reforms and many black soldiers became paratroopers too.

These reforms occurred even though the core tenets of professionalism – advancement premised upon meritocracy, competency, and expertise – clearly clashed with Rhodesia's institutionalised racism, as discussed in Chapter 4. However, Rhodesia was not the only racist society in which the army adhered to a professional ethos that contrasted with the state's practices in wider society. Peled argued that, in such instances, when 'given a chance to serve their countries', regular soldiers serving in a 'professional' army 'are almost always loyal soldiers'.[71] Here I argue that professionalism was key to the soldierly loyalties of black troops in Rhodesia too.

Modern standing armies prize professionalism above almost all else and seek to instil this through continuous training and exercising in weaponry, tactics, and battlefield skills such as map-reading and first aid. In professional armies, training is exacting in the extreme, so that by comparison actual combat seems easier, as the 'widely used military aphorism: "Train hard, fight easy"' summarises.[72] However, the function of this training extends beyond the competencies of the individual soldier: training is vital for units to operate effectively. As King argued, 'it is here in the domain of training that a profound divide appears

---

[69] Janowitz, *Military Conflict*, p. 121, as quoted in Segal and Segal, 'Change in Military Organization', p. 161.
[70] Ginio, *The French Army and Its African Soldiers*, p. 70.
[71] Peled, *Question of Loyalty*, pp. 4–5, 173.   [72] King, *Combat Soldier*, p. 274.

between the citizen and the professional army', and there is a close relationship between effective training and performance in combat, as training serves 'not just inculcate a series of complex individual and collective skills', but also serves to create an intense, affective bond – 'social solidarity' – of loyalty between members of the same unit.[73] This generates 'a moral obligation upon soldiers' to perform at their best in order to meet the expectations of their comrades, a view also uniformly espoused by my interviewees.[74]

This explains why other skills, not directly related to the conduct of war, are associated with professionalism too. The pressing of uniforms and shining of boots to convey a pristine and professional appearance is of little intrinsic military utility, especially when an army is engaged in COIN warfare for lengthy periods, but possesses much symbolic value, for it emphasises soldiers' conformance to a unitary standard, and it is glaringly obvious on parade if a scruffy soldier has let his unit down.

Likewise, 'drill', the military practice of marching in a synchronised formation, certainly fulfils a 'choreographic, ritualistic, perhaps even aesthetic' function, but is of little use during combat.[75] However, it serves an important purpose in training individuals to operate as a disciplined collective, and my interviewees detailed how their smartness of appearance and high standard of drill reinforced and affirmed professional standards.[76]

Inherent to professionalism is continuous retraining. King argues that commanders emphasise that the goal of training is to ensure that the basic skills of soldiering are learned and rehearsed so frequently as to become second nature. To the outside observer, 'the higher level of training in a professional force may seem like a relatively small and mundane difference', but it is vital, not only for how much more deadly it makes the individual trained soldier in terms of, say, the accuracy of his marksmanship or his skill in traversing the battlefield, but 'the experience of training fundamentally alters the relations between soldiers in an infantry platoon and the kind of association which they generate with each other' (see Figure 3.1).[77]

The Rhodesian Army's emphasis on retraining adhered to this professional ethos, and RAR officers' records detail continuous retraining in marksmanship, which one remarked saw the standard of 'shooting improved considerably'.[78] My interviewees attested that they felt reassured by the proficiency of their comrades within the platoon, and fulsomely praised their fellow soldiers in the RAR as 'excellent fighters',[79]

[73] Ibid., p. 346. [74] Ibid., pp. 266–7, 273–5. [75] Keegan, *Face of Battle*, p. 34.
[76] Interview with HZ. [77] King, *Combat Soldier*, p. 273.
[78] See, for instance, Wood, *War Diaries of Andre Dennison*, pp. 36, 98, 118.
[79] Interview with WR.

Figure 3.1 RAR soldier with FN FAL rifle (*Nwoho*, April 1976). Note the cap badge image sewn into the field cap. It features 'a Matabele war shield upon which is laid a Zulu stabbing spear or assegai crossed with a Shona digging spear both under a vertical knobkerrie with a scroll below bearing the title "Rhodesian African Rifles"' (Binda, *Masodja*, p. 42).

and as 'just excellent, above excellent, I think'.[80] WM told me that 'the RAR's training was second to none'.[81]

As King argues, the commitment to professionalism is total: 'Combat performance is self-consciously related by professional soldiers to this refinement of a myriad of military skills, each small, often apparently insignificant in themselves, but together generating a complex of battlefield competence.'[82] These skills rely 'not simply on rote learning one specific choreography but on a deeply ingrained shared professional culture' which serves to perpetuate these exacting norms.[83] For instance, the RAR placed a premium on periods of retraining for its soldiers, even those companies that had recently spent long periods on operational deployment. As LCpl

---

[80] Interview with CD. [81] Interview with WM. [82] King, *Combat Soldier*, p. 273.
[83] Ibid., p. 277.

Innocent Mutinhiri wrote, when he joined A Company 1RAR, 'the Coy was on three weeks retraining. We spent this duration in Camp doing weapons, Drill, Range and the sports'.[84] Professionalism was inculcated among soldiers in their basic training in the first instance, but was constantly reaffirmed thereafter through retraining.

The importance of this was conveyed to me by JM, who described his time as a member of Mortar Platoon with much pride. After doing his apprenticeship as the 'Number 3' man, whose role involves preparing the mortar bombs, JM moved up to being 'Number 2', who loads them into the tube, a job that requires much caution as 'if you are not very careful, you'll hurt yourself, because when you load the bomb, you must remove your arms. If you don't remove them [when the bomb is fired from the tube] your arm will go'. Later, JM was entrusted to be 'Number 1', the soldier who 'controls the aiming ... controls the bipods ... and you control the baseplate. And the elevation. Then you must make sure that you've set a good range ... using the rangefinder, then you can see. I was a good mortar-man'. JM stated that this complexity explained why Mortar Platoon commanders selected not simply those with the physical strength and stamina to carry mortar tubes and bombs in addition to their other equipment, but also those who could learn quickly, those 'with a good understanding. Fast understanding. That machine needs bright people'.[85]

The expectation that soldiers would meet high standards and demand the same of their peers permeated the professional Rhodesian Army. The mortar-man was not a solitary actor, as not only was the weapon crew served, but he was reliant upon other members of his platoon to quite literally share his burden and assist in carrying rather heavy items while on the march: extra mortar bombs, or the base plate, or the tube. Likewise, machine gunners relied upon other soldiers to carry extra ammunition and additional gun barrels (which must be replaced when the weapon overheats), a neat illustration of the mutual dependence professionalism creates between soldiers, as King argued.[86]

In 1977, the first RAR companies underwent parachute training, achieving, as Stapleton noted, 'an elite status previously the preserve' of the all-white units.[87] The RAR's journal noted how parachuting 'added a new dimension to the role of the RAR soldier. The fact that the African soldier has taken to this new development is evidenced by the enthusiasm he has shown to undergo this training and the obvious pride he takes in wearing the wings of the "para"'.[88] 'Wings', worn in many armies, are an

---

[84] I. Mutinhiri, 'My Life in "A" Company 1RAR', *Nwoho* (April 1978), p. 23.
[85] Interview with JM.   [86] King, *Combat Soldier*, p. 338.
[87] Stapleton, *African Police and Soldiers*, p. 208.
[88] 'Editorial', *Nwoho* (April, 1978), p. 5.

embroidered badge donned only by those who have passed their jumps course and denote one's status as a paratrooper.

Since its first combat use during World War II, parachuting has possessed an elite cachet among soldiers. It has been touted as one of the quintessential embodiments of military professionalism, for it promotes 'feelings of self-worth, accomplishment and personal mastery [and] tends to foster group bonds and social cohesion', alongside being a 'status passage' and 'test of manhood'.[89] As Stapleton noted, black soldiers in the RAR also revelled in this status, and those who qualified as paratroopers described themselves as 'special soldiers'.[90] Grundy said of black soldiers in apartheid South Africa:

> Once a person is armed and trained to fight, equipped with the latest skills in counterinsurgency methods [such as] parachute skills, for example, and once he is enabled to assume ... command responsibilities, a psychological and practical metamorphosis occurs – a new persona is unlocked ... Important tactical and combat proficiencies that heretofore have been the legal monopoly of the dominant group are being transmitted on a small scale to individual members of the repressed group.[91]

The RAR soldiers' testimonies demonstrate that becoming paratroopers enhanced their conception of themselves as elite, and this reinforced their self-conception as professionals.[92]

While parachuting was glamorous, mastering the bread-and-butter skills of soldiering was also important to being professional. My interviewees attested that the rigor of their training was vital to their bearing as soldiers in terms of core professional skills, but also other specialisms. DC told me:

> Personally, I benefitted – personal discipline, I benefitted, you know? My knowledge of the environment, of weapons – how to handle weapons and all the like. I benefitted a lot. And a lot of courses – administration, medicine-wise, and all that we did. And being an administrative officer I had a chance to go through [courses of instruction in] military law – I went through that trying to find out which is right and which is wrong. And I learned a lot from that.[93]

This ethos was also prevalent among non-front-line troops. Those employed in non-infantry trades were also required to be trained in the generic military skills which they were required to perform professionally, even if most of them did not engage in combat during the war. For instance, MN, an electrician, recounted how 'you know in the army you

---

[89] Cockerham, 'Attitudes towards Combat among US Army Paratroopers', p. 4, as quoted in King, *Combat Soldier*, p. 72.
[90] Stapleton, *African Police and Soldiers*, p. 208.
[91] Grundy, *Soldiers without Politics*, p. 123.
[92] See, for instance, D. Wushe, '1RAR Para Profiles', *Nwoho* (April 1978), pp. 40–3; G. Munana, 'A Coy: Personalities', *Nwoho* (April 1978), p. 57.
[93] Interview with DC.

learn a lot of things, but I was in [Rhodesian Army Corps of] Signals, see I did all my army courses like drill, weapons drilling and from there I was trained in signals as an electrician'.[94] As the numbers of black soldiers in the army increased, more opportunities opened up for specialists such as medics and signallers, whose professionalism was demonstrated by their technical competencies, rather than their infantry skills.

In regular armies that adhere to a professional ethos, promotion is premised upon competence and is, notionally, wholly meritocratic. Soldiers must pass demanding training courses where their ability to command and lead is assessed.[95] The Rhodesian Army required this of its soldiers too, although as discussed in Chapter 4, black soldiers were discriminated against by the racist structures of the wider army and could not become officers until 1977. However, my interviewees described how, within this racist system, there also existed a culture of relative professional meritocracy. DSN recounted how his first promotions proceeded:

There was a board [of officers] ... If your commander, officer, nominates you, then you go in front of the board. Well, they drill you and ask you many questions. If you pass that board, you go for a commander's course ... [it was tough, and lasted usually] about a month or so, so you'd be doing map-reading, rifle shooting, all these funny little things a soldier would do. Then they see that you are capable of doing that part of command in that rank.[96]

This emphasis upon meritocracy meant that the professional skills of black warrant officers and NCOs were of a very high standard.

Inevitably, professional ideals were not always lived up to. In the first instance, soldiers performing poorly would be severely reprimanded verbally, and sometimes physically, in order to bring them up to scratch. The accounts of RAR soldiers make clear that, during their first brushes with combat, their NCOs constantly monitored their performance and did not hesitate to chastise or threaten them if they failed to conduct their duties professionally. A new recruit to A Company 1RAR described 'following the senior troops' tactics until I became as tactically [proficient] as those senior troops'.[97] Likewise, the OC of Support Company 2RAR related how 'a large influx of new recruits' posted to the company were not yet up to scratch and 'immediately came into contact (in more ways than one) with Company Sergeant-Major Van [Rashayi Doro] who set about getting them up to standard in no uncertain terms'.[98]

GM told how once, while on patrol, one of his comrades' poor combat drills gave away his position and left him vulnerable to guerrilla fire, nearly

---

[94] Interview with MN. [95] King, *Combat Soldier*, pp. 273–4. [96] Interview with DSN.
[97] I. Mutinhiri, 'My Life in "A" Company 1RAR, *Nwoho* (April 1978), p. 23.
[98] 'Support Coy', *Nwoho* (April 1978), p. 63.

costing him his own life.[99] As with the aforementioned example, the errant soldier was left in no doubt as to the error of his ways. Yet this harsh code of discipline was not the main deterrent to soldiers acting unprofessionally, for those soldiers who failed to meet the requisite standards were quickly ostracised by their peers for their lack of care or effort. As King argued, among soldiers, 'professional failure' is the 'ultimate shame', and the fear of incurring this shame is often a far more powerful motivator than courage or fear of formal disciplinary punishment.[100]

The professional ethos also allowed the RAR to learn from its failures at an institutional level. In 1968, a platoon from E Company 1RAR was involved in a contact in the Zambezi Valley. It was led by a new platoon commander who had taken command only the day before, and who 'did not know the names of most of his men, nor did they know him. In contact, the men would not follow him, and control of the platoon broke down'.[101] This meant the platoon experienced 'multiple failures in the face of the enemy' and some 'RAR soldiers proved reluctant to move under fire and attack the enemy'. As a result one RAR soldier was killed and two more were wounded. This was a clear instance where the professional standards of the army had not been upheld. However, the RAR's adherence to a professional ethos meant that the performance of this platoon was subject to swift criticism and review, and the commanding officer of the RAR implemented the lessons learned.[102] Thereafter such incidents did not reoccur, illustrating that the professional ethos mandated introspection to identify performance failures. A virtuous cycle was thus created wherein operational mistakes were addressed by retraining.

If one doubts the importance of professionalism, a clear counter-example existed during the war. The Security Force Auxiliaries (SFA), also known as Pfumo reVanhu (Spear of the People), were black militiamen hurriedly raised by a panicked Rhodesian government in 1978. They represented a desperate last gamble by Ian Smith, who had spent much of the prior two decades opposing any expansion in the numbers of black soldiers against the advice of his military commanders.[103]

The SFA soldiers, numbering 'about 10,000 in 1979',[104] were poorly trained, receiving just six to eight weeks of lacklustre and ad hoc instruction.[105] They were wholly ineffective at combating guerrilla activity.[106] Their deployments were disastrous, they were not integrated

---

[99] Interview with GM. [100] King, *Combat Soldier*, pp. 371–2.
[101] Stewart, 'Rhodesian African Rifles', p. 39. [102] Ibid., p. 40.
[103] Flower, *Serving Secretly*, p. 231. [104] Dorman, *Understanding Zimbabwe*, pp. 20–1.
[105] Whitaker, *'New Model' Armies of Africa?*, p. 196.
[106] Alexander, McGregor, and Ranger, *Violence and Memory*, p. 206; Flower, *Serving Secretly*, p. 215.

into the military command structure until June 1979, and they were notorious for abuses against the civilian population.[107] A *New York Times* report from August 1979 gives an indication of the scale of indiscipline:

> On more than one occasion, Government troops were sent to put down mutinies by auxiliaries or to bring them to account for incidents in which local people were murdered, raped or robbed. Then, last month, the disaster that critics of the program had long feared happened: A large-scale mutiny ended in a blood bath, with Government troops killing at least 183 of the irregulars and possibly as many as 400 in two separate incidents on one day.[108]

Luise White argued that the SFA soldiers 'were ill-disciplined and highly unstable, plagued by ethnic strife and "immaturity"', and although their numbers nominally added to the strength of the RSF, they were an 'essentially fantasy army' whose deployment was not indicative of white Rhodesian might, but rather an 'embarrassing example of white desperation and weakness in post-colonial Africa'.[109]

For Jakkie Cilliers, 'the Auxiliaries were politically motivated [as] any militia-type force had to be a political and an ethnic representation. This was, of course, not the case as regards the regular black soldiers of the Rhodesia African Rifles battalions'.[110] The RAR soldiers' politics are discussed later; the salient point here is that, unlike auxiliaries, they were motivated by their regimental loyalty and professionalism, and not local ethno-political allegiance, as were the SFA members.

BM, an RAR sergeant major, was briefly tasked with retraining auxiliaries in 1979, a hasty attempt on part of the RSF to improve their disastrous record. His impression of them was that:

> Ah, they were useless [*laughs*]! Because they were civilians, without [training] They just issued them the rifles without training, you see? [They were] very dangerous, very dangerous ... there was no discipline to them, but we were trying to neutralise them. Some they were okay, but some they were still harsh, you see? When they're drunk, they want to shoot each other ... Ah [they were] a waste of time.[111]

While BM's criticism foregrounded the SFA soldiers' lack of training and discipline, he also attributed their lack of professionalism to the fact that 'they were recruited from the local', which meant that their pre-existing political loyalties, grudges, and sympathies determined how they acted as armed auxiliaries.[112] He felt that their loyalties had been bought by their salaries, which he though excessive for their low level of skill, and that they did not possess anything like the loyalties of soldiers.

---

[107] Whitaker, 'New Model' Armies of Africa?, pp. 195–8.
[108] Burns, 'Killing of Black Troops Adds to Rifts in Rhodesia'.
[109] White, 'Animals, Prey, and Enemies', pp. 15–17.
[110] Cilliers, *Counter-Insurgency in Rhodesia*, p. 214.   [111] Interview with BM.   [112] Ibid.

Auxiliaries were not well trained and thus did not possess micro-level bonds of professionalism. They had not undergone military socialisation and had no sense of loyalty to a regiment. They had no storied history of military service to fall back upon, no parades or marching songs or military messes. They fought not for the army of the state, but for their local militia, and were often guilty of settling pre-existing scores or engaging in partial conduct with civilians. According to Henrik Ellert, many SFA members were 'criminals who welcomed the opportunity to be armed and take to a life of banditry'. Others were men recruited under false pretences, or simply impressed.[113] The 'fragging' of officers was often threatened and happened on at least one occasion, along with several large-scale mutinies.[114] Unsurprisingly, desertion rates were high, and many defected.[115] In short, they were simply the antithesis of professional RAR soldiers.

Conclusion

Within the RAR, processes of initial military socialisation and continuous retraining instilled a powerful professional ethos among black soldiers. This was fundamental to creating enduring soldierly loyalty, not only in instilling essential soldierly competencies but, as per King, creating a shared normative perception among soldiers of their mutual obligation during combat. Through extensive training, black RAR soldiers acquired great confidence not only in their own abilities, but also those of their peers, who they could expect to fight for them in difficult situations.

Underpinning these professional norms was a system of military discipline that relied upon a quasi-juridical form of oversight, which my interviewees attested was rational and fair. Clearly, soldiers were not automatons and, like in many armies, the army hierarchy tacitly condoned acts of permissible indiscipline such as fighting and heavy drinking. These functioned as buffers to forestall acts of impermissible indiscipline. Lastly, the professional ethos also incubated a limited form of meritocracy within the army, wherein black soldiers were promoted based upon their competencies and experience. However, this meritocracy was fundamentally constricted by systematic Rhodesian racism. How this impacted soldiers' loyalties is the subject of Chapter 4.

---

[113] Ellert, *Rhodesian Front War*, p. 147.
[114] White, 'Animals, Prey, and Enemies', p. 17; White, *Fighting and Writing*, p. 212.
[115] ZANU Security and Intelligence Department monthly reports reveal that 111 auxiliaries defected to ZANLA between January and June 1979 (RAA Op URIC Files, CIO Document XYS 5937/100, Tembue Base Camp, Ref 03/79).

4 Racism and Soldierly Loyalty During the War

Wartime Rhodesian propaganda frequently asserted that the 'the war against the national liberation movement has nothing to do with racism but is a struggle by black and white together against "communist insurgents"'.[1] The government cited the important role of black soldiers and the later integration of most army units as evidence that the army was not racist.

As David Kenrick argued, the white 'Troubadours of UDI' penned several odes to black soldiers, reflecting 'an idealised, white, view of Rhodesia in which Africans and whites fought side by side against a common, communist aggressor'.[2] This narrative has latterly been perpetuated in neo-Rhodesian accounts. In this chapter, I use archival documents and oral history interviews to conclusively demonstrate that this propaganda was utterly false and that the Rhodesian Army was systematically racist. Furthermore, I demonstrate that some senior army officers and ministers blocked reforms of the army's racist treatment of black soldiers and sought to retain systematic discrimination.

Thereafter I argue that, despite the prevalence of racism within the army, it was not corrosive to the loyalties of black soldiers. In part, this reflected how the army's practices of discrimination were less severe than in other areas of Rhodesian life. In other contexts where marginalised troops serve in the army of an oppressive state, a professional ethos has served to minimise the military impact of wider systematic societal racism. As Alon Peled claimed, in apartheid South Africa and Israel, the treatment of soldiers was not solely determined by the policies of 'racial division and ethnic stratification' prevalent in wider society,[3] and in fact there existed 'a causal relationship between military professionalism [defined as "training, experience and expertise" in achieving combat efficacy] and ethnic integration'.[4] In other words, for Peled, the more

---

[1] Anti-Apartheid Movement, *Fireforce Exposed*, p. 13.
[2] Kenrick, *Decolonisation, Identity and Nation in Rhodesia*, p. 195.
[3] Peled, *Question of Loyalty*, pp. 4, 10.   [4] Ibid., p. 23.

professional an army, the better the treatment and prospects of those soldiers from marginalised groups. In this chapter, I contend that the professional ethos of the Rhodesian Army also served to minimise the impact of racism on black soldiers.

Furthermore, the Rhodesian Army's racist policies also underwent a glacial process of reform. In colonial armies, reforms such as improvements in pay and promotion prospects were enacted to counter waning morale among black troops and to cement their loyalties. For instance, Ruth Ginio stated that the French colonial army's reforms, carried out in the midst of wars of decolonisation, were motivated not only 'to render the African units more professional', but also to enhance 'soldiers' loyalty and sense of belonging'.[5] As this chapter shows, the Rhodesian Army enacted comparable reforms on similar grounds, meaning it was ironically within the prime coercive apparatus of the settler state that a slow and stuttering process of reform occurred, and the army was in the vanguard of reform regarding racial discrimination within Rhodesia.

However, as Stapleton argued, it was only in 1977, at the very end of the war, when 'racial segregation in the Rhodesian military started to break down because of the scarcity of manpower' and 'political need', and these reforms were largely 'cosmetic or ineffective'.[6]

Stapleton's argument is convincing in the context of the Rhodesian Army as a whole. However, as argued earlier, the post-1977 integrated units comprised only a small proportion of the army's strength, and the bulk of the regular army's manpower was still supplied by RAR until after independence. It was within the battalions of the RAR that the ethos of professionalism had its most marked impact in terms of reforming the racist character of the army. As the second part of this chapter reveals, within the RAR, a distinctive military culture flourished that attempted to mitigate the racism of the wider army and society, founded upon adherence to a professional ethos. In this regiment, relationships between black and white came to be premised upon mutual respect and camaraderie in a way that differed from the rest of the army, and which enhanced the loyalties of black soldiers. I start, however, by discussing the wider Rhodesian Army's racism.

Structural Racism in the Rhodesian Army

The starkest illustration of the systematic racism of the Rhodesian Army was found in its policies of pay, in which black soldiers received far less than white soldiers. Unlike other aspects of army life that are harder to

---

[5] Ginio, *The French Army and Its African Soldiers*, p. 77.
[6] Stapleton, *African Police and Soldiers*, p. 182.

quantify, simple and direct comparisons of the disparity can be drawn. In 1973, the most junior white private soldier received an annual salary of Rh$1,500, whereas the most senior black soldier in the army – a regimental sergeant major with more than twenty years of service – was paid just Rh$1,452.[7] Although the pay of black soldiers improved over course of the war, by 1977, junior white soldiers were still being paid more than black warrant officers,[8] and black private soldiers received just half the salary of conscripts, who were largely white.[9]

Official Rhodesian rhetoric elided this inequity. Unveiling a plaque at the site of the regiment's original, World War II–era camp in Borrowdale during April 1975, army commander Lt Gen. Peter Walls lauded the RAR as 'an elite group of fighting men, both European and African, to whom the country owes an incalculable debt for their dedication and bravery'.[10] However difficult this debt owed to black soldiers may have been to tabulate, it was one that the Rhodesian government was not willing to pay on terms equal to those of white soldiers.

This pay disparity was airily glossed over by the minister of defence in the Cabinet during 1973 as the 'different market rates for the job', an utter untruth on two accounts.[11] Firstly, this supposed 'market rate' was not the product of normal labour market dynamics, but instead the consequence of the Rhodesian government's array of racist practices and legislation geared to generate a large pool of cheap black labour,[12] and the fact that the economic consequences of UDI disproportionately affected black people.[13] In 1968, the Rhodesian minister of labour and social welfare noted that approximately 49,000 black men were reaching the age of sixteen annually, whereupon 95 per cent of them entered the workforce, but that it was estimated only two jobs were available for every five school leavers.[14] By late 1976, the minister of internal affairs estimated that the

---

[7] CL, R.C. (S) (73) 122, 'Salary Review: BSA Police and Armed Forces', Memorandum by the Minister of Finance, 5 October 1973, Appendix A.
[8] CL, R.C. (S) (77) 86, 'Pay Restraint: Effect on the Public Service and Uniformed Forces', 6 July 1977; CCC(S) (77) 1, 'Cabinet Committee on Conditions of Service', 6 July 1977, Annex A, p. 2.
[9] R.C. (S) (77) 115, 'National Service: African Apprentices and Intending University Students', 10 November 1977. This was the pay received by TF members who had completed four and a half months of basic training.
[10] Binda, *Masodja*, p. 268.
[11] CL, R.C. (S) (73) 33, 'National Servicemen: Pay and Allowances', 23 March 1973, p. 4.
[12] Arrighi, 'Political Economy of Rhodesia', pp. 39–42.
[13] Phimister, 'Zimbabwe', p. 53.
[14] CL, R.C. (S) (68) 193, 'Employment: African Youth', p. 2. The minister's prediction that these young men 'will be forced by economic necessity to look for any sort of work to feed and clothe themselves and ultimately those Africans who are unable to find work will have to support themselves from their family lands' reflected the racist and callous attitude of RF politicians to the plight of the black population.

annual number of school leavers had increased to 67,000 per annum.[15] Secondly, 'the job' of soldiering was identical whether it was carried out by black or white soldiers, a fact not lost on RAR troops.

PM told me that during the Federal era, he and his peers 'used to complain' to their white officers about the disparity, but were told 'that's the government policy; we cannot do anything about it'.[16] He further noted how 'even [though] my education was not that good, my [military] knowledge, my know-how, was better than [white servicemen]. I'm doing his job, exactly the same – but when we got to the salary it was different. So what's the difference between us? [We carry] the same rifle [in combat]'.[17] Likewise, MK loathed that racism dictated salaries and described the unfairness: 'I'm a black, you're a European' your pay is more than [mine].'[18] In 1977, an RAR sergeant of nineteen years standing conveyed his 'resentment over discrimination against blacks in the Government forces', citing pay in particular.[19] In 1964, RAR officer John Redfern, noting that he could not answer 'candidly' his soldiers' queries as to the justification for the racial pay disparity, authored a memorandum asking for this to be addressed, which was kicked into the long grass the by the Rhodesian Army's adjutant general at the time – one Peter Walls.[20] As discussed later, Walls was at the forefront of many of the army's decisions to forestall the equal treatment of black soldiers.

This pay disparity laid bare the hypocrisy and racism of many Rhodesian elites. However, this has been misinterpreted in the literature as a factor that dissuaded soldiers from enlisting. For instance, writing in the late 1970s, the political scientist Cynthia Enloe argued that 'for an African to join the RAR today ... means that his need for income must be particularly acute, especially given the wide salary disparities between black and white soldiers'.[21] This claim that salary disparities acted as a deterrent to black recruits founders on two counts.

Firstly, it elides the fact that an army salary, unequal as it was, was not only guaranteed in a time of high unemployment, but was also higher than that alternative jobs offered: even a junior RAR soldier earned double the wage of a senior agricultural worker.[22] Furthermore, the salaries earned by experienced black soldiers, or those trained in specialisms, were competitive with the wages earned by black civilians in skilled or artisanal occupations.[23]

---

[15] CL, R.C. (S) (76) 137, 'National Service for Africans', p. 1.   [16] Interview with PM.
[17] Ibid.   [18] Interview with MK.   [19] Burns, 'Reporter's Notebook'.
[20] Telfer and Fulton, *Chibaya Moyo*, pp. 86–7.   [21] Enloe, *Ethnic Soldiers*, p. 195.
[22] A point made in Chinodya, *Harvest of Thorns*, pp. 141–2.
[23] Skilled and experienced workers in the Trojan Nickel Mine earned $Rh104 a month in 1979 (Caute, *Under the Skin*, p. 321), a salary equivalent to that of an RAR sergeant, whose length of experience and amount of training were comparable.

As argued earlier, economic motivations should not be foregrounded when analysing loyalty among black Rhodesian soldiers; however, pay was an obvious enticement to recruitment in the first instance. Despite the obvious inequity, pay within the army was among the best options on offer for many young black men from the rural areas.

Secondly, Enloe's argument ignores that the pay disparity in the army was less pronounced than that in the civilian economy. In 1970, across the entire Rhodesian economy, 'the average annual income for blacks was Rh$312; the figure for whites was Rh$3,104', an approximate ratio of 9.5:1.[24] That same year, a black army sergeant earned a salary of $Rh636, compared to $Rh2,496 for a white sergeant, a ratio of approximately 4:1.[25] Clearly, these salaries were still hugely unfair, but they were markedly less inequitable than the salary disparities in civilian life. A white sergeant received four-fifths of the salary of the average white worker, whereas a black sergeant received twice the income of the average black worker.

Furthermore, one-third of black soldiers were classified as 'tradesmen', meaning they undertook specialist roles as signallers, engineers, medical assistants, and teachers and received better pay.[26] DT, a signaller, told me that 'we were given what they called "trade pay"', which increased his pay to a much higher level than that of RAR infantrymen, which for him signified that 'we were better than the RAR'.[27] Likewise, DSN told me, 'I was a rifleman [in the RAR], then from there I became a signalman,' owing to his being put on a training course in signals, 'which was a bit privileged, for people with my Form II education [*laughs*]; it was mostly the case that my fellow comrades couldn't read and write, you know? ... There was trade pay. That was the incentive'.[28] Those in such skilled roles received not only extra pay, but also accelerated promotion. For instance, both DC and TM, who were educational instructors in the Rhodesian Army Education Corps, were rapidly promoted. TM became a Warrant Officer Class II, a rank normally achieved by soldiers only after some fifteen years' service, after just five years.[29] It is also possible that 'trade pay' allowed the army to top up the pay of black soldiers, in spite of government refusals to grant wider salary increases, in order to retain well-trained black troops.

Black soldiers resented that whites were paid far more for doing the same work, but simultaneously felt that they were in a better position

---

[24] Godwin and Hancock, '*Rhodesians Never Die*', p. 46.
[25] CL, R.C. (S) (73) 122, 'Salary Review: BSA Police and Armed Forces', 5 October 1973, Appendix A.
[26] Mutangadura, *Study*, p. 17.   [27] Interview with DT.   [28] Interview with DSN.
[29] Interview with TM.

compared to most civilians, as HZ told me. He was an RAR infantry soldier and later a pay clerk at battalion headquarters and thus was intimately familiar with the levels of pay across the regiment. He told me that he felt that the pay disparity, while widely known, 'wasn't [a] very big' factor among black soldiers, as 'at that time, even if you were getting [a few dollars a day], you could buy anything [you needed], and you could easily get [enough money to support a wife and family]'.[30] This was partly the result of pay increases during the war. By 1979,

> An African private [the lowest military rank] in the RAR will receive a salary of over Rh$1,000 a year, plus free medical facilities for himself and his family, free accommodation, a guaranteed pension, free schooling for his children plus many other fringe benefits. The average annual income in 1978 for African males employed in urban areas was Rh$630, and for agricultural and forestry workers, Rh$360, according to official statistics.[31]

These concomitant benefits had an important implication, for a large proportion of the salaries of black soldiers were thus disposable income. This meant that their net income relative to civilians, who did not receive such free benefits, was significantly higher. Furthermore, as TM told me, 'you were assured of getting' these benefits, and the army also offered job security, whereas 'for those in the private sector, for failing to turn up for a day's work you could be gone for good'.[32]

As the old adage goes, an army matches on its stomach, and many of my interviewees, such as MSW, emphasised the importance of the benefit of free food. 'They gave us good food – breakfast, lunch, supper, everything.'[33] He also highlighted that the army provided alcohol: 'by that time, also even the beer was cheap in the military cantonment … Castle lager, Lion, we had all types of alcohol. I used to go for a Castle'.[34] As noted in Chapter 3, alcohol was important to the RAR's military culture for the purposes of relaxation and group bonding. When consumed outside the army, alcohol also signified status and the possession of disposable income: in 1977, Colour Sergeant S. Chiwocha wrote that, during his downtime, he was 'usually found within the outskirts of Fort Victoria if not in the famous Chevron Hotel for some Brandy and Coke'.[35]

Some aspects of the soldiers' diet were not met with approval, however. Ration packs had long been differentiated upon racial lines, as they were in other state institutions. TM told me, 'the European's pack had better [contents] than the black man's pack'.[36] HZ, however, understood the

---

[30] Interview with HZ. [31] Anti-Apartheid Movement, *Fireforce Exposed*, p. 41.
[32] Interview with TM. [33] Interview with MSW. [34] Ibid.
[35] S. Chiwocha, 'Life in B Coy (Chibaya Moyo) 2RAR', *Nwoho* (October 1977), p. 43.
[36] Interview with TM.

difference not as one of quality, but rather as an attempt by the army, as was the norm in state institutions, to cater for what were cast as different dietary needs: 'In terms of food, only what kind there was African ration and European ration. The reasons were, Africans would get mealie-meal, when the whites were not allowed to get mealie-meal... because, you see, most whites didn't want to cook *sadza*, so this is why.'[37]

Some black soldiers made it known 'that they wanted the same ration as what the whites are getting. And that was done'. However, they later rued the change, finding rice insufficiently filling: 'you know, when you're [used to] eating *sadza*, for you to eat rice only – it's tough within a few hours! And so they complained again, to say, "Ah, no, we want to go back to our old rations"', which were issued once more.[38] HZ felt that the existence of two different ration packs was not the result of an army policy to give black soldiers worse-quality food, but instead reflected racist Rhodesian conceptions which deemed some foods 'African' and thus socially unacceptable for whites to eat. He noted that many white officers actually preferred *sadza* over other forms of carbohydrates and would swap their rice with black soldiers who preferred it, while ensuring that they were not observed doing so by other whites, even on operations.[39]

My interviewees recalled army benefits favourably, for they constituted a significant monthly saving, particularly for those with children. HZ noted that 'children of soldiers had their school here in camps where they don't pay anything. Free books, free everything, free transport if that person has got to go out of camp for school, like those in secondary education'.[40] GM also told me, 'I was thinking the army was the best' as it provided 'free accommodation' and education for his family.[41]

The free accommodation on offer was, like pay, of a lesser standard than that provided for white soldiers. The 1977 figures from the minister of works show that the money spent on 'African married quarters' compared to 'European single quarters' was just 65 per cent in gross terms, and 69 per cent of the spend per square metre.[42] Prior to 1975, accommodation built for government employees such as soldiers and civil servants included 'full electrics' (i.e. access to hot water and the ability to power domestic appliances) for white residents. Black residents were restricted to cold showers and:

[I]n areas where electricity is available the procedure has been to either withhold this facility or restrict the supply to electric lighting depending on the grading of the occupant. Where lighting is provided, consumption is controlled by a load limiter

---

[37] Interview with HZ.   [38] Ibid.   [39] Ibid.   [40] Ibid.   [41] Interview with GMH.
[42] CL, R.C. (S) (77) 60, 'Standards of Building Construction for the Uniformed Forces', 13 May 1977.

which confines usage to lights and one power point of 560 watts. The latter permits low-powered appliances only such as a radio or low wattage electric iron, but excludes the use of electricity for cooking appliances, electric fires, kettles, etc.[43]

While the minister of local government and housing pressed for rapid reform of this racist policy, the minister of finance disagreed, citing cost. Black Rhodesian soldiers were relied upon to risk their lives for the state, a fact of which the Rhodesian government made great fanfare. Yet this appreciation for what Lt Gen. Walls called an 'incalculable debt' did not extend to providing black soldiers with the means to use an electric kettle in their home.

As with pay, the disparity in the provision of accommodation was obvious to black soldiers, a stark illustration of Rhodesia's systemic racism. However, this unfair treatment was not corrosive to the solidarities of these troops for, just as with pay, the army's provision was much better than that on offer in civilian life. GM told me that the army was a good place to be, as 'during this time, we were given marriage quarter, three-roomed house; if you are lucky, four-roomed house', and that the houses were of a good standard.[44] HZ said, 'you could get a nice house, your own house'.[45] MC, a teacher and the wife of a soldier, told me, 'you automatically get accommodation. So it was easy for us; straightaway we were given a house to stay in, so that's where we moved'. Her husband, DC, added that it was 'a three-roomed house. *Three!*', emphasising that this housing was far better than that available in civilian life.[46]

It is difficult to properly cost these concomitant benefits in retrospect, although they did not amount to more than a fraction of the salary differential between black and white soldiers. Tellingly, the army did not offer these benefits to white soldiers, but simply paid them more. Furthermore, it made a concerted effort to publicise the benefits offered to black soldiers, particularly accommodation, as 'an inducement to recruitment' in the words of an army spokesman.[47] While attracting recruits was, for the army, a useful secondary effect of its provision of benefits, they were primarily intended for retaining the loyalties of black soldiers throughout the war, as the army was acutely aware of the necessity of meeting its end of the social contract between itself and its soldiers. This is not to imply that the army's provision of benefits was motivated by progressive views among its top brass, for in fact the opposite was the case.

---

[43] CL, R.C. (S) (75) 39, 'Standards of Housing: Government African Employees', 27 March 1975.
[44] Interview with GM.   [45] Interview with HZ.   [46] Interviews with MC, DC.
[47] Maxey, *Fight for Zimbabwe*, p. 32.

It was only after the first armed attacks of the war that the RF government started to pay closer attention to the service conditions of black soldiers, which had historically been poor. A 1966 memorandum by the minister of defence argued that the disparity in pay had 'been particularly noted by the African soldier because he believes he carries out identical duties at a very considerably lower rate of pay'.[48] Successive defence ministers expressed anxiety in the Cabinet as to the volume of complaints concerning the pay disparity that reached their desks and the potential damage this could do to black troops' morale. Later in the war, some ministers expressed concern over the propaganda value of the disparity to the liberation forces. Reporting in 1977, the Committee on Conditions of Service noted that ZANU propaganda broadcasts on Radio Mozambique 'harp on the disparity in rates of pay between Africans and their European counterparts' to undermine the morale of black soldiers, and recognised 'an urgent need to improve the salaries of African soldiers'.[49]

The relatively good pay of black soldiers was a direct product of the Rhodesian government's desire not to break the social contract in this regard. Pay increases were forced through by various ministers of defence explicitly on these grounds, and they had to overcome the strong and continual objections of other RF ministers. For instance, in 1966, a small pay increase for black soldiers was hammered through Cabinet opposition on the grounds that it was 'not only necessary but overdue'.[50] The next pay review, in 1973, awarded a 20 per cent increase for black soldiers.[51] The next review, in 1977, endorsed larger increases for black soldiers in particular, as the increments at which their salaries increased (either annually or on promotion) were meagre in comparison with those of other government employees.[52]

These increases seem to have functioned as intended, for as Stapleton argued, 'in the mid-1970s it was not uncommon for African soldiers to leave the army upon completion of their contracts but then return a few months later because of the increased military pay and frustration with civilian life'.[53] My interviewees welcomed these increases, although they

---

[48] CL, R.C. (S) (66) 178, 'Pay Review: African Soldiers and Airmen', 4 June 1966.
[49] CL, CCCS(S) (77) 1, 'Cabinet Committee on Conditions of Service', 19 May 1977, Annex A, p. 3. The committee did not recommend 'substantial' increases for fear of 'repercussive effects on the other Uniformed Services'.
[50] CL, R.C. (S) (66) 99, 'Extension of National Service', 21 March 1966; R.C. (S) (66) 177 'The Rhodesian Army: Additional Maintenance Costs 1966/67', 13 May 1966; R.C. (S) (66) 178 'Pay Review: African Soldiers and Airmen', 14 June 1966.
[51] CL, R.C. (S) (73) 120, 'Salary Review: BSA Police and Armed Forces'. 5 October 1973, p. 3; R.C. (S) (73) 123 'Salary Review: BSA Police and Armed Forces', Appendix A; R.C. (S) (73) 122, 'Salary Review: BSA Police and Armed Forces', 5 October 1973.
[52] CL, CCCS(S) (77) 1, 'Cabinet Committee on Conditions of Service', 19 May 1977, Annex A, p. 3.
[53] Stapleton, *African Police and Soldiers*, p. 31.

were not overawed by them. TM told me, 'there were salary reviews; we got something, though not as attractive as we would have liked'.[54] The Rhodesian state did not seek to match its rhetoric that the conflict was one of black and white fighting side by side with a material reflection of this equality created by sharing the burdens of combat. Instead, it raised the salaries of black soldiers just enough, and only after prolonged intra-ministerial wrangling, to ensure that the contract it had forged with them did not lapse.

The Increasing Military Importance of Black Soldiers

Maintaining the contract with black soldiers became ever more important as Rhodesia became increasingly dependent upon them. However, despite obvious military need, the number of black soldiers increased rather slowly. As argued earlier, in the 1960s, Rhodesian cabinet ministers had vetoed proposals to recruit more black troops. This continued even after the army became utterly overstretched and the well of white manpower ran dry. In December 1972, the minister of defence noted with panic that 'we are faced also with substantial problems arising from shortages in the establishments of the Regular Forces', and requested fourteen additional rifle companies – approximately 1,600 more soldiers.[55] The RF's insistence upon a 'balanced' 1:1 ratio of black to white troops, discussed in Chapter 2, made it quite impossible to recruit this number.

One year later, the same minister argued that the failure of the 'previous policies', owing to their reliance upon a 'preponderance of European national servicemen' and the TF, meant that '2RAR must be raised'.[56] Military necessity had finally overcome the RF's racism and paranoia over the loyalties of black troops. Ten years after its initial refusal to raise a second black battalion, the Cabinet authorised the creation of 2RAR, which was established in Fort Victoria at the end of 1974 from a nucleus of 1RAR officers and NCOs.[57]

This was still insufficient for the military's needs and securocrats lobbied for more black troops, and for them to take on more senior roles, with intelligence chief Ken Flower foremost among them. In a 1975 memo, seemingly written in response to the objections of RF ministers, he argued vociferously for the rapid inclusion of more black personnel in the security

---

[54] Interview with TM.
[55] CL, R.C. (S) (72) 176, 'National Service: Extension of', 8 December 1972, p. 3.
[56] CL, R.C. (S) (73) 162, 'National Service: Territorial Training: Priorities in the Organisation and Utilisation of Defence Manpower', 7 December 1973, p. 1.
[57] CL, R.C. (S) (74) 95, 'National Service: Territorial Training: Priorities in the Organisation and Utilisation of Defence Manpower', 17 May 1974.

forces, including in an expanded TF. 'If one doubted the effectiveness of African troops', they should refer to 'the achievements ... of our Rhodesian African Rifles in the Second World War and since'.[58] In 1976, he contended that the Rhodesian top brass should have overseen a 'far greater integration by Blacks [in the security forces] and at a much higher level'.[59] In 1977, he argued in the Cabinet that 'urgent consideration should be given to ways and means of utilising African manpower'.[60]

This impetus for expanding the number and role of black soldiers came too late to have any significant military effect upon the trajectory of the war. As argued earlier, professional soldiers take considerable time and resources to train. For instance, a 1977 Rhodesian policy paper stated that '2500 A/S' (African soldiers) were to be recruited in the following year.[61] That same year, the RAR held its 'largest passing out parade in history', achieved by entirely omitting the conventional war aspect of a recruit's basic training. Yet the number of troops passing out was a mere 400.[62]

Furthermore, the army's refusal to commission black officers prior to 1977 imposed an upper limit on the number of regular officers available, meaning that there were simply not enough officers to command any great expansion of soldiers.[63] While 2RAR was operational by 1975, it was several months until its full complement of companies were ready, and 3RAR only came into existence right at the end of the war in November 1979.[64] Just some 1,500 black soldiers were added to the regular army's strength between 1976 and 1980, a time when the war was rapidly escalating and the liberation armies expanded at a dramatic rate. According to Rhodesian intelligence, by March 1979, ZANLA had a trained strength of 21,000 and ZIPRA 20,000.[65] The regular Rhodesian Army was just some 5,500 strong.

This shortage of black soldiers was not solely the product of RF politicians' racism. As Stapleton argued, as late as 1975, influential whites within the military still espoused concerns as to 'the loyalty of African troops', despite there being no grounds for doing so.[66] The most

---

[58] PKF, A/3, Memorandum from Director CIO, 'Commitment of Africans in the National Interest', 2 September 1975.
[59] PKF, A/3, Memorandum from Director CIO, 'Morale and Leadership in the Security Forces', 20 December 1976, p. 4.
[60] Flower, *Serving Secretly*, p. 188.
[61] RAA Box 2001/086/227, 'Strategy: Courses of Action to Be Adopted until September 1978', Undated and Uncatalogued Draft.
[62] Reynolds, 'Army Crash Course for Africans', p. 1.
[63] Brownell, *Collapse of Rhodesia*, p. 81.   [64] Binda, *Masodja*, p. 366.
[65] Flower, *Serving Secretly*, pp. 175, 221.
[66] Stapleton, *African Police and Soldiers*, pp. 176–9.

important Rhodesian military officer of the war, Lt Gen. Peter Walls (army commander 1972–7, overall Rhodesian commander 1977–80), personified this tendency among the top brass to mistrust black soldiers in favour of white units. Walls wielded huge influence, and his prejudiced views towards black soldiers illustrate how hostility at the highest levels of the army persisted throughout the war.

Walls' discriminatory views were displayed over a long period of time. For instance, in 1963, he was army representative of the (Southern) Rhodesian delegation to the Central African Conference that met in Victoria Falls to dissolve the Federation, which made a concerted effort to retain as many white Federal Army soldiers as possible from Nyasaland (Malawi) and Northern Rhodesia (Zambia) in the (Southern) Rhodesian Army, but actively sought to prevent black Federal soldiers from following suit.[67] In 1964, Walls, then the army's adjutant general, received a proposal from a white RAR officer to increase the salaries of black soldiers, but rejected this on the grounds that the air force would not accept it.[68] This was a spurious claim given the relatively small number of black airmen in the RhAF.

That same year, Walls, now CO of the all-white RLI, had allowed his soldiers to wear Christmas party hats emblazoned 'RLI for UDI', a clear indication of support for white-minority rule and a gross violation of the army's apolitical norms.[69] In 1968, Walls made 'heavy criticism' of the RAR after difficulties experienced by a single RAR platoon on operations.[70] A white ex-RAR officer told me that, throughout the war, well-known senior army commanders had continually scotched the raising of more RAR battalions, and also prevented the implementation of equal pay and the commissioning of black officers.[71] He strongly inferred Walls was among their number.

It was no coincidence that Walls' hostile views of black soldiers accorded with those of the RF. Although Walls had earned a reprimand from Maj. Gen. Putterill, then army commander, for the 'RLI for UDI' incident, it made him 'popular, particularly among' the RF and Ian Smith.[72] Walls 'was committed to UDI', and it was widely known that Smith liked Walls, who had also been born in Rhodesia (a factor of importance for Smith, the first Rhodesian-born prime minister, a fact he highlighted frequently for political gain) and whose father Smith had

---

[67] CL, S.R.C. (F) (63) 313, 'Report of the Inter-governmental Committee on Defence', 1 October 1963, pp. 2–3, 6, and Annex J.
[68] Telfer and Fulton, *Chibaya Moyo*, pp. 86–7.
[69] Wood, *So Far and No Further!*, p. 244.   [70] Stewart, 'Rhodesian African Rifles', p. 39.
[71] Interview with anonymous white ex-RAR officers, Harare, 2018.
[72] 'Obituary: Lieutenant-General Peter Walls', *The Telegraph*, 27 July 2010.

been friends with in the air force.[73] When Smith appointed Walls in charge of the army in 1972, it was 'a promotion that came as no surprise [as Smith] needed an army commander he could trust to support him',[74] having purged several senior officers in the wake of UDI for suspecting their enduring loyalty to the Crown over the RF.[75] Walls' meteoric rise from major to lieutenant general in just eight years was clearly facilitated by both Smith's favouritism and his political support for minority rule.

In 1977, Smith promoted Walls once more, to Commander Combined Operations (COMOPS), the first time one commander had control over the entire RSF apparatus. Tellingly, at this juncture, the 'special forces', comprising the RLI, RhSAS, and Selous Scouts, were removed entirely from the army chain of command and reported only to COMOPS, while the army commander 'only retained command of black regular units such as the Rhodesian African Rifles' and the TF.[76] Walls had made overtly clear that these units, which included the white 'Praetorian guard' of the RhSAS and RLI, took orders only from him, to the chagrin of other army commanders, with whom he clashed over the matter.[77]

Walls had previously intervened to make sure that these white units, both of which he had previously commanded, were not opened to black soldiers. Barbara Cole detailed how the RhSAS, a special forces unit, wished to drop its policy of segregation and recruit black soldiers. Its missions typically comprised clandestine reconnaissance or operations by small teams relying upon stealth, almost all of which occurred within Mozambique or Zambia. White RhSAS troops struggled to operate owing to their lack of language skills and the fact that their spoor and appearance readily gave them away as white, which compromised them.

Consequently, in the mid-1970s, black soldiers from 1RAR were seconded to RhSAS patrols:

[A]nd the operational results were greatly improved. RhSAS troops were generally full of praise for the professionalism of these attached African soldiers and what interested [RhSAS CO] Brian [Robinson] was the great mutual affection exhibited between them all when off duty ... it convinced the RhSAS hierarchy sufficiently to approach the Army Commander, Lieutenant-General Peter Walls, and formally request they be allowed to embody African troops into the unit who

---

[73] D. van der Vat, 'Lt Gen Peter Walls Obituary: Commander of the White Rhodesians Who Resisted Black Rule', *The Guardian*, 28 July 2010.
[74] Ibid.
[75] Kenrick, *Decolonisation, Identity and Nation in Rhodesia*, p. 146; Moorcraft, *Short Thousand Years*, p. 13.
[76] Cilliers, *Counter-Insurgency in Rhodesia*, pp. 66–73.
[77] See Beckett, 'Rhodesian Army'.

had successfully passed the selection course and the parachute and SAS skilled-training courses. They were turned down flat.[78]

Walls' refusal to allow black soldiers to become special forces had no military rationale, and was indeed counterproductive to the combat effectiveness of the RhSAS, the Rhodesians' most elite unit. This conformed to Walls' long-standing attitude towards black soldiers, which was one of hostile prejudice that persisted irrespective of the high levels of loyalty and proficiency continually demonstrated by black soldiers.

The Integration of the Rhodesian Army

Despite the enduring hostility of many Rhodesian elites towards black soldiers, the increase in their number after 1974 did have some impact on their treatment within the army. As Stapleton argued, 'in the late 1970s racial segregation in the Rhodesian military began to break down', most noticeably with white national service conscripts being integrated with those newly trained RAR recruits that were not posted to the main RAR battalions.[79]

It had long been known among black troops that integrating the army would increase its effectiveness. A 1977 RAA document noted that 'many African regulars suggested that if African, Coloured and white troops went through basic training together, the army would be much more efficient'.[80]

Although 'the decision to create an integrated security force with black officers was heralded as proof of Ian Smith's desire to create a co-equal bi-racial society', it was in fact taken 'only after the strength of the insurgent forces' was such that 'the army was in danger of being overrun'.[81] While the reform was borne more out of Rhodesian desperation than egalitarianism, the increasing number and seniority of black troops in the army ended some forms of discrimination.

---

[78] Cole, *Elite*, p. 92. I find Coles' account convincing as her book is meticulously well researched and, unlike many such texts chronicling the Rhodesian side of the war, contains hardly any inaccuracies. However, a contrasting version was offered by Ron Reid-Daly, Selous Scouts founder and CO (and who had previously served under Walls in Malaya and in the RLI), who developed a highly intense personal and professional rivalry with the RhSAS during the war that was reciprocated by the RhSAS, which loathed him. Writing in retrospect, he alleged that when the 'pseudo-gangs' that would eventually become the Selous Scouts were trialled in 1973, 'RhSAS commanders "refused to take Africans into their ranks and hinted the RhSAS would break up if forced to do so"' (as quoted in Stapleton, *African Police and Soldiers*, p. 203). Reid-Daly had a history of making extravagant and self-aggrandising claims, and given the enmity he harboured towards the RhSAS, his account seems dubious. Peter Baxter made similar claims to Reid-Daly in his own book on the Selous Scouts, but no references or sources are provided to verify this claim (*Selous Scouts*, pp. 65, 89).

[79] McLaughlin, 'Thin White Line', p. 180; Stapleton, *African Police and Soldiers*, p. 182.

[80] White, *Fighting and Writing*, p. 229.   [81] Lohman and MacPherson, *Rhodesia*, p. 38.

Nonetheless, just as racist paternalism was widespread in white Rhodesian society and civilian perceptions of black soldiers essentialised them as the 'martial askaris of the RAR',[82] such perceptions were commonplace among whites in the TF and RLI, many of whom, as Stapleton noted, attributed the tracking ability of black soldiers to their supposedly superhuman eyesight and powers of navigation, while simultaneously black soldiers were supposedly poor shots.[83] This was, of course, untrue and reflected the racist colonial conceptions commonplace among whites.

For instance, BM was sent to the Wafa Wafa training school on a tracking course.[84] Laughing, he recalled that he found this course, widely reputed as difficult, as 'fine and easy', owing to his long experience of tracking cattle in rural areas; however, many of his black peers, who did not possess such experience, struggled. To BM, it was self-evident that tracking ability was determined by experience and training, as it was to Chris Cocks, an RLI soldier, who noted that whites could become proficient trackers too.[85] Yet these racist preconceptions remained prevalent in the minds of many Rhodesian whites.

Likewise, black soldiers were not poor shots and varied in their ability to shoot just like any group of soldiers the world over. Their supposedly poor marksmanship was, in reality, the product of the Rhodesian prohibition of Africans owning or using firearms in the aftermath of the wars of the 1890s.[86] As CD told me, 'many whites they had [more] experiences with guns than us; they were better off with guns than us' having handled and used them from a young age, but that after training black soldiers became excellent marksmen, discussed further in Chapter 5.[87]

Within the newly integrated units, for the first time in the history of the army, blacks commanded whites on a regular basis. To many Rhodesian whites, this represented a shocking change, as: 'Racial divisions in Rhodesia were almost absolute, and although to some degree this was loosened in the field of military service ... the notion of a white recruit being berated by a black drill instructor, or a white trooper saluting and calling a black officer "sir", was very difficult for many in the establishment to swallow.'[88]

---

[82] Lowry, 'Impact of Anti-Communism', p. 184.
[83] Stapleton, *African Police and Soldiers*, pp. 65–6.
[84] Wafara Wasa translates as 'if you die, you die.' Wafa Wafa was used extensively by the Selous Scouts and remains in use today as an elite ZNA camp where One Commando Regiment (the successor of the RLI) trains, its notorious reputation still intact. See Kawadza, 'ZNA Sticks to Its Guns on Training'; Manzongo, 'Wafa Wafa'; Manzongo, 'Zimbabwe Army Commandos Graduation'.
[85] Cocks, *Fireforce*, p. 157. For other examples of this point, see White, *Fighting and Writing*, pp. 84–5.
[86] Stapleton, *African Police and Soldiers*, p. 7; T. Ranger, *Revolt*, p. 114.
[87] Interview with CD.   [88] Baxter, *Selous Scouts*, p. 95.

The discourse of professionalism was widely incorporated by both blacks and whites to overcome these reversals of racial hierarchy. As Flood noted of her white interviewees, after these reforms, 'whilst rank prevailed over race, the [white RLI] soldier acknowledged that: "It felt funny to start with." Another RLI soldier remembers his white troop Sergeant deferring to the black Warrant Officer of a black platoon they were with, the Sergeant explaining that "he's [the Warrant Officer] been around forever, he outranks me"'.[89] Many whites from the RLI or TF, as Stapleton has noted, expressed 'initial dislike of black soldiers' which was later 'followed by a change of heart' after serving alongside them; one TF soldier recalled that 'compared to them, we were a bunch of farmers with weapons. They were true professionals'.[90]

Drawing upon interviews with white veterans, Stewart recounted a similar story in which two white TF soldiers 'of Afrikaans descent' who 'each owned farms which employed hundreds of blacks [and] were not accustomed at all to taking orders from black men' had 'initially expressed their hesitation at spending time in the bush under the command of a black NCO', but after six weeks under the command of RAR soldiers, had 'a new-found respect for their black counterparts. They had learned the ability of the RAR soldiers to conduct extended patrols over long distances in the Rhodesian bush, and had trouble keeping up. They came away with an intimate knowledge of this and learned to respect their black colleagues' capabilities'.[91]

My interviewees also used the language of professionalism. They noted that while they sometimes experienced difficult interactions with whites from outside the RAR, these could be overcome by invoking professional values as embodied in the military chain of command. MN told me that, after being promoted as an NCO:

[S]ome of the Europeans they couldn't respect [black soldiers initially as they had not served with them before] ... but they could respect your rank ... if I give orders and I'm the senior man there, it doesn't matter who you are, they've got to respect, take those orders ... I've been given the appointment, I'm the senior man [and would order white recalcitrants in a commanding tone, saying] 'Let's go, gentlemen'. And that was my way. 'Let's go, gentlemen. Let's go and fight; let's do our job'.[92]

Likewise, DSN noted that, on his commissioning course, white soldiers treated him 'very well' and there was 'no problem' as 'the instructors were ORs [Other Ranks, enlisted personnel], they knew that they are training

---

[89] Flood, *Brothers-in-Arms?*, p. 43.   [90] Stapleton, *African Police and Soldiers*, pp. 67–8.
[91] Stewart, 'Rhodesian African Rifles', p. 72.   [92] Interview with MN.

you to be an officer, so one day they'll salute you, so there was no problem at all'.[93]

The experience of combat itself also served to enhance the bonds between black and white soldiers. Flood noted, 'Combat acted as a great leveller, both of rank and of race ... the lifestyle demanded by bush warfare meant that soldiers, both black and white, and often junior officers and the rank and file, lived in very close quarters, where "everything was done together" including "eating, sleeping, drinking and fighting"'.[94] BM, an RAR warrant officer, served with 1 (Independent) Company, an integrated unit of black and white soldiers that predominantly fought around the Beitbridge area during the latter, intense period of the war. His recollection illustrates how combat served as a leveller that trumped over Rhodesian racism:

> 1 Indep, we were combined – European and African. We were soldiers, African soldiers and European soldiers. We were staying in the same barracks. We were eating in the same kitchen. At the operation we used to be doing two European, two African – go together as a stick of four, you see? That's why 1 Indep was strong, yeah ... we were strong, and we liked each other. There was no segregation. We were together. We were working as a team. If there was a European section commander, if there was an African section commander, [it was] no problem. We were together, like eating *sadza* together in the same plate ... Some [of the whites] were speaking Shona, some were speaking Ndebele.[95]

BM also remarked that, had the war continued beyond 1979, these integrated companies were 'the model army for the future'.[96]

The formation of new companies and the expansion of the RAR created a large number of vacancies for warrant officers and NCOs, and opportunities for promotion increased markedly. My interviewees remarked that, before this increase, even if one were qualified for promotion it could be a case of waiting for a vacancy to arrive – or 'dead man's shoes'.[97] As WM recalled: 'Since I was the best recruit [during basic training], I was looking forward to early promotion, but there were still very senior people who had to retire first to create vacancies so I stayed as a private for five years from '64 to '69; that's when I became a lance corporal.'[98] By 1975, WM was a warrant officer, a promotion trajectory other RAR interviewees also experienced.[99]

As part of these reforms, the warrant officers' and sergeants' messes were gradually merged. As MN recalled to me, he approved of this and thought it was a good step, as 'we were combined', although in the new

---

[93] Interview with DSN. [94] Flood, *Brothers-in-Arms?*, pp. 15–18.
[95] Interview with BM. [96] Ibid. [97] Interview with SM. [98] Interview with WM.
[99] Interviews with BM, MS, and GMH.

merged mess 'instead of drinking Chibuku [opaque sorghum beer popular in Zimbabwe] you now ended up with [small glasses] of lager', much to his dismay. He thought the combined mess was better as 'if you are in a community you have got to do the same thing. You can't be somebody who wants only his own'.[100] Those, such as GN, who had become officers automatically joined the extant officer's mess, which had previously been all white.[101]

In the late 1970s, African soldiers like GN were able to purchase houses in formerly white-only suburbs and were given private mortgages to do so, a facility previously unavailable.[102] In 1976, guerrilla forces destroyed MN's home in the rural areas. He told me he was 'working with some very good Europeans' in his unit, who lobbied the city council on his behalf and managed to secure him a council property. The next year, his OC convinced him to purchase a house in the formerly white-only suburbs and assisted him in completing the mortgage application, filling out the administrative paperwork, and connecting the utilities and delivering furniture to the property. MN's neighbours in barracks:

heard we have bought a house in the suburbs where Europeans are staying. They were *laughing* at my wife. 'Do you think *you* can go and stay with the Europeans?' But, a few days later, they wanted to know how I did it ... I can say I was the first African to leave barracks and stay in the suburbs with the Europeans.[103]

MN praised the whites who assisted him in acquiring a property. He demonstrated how black soldiers acquired status and an increasing amount of disposable income by the end of the 1970s, as well as how some white officers sought to help black soldiers. These slow reforms did improve my interviewees' perceptions of the army and Rhodesian society, and in this manner buttressed their macro-level loyalties.

However, MN's experiences were exceptional. They highlight the extent of direct intervention by white officers required to gain access, in the last years of the war, to Rhodesia's almost entirely still segregated suburbs. There are similarities in this to how the apartheid-era South African Army's boast that its black soldiers did not need to carry passes within military cantonments simply highlighted the 'unstated reality ... that they do need a pass outside of camp'.[104]

Another anecdote is telling in this regard: Luise White retold the story of Graham Atkins, a white Rhodesia Regiment conscript. By 1979, 'white society, he lamented, had not yet caught up to the Rhodesian army'.

---

[100] Interview with MN. [101] Interview with GN. [102] Ibid. [103] Interview with MN.
[104] Grundy, *Soldiers without Politics*, p. 222.

In order for Atkins and his white friends to get 'their African comrade Moses' into a wedding reception, they had to pretend he was a waiter.[105]

The swift change in how the RF perceived black soldiers was epitomised by a 1978 proposal from the minister of defence to create a military school, named the Army Potential Leaders Education programme, as the army 'was anxious to set up a military academy to provide future black army officers'.[106] This scheme, which echoed similar programmes that commenced during the Federal era but were abandoned after UDI.[107] This was a clear imitation of the white-only boarding schools which were imbued with a masculine-martial ethos and churned out Rhodesia's white officers. The school was to be staffed with the same teachers from the Army Education Corps that provided education to the RAR.[108] As the time period covered by the Smith Papers ends immediately after this cabinet meeting, it is unknown whether this scheme materialised prior to independence, although I found no other records of it.

However, the fact that it was proposed by the army and discussed at the cabinet level is indicative of a change in official white attitudes. Recall that voices within the senior levels of the Rhodesian Army and the ministry of defence had lobbied to disband the RAR at the end of World War II, again at the end of Federation, and once more on the eve of UDI, and that in 1964, white officers had ridiculed 'day dreams of rapid African advancement in the armed forces'.[109] Fourteen years later, a permanent military academy to train black officer cadets was proposed which, even if its primary purpose was to create loyal cadres who would defend white political and economic interests, illustrated how important black soldiers had become to the Rhodesian military and political establishments.

'No Second-Class Officers': The First Black Officers in Rhodesia

Aside from improvements in pay and the integration of some units, the other most tangible army-wide reform was prompted by the June 1976 release of the *Report of the Commission of Inquiry into Racial Discrimination*,[110] commonly also referred to as the Quenet Report after its chairman.[111] Its conclusions were not radical and, as D. G. Baker

---

[105] White, *Fighting and Writing*, p. 53.
[106] CL, R.C. (S) (78) Rhodesian Cabinet Minutes, 4th Meeting, 24 January 1978.
[107] Stapleton, *African Police and Soldiers*, pp. 175–6.
[108] CL, R.C. (S) (78) Rhodesian Cabinet Minutes, 5th Meeting, 31 January 1978.
[109] Stapleton, *African Police and Soldiers*, p. 176.
[110] CL, Cmd. R.R. 6, 'Report of the Commission of Inquiry into Racial Discrimination' (Salisbury, Government Printer, June 1976).
[111] 'Rhodesia Revising Laws on Blacks', *New York Times*, 15 June 1976, p. 7.

argued in 1979, were largely a rehash of the paternalistic 'liberal' reforms of the 1950s: 'but another effort by the Rhodesian Front and White society to suspend time and thereby preserve White power and privilege by granting concessions to Blacks, concessions which, however, did not

Figure 4.1 Lt Tumbare presented with Lt Col. Rule's sword, 1977 (*Nwoho*, October 1977). Mrs Rule presents the officer's sword of her late husband, Lt Col. Kim Rule (CO 1RAR 1951–5), to Lt Tumbare, the first black officer to be commissioned (and a former 1RAR regimental sergeant major). Lt Col. Rule had bequeathed his own officer's sword to the first black officer to be commissioned.

threaten White power'.[112] Even this markedly partial commission's report was damning of Rhodesia's systematic racism, and mandated the government to undertake sweeping political and economic reforms.[113] Yet the report's statement that black officers should be commissioned was couched in rather timid language: 'persons of proved ability and character should be considered for appointment to commissioned rank and should be encouraged to achieve it if they satisfy the qualifications required'.[114]

This was revealing, for the requirement for 'proved ability' and to meet 'qualifications' were euphemisms long used by the army to refuse to commission black officers. After UDI, the army had abandoned previous Federal-era initiatives to commission African officers.[115] It subsequently insisted that no candidates met the required 'qualifications', an obvious lie. As Stapleton argued, black recruits often concealed their qualifications 'out of fear of being rejected by insecure white officers', who were themselves not as educated.[116] TM told me that he and many of his peers met the qualification criteria, but:

It was something taboo, not to talk of. In fact, at one stage, we were led to believe that if one had O-Levels, or [the] equivalent of four years secondary, he would be eligible for selection to train as an officer. But I, for one, had [these qualifications] through private study [in his spare time] as early as 1968, but kept it a secret as if I had exposed myself, they would have kicked me out of the army.[117]

Securocrats also noted that the army's refusal to commission black soldiers was an obvious instance of racist prejudice. Ken Flower, head of Rhodesian intelligence, remarked in a memorandum to the Cabinet in 1975 that even apartheid South Africa had commissioned black officers, and 'Rhodesia now has the unenviable reputation of being the ONLY COUNTRY IN AFRICA that debars Africans from personal advancement in this sphere.'[118]

The army's evidence to the Quenet Commission was provided by Lt Gen. Walls. He requested that the evidence he provided to the commission 'be expunged' from the final report for, notionally, security reasons.[119] Cabinet memoranda reveal that, in fact, the reason Walls requested this censorship was that he felt publication of his comments would arouse 'discussion and controversy ... which would compound the difficulties

---

[112] Baker, 'Time Suspended', p. 252. [113] Ibid., p. 243.
[114] R.C. (S) (76) 46, 'Report of the Commission of Inquiry into Racial Discrimination', 23 April 1976, p. 5.
[115] Stapleton, *African Police and Soldiers*, pp. 174–6. [116] Ibid., p. 86.
[117] Interview with TM.
[118] PKF, A/3, Memorandum from Director CIO, 'Commitment of Africans in the National Interest', 2 September 1975. Emphasis as per original document.
[119] CL, R.C. (S) (76) Cabinet Minutes, 19th Meeting, 11 May 1976, p. 2; CL, R.C. (S) (76) Cabinet Minutes, 21st Meeting, 25 May 1976.

which would inevitably occur in the commissioning of Africans'.[120] It is not clear as to what these supposed 'difficulties' comprised, as the censored pages are not found in the Smith Papers. Given that Walls who, as argued, was persistently prejudiced towards black soldiers, deemed his comments too controversial infers that he opposed the creation of black officers.

Later cabinet memoranda reveal that the army had attempted to subvert the conclusions of the Quenet Report by refusing to commission black officers on the same basis as whites, and had forwarded a proposal to create 'second-class officers'.[121] It was forced into a swift about-turn by the government and belatedly 'accepted there would be no second-class officers and therefore all amenities would be open to African officers', although a special three-month course would be necessary to instruct them in administrative duties and to 'teach them the correct deportment as officers'.[122] Clearly, the latter was not a military prerogative, but instead reflected how white settler elites placed an enormous emphasis upon 'manners'.

As Alison Shutt argued, 'manners mattered' in Rhodesia, and white elites devoted much effort to arcane 'rules of etiquette' that denoted status and served to reinforce the racist colonial hierarchy.[123] The commissioning of black officers put them at the apex of colonial power – command of army units – for the first time (see Figure 4.2). Given that 'settlers were obsessed with prestige, especially its vulnerability',[124] it is unsurprising that the army's first reaction to being ordered to train black officers was not to instruct them in command or tactics, but to attempt to ensure that they maintained the 'correct deportment'.

The army's reluctant embrace of black officers as not 'second-class' extended to pay, status, and entitlements. As GN, one of the first to be commissioned, told me: 'there was no difference in pay between the white officer and black officer and the respects paid were exactly the same throughout the army ... The whites they used to respect the black officers as normally as they respected white officers'.[125] In 1979, a journalist spoke with an African RAR lieutenant, who was of diminutive stature, 'as he strode down a gravel path toward lunch in the Officers' Mess, returning a salute from a white along the way [saying] "The only thing that separates me from the white officers in this regiment is that I wear a smaller uniform!"'[126]

---

[120] CL, R.C. (S) (76) Cabinet Minutes, 22nd Meeting, 1 June 1976.
[121] CL, R.C. (S) (76) Cabinet Minutes, 21st Meeting, 25 May 1976.   [122] Ibid.
[123] Shutt, 'The Natives Are Getting Out of Hand', p. 655.   [124] Ibid., p. 656.
[125] Interview with GN.
[126] Burns, 'How Blacks View Their Larger Role in Rhodesia's Army'.

Figure 4.2 Newly commissioned officer receiving a prize from Maj. Gen. John Hickman. One of my interviewees as a newly commissioned officer on 6 March 1978, the day of his passing out parade. As the sword of honour recipient he is receiving a prize from army commander, Maj. Gen. John Hickman. This image featured on the front page of the state-controlled Herald newspaper the following day (copy of interviewee's original photograph by author).

Black officers were not treated as second class, but they were commissioned into an army that remained systematically prejudiced towards black troops. The army invoked professional discourse in an attempt to overcome this. In November 1976, speaking to the press during a selection course of potential black and white officers, Brigadier Sandy Maclean told a journalist, 'we already have circumstances where European and African soldiers work quite happily together with African soldiers giving the orders: in operations, in places like signal centres, and I see there's no difference here. If these chaps qualify and pass the course they'll be officers in the true sense of the word'.[127]

My interviewees affirmed that this was the case in their experience. DSN told me that he and a peer from his commissioning course were 'the first black officers' in Grey's Scouts, and that at 'first we felt out of place', but that the white officers 'were so friendly, especially Colonel

[127] Associated Press, 'Rhodesia War or Diplomacy?'

Fitzgerald'.[128] TM told me that newly commissioned black officers were made to feel welcome, were treated no differently from their peers, and that 'when we took our wives to the mess, they appeared to be very welcome; we saw no signs of resistance or being unwelcome'.[129] The commissioning of black officers was given full propaganda treatment, and the army very deliberately chose to announce it so as to 'coincide with the release of the [Quenet] Report' in what it called a 'tactical' move to gain favourable coverage.[130] TM commented that 'they gave us a lot of publicity when we were commissioned. It was headlines in the newspaper. We saw it as a way of building bridges between blacks and whites'.[131]

While the commissioning of black officers was symbolically important, it seems that only some sixty were commissioned prior to 1980.[132] The first cohorts were drawn from serving soldiers of the rank of sergeant and above, of whom many were sergeant majors with more than twenty years' service, and thus too old to command fighting formations.[133] They were commissioned as training and administration officers, while younger soldiers were commissioned as general duties (GD) officers and commanded combat units.[134] DSN told me that he was commissioned as a GD officer in 1978, and 'I was given a platoon, it was a fighting platoon [that he led on] operations in Marondera, Bikita, and Mash[onaland] West.'[135]

Black officers 'soon became well respected' according to Moorcraft, although it seems that none commanded a unit above platoon level,[136] and by the end of the war, major was the highest rank a black soldier had achieved.[137] Despite this, the commissioning of black officers was

---

[128] Interview with DSN.   [129] Interview with TM.
[130] CL, R.C. (S) (76) Cabinet Minutes, 21st Meeting, 25 May 1976.
[131] Interview with TM.
[132] As the astute reader will have noticed by now, the scholarly war literature often provides slightly different or sometimes simply contradictory figures. This is not particular to this conflict – for example, 'enormous statistical discrepancies were frequent during' Algeria's war of independence (Crapanzano, *Harkis*, pp. 60, 69). The number of black officers prior to 1980 is no exception. Beckett stated there were thirty ('Rhodesian Army', p. 174). Ehrenreich said that black officers formed 10 per cent of the total Rhodesian Army officer corps – that is, approximately sixty-five by 1980 (Ehrenreich, 'National Security', p. 256). Ehrenreich's estimate seems the more accurate, given that by January 1979, there were already thirty black officers (Burns, 'How Blacks View Their Larger Role in Rhodesia's Army'), that my interviewees' described to me that their commissioning courses were eighteen to twenty strong (Interviews with GN, DSN, TM), and that after 1978, the annual regular officer's intake started to accept black cadets (Interview with WR), meaning it is likely there were approximately sixty black officers by end of the war.
[133] See, for instance, 'A Moment in History', *Nwoho* (October 1977), pp. 55–8.
[134] Interview with GN.   [135] Interview with DSN.
[136] Moorcraft, *Short Thousand Years*, p. 175.
[137] Interview with DSN. Whitaker asserted that captain was the highest rank (*'New Model' Armies of Africa?*, p. 210). Either way, no black officer commanded more than a subunit by the end of the war.

remembered by my interviewees as a sign that the army could reform, even those who did not aspire to become officers, such as JM, who told me: 'Lieutenants from the blacks, yes. It changed, it looked nice, it was fairer... We used to work with [those African soldiers now commissioned], we used to hear that "so-and-so" has been picked up for an officer's course. We used to look at their testimonials from when they joined the army.'[138] Nowhere was the commissioning of black officers better received than the RAR, which had developed a unique military culture.

Race and Professionalism within the RAR

While the army's reforms met with the approval of black soldiers, they occurred at a snail's pace and structural racism remained. Yet the soldierly loyalties of black soldiers remained strong. An important factor in explaining this was the unique military culture of the RAR, in which most black soldiers served.

The RAR troops did not routinely serve directly alongside whites, and thus did not experience racist views and behaviour frequently. For thousands of black soldiers, aside from occasional joint operations with white units,[139] the only regular interactions with whites were with the small number who were their own officers.[140] It is not unreasonable to presume that these white officers could have acted as lightning rods for black soldiers' frustrations at the inequities that prevailed in Rhodesia, as was the case among black soldiers in the colonial French Army during its COIN wars in Indochina and Algeria.[141]

Yet the contrary was the case. As Jakkie Cilliers argued, white RAR officers 'had a very good relationship with their black subordinates. To a black troopie it was very difficult to see his platoon leader as symbol and a part of the white regime'.[142] None of my interviewees expressed

---

[138] Interview with JM.
[139] See, for example, Wood, *War Diaries of Andre Dennison*, p. 17.
[140] The exact number of white RAR officers is not known. The only source I have found that provides a number is Rupiya, 'Demobilization and Integration' (p. 2), which stated that the number of whites in the RAR (most of whom would have been officers) was 100 at the end of the war, which seems somewhat low given that he also states there were 4,000 RAR soldiers. Modern armies would typically have a far higher officer-to-soldier ratio – for instance, the Wehrmacht in World War II, acknowledged as an 'under-officered force', had a ratio of 1:34, whereas the ratio in the US Army during the Vietnam War was 1:5.7 (Sevy, *American Experience in Vietnam*, pp. 91–2). Even allowing for the ratio of the Rhodesian Army to be closer to the World War II–era Wehrmacht than the Vietnam War–era US Army, a more realistic total number of RAR officers by the end of the war would be approximately 210, of whom perhaps 150 would have been white.
[141] See Ginio, *The French Army and Its African Soldiers*, chapter 4 and chapter 5, p. 89, in particular.
[142] Cilliers, *Counter-Insurgency in Rhodesia*, p. 214.

resentment towards their white officers; instead they recounted favourable opinions of their professionalism and described strong relationships with them in terms of kinship and respect. This military culture was, I argue, particular to the RAR and formative to its fighting prowess.

Zoe Flood, who interviewed white ex-RAR officers, noted they 'established with their black comrades perhaps the closest interracial relationships they had ever experienced' and that they 'respected and admired fellow black soldiers, and cited a deep comradeship that developed, irrespective of race'.[143] For Flood, these strong relationships were generated by the intense relationship that developed within 'primary groups' of soldiers, as discussed in Chapter 3. For white officers, these bonds were rooted in the reciprocal 'moral obligation' also discussed earlier. For instance, the commander of A Company, 2RAR was described by a British war correspondent as 'a typical fighting man, utterly devoted to his men, who in turn are immensely loyal to him'.[144]

Flood records a sea change in attitude among regular white officers who served alongside black soldiers during the war, as 'ideas about race bred in a white settler community directly contradicted the experiences shared by black and white'. Many expressed fulsome praise for black troops, one recalling them as: '"pretty exceptional", another that he "would serve with them anytime, anywhere in preference to the white soldier". Such interracial closeness was unusual in civilian society in Rhodesia, suggesting a cohesion amongst small groups of men stemming from training and combat experiences'.[145]

The white officers who served alongside black troops were relatively small in number. As noted earlier, the majority of whites in the army were in the TF or regular units such as the RLI, and did not ordinarily serve with black soldiers. They did not seem to have reformed their racist attitudes and behaviour. For instance, a British officer, part of the Commonwealth Monitoring Force in Zimbabwe from 1979 to early 1980, 'struggled to find words to describe the whites he encountered', noting that they displayed 'incredible antagonism' towards members of the liberation armies and were uniformly 'appalling, with the notable exception' of what he termed the 'white Africans', those white Rhodesian officers in units such as the RAR and Grey's Scouts.[146]

'White African' is a problematic term, for it has often been used to connote a spiritual connection between white settlers and the land and wildlife. This has been argued as a functioning as a 'subtle form of exclusion' of black people, and one invoked after independence by whites

---

[143] Flood, *Brothers-in-Arms?*, pp. 3, 15.   [144] Downie, *Frontline Rhodesia*, 7m:5s.
[145] Flood, *Brothers-in-Arms?*, pp. 3, 17.
[146] Kriger, *Guerrilla Veterans in Post-war Zimbabwe*, p. 105.

who 'gained a sense of belonging, negotiated with the land and circumventing the people'.¹⁴⁷ In the context of the Rhodesian Army, the term had different meaning, which still varied. The arch-'neo-Rhodesian' scribe Peter Baxter, for instance, referred to whites in the Selous Scouts as 'acculturated "white Africans"', meaning they could disguise themselves as black people sufficiently well to infiltrate guerrilla units.¹⁴⁸ Here I use the term 'white African' solely to denote white officers who routinely served alongside black soldiers, generally in the RAR, and explicitly not in the mythic construction of much of the neo-Rhodesian literature.

'White African' officers were often specifically selected by the army for service in the RAR on the basis of their linguistic skills and experiences of working with African labour on farms and sometimes in mines, on the assumption that this would make officer-soldier relationships and communication as frictionless as possible.¹⁴⁹ These relationships were vital for, as King argued, the 'treatment of professional soldiers by their superiors ... can generate a sense of community and wellbeing which reduces discipline problems and increases performance'.¹⁵⁰ Thus cadets familiar with what the army deemed 'African' customs, and life outside the white (sub)urban enclaves, particularly those who could already speak chiShona or isiNdebele, were encouraged to select the RAR as their first choice of unit.¹⁵¹ These skills were among Rhodesian whites, given that 71 per cent lived in the four major cities.¹⁵²

My interviewees described their appreciation of the linguistic skills of their white officers. For instance, DSN told me that many white officers he knew hailed from rural areas, meaning they were bilingual: 'the CO spoke Ndebele ... the rest [of the officers] used to speak Shona because their farms were right in Mashonaland'.¹⁵³ Black soldiers respected white officers' familiarity with the vernacular. CD remembered how during his 'first operation, my platoon lieutenant ... you'd think he was Ndebele, he would speak my language better than myself!'.¹⁵⁴ This fluency enhanced the officer's qualities of leadership: 'that guy, he was on top of things ... he was a tough guy, he never feared anything that one. When you had such people like him as your commander, you really felt "Yes, we have it!" You

---

[147] Hughes, *Whiteness in Zimbabwe*, pp. xviii, 12. See also Harris, 'Writing Home', pp. 103–17.
[148] Baxter, *Selous Scouts*, p. 75. Luise White also discusses this topic extensively. See White, *Fighting and Writing*, chapter 3.
[149] Stewart, 'Rhodesian African Rifles', p. 22. See also White, *Fighting and Writing*, p. 87.
[150] King, *Combat Soldier*, p. 362.
[151] Interviews with anonymous white ex-RAR officers: Harare, 2018; Bulawayo, 2016 and 2017.
[152] Stedman, 'End of the Zimbabwean Civil War', p. 129; Baxter, *Selous Scouts*, p. 32.
[153] Interview with DSN. [154] Interview with CD.

don't fear anything, he is a fearless guy ... When he says "run" you run and you are done, you overcome all the odds'.[155]

In their accounts, my interviewees drew a distinction between their own white officers, of whom they were fond, and whites they encountered from elsewhere in the military, particularly officers from the TF, who they remembered as not only overtly racist towards them, but also less competent, which – as Chapter 2 argued – they generally were.[156]

The skills and training of the RAR's white officers (and officers in other regular units) marked a strong contrast and formed a key element in their relations with black soldiers. In contrast to the TF officers, regulars had passed a rigorous selection board, for which the pass rate was around 25 per cent.[157] Rhodesian officer training was based on Britain's Sandhurst (where the crème of Rhodesian officer cadets had been instructed prior to UDI), and comprised thirteen months of intensive training at the School of Infantry in Gweru, more than double the duration of that of the US Army's Officer Candidate School of the time.[158] During officer training intakes were further pruned. One white ex-RAR officer recalled how his 1976 intake saw only ten of the twenty-eight officer cadets who had commenced training pass out.[159] In the 1977 intake, '650 candidates applied, 178 went to a selection board, and 45 were selected as officer cadets. Of these, 18 actually passed out of training as Second Lieutenants'.[160]

Given this selectiveness and the duration and intensity of training, regular army officers tended to be effective leaders. As JC told me, 'we can say the relationship [between black soldiers and white officers] was too good because they were our mentors'.[161] My interviewees described their respect for the professionalism of their officers, calling to mind how a captured German Army officer during World War II:

once tried to summarize to his interrogator what made the German Army 'work': political indoctrination and 'pep talks' were 'all rot'; whether the men would follow him depended upon the personality of the officer. The leader must be a man who possesses military skill: then his men will know that he is protecting them. He must be a model to his men; he must be an all-powerful, and still benevolent, authority. He must look after his men's needs, and be able to do all the men's duties better than they themselves in training and under combat conditions. The men must also be sure that their officer is duly considerate of their lives: they must know that he does not squander his human resources, that the losses of life which occur under his command will be minimal and justified.[162]

---

[155] Ibid. [156] Interview with TM. [157] Telfer and Fulton, *Chibaya Moyo 2*, pp. 87–9.
[158] Whitaker, *'New Model' Armies of Africa?*, p. 162.
[159] Telfer and Fulton, *Chibaya Moyo 2*, pp. 90–2.
[160] Stewart, 'Rhodesian African Rifles', p. 22. [161] Interview with JC.
[162] Shils and Janowitz, 'Cohesion and Disintegration', p. 297.

Similar professional dynamics – premised upon personal, demonstrable skill and competence – were inherent to the officer-soldier relationship in the RAR in the descriptions of black soldiers. Indeed, one could simply amend this quote, replacing 'German Army' with 'Rhodesian Army', and it would remain an accurate depiction.

These bonds of respect were not one-way ties. My interviewees remembered them as reciprocal. BM effusively elaborated: 'in fact the European officers they were very good, and myself I was liking them like something! The [white officers] were also liking me! They were respecting me very well'.[163] Regular white officers were described as having particular respect for senior black troops. WM told me that, while white subalterns were well trained, they were still often young and inexperienced. He, as a platoon warrant officer (PWO), was not merely the officer's second in command, but also his confidant, teacher, and mentor: 'I think I served under ... four platoon commanders. All were very young [straight] from training, they relied upon my experience. Much of the time I was the one giving orders instead of him giving orders to the platoon so they really relied on me.'

For subalterns, this reliance upon black senior NCOs or PWOs was commonplace.[164] It was widely acknowledged that these experienced troops were capable platoon commanders in their own right, and many would have been already commissioned as officers but for the army's policies.[165] My interviewees often acted as platoon commanders for long periods on operations, such as when there was no subaltern posted to their platoon, or when the platoon commander was away on a course or on leave.[166] As WM explained, respect was very important in allowing these relationships to function: 'they [white officers] were respecting me, I could not find anything bad about them'.[167] This encapsulated the mutuality of the relationships between black soldiers and white officers. Although framed by the hierarchical nature of the army, it was not sufficient for a white officer to merely be professional in the sense of technical competency. Black soldiers expected white officers to form an affective bond with them, a bond they rendered as 'respect'.

Black soldiers often recalled this relationship with fondness. SM told me, 'the white officers in the RAR were very friendly to the African soldiers ... like brothers'.[168] Likewise CD told me of an officer he described as 'like a brother but he was also my OC', and other white officers he knew who 'were never racist. You know, a black guy is injured, he will cry. He would

---

[163] Interview with BM. [164] Stewart, 'Rhodesian African Rifles', pp. 20–1.
[165] Interview, anonymous white ex-RAR officer, Bulawayo, 2016.
[166] Interviews with BM, WM, and HZ. [167] Interview with WM.
[168] Interview with SM.

cry as if [it is] his own son. He would visit this guy mornings, afternoons, evenings. With his family. What more do you ask for [from] a brother?'.[169] Similarly, HZ told me how 'we had a very good relationship with our officers. You could find those who used to be with us, you could go together, drinking in pubs and doing whatever you do. But when they get to duty they do what the duty was. We didn't segregate that 'This is a lower rank' and what-what, no. We worked very well together'.[170]

'White African' officers also contrasted their own relationships with black troops with those of white South Africans, who were known for their hostility towards black troops. For instance, in the late 1970s, white South African paratroopers operated jointly with the RAR on Fireforce operations in the south-east of the Lowveld near Nuanetsi. A white RAR officer described the white South Africans' 'reluctance to serve with African soldiers. We had attached an RAR soldier to each of their sticks and they didn't like it at all, rationalising the concept only in terms of our soldiers having some value as interpreters'.[171] In contrast, the contemporary accounts of white Rhodesian officers demonstrate that many 'white Africans' were devoted to their soldiers and rooted for them to receive promotions, taking great pride in their soldiers' successes.[172]

Indeed, some white RAR officers had long willed for a black soldier to be commissioned. One white ex-RAR officer told me that 'any "real" RAR officer would tell you there were always officers amongst our NCOs' and that it was the prejudice of the army top brass, not that of the RAR, that precluded black soldiers being commissioned earlier.[173] Upon retirement, Lt Col. Rule, CO 1RAR 1951–5, bequeathed his own officer's sword to the first black officer to be commissioned.[174] It is likely he did not expect to have to wait so long, as he predeceased its occurrence; however, his widow did present his sword to Lt Tumbare, former 1RAR regimental sergeant major, in 1977, an occasion much celebrated in the regiment (see Figure 4.1).

These relationships between black and white were unparalleled in civilian society, as recognised in 1975 by the Rhodesian government, which stated that 'a sense of brotherhood and of racial understanding existed [in the military] to a degree probably not repeated elsewhere in Rhodesia'.[175] As King argued of Western regular infantry soldiers, 'the

[169] Interview with CD.   [170] Interview with HZ.
[171] Telfer and Fulton, *Chibaya Moyo*, p. 245.
[172] See, for instance, *Nwoho* (April 1978), pp. 13, 18, 24; Wood, *War Diaries of Andre Dennison*, pp. 190–1.
[173] Interview with anonymous white ex-RAR officer, Bulawayo, 2016.
[174] Binda, *Masodja*, p. 321.
[175] CL, R.C. (S) (75) Cabinet Minutes, 30th Meeting, 6 August 1975, p. 2, as quoted in Kenrick, *Decolonisation, Identity, and Nation in Rhodesia*, p. 195.

basis of comradeship and solidarity has become professionalism itself', and I argue that a similar basis existed within the RAR.[176] The high esteem in which black and white soldiers held each other served to cement micro-level soldierly bonds, described in terms of respect and brotherhood, that diffused the potential for racial tensions, and bolstered wider regimental loyalty among black and white alike. Ironically, it was within these regular army units, the vanguard of the Smith regime's military machine, that many 'white African' officers refuted the racist views they had been socialised into, and where genuine friendships were established between black and white. These relationships were also boosted by combat experiences on active service, as discussed in Chapter 5.

While the memories of the RAR's black soldiers were notable for the lack of overt racism that characterised Rhodesian society as a whole, even within the RAR, racist views remained pervasive. As Flood argued, many 'white African' officers' conception of black soldiers continued to be rooted in a discourse premised upon 'colonial and white settler assumptions about Africa and the African'. Black soldiers were treated with respect and affection, always deemed as loyal allies, but this discourse simultaneously rendered 'the white soldier as dominant in his relationship with fellow black soldiers'. Many white officers held a 'conviction' that it was possible to 'know the Africans' through invocation of racist 'tribal stereotypes' and 'biological and cultural generalisations' which recreated 'the racial hierarchy that was lost in the equality of combat'.[177] This implies a gap between black soldiers' perceptions, or renderings, of the lack of racism among white officers, and the views held by many white officers. It is likely that these divergent perceptions and attitudes existed concurrently.

These deeply embedded racial views notwithstanding, black soldiers in the RAR often believed that they had forged close bonds with their white officers and told stories of solidarity. TM recalled, 'there were some whites who really sympathised with the lot of the black man' and who supported majority rule, 'and some had ways of putting this across'. One officer in particular protested against the army's unequal treatment of black soldiers up the chain of command: 'he had put across his feelings but was not entertained. That is why he left the army. He told the blacks [who] were close to him that he was not happy'.[178] White ex-RAR officers told me of how they forcefully argued with the chain of command as to the unacceptability of

---

[176] King, *Combat Soldier*, p. 421.   [177] Flood, *Brothers-in-Arms?*, p. 32.
[178] Interview with TM.

discriminatory pay and racism in the army, but that they were ignored or forced to be quiet.[179]

As noted, 'white African' officers were also few in number, a drop in the ocean of white society. Although they created a harmonious atmosphere within the RAR, they could not effect change on a wider scale. DSN described this dynamic when I asked him if he thought that black soldiers were treated better than black civilians. He responded matter-of-factly: 'Yeah. Yeah because these [white] people [in the army] were friends, you know? You know, civilians were never friends. In the bush, you could be together with your [white] platoon commanders, share jokes together, because of training. But in civilian life? In civilian life you can't do that.'[180] DSN's point highlights how relationships between blacks and whites within the army were exceptional. While a professional ethos prevailed among men in uniform, black soldiers were still subjected to racism in wider society. Although Rhodesian authorities used the integration of the army in propaganda pieces to convey a narrative that Rhodesian society was non-racist, this was clearly not the case.

While experiences of racism remained prevalent for these soldiers throughout the war, they also described some shifts that they found striking. CD told me that although he knew many of his peers had suffered abuse and discrimination, his own experiences a soldier in the later years of the war had differed:

> We used to have 'Forces Canteens'. They were run by whites, they were dotted everywhere... in the bush, run by women – whites – [where] you get a hamburger, you get coffee... I think they were charitable organisations. They were set up, say, along Gwanda Road... we just drive there, whether you are off duty [or not], you drive there you have your ID card, you get a meal, free of charge... Served by whites, there were no blacks [serving meals] there... There was never discrimination – they never used to look at your and say you were a black or whatever, we get there we are all white and black, we are served, we sit down and eat, we relax for some time then we go. So what other guys really experienced I never did, I never experienced racism anyway by whites, both male and female, everywhere I went they accepted me for who I was.[181]

CD felt that he had come to be valued by whites as a soldier fighting on their behalf. This should not be taken to imply that these whites were suddenly committed to equality, but more likely indicative of how white civilians recognised that the Rhodesian state was now dependent upon black soldiers to avoid military defeat.

---

[179] Interview with anonymous white ex-RAR officers: Bulawayo, 2016 and 2017; Harare, 2018.
[180] Interview with DSN.   [181] Interview with CD.

Conclusion

In this chapter, I have argued that, contrary to Rhodesian propaganda and neo-Rhodesian narratives, the Rhodesian Army was structurally racist, as evidenced by the clear disparities demonstrated in archival documents. I contend that while black soldiers were aware of and loathed these racist disparities, they concurrently felt that the army's provision for them was better than that on offer in civilian life. Thus the social contract between black soldiers and the army itself was not significantly corroded by the army's racism, as black troops felt that they were, relative to civilians, well treated. The Rhodesian government paid close attention to the pay and conditions of black troops and improved them throughout the war in order to maintain the social contract and retain their loyalties.

Despite the Rhodesian Army's increasing dependence upon black troops, and the pressing military need for more soldiers, the racist views of senior army officers and government ministers forestalled the recruitment of more black soldiers. This meant that additional battalions of the RAR were not raised until the war had markedly escalated, and limited the RAR's later capacity for expansion. The prejudice of Lt Gen. Walls in particular hindered the improvement of the service conditions of black troops. Furthermore, the army's reforms of the late 1970s occurred too late to have any significant impact upon the course of the war, but my interviewees noted their symbolic importance and several described to me how they personally benefitted from them. These reforms bolstered the social contract between black soldiers and the army and signified that they were of vital military importance, epitomised above all by the commissioning of black officers.

Lastly, I have argued as to the importance of the RAR's own particular military culture. This was distinctive, characterised by strong relationships built upon comradeship and mutual respect between black soldiers and the small number of white officers. While still premised upon colonial understandings of race, interracial bonds within the RAR were exceptionally strong and played a key role in undergirding the loyalties of black soldiers. These solidarities were further enhanced by the experience of combat.

5 The Impact of the War upon Soldierly Loyalties

Combat and the type of warfare experienced also bolstered the extant loyalties of black Rhodesian soldiers. It is clear from the testimony of black veterans that they felt they had triumphed during their clashes with the liberation forces, and this informed their understanding that they were militarily on top throughout the conflict.

After the mid-1970s, this perception did not match the strategic reality of the situation, as the war escalated quickly with the liberation movements having grown enormously in strength and capability.[1] The RSF 'could not expand fast enough to match the growth of ZANLA and ZIPRA, and were soon outnumbered except at times of total mobilization'.[2]

As early as 1977, the highest command echelon of the Rhodesian war effort assessed that the war was being lost, and in March 1979, Rhodesian intelligence told the government that it assessed the trained strength of ZANLA as 21,000, and of ZIPRA at 20,000[3] – numbers far superior to the Rhodesian Army's 6,000 regular soldiers[4] – and 15,000 reservists.[5] A mid-1979 Rhodesian Army briefing stated that, given its soldiers were outnumbered one to three, 'in classical COIN [counterinsurgency] terms, this is a no-win [war] or rather, a sure lose equation'.[6]

Yet black soldiers' perceptions that they were not losing the war are understandable, for they reflect their unique perspective as elite infantry troops, as this chapter shows. Furthermore, the escalation of the war altered the perception black troops held of the liberation forces. Their exposure to incidents of guerrilla violence against civilians, and the widespread targeting of off-duty soldiers and their families, meant that many came to despise elements of the liberation armies.

---

[1] Mtsi, Nyakudya, and Barnes, 'War in Rhodesia', pp. 141–2.
[2] Wood, 'Countering the Chimurenga', p. 199.
[3] Flower, *Serving Secretly*, pp. 175, 221.
[4] Rupiya, 'Demobilization and Integration', p. 31.
[5] Moorcraft and McLaughlin, *Rhodesian War*, p. 57.
[6] Cilliers, *Counter-Insurgency in Rhodesia*, pp. 239–40.

143

This also served to solidify the notion that the RAR and the wider army were on the 'right side' of the war and that they protecting civilians against the violence of guerrillas. In this manner, their 'regimental loyalties' were boosted, as they came to deem the RAR a more moral actor than guerrilla forces.

As with soldiers' perceptions of the military balance of the war, this reflected the limited perspective of the RAR soldier on the ground, and was not an accurate depiction of the overall situation as other Rhodesian units used wanton violence against civilians and killed thousands. The Rhodesian state carried out a 'draconian' COIN campaign premised upon the use of 'maximum force' against guerrillas (both real and suspected), where 'kill rate' statistics were deemed the key metric of operational success.[7] The overall Rhodesian approach was aptly summarised as 'a counter-guerrilla doctrine rather than a counter-insurgency one' for the primacy it placed upon tactical military successes at the expense of a political strategy.[8]

In rural areas, the latter stages of the war saw the Rhodesian government implement martial law and dawn-to-dusk curfews, collective punishment, 'special' courts, and the forced resettlement of 250,000 people into 'Protected Villages'.[9] While the acts of violence, torture, and murder that guerrilla forces carried out were given ample coverage in the Rhodesian press, Rhodesian atrocities went largely unreported at the time including, inter alia, the use of chemical and biological weapons, the poisoning of food supplies and clothing, and the extensive deployment of Selous Scouts infiltration units, disguised as guerrillas, who killed thousands.[10] However, as a regular infantry unit, the RAR was not involved in these operations – which were conducted by clandestine units such as the CIO, BSAP Special Branch, and Selous Scouts – and very likely did not have knowledge of them.

---

[7] Evans, 'Wretched of the Empire', p. 188.

[8] Preston, 'Stalemate and the Termination of Civil War', p. 72.

[9] For draconian tactics, see Evans, 'Wretched of the Empire', p. 188. For martial law, see Hove, 'War Legacy', p. 198. For collective punishment, see Ellert, *Rhodesian Front War*, pp. 24–6. For special courts, see Weitzer, 'In Search of Regime Security'. For forced resettlement, see Weinrich, 'Strategic Resettlement in Rhodesia'; Kesby, 'Arenas for Control', p. 564; Abbott and Botham, *Modern African Wars*, pp. 15–16, and Ellert, *Rhodesian Front War*, pp. 24–7.

[10] For chemical and biological weapons, see McGregor, 'Containing Violence', pp. 131–5; Martinez, 'History of the Use of Bacteriological and Chemical Agents'; Ellert, *Rhodesian Front War*, pp. 27, 112–13; Moorcraft, 'Rhodesia's War of Independence'; Hove, 'War Legacy', pp. 198–9, Cocks, *Fireforce*, pp. 62–4. For food contamination, see McGregor, 'Containing Violence', and for the Selous Scouts, see Ellert, *Rhodesian Front War*, p. 93; Melson, 'Top Secret War', p. 63; and Preston, 'Stalemate and the Termination of Civil War', p. 72.

The Absence of 'Disloyalty' among Black Rhodesian Troops

Prior to arguing as to how the war fortified black Rhodesian soldiers' loyalties, this chapter contends they were not 'disloyal'. This may seem counter-intuitive, but this approach highlights how the factors that motivated 'disloyalty' among soldiers elsewhere were not prevalent among black soldiers in Rhodesia, which in turn offers us an understanding as to the reasons for their enduring loyalty throughout the war.

I define 'disloyalty' as those major acts of disobedience – desertion, mutiny, refusing to soldier, or the fragging of officers – which comprise an explicit renunciation of the core tenets of soldierly identity and professionalism as outlined in Chapter 3. This definition deliberately omits comparably minor transgressions such as off-duty fighting or the use of marijuana, referred to previously as permissible indiscipline, which while undoubtedly commonplace, have negligible impact upon a unit's combat efficacy.

Perhaps the most obviously comparable instance of disloyalty among African colonial troops took place in late January 1964, when mutinies occurred almost simultaneously across newly independent Uganda, Tanzania, and Kenya among the battalions of the KAR, a colonial *askari* regiment highly similar to the RAR which had fought in the same campaigns during World War II and the Malayan Emergency.

As Parsons argued, the KAR mutinied over the continued presence of British officers and the slow pace of the Africanisation of their regiments, poor pay and conditions, the preferential treatment afforded to those deemed to come from colonially constructed 'martial' ethnic groups, and the lack of respect post-independence governments displayed towards their professional skills and experience.[11] In other words, KAR soldiers were contesting a perceived violation of the contract that bound them to the army and government.

Army mutinies in Africa during the 1960s and 1970s were generally not driven by wartime experiences but were instead, as Maggie Dwyer argued, a tactic marginalised soldiers used to convey their grievances to the government and force improved treatment.[12] The context in Rhodesia differed from these instances for, as argued earlier, the Rhodesian government's dependence upon black soldiers during the war meant it paid assiduous attention to their pay and conditions in order to maintain the social contract. It is likely that the Rhodesian

---

[11] Parsons, *1964 Army Mutinies*, pp. 95–143; Parsons, 'Lanet Incident'.
[12] Dwyer, *Soldiers in Revolt*, pp. 2–3.

Army's reforms forestalled the development of grievances comparable to those that compelled troops in the KAR to mutiny.

Black Rhodesian soldiers' loyalties were all the more remarkable as they experienced a prolonged period of COIN warfare. As argued in Chapter 1, combat requires the highest form of soldierly loyalty, including that troops regularly and willingly expose themselves to mortal danger. In this context, acts of disloyalty not only denude the fighting power of a unit, but also serve to compromise its binding social fabric by rending the all-important bonds of mutual trust. Soldiers fighting in comparable COIN conflicts have sometimes committed such acts. For instance, during the US military's COIN war in Vietnam, fifty-seven officers were murdered and hundreds more were injured by enlisted men under their command in incidents of fragging.[13] During the earlier French COIN war in Indochina, soldiers from west Africa murdered 'at least three French commanders between May 1953 and March 1954'.[14] In contrast, no incidences of fragging by black Rhodesian soldiers were ever recorded, likely a consequence of the strong relationships between officers and soldiers in the RAR.

African soldiers in the French Army were discriminated against by their white officers, deployed 'almost entirely in small, static garrisons' – tedious, low-status, and unrewarding duty, in contrast to the combat troops of the RAR. The Tirailleurs Sénégalais of the French Army were 'the worst led and the worst treated', who 'came to resent their very low pay, their lowest priority for every necessity and reward, and their treatment' by low-quality white NCOs whose 'dull-witted racism did great damage' to their military efficacy, and white officers from the metropole who discriminated against and verbally and physically abused African soldiers.[15] Ginio argued that such racist treatment was a significant factor in the disloyalty of these soldiers. As we have seen, the Rhodesian Army made efforts to sustain the social contract with its soldiers in order to forestall the development of such disaffection. Furthermore, in the RAR, relationships between black and white were instead premised upon mutual respect, and its military culture, as outlined earlier, functioned to maintain soldierly loyalties.

There are, however, two instances described in the literature of RAR troops refusing to soldier during the war. The rarity and nature of these incidents demonstrate a particular aspect of how the RAR's military culture forestalled acts of disloyalty. The first occurred in 1968, when a section of soldiers from 14 Platoon, E Company, 1RAR 'experienced

[13] Lepre, *Fragging*. [14] Ginio, *The French Army and Its African Soldiers*, p. 89.
[15] Windrow, *Last Valley*, pp. 201–2.

multiple failures in the face of the enemy [having] proved reluctant to move under fire and attack', as there had been a breakdown in command and communication, largely caused by the fact that the platoon commander 'had only taken command of his platoon the day before [and] did not know the names of most of his men, nor did they know him'.[16]

As King noted, instances of disloyalty are inevitable in any army, and even among 'today's professional forces' of the Western powers – quite possibly the most expensively and extensively trained soldiers in the history of warfare – there have 'certainly been cases of "combat refusals"' during operations in Iraq and Afghanistan.[17] King's point is not that professional soldiers are inured against fear, although their training and socialisation mean that such incidences are far more uncommon.

He argues that, unlike in the non-professional citizen armies of the twentieth century, in which 'even small panics recurrently caused' catastrophe as fear and disorder spread like a contagion among the ranks, in professional forces, the quantity and quality of training mean that indiscipline and fear are contained, for 'the cowardice or non-performance of a single soldier is simply that. The other soldiers are so tightly bound to the performance of their drills by their training that they are far less prone to panic as a group'.[18] This was the case with the RAR, as the 'refusal to soldier' of these six troops in 1968 did not spread to the rest of E Company. Furthermore, a subsequent inquiry by the commanding officer established the cause of the failings and swiftly implemented training and procedures to rectify them. In this manner, the army's professional ethos was self-reinforcing.

The second instance of disloyalty occurred in 1973, when six RAR soldiers refused to 'participate in cross-border raids', for which they were sentenced to prison sentences of twenty-five years' duration.[19] The army's reaction was harsh, and my interviewees recalled that these punitive sentences seemed intended as deterrents to others.[20] As argued earlier, such punishments were highly rare, for it was generally not the threat of sanction that dissuaded soldiers from disloyal acts: the real deterrent was the shame of violating professional norms and letting down their comrades. These two instances of disloyalty are notable for how exceptional they are as – with the exception of one further anecdote – in the rest of my interviewees' testimony, and within the vast literature on the war, no other such instances are noted.

---

[16] Stewart, 'Rhodesian African Rifles', p. 39.   [17] King, *Combat Soldier*, p. 368.
[18] Ibid.
[19] Maxey, *Fight for Zimbabwe*, p. 34; Stapleton, *African Police and Soldiers*, pp. 180–1.
[20] Interview with MSW.

A clear demonstration of how exceptional incidences of disloyalty were among black Rhodesian soldiers is their low level of desertion, which itself is historically the most commonplace form of disloyalty among troops at war. As documented since at least the eighteenth century, disobedient troops will most frequently desert in order to escape punishment, rather than refuse to soldier or attack their officers, which would immediately incur the wrath of military authorities.[21] Scholars estimate that, during the American Civil War, some 200,000 Union and 104,000 Confederate soldiers deserted.[22] During World War II, 150,000 American and British troops deserted from the European theatre alone,[23] and in that same conflict, Soviet forces 'recorded 2,846,000 men and women as deserters and draft dodgers'.[24] In the recent Syrian Civil War, the number of deserters from the Syrian military are estimated at between 50,000 to 100,000: 'up to one-third of pre-war active military personnel'.[25]

During the French *sale guerre* against the Vietminh, colonial troops provided three quarters of the soldiers of the Far East Expeditionary Corps, including 30,000 soldiers from north Africa and 18,000 from west Africa.[26] In the major battle of the war, Dien Bien Phu (March–April 1954), 'a large number' of colonial soldiers, estimated at between 2,000 and 3,000,[27] 'burrowed themselves in holes in the banks of the little river which traversed the *enceinte* of the fortress and pilfered what they needed to live from the loads parachuted inside the perimeter each night, sometimes fighting the combatants for shares. At the end of the siege they were believed to have outnumbered the active garrison'.[28]

These acts of 'internal desertion' were clear instances of disloyalty. Not only did these troops abandon their comrades, but they also cannibalised the supplies meant for the remaining forces.[29] It is clear that the loyalties of these deserters had been frayed by their poor equipment, battlefield

---

[21] Gilbert, 'Why Men Deserted from the Eighteenth-Century British Army'; Garnham, 'Military Desertion and Deserters in Eighteenth-Century Ireland'.
[22] Lonn, *Desertion during the Civil War*, p. 226.   [23] Glass, *Deserters*.
[24] Reese, 'Motivations to Serve', pp. 269–70.
[25] Albrecht and Koehler, 'Going on the Run', p. 180.
[26] See Windrow, *Last Valley*, chapter 5, and in particular page 170.
[27] Windrow, *Last Valley*, pp. 481–3. This number certainly included 'a few white soldiers' from metropolitan France and likely a number of white Foreign Legion troops too. As Ginio argues (*The French Army and Its African Soldiers*, pp. 100–1), the exact number of African deserters is difficult to establish. Desertions had also occurred prior to the debacle of Dien Bien Phu. For instance, 'many Laotian troops' deserted in April 1953 after the French officer General Salan ordered the garrison of Sam Neua abandoned (Windrow, *Last Valley*, p. 126). See also Roy, *Battle of Dienbienphu*, p. 229.
[28] Keegan, *Face of Battle*, p. 311.
[29] These 'internal deserters' were a minority, albeit a substantial one, and it should be noted that most French colonial troops 'fought to the end' (Windrow, *Last Valley*, p. 692).

reverses, and the high numbers of casualties.[30] All of these are factors that, as I will show in this chapter, did not apply to black Rhodesian troops.

High rates of desertion are considered by scholars as signifying the dissolution of soldierly loyalty. As Branislav Slantchev argued, rates of desertion are highly indicative of discontent among soldiers.[31] Shils and Janowitz argued that 'army units with a high degree of primary group integrity suffered little from desertions or from individually contrived surrenders'.[32] Peter Bearman argued that 'desertion has historically been inversely related to company/unit solidarity'.[33] Likewise, Theodore McLauchlin contended that 'characteristics of military units impinge on the individual. Even a relatively committed combatant may desert if he or she does not trust his or her fellow soldiers; even a lukewarm combatant might keep fighting given enough pressure from a generally unified military unit'.[34] Building upon this scholarly consensus, I argue that the low rates of desertion among black Rhodesian soldiers during the war are indicative of high levels of soldierly loyalty.

It seems that desertions among black Rhodesian soldiers were vanishingly rare. The former CO of 1RAR told Flood that there 'would never have been any trouble from the African troops' as 'they were very good'; likewise, the former second in command of 2RAR stated that he 'never ever encountered any situations where he felt that [African soldiers] were being disloyal'.[35] My interviewees also stated that desertion was highly rare. The only such incident BM was aware of occurred during 1978, when his platoon had crossed the Zambezi and were fighting in Zambia: '[We were] attacked by ZIPRA people ... The two soldiers ran away from Zambia to Zambezi river [because] they were scared. Because we were attacked by bazooka, everything, mortar fire, everything. But we had a platoon commander from America who didn't ran away. But only [those] two, they ran away and left their guns behind.'[36]

In this instance, the two soldiers had fled as a result of battlefield terror, rather than making a premeditated decision to commit a disloyal act. They had not expected the remainder of their platoon to survive the fierce ZIPRA attack on the RAR position and, after their panic and fear had subsided, the deserters returned to their barracks in Rhodesia.

---

[30] Ginio, *The French Army and Its African Soldiers*, pp. 88–9; Windrow, *Last Valley*, pp. 178–9.
[31] Slantchev, *Military Threats*, pp. 69, 71.
[32] Shils and Janowitz, 'Cohesion and Disintegration', p. 285.
[33] Bearman, 'Desertion As Localism', p. 323.
[34] McLauchlin, 'Desertion and Collective Action in Civil Wars', p. 669.
[35] Flood, *Brothers-in-Arms?*, p. 23.   [36] Interview with BM.

BM recalled that, after some time, his platoon managed to fight their way out: 'there is not one who got shot that day, all of us we went back home, no problem'. BM and his comrades arrived back at their barracks to find the two deserters there, to mutual astonishment. The deserters were dealt with harshly. BM described them, with some relish, as being 'squashed' for 'doing rubbish ... they went for court-martial. The two of them [were given] twenty-five years. They were supposed to be hanged'.[37] BM was evidently pleased that these deserters had been severely punished.

BM's reaction was not schadenfreude, but reflected how soldiers viewed violations of their professional normative ethos as taboo. Juridical sanctions do, to an extent, dissuade soldiers from disloyal acts, and my interviewees were aware of the strict punishment that desertion incurred.[38] However, the stigma against violating soldierly ethics can be more powerful than formal punishment. As King argued, punishments such as that detailed by BM are rarely required, for the 'prime motivating and disciplining factor in combat is that [soldiers] will be respected by their peers for upholding professional standards'.[39] This understanding of desertion as a cardinal sin, a violation of the professional ethos under which soldiers were mutually dependent, explains the depth of BM's contempt for these deserters.

DC, who often acted as a military prosecutor in Mashonaland West during the war and partook in many courts-martial, also told me that desertions were rare and 'there were not many'.[40] He told me that those which did occur did not stem from combat or a breakdown of discipline within a unit, nor were there any defections, for 'soldiers did not actually desert to go and join the liberation army'. Instead, in DC's experience, deserters were generally those who had committed serious criminal acts, such as robbery or rape, and fled to evade the authorities:

> People deserted when they had committed a certain crime and they know 'this is not going to take me far' and they just [*claps*] go. Sometimes they went to Mozambique just to work in the street, sometimes they went to South Africa, sometimes they just roamed around here in the [rural] districts. Ah, but they were not very many, but they used to happen.[41]

Desertions were, then, not prevalent among black soldiers, which is indicative of a high level of soldierly loyalty. That the professionalism and regimental loyalties of these troops ensured the integrity of the primary group offers a convincing explanation as to these low rates of

---

[37] Ibid. [38] Interview with MSW. [39] King, *Combat Soldier*, p. 368.
[40] Interview with DC. [41] Ibid.

desertion. However, other factors were important too in explaining why black soldiers remained so loyal.

To illustrate this, I incorporate the typology advanced by Holger Albrecht and Kevin Koehler as to why soldiers do or do not desert.[42] Based upon fieldwork with deserters from the Syrian army during the recent civil war, they argue that motives can be broken down into two categories: individual dispositions, or 'push' factors, and intersubjective opportunities, which they refer to as 'pull' factors.

'Push' factors are those which generate disaffection in the first instance. These include the breakdown of the primary group or a dearth of morale, a lack of faith in the efficacy of the army and thus prospects of victory, fear of death in combat or returning to combat, 'moral grievances' as to the ethics of the war, and instances of persecution by military authorities.[43] 'Push' factors are compounded by 'pull' factors, such as being able to desert to safe hinterland areas where it is unlikely military authorities can trace deserters, and the existence of strong ties to networks of sympathisers. These 'pull' factors often determine 'whether soldiers would translate disaffection into desertion'.[44] Starting with 'push' factors and thereafter addressing 'pull' factors, here I argue as to why these factors did not exist or were not prevalent among black Rhodesian soldiers.

Black Soldiers' Faith in Their Military Prowess

Writing in 1975, Kees Maxey, a scholar at Leeds University, predicted that 'African supporters of the regime, including the RAR, will have little enthusiasm for fighting an obviously losing battle. The Europeans in the security forces, especially the national servicemen, and the members of the Territorial Force, will also have little incentive.'[45] The latter part of this forecast was accurate – white morale and combat efficacy plummeted, as discussed later – but the initial part proved utterly incorrect.

My point here is not to use hindsight to criticise Maxey's almost half-century-old prediction, but instead to highlight that the reason *why* it proved so wide of the mark is of utmost interest in understanding an aspect of the loyalty of black Rhodesian troops. Contrary to Maxey's

---

[42] Albrecht and Koehler, 'Going on the Run'.
[43] Ibid. For a case study of desertion in today's ZNA caused by political persecution, see Maringira, 'Politics, Privileges, and Loyalty'; for accounts of the moral grievances of Soviet troops during the Soviet-Afghan War, see Borovik, *Hidden War*.
[44] Koehler, Ohl, and Albrecht, 'From Disaffection to Desertion', p. 453. See also Clark, *Soviet Military Power in a Changing World*, chapter 8, for an outline of how the dissolution of the Soviet Union facilitated the mass desertion of disaffected troops.
[45] Maxey, *Fight for Zimbabwe*, p. 172.

expectation, the 'push' factor of a lack of faith in the fighting prowess and prospects of the army was simply not present among black soldiers.

Indeed, as combat intensified, their loyalties were in fact strengthened, and their combat experiences informed a firm belief that they were militarily stronger than the guerrilla forces and that they were winning the war. Thus they did not think that the war was 'an obviously losing battle', and my interviewees, such as SM, told me that even as the war escalated to its highest pitch in 1979 they still felt that the conflict would continue for an indeterminate period of time.[46] JM told me, 'we never thought [the liberation forces would win]. We thought we were going to win, that it was going to go on forever!'.[47]

A comparable trend was apparent in Algeria, where desertion rates among colonial troops declined 'as the tide of the military balance swung in favour of the French'.[48] This improvement in French military performance particularly boosted the morale of regular soldiers, which 'strengthened the longer hostilities continued'.[49] The military proficiency and battlefield success of the RAR functioned to boost their morale in a comparable manner. My interviewees attributed their combat performance to their high level of military training and proficiency – their professionalism – and also maintained that they were not defeated militarily during the war, as discussed later.

It is important to understand the nature of combat black soldiers experienced if we are to grasp why they felt they were winning. Although the general experience of the war was one in which violence was only experienced on a widespread scale after the escalation of the war in the mid-1970s, for the RAR, the war had been 'hot' since 1966.

As the dominant component of a small army, black soldiers were continually tasked to patrol areas of suspected guerrilla presence, and frequently directly deployed in response to guerrilla sightings. Thus even during the 'phony war' of the late 1960s and early 1970s, when violence simmered at a relatively low level throughout Rhodesia as a whole, black soldiers were constantly deployed at the sharp end where conflict occurred and experienced a high proportion of the war's combat.

Lt Col. Shute, 1RAR CO, wrote in 1976 that the regiment considered the war to have been ongoing for a decade, for it first suffered combat fatalities in 1966. For Shute, this meant that 'all the African soldiers with over ten years' service have been continually on operations, except for leave, R&R and courses, for ten years ... it goes without saying that they

---

[46] Interview with SM.   [47] Interview with JM.
[48] Gortzak, 'Using Indigenous Forces', pp. 318–19.
[49] Alexander, Evans, and Keiger, 'The "War without a Name"', pp. 26–7.

have given ten years of damned fine soldiering'.[50] Thus the experience of RAR soldiers differed from that of many other protagonists in the war. My interviewees attested as to its relentless pace. GM recalled that it was 'two months out' on deployment, then back for some R&R, before swift redeployment, for years at a time.[51] DSN recalled once having to deploy eight times consecutively to the 'hot' area of the Mozambican border, which often involved having to operate across the border too, with just fourteen days of R&R between each deployment, itself often truncated.[52]

During this period, black soldiers experienced hardly any battlefield defeats. This can be quantified by examining how the RAR experienced few casualties relative to other comparable wars. Losses for 1RAR, 2RAR, Depot RAR, and the Independent Companies were approximately 200 men killed in action throughout the war.[53] In contrast, during Algeria's War of Independence, '1,345 regular Muslim servicemen were killed' fighting the French Army.[54] When allowing for the marked increase in intensity of the war in the late 1970s, a comparison with the war in Vietnam is also apt: those US forces killed in action from the US Army alone numbered 38,224, the vast majority occurring during that conflict's peak years (1966–70).[55] During the peak years of Zimbabwe's War (1975–9), 57 soldiers from 1RAR and 52 soldiers from 2RAR were killed in action.[56] This is not to say that being a Rhodesian soldier was not dangerous, but it does suggest that the Rhodesian Army suffered few casualties relative to other comparable wars, and it infers a strong RAR military capability vis-à-vis its battlefield adversaries.

My interviewees resoundingly perceived themselves as a militarily potent group, members of a cohort whose loyalties were strong. This accords with the aforementioned scholarly consensus that high levels of intergroup solidarity beget further loyalty and enhanced soldierly performance. In essence, the RAR's adherence to professionalism and the instillation of regimental loyalties created a virtuous cycle wherein black soldiers' confidence in their comrades and pride in their regiment served to further motivate them to strive for the best military performance possible.

---

[50] 'Editorial', *Nwoho* (April 1978), p. 8.   [51] Interview with GM.
[52] Interview with DSN.
[53] There are no official figures that I am aware of; the RAA may have authoritative numbers, however. Binda's RAR book, which was researched with RAA access, lists 191 RAR servicemen killed in action in its Roll of Honour appendices (Binda, *Masodja*, pp. 404–7). Although these figures contain names, dates, and service numbers – indicative of compilation from official data – no original source is cited, nor are scans or excerpts provided.
[54] Alexander et al., 'The "War without a Name"', p. 5.
[55] Data extracted from the US National Archives, 'Vietnam Conflict Extract Data File', April 2008. https://catalog.archives.gov/id/2240992 [Accessed March 2020].
[56] Binda, *Masodja*, pp. 405–6.

As argued earlier, RAR soldiers were well trained and their professionalism and combat experience were important to their tactical military successes during the war. However, this strong performance was not solely derived from these factors, as they also enjoyed a considerable military advantage over the liberation forces in that the Rhodesian Air Force (RhAF) controlled the country's airspace. I discuss in detail later how Rhodesian control of the skies had particular implications for the nature of fighting during the war.

For now, it is sufficient to state that the liberation forces did not deploy anti-air defences on a large scale within Rhodesia, meaning that the RSF could conduct aerial surveillance and bombardment and possessed the ability to rapidly ferry troops by air throughout the country. This also meant the army could quickly and easily reinforce troops on the ground in contact. Consequently, guerrilla units that engaged in combat or that presented themselves outside cover for a prolonged period risked being attacked by Rhodesian aircraft, whereas Rhodesian forces were never attacked from the sky.

Thus, while my interviewees disparaged guerrilla forces for how often they 'ran away', for them to not do so would have been suicidal in most instances. Commanders in modern professional militaries are taught to seek three-to-one numerical superiority before attacking an enemy, as a ratio lower than this greatly reduces the chances for success. The liberation armies knew from painful experience of the efficiency of the RhAF and its Fireforce, discussed later, which could rapidly drop soldiers directly into ongoing combat. This markedly altered relative combat strengths in any battle and meant that RAR troops' combat experiences should be taken in context: not only were they were a well-trained and experienced force, but they could also rely on complete air superiority and rapid reinforcement to ensure they outnumbered and outgunned any guerrilla units they encountered.

As David Caute argued, the Rhodesian obsession with the ratios of guerrillas killed to RSF personnel glossed over the asymmetric nature of the war: 'How would the white commandos have fared against an enemy enjoying total dominance of the sky, exclusive possession of the deadly air strike; an enemy able to ferry out its wounded by helicopter rather than drag bleeding shattered limbs through hundreds of miles of bush?'[57] This is not to say that black soldiers were not brave, or that they could rely on aerial reinforcement at all times, or that they were never outnumbered. But it should be understood that, in the main, black soldiers held

---

[57] Caute, *Under the Skin*, p. 48.

a decisive advantage in training, equipment, weaponry, reinforcements, and medical provision over their foes in the guerrilla forces.

A secondary effect of the Rhodesian dominance of the air is that guerrilla units infiltrating the country had to be highly careful not to be spotted, so as to avoid aircraft being dispatched to their location. This meant that they often travelled within the rural areas incognito and thus could not carry large amount of ammunition or heavy weapons. Contrastingly, an RAR platoon would deploy with at least three machine guns and could often call upon immediate support from its company's mortars.

Consequently it would frequently be suicidal for lightly armed guerrilla units to directly engage regular units such as the RAR. TM told me, 'the moment [guerrillas] heard that the RAR was in the area, they tried by all means to avoid us'.[58] Instead, guerrilla operations typically comprised small-scale attacks on settler outposts, vital infrastructure, and the isolated elements of the security forces, which relied upon the element of surprise and the ability of the guerrillas to swiftly exfiltrate themselves before reinforcements could arrive.[59] Within the country, there were no large-scale battles and there was no Rhodesian equivalent to Dien Bien Phu, or even the Battle of Algiers.

Fighting largely occurred in the marches, with very little combat in the urban and suburban areas of the country, for guerrillas relied upon the concealment these remote regions offered and their low RSF presence. As the ZANLA commander Josiah Tongogara described, the topography of the forest-covered, rugged highlands provided ample cover, meaning the east and north-east of the country were ideal for guerrillas infiltrating the border.[60] Weather also dictated when much of the fighting would occur: the rainy season spanning November through until March produced dense foliage that offered cover from aircraft to guerrilla fighters. Likewise, guerrillas often opted to engage in combat at dawn, dusk, or during the night in order to reduce their vulnerability to Rhodesian aircraft.[61]

This meant that black soldiers' primary experience of fighting during the war was that of bush COIN warfare, which involved them attempting to interdict guerrilla units that often sought to avoid the RAR when possible. Combat occurred during 'meeting engagements', when they

---

[58] Interview with TM.
[59] Such tactics were common to liberation movements across Africa. See Reid, *Warfare*, p. 166.
[60] Pandya, *Mao Tse-tung and Chimurenga*, pp. 59–61.
[61] Interview with FM, ZIPRA soldier 1975–9, policeman in the ZRP, 1980–2009, Bulawayo, 2017.

were deployed in response to reported guerrilla sightings, or had simply chanced upon a guerrilla unit.[62] This meant that fighting was often confusing and chaotic, occurring at close quarters, in poor visibility, and among ample cover.

In the bush, being caught unawares could make the difference between winning a firefight or death, as the first of the belligerents to get eyes on their enemy would gain the upper hand. Combatants on both sides placed enormous emphasis upon being able to detect the enemy. As King argued, these seemingly uncomplicated aspects of soldiering are vital, including the ability to move at night without making noise, and such 'apparently very simple drills' are in fact crucial.[63] CD emphasised how important these skills were during combat in the bush, where stealth and surprise were supreme.[64]

A key reason for this was that guerrillas relied upon a network of intelligence provided by people in the rural areas, particularly *mujibas* (young scouts), to gauge the strength of Rhodesian forces when deciding whether to engage them or withdraw, as WR, an officer from the small 'Coloured' community, told me.[65] For my interviewees, this was a key part of their professional toolkit. The ability to glean information from a seemingly normal vista could make the difference between pre-empting a guerrilla attack and being surprised in an ambush.

My interviewees did recall how, on occasion, they were let down by peers acting unprofessionally. JM remembered how members of his platoon crossing a river had done so in a noisy fashion, and nearby guerrilla

---

[62] See Preston, 'Stalemate and the Termination of Civil War', pp. 67–9, for a review of the literature on the nature of the fighting.
[63] King, *Combat Soldier*, p. 275.   [64] Interview with CD.
[65] The 'Coloured' community were a small group, perhaps only 15,000 strong in 1975 (R.C. (S) (75) 24, 'Cabinet Committee on Decentralisation', 14 February 1975), who 'either did not fit easily into the principal "races" [themselves created by racist colonial discourses that "produced a taxonomy predicated on presumptions of racial purity and fears of transgressed racial boundaries"], or who were the children of inter-racial relationships' (Seirlis, 'Undoing the United Front?', p. 73). 'Coloured' men were conscripted as whites were, although only into specific units allocated unglamorous guarding and transport duties. Rensburg was the first 'coloured' person to join the regular army and also the first to secure an officer's commission. The army initially refused Rensburg's application to become an officer, in accordance with its long-standing racist policies which, while illegal, had never been challenged. The army's refusal letter explicitly outlined the racist logic behind this decision. Rensburg noted that 'they put it in writing, so I had proof', and took the letter to Defence Minister Roger Hawkins, who was also from Shurugwi. Hawkins then forced the army to accept him for regular officer training. I asked Rensburg if he thought Hawkins was a reformer, and he replied that he thought it was more the fact that Hawkins had known him since he was a baby, and that 'I don't think there was much reform for other people he would have allowed, but he did make me the first; he did set a precedent.'

forces had 'heard them coming from behind', which placed them in danger.⁶⁶ These 'unprofessional' soldiers were held in the highest contempt by their peers and quickly forced to improve their skills for, as noted earlier, the fear of being ostracised in this manner and the attendant shame in being deemed unprofessional were highly powerful motivating factors.

When operating in the bush, being forewarned of guerrillas was key for RAR soldiers. As noted earlier, they overwhelmingly hailed from the rural areas and were very familiar with what sorts of behaviour accorded with the everyday, and what was out of place. WR told me how he had grown up in the rural environs near Shurugwi (colonial name Selukwe), meaning that sometimes 'just by the manoeuvres of the locals' he could determine, with a high degree of accuracy, that 'enemy are near'.⁶⁷ Furthermore, what one person unfamiliar with the rhythm and pitch of rural life would deem quotidian could in fact have significant implications:

> I understood the rural environment ... To give an example, when the freedom fighters approached the village, they looked for food to eat. So I identified that whenever you saw the three-legged pot they cooked in, it was a good sign that the enemy were nearby. And all I did was concentrate on following where the pot went in and that led me to where the enemy were. And also, I noticed that whenever they started calling the chickens to cook – you know, the rural people are very restricted in their cooking and killing of chickens – so that was another sign; if you saw them taking maize and calling the chickens around to catch them, that was another sign. So you follow the chicken into the pot, and from the pot, wherever it went, you knew you definitely had contact.⁶⁸

Seemingly small details sometimes had key military importance. Black soldiers were familiar with the rural environment and the vernacular, and the Rhodesian authorities placed great value on this.⁶⁹ Black troops' ability to detect guerrilla forces gave them a key combat advantage in the bush, which informed their perception that they were militarily on top during the war.⁷⁰

Observing signs of guerrilla activity was formalised by the Rhodesian Army's creation of a school, the notorious Wafa Wafa, to train troops in combat tracking.⁷¹ This was the practice of observing, in forensic detail, disturbances in the bush – such as trampled grass, remnants of food,

---

⁶⁶ Interview with JM.   ⁶⁷ Interview with WR.   ⁶⁸ Ibid.
⁶⁹ Maxey, *Fight for Zimbabwe*, p. 33. See also White, *Fighting and Writing*, p. 77.
⁷⁰ Most white units were not as proficient because, despite official settler-farmer mythologizing, most Rhodesian whites – 71 per cent – were urbanites living in the four major cities and were unfamiliar with rural areas. See Stedman, 'End of the Zimbabwean Civil War', p. 129.
⁷¹ As noted earlier, Wafara Wasa means 'if you die, you die'. Wafa Wafa was used extensively by the Selous Scouts, and remains in use today as an elite ZNA camp where One Commando Regiment (the Zimbabwean successor of the RLI) trains, its notorious

smells or smears of foodstuffs or bodily fluids, snapped twigs and branches, and footprints in the ground – that gave an indication of enemy presence. Such signs were referred to as spoor.

Experienced and proficient trackers, known as 'sparrows' in the Rhodesian Army, could derive a great deal of information from even small signs of spoor, and could give a good indication of the approximate strength of the enemy unit, whether any of their number were wounded, and the type of equipment they were carrying. In a war often fought among dense foliage where an adversary might not be glimpsed until he was within fifteen or twenty metres, such information was crucial.

Black soldiers were generally the best trackers in the army, owing to their familiarity with the rural environment.[72] BM recalled that, to him, military tracking was merely an extension of the skills he had learned as a young boy, when he was required to 'look after the cattle in the rural areas' and sometimes to locate and return cattle that had strayed, and he told me that he was one of the best trackers in the RAR.[73] This was not bluster: an officer reminisced that he 'honestly believed him capable of following spoor on water'. On operations, BM would patrol at the head of his four-man stick as they moved through the bush, seeking out spoor and following it to pursue enemy forces. This was an intimidating prospect, as being at the tip of the spear rendered him the first target that any guerrillas lying in wait would see, and thus he was the most likely to be shot at in any ambush. At first, BM 'was afraid, but as time goes I was not ... I went to the war, I never give up'. BM was evidently highly proud of both his bravery and his proficiency in tracking, which went hand in hand. This lent itself to a gung-ho, macho approach to combat patrols: 'I was tracking very well, once I get the spoor we used to go straight to the enemy position and we made a contact. No come back, go forward!'.[74]

Thus the proficiency of RAR soldiers in tracking bolstered their confidence while on operations. It gave them a sense that they had foreknowledge of their enemy's movements and that this would be decisive for, as argued earlier, the first-mover advantage was key in bush warfare. BM told me that throughout more than a decade of continuous wartime service, much of it as a tracker, he always felt he knew where the enemy were, and as a result 'none of my troop were killed' in contacts with guerrilla forces.[75]

---

reputation intact. See Kawadza, 'ZNA Sticks to Its Guns on Training'; Manzongo, 'Wafa Wafa; Manzongo, 'Zimbabwe Army Commandos Graduation'.

[72] The army's best tracker, a 1970s magazine article claimed, was a black Selous Scout. See Melson, *Fighting for Time*, p. 43.
[73] Interview with BM.   [74] Ibid.   [75] Ibid.

Tracking was only the precursor to fighting. In combat, my interviewees felt that their professional skills, instilled through training, gave them a decisive advantage over guerrilla forces. This was typified by their accounts of their marksmanship. In particular, many black soldiers became renowned for their proficiency with the FN Mitrailleuse d'Appui Général (MAG), the army's Belgian-manufactured 7.62-millimetre general purpose machine gun. This was a potent weapon, and until late in the war, many guerrilla units had no response to the powerful fire it could lay down. Many RAR soldiers could fire the MAG from the shoulder. CD told me:

[M]y role, I was a gunner. That's the MAG, the machine gun. I loved that MAG. So I was a gunner ... we were young guys; we would go to the gym. I would hold the gun with one hand! We would go to the gym, work out, we sort of created a, a kind of, our own guys. Our own tough guys ... So you were actually prepared to carry these heavy guns ... I enjoyed being a gunner. I loved that. [I was picked to be a machine gunner] not because I was strong. I was kind of a marksman. I was kind of, you know, you throw a coin, I will hit it. So the gunner would hit anything with the gun. I would've hit anything with the gun.[76]

CD's marksmanship was refined through such training. This was essential to become proficient, for firing a such a weapon from the shoulder is highly difficult, as the MAG is usually deployed upon its bipod, owing to its weight (approximately 12 kilograms unloaded), and the recoil generated by discharging its powerful round, which exits the muzzle at a velocity of 842 metres per second.

Not only could black soldiers manipulate the machine gun in this way, but they could do so with fearsome accuracy. WR told me:

[The RAR machine gunners in my platoon] could take a whole band of fifty rounds that were on a belt and fire singly, one round at a time; that's how good they were. You know you even *touch* the thing [trigger], it's on permanent automatic, you know you've used all your [ammunition, as the weapon has a rate of fire of over ten rounds discharged per second]. But these guys could use it as a rifle.[77]

Andre Dennison, a former British special forces officer who commanded A Company, 2RAR, described in glowing terms how an RAR soldier, Lance Corporal Mawire, single-handedly killed seven guerrillas with his MAG and how 'one was captured unhurt' after Mawire had 'intimidated him with a burst of fire around his feet and then shot his rifle out of his hands'.[78]

---

[76] Interview with CD.   [77] Interview with WR.
[78] Wood, *War Diaries of Andre Dennison*, p. 211.

WR recounted to me how, as a trepidatious young RAR lieutenant on his first operation in 1978, he was ordered to advance towards a known guerrilla position in a sweep line formation. He recalled how he was astounded by the marksmanship of his black soldiers:

> As I start moving, next minute my machine gunner, he opens up. I had two machine gunners in my stick being the commander [so he could direct their fire to where his platoon most needed it]. One of the gunners opens up [*makes sound of a short machine gun burst*] and a few feet away the enemy falls down. I think, 'Oh, shit, I didn't see that.' I didn't see [the enemy at all]. You know, it's so difficult; you have to train your eye not to look for movement, because your eyes, you know – urban wise there's cars moving, people moving, so that's why your eyes [are] initially [not] trained. But you have to look through the bush, pick out the green sock, the red piece of cloth; that is how you pick up [guerrillas]. Because these guys [guerrillas] are hiding, waiting for you to walk. So I thought, 'Oh, shit, that's my channel' – we were walking channels, so he's shooting somebody in my channel. We walk again, a few minutes [*makes sound of a short machine gun burst*] – my second machine gunner, he shoots, and the guy tumbles out of the bush. I thought, 'Oh, shit, I never saw that as well!' and it's again in my lane. So the first contact, I don't lie; I didn't see any [enemy].[79]

The presence of such proficient machine gunners served a dual purpose in combat. Not only did it boost their fellow soldiers' morale immeasurably, knowing that they had such powerful and accurate firepower supporting them, but it also intimidated the RAR's opponents. WR recalled that the MAG's powerful rounds could cut smaller trees down, shredding the cover used by guerrilla fighters.[80] As JC recounted, even the noise that the MAG made when fired 'frightened a lot of people'.[81] So effective were the RAR's machine gunners that, according to WR, when the guerrillas were given information as to the location of the RAR by *mujibas*, they 'always asked, "how many guns that had legs?", because the MAG had a bipod. And if they were told that they were there, they kept away'.[82]

Later in the war, as fighting intensified, the RAR increasingly deployed a large number of MAGs. One white RAR officer, in his account of operations in Beitbridge during 1978, wrote how 'to this day the firepower this particular 2RAR callsign led by WOII Dick Mandava had amazes me', as it was a fifteen-strong group of RAR paratroopers, of whom fourteen carried MAGs.[83] Such a heavy concentration of machine guns is highly unusual in COIN warfare and is indicative of how the Rhodesian Army was overstretched and reliant upon the use of overwhelming firepower to compensate for its shortage of soldiers.

---

[79] Interview with WR.   [80] Ibid.   [81] Interview with JC.   [82] Interview with WR.
[83] Telfer and Fulton, *Chibaya Moyo 2*, p. 253.

The disparity in firepower meant that guerrilla units typically tried to avoid fixed combat with regular army units unless left with no other resort. Instead, guerrilla forces sought to use the element of surprise and frequently carried out ambushes or shock attacks that enabled them to swiftly attack and withdraw before Rhodesian reinforcements could arrive. The most opportune areas for the guerrillas to mount these attacks were those that offered them ample cover to conceal their ambush site and post-contact withdrawal. Typical sites included roads flanked by dense bush, which meant that Rhodesian military vehicles could be safely observed, as SJM told me.[84] The vehicle would then be disabled with an RPG or a mine, rendering it a static target for follow-up small-arms fire.

JM described how guerrilla units would attempt to entice Rhodesian soldiers into ambushes in predesignated killing zones. He recalled how during 1972, he was on patrol between the Zambezi River and Musengezi Mission in the north-east of the country as part of D Company, 1RAR. Local civilians approached his patrol at night, telling them that 'enemies were nearby', and encouraged them to cross the river; however 'it was dangerous, because to cross the Musengezi River to where they were, they would kill us in the water – for sure'. Instead, his unit waited until sunrise and used trackers to follow the spoor of the guerrilla unit, who were lying in wait for them.

In fact they did us an ambush. They heard that we were coming behind. They are cutting, so that one of a dog's leg [a form of ambush that uses a sudden deviation in route to deceive a pursuing enemy into walking adjacent to an ambush position]. We went there, then the first round [fired by the guerrillas], hit our platoon commander, Henry Huddle. Then they ran away.[85]

Although spending long periods patrolling in the bush, never knowing when one might be attacked, was nerve-wracking, the guerrilla tactics the liberation forces used did not neutralise the RAR's military advantages.

My interviewees told me that, once ambushes were sprung, they could fight the guerrillas with ease. For instance, BM told me that his own first experience of combat occurred in 1972 as part of A Company, 1RAR in Chesa (in Rushinga, in the north-east of the country). His section was tracking a guerrilla unit when they were attacked. Despite being ambushed, none of his patrol were killed, and he remarked that this was not untypical, as throughout the rest of the decade he experienced numerous ambushes, but 'none of my troop were killed' in these contacts.[86]

---

[84] Interview with SJM.   [85] Interview with JM.   [86] Interview with BM.

162   The Impact of the War upon Soldierly Loyalties

Likewise, WR told me, 'I think I had only one loss of life during my campaign at the RAR.' He attributed this not only to the RAR's professionalism, but also to the low standard of marksmanship of the guerrillas. In a 1979 incident, after an initial contact, WR was leading his platoon back to their vehicles when they came across a tree that ZANLA had cut down to block the road:

> I get up and I swing my leg over, so I was actually sitting on the tree, and I'm not lying to you, the next [thing I saw was a guerrilla fighter] rise up, this guy opens up with an RPD [Soviet 7.62-millimetre light machine gun] with a drum magazine and empties his magazine at me. I couldn't put my foot down because there were just bullets landing near me. Eventually, he ran out of bullets, so that's about fifty rounds missing me sitting in the clear. You know... I can still remember he had a black bandana around his head, and perspiration was coming out, and he's holding this gun. I can see him clearly. And fifty rounds later, he's finished his rounds; he gets up and runs away. Do you know, that night I never slept [*laughs*]. Was I into the Hail Marys and Our Fathers! [*laughs again*] I promise you, I should've been dead.[87]

WR's close brush with death was a lucky escape. It also demonstrated that some ZANLA guerrillas were not skilled marksmen. This was a marked contrast to the RAR's machine gunners, who, as noted earlier, prided themselves on the discipline of their fire control and the accuracy of their shots. That a guerrilla missed a static target with a full drum magazine from short range implied that his training was limited.

The lack of professionalism among ZANLA fighters was highlighted by my interviewees, who made a qualitative distinction between the two liberation armies. ZANLA's Maoist strategy had created a huge guerrilla army, trained by the Frontline States and Eastern Bloc, that deeply penetrated the country.[88] However, as discussed later, many ZANLA fighters were poorly trained and equipped. Contrastingly, ZIPRA had a reputation for a very high standard of training, including a formidable regular army largely by Cuban, Zambian and Soviet instructors, equipped with an array of heavy weapons.[89]

By the late 1970s, ZIPRA's strong military presence in the Zambezi Valley had driven Rhodesian forces away from the escarpment and back to their garrisons.[90] Stood up in 1978,[91] ZIPRA's regular army's strength was demonstrated when it repulsed a raid on one of its bases across the

---

[87] Interview with WR.   [88] Tungamirai, 'Recruitment to ZANLA', pp. 42–5.
[89] Alexander and McGregor, 'Adelante!'; Brickhill, 'Daring to Storm the Heavens', pp. 48–72.
[90] Brickhill, 'Daring to Storm the Heavens', pp. 51–2.
[91] Dabengwa, 'ZIPRA in Zimbabwe's War of National Liberation', p. 35.

Zambezi by the special forces of the RhSAS in October 1979.[92]

Unlike Rhodesian propaganda, which did not mention the efficacy of the liberation forces, my interviewees recalled how potent ZIPRA's well-trained guerrilla fighters and conventional soldiers were, and often juxtaposed these statements with unfavourable comparisons to ZANLA.

GMH told me, 'I remember at Nkayi, we had a big contact, a very, very big one. We have got a very big fight. They were ZIPRAs. *Oh!* They used to fight, those guys.'[93] By the end of the war, ZIPRA was fielding well-armed and well-trained conventional units within Rhodesia, which executed sophisticated attacks using indirect weapons and fire-and-manoeuvre tactics. As BM told me of one such attack, 'we were attacked by bazooka, everything, mortar fire, everything'; however, he maintained that the RAR was not defeated, but merely performed a tactical withdrawal, having suffered no casualties.[94]

WR told me, 'I believe the ZIPRA were better equipped and better trained than the ZANLA,' and GM affirmed the same, stating that 'the difference, you can see it ... [ZIPRA] were very strong, they were real soldiers'.[95] Describing their wartime adversaries as 'real soldiers' was a notable compliment, perhaps the highest accolade my interviewees could bestow upon ZIPRA.

For BM, ZIPRA were not only well trained and disciplined, but also had access to heavier weapons such as mortars and machine guns.[96] He stated that ZIPRA troops frequently fought RAR units very effectively: 'Ah, [in Hwange it was] very dangerous. Because the ZIPRA they would stand still [i.e. hold their ground] in fighting ... But we called reinforcement to come help us as soon as possible. [ZIPRA were] very, very dangerous – [but] not ZANLA. Ah, nah, nah; those [ZANLA] are weak, very weak.'

I asked him why ZIPRA were so strong and why ZANLA were a less intimidating foe. The ZANLA groups that BM encountered were not only poorly trained, but badly equipped – he said that ZANLA guerrillas 'wore no boots, no shoes', a huge disadvantage when fighting in the bush.[97] However, while my interviewees respected ZIPRA, they did not feel that they were on the back foot for, as discussed later, ZIPRA were still vulnerable to aerial assault within Rhodesia.

The root cause of ZANLA's lack of training seems to have been its overwhelmed training and logistics infrastructure. As Miles Tendi argued, in the late 1970s, 'the pace and quality of ZANLA training struggled to keep up with the rate at which camps were swelling with

---

[92] Cole, *Elite*, pp. 378–93. [93] Interview with GMH. [94] Interview with BM.
[95] Interviews with WR and GM. [96] Interview with BM. [97] Ibid.

converts ... ZANLA lacked adequate resources to train, equip, feed, shelter and clothe its ever-inflating recruits to a high standard'.[98] Dumiso Dabengwa, a senior ZIPRA intelligence officer, levelled criticism towards ZANLA for this in 1995. 'ZANLA deployed people inside Rhodesia who were not well trained or even completely untrained. Some recruits were trained using sticks and were only given a gun on the day of crossing into Rhodesia. Most of these people were literally butchered by the enemy.'[99]

This criticism echoes aspects of my interviewees' disdain for ZANLA fighters, and many black Rhodesian soldiers were contemptuous of ZANLA guerrillas' lack of professionalism. In Nick Downie's 1978 war documentary *Frontline Rhodesia*, RAR soldiers inspect the weapon of a ZANLA commander killed in a firefight, whose Kalashnikov rifle 'is not merely dirty; it simply doesn't work', and it was claimed the discovery of ZANLA weapons so ill maintained that they failed to fire happened 'frequently, and reinforces the professional contempt the Rhodesian soldiers feel for their enemy'.[100] Such a lack of application of rudimentary soldierly skills would land an RAR soldier with a serious charge, for among professionals, failure to maintain an operable weapon is a cardinal sin. These interactions with poorly trained ZANLA cadres, prematurely sent to the front and grossly ill prepared, explains the disdain many of my interviewees expressed for their adversaries in ZANLA, and why they disparaged their martial capabilities. These perceptions informed black soldiers' sense of their military prowess and their understanding that the military balance was skewed in their favour.

Rhodesian Air Power Informing Black Soldiers' Perceptions of Combat

The gulf in training and equipment on the ground between black soldiers and many of the guerrillas they encountered was compounded by the Rhodesian monopoly of the skies. The liberation forces' Achilles' heel throughout the war was a lack of effective anti-air capability within Rhodesia, with a total lack of air defence prior to 1976.[101]

While the liberation forces did improve their air defences significantly as the war intensified, these weapons were concentrated in their external bases.[102] The ZANLA air defences were those protecting its large camps

---

[98] Tendi, *Army and Politics in Zimbabwe*, p. 100.
[99] Dabengwa, 'ZIPRA in the Zimbabwe War of National Liberation', p. 34.
[100] Downie, *Frontline Rhodesia*, 13m:30s–14m:25s.
[101] Melson, *Fighting for Time*, p. 59.
[102] Moorcraft and McLaughlin, *Rhodesian War*, pp. 96–7.

in Mozambique, such as New Chimoio, which installed ZU-23 anti-air guns in 1978 that later proved effective against Rhodesian aircraft.[103] In the late 1970s, ZIPRA established nine fortified bases across the Zambezi with very good anti-aircraft cover.[104] During the RhAF's attacks on one of these bases, Chinyunyu Camp, in October and November 1979, ZIPRA leaders claimed that the Rhodesians 'lost at least five aircraft'.[105] It is likely that, had the war continued, the liberation armies would have deployed their anti-air capability well inside Rhodesia, challenging the RhAF's control of the skies.

However, within Rhodesia, the liberation movements did not possess good anti-air coverage. Although official figures are not available, it seems that most RhAF helicopters downed within the country were in fact struck by warheads or air-bursted shrapnel from RPG-7 (a Soviet anti-tank rocket-propelled grenade) fire: the RhAF 'lost a number of aircraft to what is essentially an anti-tank weapon'.[106] The ZANLA fighters did not field anti-air assets within Rhodesia, although ZANLA's guerrillas likely first shot down an Alouette helicopter with an RPG in late 1973,[107] and in 1974, the ZANLA detachment commander for Chiweshe, Clever Mabonzo, single-handedly downed a low-flying Alouette with an RPG-7.[108] In November 1976, ZANLA fighters again attempted to down an Alouette with an air-bursted RPG-7 warhead, but were not successful.[109] This tactic was of limited efficacy, for RPG-7 warheads are highly prone to inaccuracy at anything beyond short range.[110]

ZIPRA fighters began to deploy a dedicated anti-air capability within Rhodesia towards the end of the war. Brickhill wrote that by mid-1978,

---

[103] Tendi, *Army and Politics in Zimbabwe*, pp. 107, 110–12. Cilliers noted that the Mozambican army also deployed its own Strela missiles to protect ZANLA camps (*Counter-Insurgency in Rhodesia*, p. 181).

[104] This capability was envisaged as massively expanded as part of the ZIPRA 'Turning Point' strategy, wherein an operation codenamed 'Zero Hour' was to see the conventional invasion of Rhodesia by ZIPRA units that possessed organic anti-anti cover, although the Rhodesians, having discovered the plans, destroyed the Chirundu, Lufus, Kaleya, and Chongwe bridges this armoured assault would require (Cole, *Elite*, pp. 393–410). Zero Hour was shelved when the ceasefire was agreed at Lancaster House (Brickhill, 'Daring to Storm the Heavens', p. 53).

[105] Brickhill, 'Daring to Storm the Heavens', p. 63.

[106] Brent, *Rhodesian Air Force*, p. 34, as quoted in Wood, *War Diaries of Andre Dennison*, p. 255. See also Wood, 'Fire Force'.

[107] It is likely that the earliest such incident occurred in February 1973 when an RhAF Alouette 'was lost, and its two crew members killed, in unexplained circumstances' near northern Mozambique. Strelas were not possessed by ZANLA, making an RPG strike the probable cause (Good, 'Settler Colonialism in Rhodesia', p. 13; see also Moorcraft and McLaughlin, *Rhodesian War*, p. 97).

[108] Ellert, *Rhodesian Front War*, p. 136.

[109] Wood, 'Counter-punching on the Mudzi', p. 77.

[110] US Army Training and Doctrine Command, *Range and Lethality*.

'ZGU anti-aircraft guns and SAM [surface-to-air missiles] were attached to guerrilla units in the north of the country and provided the guerrillas with their first real air defence capacity.'[111] However, Brickhill caveated this capability as being hampered within Rhodesia by the 'poor defensive character and capacity of guerrilla units, who were not trained to hold defensive positions'.[112] The ZIPRA SAMs were Soviet Strela-7s, which it used to shoot down two Air Rhodesia Viscount passenger jets in September 1978 and February 1979.[113] Moorcraft and McLaughlin noted that the Strelas were less effective against military aircraft which had been fitted with countermeasures: 'before the Viscounts were brought down there had been some 20 reports of SAM-7 firings at military aircraft, but no successful hits resulted', and that ZIPRA deployment of the Strela-7 was 'limited to border regions because of its vulnerability to poor maintenance and the short life of its specialized batteries'.[114]

Thus while ZIPRA's anti-air capability, comprising ZPU and Strela-7, was clearly potent when deployed in prepared defensive positions across the Zambezi, within Rhodesia, it had limited coverage and efficacy before the war's end. It is likely that, had the conflict continued, the liberation forces would have brought their anti-air capabilities to bear within Rhodesia. However, by the time the war ended, their anti-air defences did not challenge the RhAF's freedom of movement within Rhodesia.

Consequently, while the RSF's aircraft were certainly under greater threat later in the war, the RhAF could routinely use its aircraft within the country, often to devastating effect against guerrillas lacking anti-air weapons. For the Rhodesians, 'immediate air support was available at all times on one- and two-hour standby with standard loads of ordnance; preplanned air support could reduce this to 15-minute strip alert or even airborne over the target area'.[115]

WR told me of a contact he was involved in during 1979 in Masvingo, where guerrilla fighters had taken a well-defended position in a ravine and repelled the RAR's attempts to dislodge them. In response, an air strike was called in from jets based at Thornhill in Gweru:

---

[111] Brickhill, 'Daring to Storm the Heavens', p. 53. There is no weapon called a 'ZGU'. It is likely Brickhill meant the ZPU, a 14.5-millimetre Soviet towed anti-air gun. It is also possible ZIPRA were additionally supplied with the ZPU's successor, the ZU-23-2, a 23-millimetre towed anti-air gun. Ethiopia donated the ZU-23-2 to ZANLA, and ZANLA used it to great effect in the defence of Chimoio during the Rhodesian Operation Miracle (Tendi, *Army and Politics*, pp. 110–12).
[112] Brickhill, 'Daring to Storm the Heavens', p. 53.
[113] Ellert, *Rhodesian Front War*, p. 49.
[114] Moorcraft and McLaughlin, *Rhodesian War*, p. 100.
[115] Melson, *Fighting for Time*, p. 82.

I think it took them about five minutes to [to arrive] and I actually witnessed a jet strike onto ground troops – you didn't stand a chance [against the] cannons and bombs. By the time [one aircraft] came round [on its attack vector], the other [aircraft] was attacking, so it was like constant fire on that position [from multiple aircraft attacking sequentially]. You know, when we were told to sweep [the position afterwards], we found no one alive. The trees, everything was just totally shattered with the fire ... there were about eighteen casualties.[116]

The 'fire' referred to was the napalm (which the Rhodesians called 'frantan') dropped by the RhAF, which was devastating and had gruesome to behold, as WR recalled with disgust.[117] However, air strikes on guerrilla positions were relatively rare, owing to the cost of munitions.[118]

The real military significance of the Rhodesian air monopoly was that it meant the army's small number of regular troops could be rapidly ferried around the country. For the Rhodesian Army, this capability was utterly vital as, throughout the 1970s, it could deploy only 1,400 soldiers in the field concurrently.[119] Guerrillas had infiltrated vast areas of the country after the mid-1970s, meaning the army's few regular troops were stretched thinly. As the war intensified, guerrillas increasingly fully or partly controlled these areas as 'liberated zones' to the extent that the 'security forces could venture into them only in strength'.[120] The regular army's small size meant that it was perpetually short of this strength in numbers.

In direct response to this attenuation of its forces, the RSF developed the 'Fireforce' tactic in 1974, which maximised the reach of its regular troops by quickly deploying them directly into areas of sighted guerrilla activity, or ongoing combat, by air.[121] Fireforces were comprised of RAR or RLI companies pre-deployed to one of ten Forward Air Fields (FAF) dotted around the periphery of the country for six weeks at a time, and were required to be airborne in eight minutes from first alert (see Figure 5.1).[122] Reporting from the war emphasised how RAR units manning Fireforces during six-week stints could be called out from sunrise to sunset.[123]

---

[116] Interview with WR.   [117] Ibid.
[118] The RSF's budget was highly strained. J. R. T. Wood noted that Rhodesian helicopter gunners had to use 20-millimetre cannon sparingly owing to the cost of its ammunition, and that each fire force had to designate paratroopers who jumped not to fight, but were 'dropped purely to collect the parachutes [used by other soldiers] as sanctions made their replacement costly and difficult' ('Fire Force'). Likewise, Moorcraft and McLaughlin noted that the army did not use artillery bombardment as it 'could not afford' it, for '25-pounder shells cost $150 each' (*Rhodesian War*, p. 169).
[119] Wood, 'Countering the Chimurenga', p. 196.
[120] Moorcraft and McLaughlin, *Rhodesian War*, pp. 83–4, 99.
[121] Evans, *Fighting against Chimurenga*, p. 18. These sightings were most frequently made by the Selous Scouts (Baxter, *Selous Scouts*, p. 50). The RhSAS and Selous Scouts also manned Fireforces.
[122] Melson, *Fighting for Time*, pp. 31, 117–19.   [123] Ibid., pp. 121–2.

Figure 5.1 1RAR Fireforce pre-deployment preparations (*Nwoho*, April 1978)

During the late 1970s, four permanent Fireforces were available, two each manned by the RAR and RLI,[124] and each could transport thirty-five soldiers into battle at a time.[125] As a British war correspondent embedded with 2RAR commented in 1978, Rhodesian claims that its army was the finest in the world were untrue; however, it was certainly 'the most unusual', owing to its tactic of deploying its few regular troops rapidly into ongoing combat by air.[126]

Travelling in helicopters and, after 1977, C-47 Dakota aircraft, and supported by helicopter gunships and strike and bomber aircraft, Fireforce aimed to vertically envelop guerrilla fighters and force them to offer combat against the now numerically superior Rhodesian troops on terrain unfavourable to them.[127] The potency of Fireforce was widely acknowledged at the time, and in purely military terms, it was devastatingly effective.[128]

By 1977, the first black soldiers had become paratroopers, augmenting the capacity of the Fireforce by jumping from Dakotas. WM was

[124] Beckett, 'Rhodesian Army', p. 177.
[125] Downie, *Frontline Rhodesia*, 08m:05s–08m:25s.   [126] Ibid., 02m:50s–03m:05s.
[127] Binda, *Masodja*, pp. 312–13.
[128] See, for instance, Anti-Apartheid Movement, *Fireforce Exposed*.

a paratrooper, and he told me, 'I've got about nine operational jumps ... The first jump was frightening: if you can't get frightened by the first jump then there must be something wrong with you!' During training troops would jump out from 1,000 feet (304 metres). Jumps were also often frequently from a very low altitude – as WM put it, 'about fifteen seconds from the door of the Dakota to the ground so you don't give the enemy much chance to nail you'.[129] During operations, Fireforce troops would jump from as low as 400 feet (121 metres).

This was dangerous and demanding soldiering, and it served to reinforce the elite status of RAR troops. Sometimes 2RAR would parachute into operations two or three times in a single day,[130] and by 1978, some black soldiers had already 'parachuted into action over 40 times ... in no other war have soldiers parachuted anything like as often'.[131] Black Rhodesian soldiers retain a credible claim to be among the most experienced combat paratroopers in the history of warfare. Becoming combat experienced paratroopers cemented the sense of professionalism of black Rhodesian troops. For instance, Corporal Malambani from C Company 2RAR wrote in October 1977, 'I enjoy contacts especially when I am dropped as a paratrooper ... I am a well-known soldier because of my courage and ability as a paratrooper.'[132]

Fireforce also gave great reassurance to black soldiers engaged in combat that they would be reinforced. Pte T. Chipato of Support Company 1RAR wrote how, when on patrol in Victoria Province in October 1977, Fireforce was overhead within thirty minutes of a guerrilla sighting being reported (see Figure 5.2).[133] Fireforce not only provided troops on the ground with a favourable force ratio, but also afforded commanders aerial surveillance of guerrilla positions and movements, and fire support from rounds fired by the helicopters' 20-millimetre cannon, which exploded upon impact, creating lethal shrapnel bursts.[134]

Fireforce further shaped black soldiers' convictions that they were militarily on top, as it materially improved their fighting ability. For instance, A Company 2RAR spent six weeks on conducting routine ground-level infantry work during July–August 1978, and killed three

---

[129] Interview with WM.   [130] Wood, *War Diaries of Andre Dennison*, p. 258.
[131] Downie, *Frontline Rhodesia*, 07m:40s–07m:55s.
[132] Stapleton, *African Police and Soldiers*, p. 208.
[133] T. Chipato, 'My First Contact', *Nwoho* (April 1978), p. 31.
[134] Wood, 'Fire Force'.

Figure 5.2 Composite image of A Coy 1RAR on Fireforce duty, 1978. Images: 3 Pl emplaning at the Forward Air Field (FAF) in Mtoko, 3 Platoon pre-Fireforce callout 1978, 3 Platoon emplaning on Fireforce duty at Grand Reef FAF early 1978, A Coy 1RAR on board a C-47 Dakota on Fireforce deployment in early 1978, A Coy 1RAR at rest in the field playing volleyball. Ex-RAR officer Mike Matthews said of the 3 Pl pre-Fireforce callout photo, 'at least three of my platoon, including my Platoon Sgt and WOII, were killed in action the following year' (all images courtesy of Mike Matthews).

guerrillas. Its next six-week deployment was as a Fireforce, in which it killed seventy-two guerrillas.[135] Throughout that year, A Company spent

[135] Wood, *War Diaries of Andre Dennison*, pp. 234–75.

Figure 5.2 (cont.)

three months in total as a Fireforce, and during this period it was engaged in almost continuous combat with guerrilla forces in the east of the country; it recorded 100 guerrillas killed whereas just one RAR soldier was killed in action.[136]

These encounters, while being markedly one-sided, reinforced the notion among black soldiers that they outmatched the guerrillas. For instance, in 1977, Colour Sergeant Chiwocha of B Company 2RAR wrote that 'like all other Coys, B Coy has played its part in the present wars against ters. It goes without saying our present ter kill-rate explains more than words'.[137] Likewise, BM boasted to me that his stick of four men were so deadly that even if they 'made contact with forty guerrillas we can chase them away'.[138]

Such bravado echoed wartime Rhodesian rhetoric, which fetishized 'kill rates' between the RSF and the liberation forces.[139] This reflected internal Rhodesian Army thinking too: a December 1978 internal report by the Rhodesian Army Data Processing Unit, using 'somewhat incomplete' data from 1972 to 1978, said that there had been 1,519 contacts between elements of the RSF and the liberation movements (205 ZIPRA, 1,266 ZANLA). The analysis said that casualties 'were 629 (156 killed, 473 wounded) on the Rhodesian side as opposed to 3,391 (2,892 killed, 499 wounded) on the nationalist side. In addition, 544 guerrillas were captured'.[140]

According to the war correspondent Nick Downie, embedded with 2RAR during 1978, 'The kill ratio of the RSF operating in the country is roughly 10:1. This includes men killed by landmines, in road ambushes, and those serving in low-grade defence units. However, these figures can be somewhat misleading. In straight fighting with their regular companies the Rhodesians kill on average 60 or 70 guerrillas for the loss of every man.'[141]

Such numbers seem high, and it is impossible in retrospect to verify them. One wonders, for instance, how many civilians were caught in the crossfire and retrospectively classified as guerrillas. Much of the literature on the war has cited such ratios, and some of the lower numbers are perhaps not outlandish in strictly military terms if one factors in the Rhodesian aerial monopoly, the high level of training and experience of

---

[136] Downie, *Frontline Rhodesia*, 06m:30s–06m:45s.
[137] S. Chiwocha, 'Life in B Coy 2RAR', *Nzwoho* (October 1977), p. 43.
[138] Interview with BM.   [139] Evans, 'Wretched of the Empire', p. 189.
[140] Melson, *Fighting for Time*, p. 106.
[141] Downie, *Frontline Rhodesia*, 16m:45s–17m:15s. Melson wrote that RAR and RLI Fireforces had 'an 80-to-1 kill ratio' (*Fighting for Time*, p. 190).

the soldiers in the regular army, and the lack of training of many ZANLA forces, as noted earlier.[142]

Fireforce forced the hand of guerrillas, for if they did not withdraw before it arrived, they would stand little chance. BM told me guerrilla fighters would typically engage the RAR's ground patrols for only a short period of time before withdrawing as 'if we made a contact with them, we'd call a helicopter to come and help us. That's why they ran! They always ran away!' and 'when [the guerrilla forces] heard the sound of the helicopter [they would instantly withdraw]', for most guerrilla units had no viable way of defending themselves from aerial assault.[143]

Thus my interviewees' rodomontade and derogatory remarks that guerrilla fighters ran away were borne of the experience of professional troops who enjoyed high morale and decisive military advantages over guerrilla forces. They do not capture the complexity of the conflict, for the equipment and training of guerrilla units varied enormously, particularly between ZANLA and ZIPRA, as noted earlier. Towards the end of the war, the military proficiency of guerrilla units had markedly increased, and many were well trained and lethally efficient in the field, as attested to in an operational account by the commander of D Company, 1RAR who described a 'determined ZANLA assault' in 1976,[144] and by the commander of A Company, 2RAR during 1978, who noted of captured ZANLA fighters 'they fought like heroes and remained bloody but unbowed'.[145] Former Special Branch officer Henrik Ellert described the 'incredible feats of courage on the part of individual' ZANLA cadres.[146] Likewise the memoirs of former white Rhodesian soldiers also described the military prowess of some guerrillas,[147] as does the scholarly literature.[148] However, my interviewees' recollections of the conflict, aside from lauding the 'professionalism' of ZIPRA cadres, were not complimentary of the guerrilla fighters they encountered.

In sum, my interviewees' recollections consistently emphasised that they felt they were winning the war militarily. This sentiment provided

---

[142] As with many wartime figures, these are contested. Wood asserted that 'The war cost ZANLA and ZRPA 40,000 dead at a cost of 1,735 Rhodesian dead – a ratio of 23:1' ('Countering the Chimurenga', p. 202); whereas Abbot and Botham gave RSF 'kill/loss ratios of around ten to one in contacts with the PF' (*Modern African Wars*, p. 8), as did Moorcraft (*Short Thousand Years*, p. 178). Arbuckle noted that 'Rhodesian Government figures, released in December 1978, for example, showed that 6,100 guerrillas were killed between December 1972 and November 1978 compared to 1,051 members of the Security Forces, a kill ratio in the Security Forces' favour of just over six to one' ('Rhodesian Bush War Strategies', pp. 27–8).
[143] Interview with BM.   [144] Wood, 'Counter-punching on the Mudzi', p. 76.
[145] Wood, *War Diaries of Andre Dennison*, p. 299.
[146] Ellert, *Rhodesian Front War*, p. 137.   [147] See, for instance, Cocks, *Fireforce*, p. 180.
[148] Arbuckle, 'Rhodesian Bush War Strategies and Tactics', p. 32.

a clear boost to their morale and a fillip to their sense of professionalism. In contrast to other conflicts where the loyalties of colonial soldiers ebbed and serious instances of disloyalty occurred, black Rhodesian soldiers were not impacted by the 'push' factors of a breakdown in morale or a sense that they were going to be militarily defeated. These factors are important in explaining why they overwhelmingly remained loyal and why so few deserted. Another key 'push' factor was the lack of a 'moral grievance' as to the conduct of the war among black Rhodesian troops.

Black Rhodesian Soldiers' Conception of the War's Morality

In the telling of black soldiers, guerrillas were cowardly, as those they encountered in the field always ran away, and guerrilla tactics – petty skirmishing, ambushing, and surprise attacks – denoted a lack of integrity. DC commented that these tactics denied guerrillas soldierly status: 'in fact, they didn't fight much, those people. When they heard that the soldiers were there, they just ran away. All they were doing was disturb-[ing] the system. That's why I said they can never be soldiers'.[149] BM fulsomely expressed how the soldier should act in a what he deemed a 'strong' manner: 'If you are weak, you end up [running] away, but we have never ran [sic] away from the ZIPRA people. We always win the war. Myself I have never ran [sic] away with those four people who are working with me [his stick of four soldiers], no.'[150]

GMH contrasted the behaviour of the liberation forces during the war with his previous experience of COIN warfare:

You see, the Chinese in Malaya, they used to fight. They were not doing like this, our African guerrillas here. In Malaysia, they used to fight. They stand up and fight. These here they used to run away. They take their guns here, only that way trying to shoot [makes motion of trying to shoot over own shoulder while running away]. See, but Chinese in Malaya, they used to fight. They stand up and fight.[151]

The notions that guerrillas could 'never be soldiers', and 'ran away', and that RAR troops 'always win the war', imply that black soldiers understood guerrilla's tactics as unworthy. Their statements hold that to flee from combat, or to use a disguise to merge among the civilian population, was not the honourable behaviour of the soldier, who stood his ground and fought, or at least retreated under fire in an orderly and organised fashion.

These renderings evidence a particular masculine conception of warfare. As John Horne has argued, since the ascent of the nation state and the ensuing advent of the modern army, the military has been 'a source of

[149] Interview with DC.   [150] Interview with BM.   [151] Interview with GMH.

masculine authority and a privileged area of male activity'.[152] While the form this masculinity takes varies greatly by context, there are commonalities in how soldiers recruited from marginalised communities have invoked it.[153] For instance, as Lesley Gill argued, soldiers drawn from marginalised groups in Bolivia advanced a 'sense of subaltern masculinity' which foregrounded their bravery and proficiency in order to accrue status in a society prejudiced against them.[154] I claim that black soldiers in Rhodesia constructed themselves in a comparably masculine manner, one which stressed that their professionalism and bravery were honourable, in contrast to guerrillas who 'ran away' and could 'never be soldiers'. Being a soldier was explicitly associated with acting in a masculine fashion, and to 'act like a man' was the highest tribute. For instance, the OC of A Company 2RAR, writing of how 'two of our very best young NCOs were killed in action', paid tribute to them by describing how 'they died as they lived, like men'.[155]

Just as black soldiers invoked professionalism as a tactic to negotiate the racist structures of the army, I argue that, in Rhodesia's highly patriarchal society,[156] rendering oneself as masculine was a further way in which black troops could leverage their soldierly status to accrue social mobility. White officers, whose recommendations and reports were crucial to the promotion prospects of black soldiers, looked particularly favourably on aggressive and courageous soldiers.[157] It is also probable that black soldiers' emphasis upon 'masculine' traits were influenced by Rhodesian propaganda, such as an infamous army recruitment poster which 'exhorted potential recruits to be a "man among men"'.[158]

During the 1970s, Rhodesian propaganda increasingly incorporated black soldiers in its portrayals of martial masculinity, reflecting the army's increasing dependence upon black troops. As David Kenrick argued, although the portrayals of black soldiers were still rooted in settler-colonial racist-paternalism, these positive depictions of black soldiers demonstrated a marked shift in settler consciousness, as Rhodesian propaganda had previously only featured whites 'performing their settler masculinity'.[159]

---

[152] Horne, 'Masculinity in Politics and War', p. 31.
[153] See Higate, *Military Masculinities*.
[154] Gill, 'Creating Citizens, Making Men', p. 527.
[155] 'A Coy 2RAR', *Nwoho* (April 1978), p. 55.
[156] See, for instance, Law, *Gendering the Settler State*, chapter 4.
[157] Telfer and Fulton, *Chibaya Moyo*, pp. 223, 246; Wood, *War Diaries of Andre Dennison*, pp. 245, 277.
[158] Kenrick, *Decolonisation, Identity and Nation in Rhodesia*, p. 39.
[159] Ibid., pp. 228–9. Women were conspicuously absent, for they did not serve as Rhodesian combatants, unlike in the liberation forces. See Nhongo-Simbanegavi, *For Better or Worse*; Sinclair, Phiri, and Bright, *Flame*.

Renderings of soldiers as axiomatically 'men' by black troops also explicitly sought to exclude guerrillas. For instance, in 1978, Tobias Chinyere, a private in 2RAR, wrote, '[guerrillas are] destroying schools instead of building, what men are they?'.[160] Black soldiers' delineation of their soldierly conduct as that of men and that of guerrillas as cowards who ran away or attacked the defenceless, speaks to Kimberley Hutchings' argument that 'norms of masculinity are variable and enforce not only hierarchical distinctions between men and women, but also between different men'.[161] By questioning the masculinity of the tactics guerrillas used, black Rhodesian soldiers were creating this type of masculine hierarchy, which installed them at the top as protectors of the people and placed the guerrillas at the bottom.

This conception of a hierarchy of masculinity had a particular salience for black soldiers' conceptions of themselves and their legitimacy. To return to the 'push' factors, one such factor is when moral grievances as to the prosecution of the war or its conduct fracture the loyalties of soldiers. Here I argue that, among black Rhodesian soldiers, the opposite was the case. The 'masculine' notion that they were protecting civilians was, for my interviewees, grounded in their experience of guerrilla violence against rural people.

Soldiers have long rationalised their service in this manner. For instance, some vehemently anti-Stalinist Russians cited the abuse of Russian civilians by Nazi forces as justification for their fighting in the regime's army during World War II.[162] Algerians who fought on the side of the French against the Front de libération nationale (FLN) during the war of independence often have said that they did so owing to the FLN's violence against and exploitation of civilians.[163] Black soldiers fighting on behalf of apartheid South Africa in Namibia 'spoke of the importance and the professionalism of their military training', emphasising 'that the soldiers of SWATF "were not trained to kill innocent people [but] to take care of and to protect people"'.[164] In the telling of these Namibian

---

[160] T. Chinyere, 'A Coy Gives me Pride', *Nwoho* (April 1978), p. 57.
[161] Hutchings, 'Making Sense of Masculinity and War', p. 391.
[162] Reese, 'Motivations to Serve', p. 268.
[163] Crapanzano, *Harkis*, pp. 30–2. It should be noted that it is unclear whether Crapanzano is referring solely to the 55,000 *harki* auxiliaries (*supplétifs*) or whether he is also referring to the 20,000 Algerian regulars and 40,000 Algerian conscripts who served in the French colonial army during the war. This is no criticism of Crapanzano: both Algerian auxiliaries and regulars have come to be labelled using the catch-all term *harki*; the delineation has become muddled to the extent that even his own *harki* research participants used the term interchangeably for auxiliaries and soldiers alike (ibid., p. 70). A further layer of complexity is added by the fact that many *harki* auxiliaries served as soldiers in the French colonial army during World War II or the First Indochina War (1946–54).
[164] Bolliger, *Apartheid's African Soldiers*, pp. 84–5, 91–4, 168–9, 175–7, 180.

soldiers, they used their skills to fight only their enemies and sought to protect civilians from the outsiders of the liberation forces, whom they portrayed as using violent coercion against rural people.

In 1977, an RAR soldier told a journalist from *The Times*, 'I want to kill those people who are killing my people.'[165] My interviewees espoused a similar rationale, as the intensification of the war from the mid-1970s onwards brought widespread violence to the rural areas. Black soldiers frequently cast the RAR as the protector of the rural people and pointed to guerrilla violence as a motivation for joining the army or remaining loyal to it, such as DSN.[166] TM knew of many soldiers who joined the army 'having seen operational guerrillas being set loose in their home areas, local areas'.[167] Likewise, CD told me:

[W]hat made me join the Rhodesian army was what was happening to the civilians, you would hear these stories: you'd hear of a woman who was made to cut a husband [while he] sleeps in the tongue and made to fry it and eat it ... These were some of the things that really irked me, really, that's why I joined the Rhodesian army ... I believed civilians were supposed to be left out of the war altogether.[168]

Gerald Mazarire interviewed Jocks, an RAR veteran, who stated that 'he felt it his individual responsibility to protect innocent civilians from his village who were continuously exposed to the brutality and intimidation of Patriotic Front guerrillas'.[169] In 1977, Private T. Chinyere wrote, 'I had decided to become a soldier, not only because of the good conditions, but also because I was angry at the things that the terrorists were doing to our people and our country.'[170] In 1979, a journalist covering the passing-out parade of RAR recruits interviewed several newly trained black soldiers, who:

spoke angrily about the guerrillas. 'I joined to save my country from the brutal terrorist war,' said Pte David Sibanda, 22, previously a lifeguard at a Government swimming pool in the Belingwe tribal trust land, 60 miles east of here. Other recruits, clustered around in their camouflage fatigues, nodded agreement. 'The terrorists are not fighting for the people, as they say. They are fighting for themselves,' Private Sibanda said. 'They talk about liberation, but actually they are drinking beer, robbing stores, raping girls and doing all sorts of rubbish.'[171]

The black sergeant major in charge of these recruits observed, 'it will be hard out here, and some will get killed. But these men know that they are

---

[165] Ashford, 'Blacks Who Fight for the White Regime in Salisbury'.
[166] Interview with DSN.   [167] Interview with TM.   [168] Interview with CD.
[169] Mazarire, 'Rescuing Zimbabwe's "Other" Liberation Archives', p. 95.
[170] '2RAR Company Notes: How I Joined the Army', *Nwoho* (October 1977), p. 41.
[171] Burns, 'How Blacks View Their Larger Role in Rhodesia's Army'.

fighting for something worthwhile. Every terrorist they kill will be one less to attack their families, one step closer to establishing what everybody wants, which is a peaceful country'.[172] This conception of the RAR as the protectors of the people, prevalent among black soldiers, served to create a sense that their soldiering was in service of a moral cause, rather than in service of the Smith regime. Thus, far from black soldiers developing any kind of moral grievance 'push' factor as to the conduct of the war, many instead honed a powerful notion that their soldiering was in fact itself moral.

These soldiers' conception of themselves as protectors may raise eyebrows among those familiar with the myriad atrocities the RSF perpetuated, as discussed at the start of this chapter. However, it is important to understand that units in which black soldiers served were not involved in these atrocities: as noted earlier, most served in the RAR or other regular units, and there are no instances in the literature of RAR involvement or other regular army involvement with them. Contrastingly, the literature notes many instances of atrocities carried out by units including the Security Force Auxiliaries,[173] the Police Anti-Terrorist Unit,[174] and Special Branch.[175]

Furthermore, the literature records many incidents of white security force members killing civilians in cold blood, including the murder of women and children,[176] which often went unrecorded and unreported, as the security forces were almost completely immune from prosecution.[177] There are no reports in the literature of RAR involvement in such acts, nor was it involved in other incidents such as the Nyadzonia raid in 1976 by the infamous Selous Scouts in which more than 1,000 people were killed at a ZANLA camp in Mozambique.[178] Indeed the RAR's absence from the list of units involved in atrocities is conspicuous, and this had important implications for their post-war retention, as discussed later.

It was one thing for the RAR to kill its adversaries in combat, which my interviewees certainly did not shy away from recognising in their accounts. As we have seen, they boasted of their combat prowess. But these stories were always explicitly couched as part and parcel of conducting warfare against a recognised enemy.

---

[172] Ibid.   [173] Ellert, *Rhodesian Front War*, p. 148.
[174] White, 'Animals, Prey, and Enemies', p. 15.   [175] Caute, *Under the Skin*, pp. 191–3.
[176] See, for instance, Cocks, *Fireforce*, p. 92.   [177] Caute, *Under the Skin*, pp. 280–2.
[178] As noted earlier, it seems white TF servicemen in the Selous Scouts, rather than black soldiers, provided the personnel for 'external' assaults (Baxter, *Selous Scouts*, pp. 74–5). Selous Scouts involved in Nyadzonia and other comparable operations seem to have been drawn from what Melson refers to as the 100-strong 'assault group' comprised of white TF soldiers, which included a '14-man reconnaissance troop and mortar troop' (Melson, *Fighting for Time*, p. 170).

Soldiers' Conception of the War's Morality

My interviewees' iteration of their professional soldiering skills carried the clear subtext that they dispensed violence only against guerrilla fighters, unlike members of other units. Certainly, RAR soldiers did not shy away from using robust physical force and sometimes brutal methods.[179] In contrast to other elements of the RSF, this was in the course of their military duties fighting armed opponents, and not for other reasons. As Alexander, McGregor, and Ranger noted:

> In the estimation of civilians, the regular units of the Rhodesian army were judged the least bad of all government forces. Though they were often ruthlessly violent towards civilians, they were also seen as lacking prejudice, as a 'professional' fighting force. They lacked prejudice because they were outsiders, unknown to local people and unfamiliar with their personal histories and disputes. They were professional because they were primarily concerned with fighting guerrillas, not with personal gain or status.[180]

This perception of these civilians in Matabeleland was one that contrasted the army to the markedly unprofessional conduct of the Rhodesian government's auxiliaries.

Stewart, drawing upon interviews with white ex-RAR officers, argued that the RAR did not participate in 'externals' – large-scale operations against liberation forces bases in the Frontline States – because while they were 'quite capable of these types of strikes, [they] tended to be less aggressive [than the RLI] and more thorough in executing their missions. Their ability to observe and communicate with the population inside Rhodesia was crucial to internal operations', and the RLI's 'aggressive, fast–paced, initiative driven contact [was] much better suited to external operations'.[181] This statement can be read as these white ex-RAR officers implying that the RLI's overreliance upon violence caused civilian casualties, whereas the RAR's prudence and respect for civilians meant that they were less trigger-happy.

Drawing on correspondence with white veterans, Melson noted that RAR Fireforces were more effective than their 'keyed-up' counterparts in the RLI as they were more willing to 'be left overnight to ambush remaining guerrillas'.[182] The RLI soldiers on Fireforce, a former commanding

---

[179] Stapleton, *African Police and Soldiers*, p. 64.
[180] Alexander, McGregor, and Ranger, *Violence and Memory*, p. 151.
[181] Stewart, *Rhodesian African Rifles*, pp. 56, 74. The RAR did partake in its own 'externals', albeit within a shorter range of Rhodesia's borders (ibid.; Downie, *Frontline Rhodesia*, 19m:00s–19m:15s). For instance, in Operation Mardon, companies from both 1RAR and 2RAR raided ZANLA camps in Mozambique in 1976 (Wood, 'Counter-Punching on the Mudzi', pp. 64–82; see also Baxter, *Selous Scouts*, p. 91), and in Operation Murex, 'an airmobile company of 1RAR' attacked a ZIPRA camp at Kabanga Mission, eighty miles north of Lusaka, in November 1979 (Binda, *Masodja*, pp. 372–4; Stapleton, *African Police and Soldiers*, p. 205).
[182] Melson, *Fighting for Time*, p. 139.

officer said in 1989, also 'developed a "kill or be killed" nature not conducive to "hearts and minds" efforts'.[183]

There are other instances of the RAR's care to avoid civilian casualties in the literature. For instance, in 1978, a ZANLA group 'fired on an RAR patrol outside Mount Selinda mission ... because it was well known that ZANLA frequented the girls' dormitories there, the patrol did not return fire for fear of shooting young civilians'.[184]

It is unsurprising that black soldiers were more respectful of the civilian population for, as noted earlier, most hailed from rural areas similar to those in which they predominantly operated. This was recognised by Rhodesian securocrats, but not by the RF. In 1978, Ian Smith and his white ministers of defence and law and order convened a meeting with the RSF security chiefs. Ken Flower's memorandum on the meeting noted that the white ministers felt the:

Security Forces are fighting the war according to 'Queensbury Rules', whereas what we needed was something on the lines of 'Martial Law' – interpreted by the White politicians to be 'Martial Licence', and the Prime Minister asked at one stage whether more use should not be made of the RAR in an aggressive role (Blacks killing Blacks indiscriminately)?[185]

The securocrats swiftly disabused Smith and other RF politicians of the notion that black soldiers would partake in indiscriminate violence against civilians.

Indeed, many black soldiers profoundly empathised with the plight of civilians. DC outlined to me the dilemma of the civilian as perceived by a soldier:

You see, the Rhodesian army, they [deployed into rural areas, villages, and hamlets, but] they didn't stay there [for long periods of time]. But the liberation soldiers stayed there [continuously] with those people, they mobilised those people, they politicised them, told them what they wanted and all that. Some of them lies. But they [the civilians] had to believe them [the guerrillas], because they lived with them. The [RAR] soldiers went there once in a while and they left ... and [as a result the civilians] said [to the soldiers] 'no, we can't support you, because you leave us to the mercy of these people' [the guerrillas].[186]

In a dilemma commonplace to many COIN conflicts, in Rhodesia, civilians regularly faced the quandary of having both sides demand intelligence and support from them, and were coerced – or worse – if they

---

[183] Ibid., p. 140.   [184] White, *Fighting and Writing*, p. 24.
[185] PKF, 'Memorandum: National JOC Meeting with Prime Minister', 4 September 1978.
[186] Interview with DC.

refused.[187] WR described the terror he observed among civilians his RAR platoon encountered:

You know, the atrocities that were committed among the people, *ugh*. If you're a 'sell-out', you're either beaten to death, or they cut your lips or your tongue off... It was shocking. If you [civilians in the rural areas] didn't help the guerrillas, they were cruel to you – beat you up, kill you. They didn't think twice about killing you. If the soldiers came around on patrol, if you [a civilian] didn't help them they [civilians] were also beaten [by the soldiers]. So they were in between a rock and a hard place ... Knowing the rural people, I never asked an adult to give any information. I never. I just leave them alone; you could see the fear – how scared they were.[188]

WR delineated the behaviour of soldiers – who would beat civilians only to acquire information – from the behaviour of guerrillas, who he claimed would use torture and murder to coerce civilians. WR's recollections constructed a 'masculine' hierarchy of violence, as argued earlier.

For some members of the RAR, their sympathy with civilians generated a hatred of guerrillas, who were portrayed as dangerous and supported by outsiders. An RAR sergeant major told Peter Godwin, 'These people are just communists ... they are being used by the Russians. They are just greedy for power ... They are not fit to rule this country. They kill old men. Women even. You see what they do. They are cowards. I don't want to be ruled by them.'[189]

This notion that guerrillas were all recklessly violent and dangerous was invoked by black Rhodesian soldiers as demonstrative that their own service was moral, whereas that of guerrillas was not. For instance, I asked DC, a soft-spoken, reflective man, as to whether his allegiance to the Rhodesian government caused him any moral distress:

[In] my job [as a teacher with the Rhodesian Army Education Corps] anyway, I didn't see anything wrong, because I didn't go to hunt for them [i.e. engage in combat against guerrilla forces]. I didn't have to [as his day-to-day job was within barracks providing instruction to other soldiers]. But – even [for] those who were in the [field] army, it was just a job. They did not come here [and join the army to specifically] go and hunt for their brothers [in the liberation movements]. But when a crime happened, like what they [guerrillas] did – they used to burn people alive in the rural areas. Well, those were criminals; they had to be hunted down.[190]

DC's startling shift in tone and language towards the end of these remarks conveys the utter contempt many of my interviewees had for guerrillas who abused civilians. Another RAR soldier remarked that during a large

---
[187] Downie, *Frontline Rhodesia*, 22m:45s–23m:15s.   [188] Interview with WR.
[189] Godwin, *Mukiwa*, p. 296, as quoted in Stapleton, *African Police and Soldiers*, p. 200.
[190] Interview with DC.

firefight, he had killed a guerrilla who was wearing a distinctive watch, which was significant to him as:

> [A] couple of months before that [it was suspected that the same group of guerrillas had] attacked a farmhouse ... killing the [farm] manager's wife. And besides putting her [corpse] on the gate and all that for him to see when he came back, they took her watch, which I returned to the farmer. He really appreciated that; at least we got the group.[191]

The hatred some soldiers felt for their adversaries could become all consuming. As Downie remarked of 2RAR troops operating in a rural village: 'although the soldiers come from exactly this sort of background, they have little sympathy for those they suspect of harbouring guerrillas ... One Lance Corporal knowingly, and deliberately, killed his own brother in a skirmish' with guerrilla forces.[192]

In sum, black soldiers' experiences of the mistreatment of civilians by guerrillas meant that many, who had hitherto had adopted a pragmatic, professional approach to the conflict and combat with their adversaries, came to truly loathe elements of the guerrilla forces. This informed their perception of the guerrillas as immoral for preying on civilians, whereas they portrayed their own role in the war as that of masculine protectors whose use of lethal force was inherently moral. While it may be the case that these recollections have been burnished in retrospect by a desire among black Rhodesian veterans to distance themselves from the atrocities committed by other RSF combatants, contemporary sources also demonstrate that these sentiments were deeply and widely held by black troops during the war. Far from the 'push' factor of a moral grievance as to the Rhodesian conduct of the war existing, black Rhodesian soldiers' perspectives reveal a prevalent perception of their own wartime service as in fact both masculine and moral.

Solidarities Generated by Guerrilla Targeting of Black Soldiers and Their Families

As we have seen, in Rhodesia, black soldiers came to hold guerrillas in particular contempt for their treatment of civilians. However, nothing did more to engender wartime enmity than guerrilla forces targeting the family members of servicemen. As Anderson and Branch argued, during wars of liberation, violence created 'deeper divisions and greater rivalries the longer an armed struggle continued'.[193] In the eyes of nationalists, the strong loyalties of black Rhodesian soldiers to the army were treasonous and they were sell-outs. According to ZANU, they were 'Smith's

---

[191] Interviewee anonymised by author.   [192] Downie, *Frontline Rhodesia*, 05m:15s.
[193] Anderson and Branch, 'Allies at the End of Empire', p. 3.

soldiers',[194] 'black Zimbabwean traitors',[195] involved in 'criminal collaboration with the racist regime'.[196] And ZANU 'had threatened war crimes trials and other manifestations of vengefulness for whites and their "collaborators"'.[197] As the war intensified, guerrilla violence was increasingly directed towards off-duty soldiers and other employees of the Rhodesian state, or those associated with them, a commonplace occurrence in anti-colonial conflicts.[198]

To return to the 'pull' factors, scholars have observed that would-be deserters require areas of safe harbour or a network of sympathisers to translate 'disaffection into desertion'.[199] While I have argued that most RAR soldiers were not disaffected, and that my interviewees recalled high morale, it is nonetheless quite possible that some troops may have been disaffected. Here I contend that any would-be deserters did not have a safe harbour to potentially flee to, for the level of violence directed by guerrilla forces towards those associated with the army increased exponentially as the war intensified.

My interviewees told me that this violence was largely conducted by ZANLA cadres in the east of the country. These ZANLA groups targeted those with a government affiliation for murder, ranging from cattle-dip attendants, to civil servants, to chiefs, to soldiers. This is not to imply that all members of ZANLA condoned such acts. For instance, as Tendi argues, 'Tongogara's High Command' did not condone the use of violence against the family members of soldiers, as it 'saw family loyalty as divisible; just because a ZANLA guerrilla's family member belonged to the RSF did not make that guerrilla a sell-out or spy'.[200] Nonetheless, the use of violence against soldiers and their families was widespread within ZANLA strongholds from the early 1970s onwards. Later in the war, similar patterns of violence appeared in ZIPRA-controlled areas.

Those in the security forces were doubly at risk, for, as Stapleton argued, 'since African police and soldiers actively worked against the insurgency, they were seen as traitors to the nationalist cause', and they were frequently abducted and murdered or shot in cold blood, with their corpses displayed 'as an example for other "sell-outs"'.[201] A vast majority

---

[194] ZANU PF, *Zimbabwe News*, 10, 5 (1978), p. 21.
[195] Zvobgo, 'For Black Zimbabwean Traitors This Is a Time of Crisis and Decision'.
[196] Raftopoulos, *Hard Road to Reform*, p. 101.
[197] McLaughlin, 'Victims As Defenders', p. 270.
[198] This was widespread in Algeria, for instance. See Evans, 'Harkis', pp. 124–5; Crapanzano, *Harkis*, pp. 30–2; Ferdi, *Un Enfant Dans La Guerre*. For Zimbabwe, see Alexander, 'Loyalty and Liberation', p. 6.
[199] Koehler et al., 'From Disaffection to Desertion', p. 453.
[200] Tendi, *Army and Politics*, p. 45.
[201] Stapleton, *African Police and Soldiers*, pp. 208–9.

of black troops were 'country lads' who hailed from the rural regions.[202] Prior to the mid-1970s intensification of the conflict, many would frequently travel from the main garrisons, located in the vicinity of the urban centres, to visit their families during leave periods. Many came from the eastern regions of the country, which were long-standing army catchment areas as discussed earlier, but during the war had also become ZANLA bastions. This made them particularly vulnerable.

MSW told me, 'you see we couldn't go to TTL [Tribal Trust Lands]. Because villagers [were compelled to] to tell the guerrillas, "in this village, there were so many young men who went to war [i.e. were in the Rhodesian Army]". So those families were now enemies [and the guerrillas asked them] – "Why did you let your youngsters go and join the army?"'.[203] Relatives and friends of soldiers were also often targeted too.[204]

The methods of violence used against those associated with the state were sometimes cruel and spectacular, including, inter alia, the amputation of limbs, sexual violence, torture with implements, and torture with fire.[205] If guerrillas could not attack people associated with the army or their relatives, they instead destroyed their property, such as their homes and their animals, as MS, the wife of an RAR soldier, relayed to me: 'they even went on to kill their cattle in the reserve because the owner of the cattle is in the army. They killed them *all*. They didn't like to see people from the army – from all government departments'.[206] Likewise, an RAR sergeant in 1979 stated 'that his wife and children were safe, in an army barracks in Bulawayo', but that 'other relatives, including cousins, have been threatened with death because of their connection to him . . . people in his home village are so frightened that nobody will any longer look after his cattle'.[207]

This caused immense difficulties for the families of soldiers, as it meant they could no longer visit their relatives in the rural areas safely. MZ, the wife of an RAR soldier, told me that 'in the rural areas, we didn't used to go there to see parents, because if they saw you they'd go and tell the guerrillas "She's here, he's here", so they maybe come at night at home and kill you'.[208] MS, also the wife of an RAR soldier, recounted that this

---

[202] Downie, *Frontline Rhodesia*, 5m:10s.   [203] Interview with MSW.
[204] 'Editorial', *Nwoho* (April 1978), p. 5. The opposite was also the case – the Rhodesians pursued the families of nationalists and guerrillas, meaning that it was both ZIPRA and ZANLA policy for fighters to use a nom de guerre.
[205] See, for example, Pandya, *Mao-Tse-Tung and Chimurenga*, p. 5. As noted earlier, the Rhodesian forces also carried out many war crimes and targeted the families of known guerrillas.
[206] Interview with MS.   [207] Burns, 'Reporter's Notebook', p. 1.
[208] Interview with MZ.

Guerrilla Targeting of Black Soldiers and Their Families 185

period was tough: 'it was definitely very difficult. You could sneak in and out, but privately – secretly'.[209] These clandestine trips were highly dangerous and placed immense strain upon families.[210]

The Rhodesian government recognized the level of threat. The BSAP Support Unit, a paramilitary force similar in some respects to the RAR, suffered a shortage of married accommodation at its barracks, meaning many of its constables refused to marry in their home areas as they:

> did not see marriage to a wife in a tribal area as satisfactory or secure whist they themselves remain members of the Security Forces. Those men ... whose wives are in sensitive tribal areas do not, for example, go home on returning from operations ... One constable in the Support Unit suffered the murder by terrorists of his immediate parents in the Kandeya TTL. This has not been forgotten.[211]

By 1974, the threat to soldiers was critical, with General Walls remarking to the *Rhodesia Herald* that RAR troops 'had done very well considering the "tremendous pressures"' on them. 'It must be appreciated that the terrorists are using all possible means to "get at" African soldiers.'[212]

These pressures increased in parallel with the intensification of the war. In 1976, the RSF high command 'was notified that many African troops were receiving letters from their relatives in their home districts, notably Gutu and Buhera, stating that they were being questioned about their army connections and asking the soldiers to return home'.[213] The RAR companies issued small 7.65-millimetre pistols to black soldiers going on R&R.[214] This indicated that the threat was so severe that troops on leave routinely carried concealed arms if heading to the rural areas.

In 1977, the Rhodesian Cabinet noted that black soldiers were particularly at risk, as they were unpopular in their 'own community and [are] under considerable physical and psychological pressure from nationalists'.[215] DC recalled:

> You couldn't go and visit the rural areas if you were working in the army then, because they took you as an enemy ... and so many people died for that ... one of our soldiers from Bikita his parents, the father and the brother who had just

---

[209] Interview with MS.
[210] Kanaaneh observed a similar dynamic in Arab soldiers in the IDF visiting their families (*Surrounded*, pp. 18–19).
[211] CL, R.C. (S) (76) 35, 'Cabinet Committee on Decentralisation: BSAP and Training Schools', 26 March 1976.
[212] Maxey, *Fight for Zimbabwe*, pp. 34–5; Stapleton, *African Police and Soldiers*, pp. 180–1.
[213] Flood, *Brothers-in-Arms?*, p. 27.   [214] Hopkins, 'Organisation of an RAR Battalion'.
[215] CL, R.C. (S) (77) 86, 'Pay Restraint: Effect on the Public Service and Uniformed Forces', 6 July 1977; CCC(S) (77) 1, 'Cabinet Committee on Conditions of Service', 19 May 1977, Annex A, pp. 2–3.

written O-Level, they were slaughtered just like that, just because your son is in the army. And so many people died because of that. For what reason? Well, it was a silly war. It was a silly war.[216]

In saddening and heart-wrenching testimony, JC told me of an incident that occurred in 1977:

They knew that I was a soldier. And that is why my father was killed. Because when the comrades which were out, when they came here to our area there, they wanted to know if there is somebody who is a soldier. So people at our area sold [out] my father, that he has got a son, JC, who is in the army, and he was killed.[217]

In 1978, Rhodesian officials were concerned as to the potential for this violence to prompt black soldiers to seek discharges.[218] However, it seems very few soldiers actually left the army, as discussed later in this chapter, for the RAR was concurrently lobbying the army to rehouse soldiers' families.[219] By the end of the year, a rapid programme of resettlement was instigated.[220] Several of my interviewees had their family members moved, often to accommodation within one of the military cantonments. After MN's rural home was destroyed, his family moved into barracks near Bulawayo.[221] After JC's father was murdered, his CO ordered 'JC's family should be taken to be safeguarded in RAR' at Llewellin Barracks.[222] Other garrisons, such as that of 2RAR, had family accommodation built adjacent to barracks that was continuously guarded.

In 1978, it was reported that 'a hundred African soldiers had been killed by insurgents while on leave',[223] and the next year, another journalist reported that 'more than 100 black soldiers on vacation in the tribal reservations have been killed by guerrillas'.[224] This number is roughly similar to that in other branches of the security forces – for instance, a November 1977 memorandum from the minister of internal Affairs outlined that 'to date, 107 District Assistants and District Security Assistants and 110 of their relatives have been murdered by terrorists. This is in addition to those killed in action'.[225] When one considers that, throughout the whole of the war, RAR

---

[216] Interview with DC.   [217] Interview with JC.
[218] PKF, SC (78) 26th Meeting, 'Security Briefing', 8 August 1978.
[219] 'Editorial', *Nwoho* (April 1978), p. 8.
[220] Caute claimed that in 1978, three 'rest camps' had been 'established near Salisbury, Bulawayo, and Fort Victoria' (*Under the Skin*, p. 190).
[221] Interview with MN.   [222] Interview with JC.
[223] Stapleton, *African Police and Soldiers*, p. 210.
[224] Burns, 'How Blacks View Their Larger Role in Rhodesia's Army'.
[225] CL, R.C. (S) (77) 116, 'National Service: African Apprentices and Incoming University Students', 10 November 1977.

soldiers killed in action numbered 191 in total, of which 136 were from 1RAR and 2RAR,[226] by the end of the war, black soldiers were almost as much at risk off duty in rural areas as they were on combat operations.[227]

Despite the immense threat posed to black soldiers, it seems few left the army, although without full access to the RAA, it is difficult to know with certainty. None of my interviewees sought discharges, nor did they know of many who did so. A 1977 study of 500 black soldiers demonstrated that just 15.8 per cent intended to leave the army within the following one or two years, 34.1 per cent intended to leave within the following two to five years, and more than 50 per cent intended to serve for at least another five years.[228]

It is likely that the combination of these soldiers' extant loyalties and the RAR-driven programme to rehouse the families of black troops forestalled an exodus of black soldiers leaving the army at the end of their enlistment. Furthermore, deserting was likely not an option for these troops, and even this act would not have purged them of their sell-out status. To return to the typology of desertion, the 'pull' factor of safe harbour was not present. As WM told me, he did not know of any RAR deserters, but even if black soldiers were to entertain the idea, 'we had nowhere to desert to anyway! Nowhere to go'.[229] Likewise, given that many soldiers' families increasingly lived in barracks and cantonments, the kinship networks within rural areas that provide a network of sympathisers, as scholars have of observed other conflicts, did not exist to the same extent within Rhodesia.

My interviewees reasoned that they (and their families) would be safer if they remained serving, despite the risks of combat duty, than if they returned to their home areas.[230] MSW told me his wife 'wasn't happy – she used to tell me, "Why can't you quit?" but I couldn't... because by that time I was already registered as an enemy... if I quit and [went] home I was going to be killed'.[231] Thus the 'push' factors of a safe haven or network of sympathisers simply did not exist for black Rhodesian soldiers.

---

[226] One hundred and ninety-one were killed in action from 1RAR, 2RAR, 3RAR, Depot RAR and the Indep Coys (Binda, *Masodja*, pp. 404–7).
[227] In addition to those 191 soldiers killed in action, many more RAR soldiers were killed on active service, but not by guerrillas (e.g. in vehicle accidents or through injuries otherwise not sustained in combat such as in training), or were murdered when off-duty by guerrillas. Their number remains unknown.
[228] Mutangadura, *Study*, p. 18.   [229] Interview with WM.
[230] Similar sentiments were expressed by SWATF soldiers. See Bolliger, *Apartheid's African Soldiers*, pp. 104–7.
[231] Interview with MSW.

Conclusion

Having outlined 'push' and 'pull' factors, this chapter has argued that black Rhodesian soldiers did not possess the motivations that scholars have observed of deserters in other conflicts. The loyalty of black soldiers to the army was not seriously challenged by their experiences of conflict, for these troops felt that their professionalism and martial qualities had afforded them a decisive military advantage. They did not feel that the war was being lost and came to regard many guerrilla fighters with contempt. While black soldiers did afford ZIPRA's well-trained forces begrudging respect, their generally contemptuous perspectives of guerrillas reflect the particular combat experiences of the RAR, which were shaped by the nature of their wartime tasks, and should not be considered a comprehensive account of the war.

Furthermore, the rodomontade of black soldiers should be understood as those of soldiers who fought while enjoying air superiority over their adversaries, and who could be quickly reinforced, resupplied, and medically evacuated during combat, unlike guerrilla forces. I have argued that the combat experiences of my interviewees cemented their extant conceptions of their professionalism and bolstered their solidarities to their comrades, the regiment, and the wider army.

As the war intensified and violence became more prevalent in the rural areas, black soldiers increasingly came to hold guerrillas in contempt for what they perceived as their widespread abuses of the civilian population. This forged a notion among black soldiers that their soldiering was moral and masculine, in contrast to what they portrayed as the cowardly tactics of guerrillas. The widespread use of guerrilla violence against off-duty soldiers and their families sharpened the hostilities of black soldiers towards their adversaries, and likely forestalled any potential desertions among black soldiers. Thus the loyalties of black soldiers to the army were not corroded by their wartime experiences and were in fact reinforced and boosted by them, particularly as the conflict intensified. Chapter 6 argues that these troops also adopted an apolitical ethos with one eye on the conclusion of the war and their post-war future in an independent Zimbabwe.

6 'They Just Follow the Government of the Day'
The Politics of 'Apolitical' Black Rhodesian Soldiers

This chapter argues that black Rhodesian soldiers professed an apolitical ethos, which they deemed inherent to their status as professionals. The Rhodesian Army implemented its British-inherited apolitical norm selectively and policed black soldiers' political expression in a manner from which white troops views were exempted. However, black soldiers also played a large role in the construction of this apolitical identity. By couching their service as apolitical, black soldiers avoided political party or ethnic allegiances, thus distancing themselves from politicised factions such as the auxiliaries, and their use of partisan violence against civilians in pursuit of narrow ethno-political aims, and white units that expressed an open allegiance to minority rule. As we have seen, the loyalties of black soldiers to the Rhodesian Army became highly contentious during the war in the eyes of nationalists, who labelled them as sell-outs for what they saw as their collaboration with the Smith regime. Black soldiers rejected this portrayal and positioned themselves both during and after the war as apolitical troops who served their country and the 'government of the day', regardless of its political orientation.

For black soldiers, asserting that one was apolitical was thus accomplished through directing their loyalty to the RAR (or other regiment) and the army. As argued earlier, this did not constitute macro-level loyalty to the Smith regime: in fact, privately, many RAR soldiers supported majority rule. The term 'apolitical' in their usage distinguished between their loyalties as soldiers and their personal political preferences, enabling them to retain their effectiveness as a fighting force.

In this there was a stark contrast to white soldiers, whose loyalties were often premised upon political support for minority rule. As a result, their commitment to the war and the country waned as the inevitability of decolonisation became clear.

Conversely, RAR soldiers had strong instrumental reasons following the war to portray their loyalty as apolitical and distance themselves from accusations of collaboration. However, I contend that there is a great deal of evidence that this stance was both genuine and contemporary and, furthermore, that the liberation movement leadership also recognised it.

It may also be the case that RAR veterans have emphasised the apolitical aspect of their service in retrospect, so as to defuse accusations levelled against them of being sell-outs during the politically charged post-2000 crisis years in Zimbabwe, in which wartime allegiances were instrumentalised by ZANU(PF). This does not detract from its historical reality and significance, but is demonstrative of how wartime narratives have been adapted in response to political changes.

Lastly, this chapter argues that black RAR soldiers' positioning of themselves as apolitical and militarily effective meant that they could become the acceptable face of the Rhodesian Army. Thus the apolitical stance of black troops also functioned as a way to display their professionalism and regimental loyalty, so as to ensure their safety from persecution, and post-independence retention as soldiers. I start by discussing the class background of black soldiers and how this impacted their political views.

Regional and Class Backgrounds As Influencing the Politics of Black Soldiers

Black soldiers' socio-economic status placed them in a black middle class that one might expect to be sympathetic to nationalism, as much of the black middle class was. Here I show that the combination of deliberate army recruitment in rural areas and social isolation in military institutions worked against such involvement, though support for majority rule was nonetheless widespread among soldiers.

Michael West argued that although the Rhodesian settler-colonial system 'was hardly conducive to upward social mobility . . . a small minority of Africans managed to defy the odds', becoming what he termed the African middle class.[1] Some parallels between this cohort and black troops are apparent, principally soldiers' relatively high standard of living and disposable income, as we have seen. The initial motivations of black soldiers to enlist in the army included a desire to learn new skills and trades, obtain a well-paid and secure job, and acquire a role that bestowed status.[2] These factors were prevalent among the middle class too, and Stapleton argued that as 'educational achievement was related to social status' in Rhodesia, 'some soldiers, particularly senior ones, and their wives and children, entered the emerging African middle class'.[3]

Black soldiers, however, were not part of the middle class in an important way. West argued that 'a strong urban bias' existed among members

---

[1] West, *Rise of an African Middle Class*, p. 1.
[2] Stapleton, *African Police and Soldiers*, pp. 28–33.   [3] Ibid., p. 87.

of the middle class, and almost all of them lived in or around the cities.[4] They were defined not solely by their 'material reality', but also by a 'shared consciousness of class' which embraced nationalism, notably after the RF came to power, and their urban interconnectedness was pivotal in its social construction. This was important, as the urban and peri-urban areas of Rhodesia were not only where nationalist politics first took root in trade unions and urban associations, but also remained the primary fora for democratic debate, and the strongholds of its leadership and intelligentsia.[5]

In contrast, most black soldiers were 'country lads', as we have seen. Their rural backgrounds meant that they were less likely to be exposed to nationalist discourses or occupy roles in the nationalist movement in the 1960s and early 1970s, before the spread of the guerrilla war throughout the rural areas. DSN told me that, in the RAR, 'you could get two or three people who like to talk about politics. But mainly we didn't know [what nationalist] politics was'.[6] Black soldiers were also, in the main, not well educated, largely owing to the chronic underinvestment and low capacity the Rhodesian government provided for black education in the countryside, which meant that only 20 per cent of black students could find a place at a secondary school.[7]

While three of my interviewees – HZ, BM, and DSN – had attended mission schools and were able to continue their education after Standard VI (meaning they possessed more than eight years' total schooling) prior to enlisting, most of my interviewees had only a few years of formal education.[8] Most black soldiers had not received much education and did not perform the roles typical of the middle class prior to enlisting, which typically included 'clerks, teachers, preachers, social workers, journalists, businessmen, nurses, lawyers, and doctors' – jobs available to those who had completed secondary school and often further education too.[9] A 1977 study of 500 regular black soldiers demonstrated that all those who had been in the workplace prior to enlisting had worked in low-skilled roles, with the exception of 'eight teachers and one medical assistant'.[10] Most black soldiers were not members of the middle class prior to enlisting. Thus while their salary and perks meant that black soldiers may have shared aspects of the material reality of the middle

---

[4] West, *Rise of an African Middle Class*, pp. 2–3.
[5] Scarnecchia, *Urban Roots of Democracy*, chapter 6. Nationalist ideology was thus prevalent within the urban areas, although there were important regions of rural nationalism too. See Alexander et al., *Violence and Memory*, pp. 84–102.
[6] Interview with DSN.   [7] West, *Rise of an African Middle Class*, pp. 48–51.
[8] Interview with TM.   [9] West, *Rise of an African Middle Class*, pp. 6–7.
[10] Mutangadura, *Study*, p. 16.

class, they did not share its socially constructed consciousness of class. Consequently, there were far fewer nationalists among black soldiers than among the wider middle class.

This was also influenced by the recruitment policies of the Rhodesian Army, which deliberately did not recruit from the middle class. My interviewees told me that white officers viewed educated black soldiers with suspicion as possessed of potential nationalist sympathies, and as a potential rivals for their own jobs and career prospects.[11] This was well known among black recruits, and the few who possessed O-levels (who in the main joined as teachers or medics) concealed their education.[12] As discussed earlier, the army's practices of recruitment emphasised regional traditions of service, and its rural catchment areas were conspicuously not middle-class strongholds.

This cleavage between black soldiers and the middle class was decisively compounded by the detached nature of army life. The scholarly literature has long asserted that the regular soldier is 'almost by definition a social isolate, for his values and norms, his sense of commitment, his socialization and his self-realization seem to distinguish him from other members of society'.[13] As argued earlier, the Rhodesian Army deliberately encouraged this detachment among its soldiers, and elaborate processes of 'military socialisation' moulded the loyalties of its recruits to their comrades and regiment, and prohibited overt political allegiance. Furthermore, as nationalism became more popular in the 1960s, the army also began to actively suppress even the smallest signs of political consciousness among its soldiers.

The Army's Policing of Politics among Black Soldiers

Despite the Rhodesian Army's nominal adherence to British-derived political impartiality, after UDI, its upper echelons became fundamentally politicised in support of minority rule. This filtered down to the company and platoon level, and the British norm of soldiers not espousing political views was widely ignored among whites, many of whom stated support for the RF. However, the institutional racism of the army, as we have seen in Chapter 4, meant that the political views of black soldiers were treated very differently by the army, which policed their politics by the use of surveillance and punishment. In this manner, the supposedly impartial norms of the army were in fact political.

---

[11] Interview with TM.   [12] Stapleton, *African Police and Soldiers*, p. 86.
[13] Harries-Jenkins and Van Doorn, 'Armed Forces and the Social Order', p. 17.

The Army's Policing of Politics among Black Soldiers 193

In the Western military tradition, the normative expectation is that the army does not involve itself in political matters and that professionalism is the guarantor of the army's impartiality.[14] While the Rhodesian Army inherited this British ethos prior to UDI, its adherence to it quickly became a mere veneer.[15] UDI fundamentally ruptured adherence to it among the army top brass, not least because the RF purged it of senior officers it deemed as loyal to the Crown during the 1960s.[16] The army's officers corps was all white until 1977, and much of it, particularly those that joined after UDI, were 'avid supporters of the Rhodesian Front government'.[17] Thus from UDI onwards, the army's enforcement of the norm that soldiers do not engage in politics was largely applied to black soldiers and rarely to whites, many of whom were politically outspoken supporters of minority rule.

The inherited impartial ethos may have persisted to an extent among ordinary white soldiers. For instance, a white deserter who had served as a private soldier on the front line, interviewed by an academic in 1977, stated that 'there is no political indoctrination given to black or white troops' because 'the Army has a very British structure' and 'the military machine thinks like a military machine, pure and simple'.[18] This discourse remained prevalent among black soldiers too. My interviewees characterised the army as 'not interested [in politics] and apolitical' and told me that as soldiers, 'we were apolitical' and the RAR especially was 'apolitical'.[19] However, I argue, this discourse fails to account for the particular way in which this supposed British-derived norm was actively shaped by the army through coercion.

While TM described the army as apolitical 'in general', he noted that this ethos was flouted by white officers, particularly those from the TF and white-only units:

You also had quite a number [of whites] who expressed their feelings that they would not tolerate black-majority rule ... They were privileged, they would say what they like and whoever was listening was a black man [and so] had no way of putting across his feelings or reaction [without risking punishment]. We sort of

---

[14] See, for instance, Janowitz, *Professional Soldier*; Finer, *Man on Horseback*; Huntington, *Soldier and the State*. Some scholars have questioned whether this maxim reflects the historical reality of British political-military interactions, particularly when one factors in that give and take between political and military elites is inevitable, and that the top echelon of military commanders will always enjoy political power and influence by virtue of their rank and appointment – see Tendi, 'Soldiers contra Diplomats', pp. 939–40.
[15] McLaughlin, 'Thin White Line', p. 182.
[16] Kenrick, *Decolonisation, Identity and Nation in Rhodesia*, p. 146; Moorcraft, *Short Thousand Years*, p. 13.
[17] Whitaker, *'New Model' Armies of Africa?*, p. 165.
[18] Cohen, 'War in Rhodesia', p. 484.   [19] Interviews with TM, CD, and WR.

suffered in silence. The whole idea was not to let the feeling spread or grow ... No matter how carried away you may be, not politics ... the fact that blacks were anxious and looking forward to the day when a black man would rule Zimbabwe, rule this country, was never to be entertained ... A few [whites] would express these [racist] feelings upon any occasion. Say, if a black man made a blunder, one would say, 'Now you think you blacks can rule this country and expect us to live under your rule.'[20]

Black soldiers widely observed this double standard. JM recalled how he was once in conversation with a white officer who asked him, '"Did you meet any African government [officials]?" I said no. He said, "I met one in Zambia. They'll take all your cattle, they'll take even your wife, even take your children ... they're there killing each other."'[21] Of course, not all black soldiers believed these made-up stories, and many saw through this racist fearmongering, as was the case for JM and TM.

TM's allusion to 'suffering in silence' referred to the army's increased used of coercion to forestall any expression of political consciousness among black soldiers. Stapleton has described in detail the Rhodesian Army's institutional practices of political censorship and surveillance of nationalist sentiment. In the late 1950s, authorities placed RAR NCOs under surveillance for suspected 'subversive talk', although it seems no official action was ever taken.[22] In the late 1950s and early 1960s, a handful of soldiers were seemingly reprimanded for engaging in political discussion.[23]

This mirrored the Rhodesian government's wider clampdown upon nationalism among civil servants, such as the 1959 Native Education Act that '"forbade teachers" from "taking an active part in political matters"'. In this way, the colonial authorities hoped to detach teachers, traditionally an important leadership element within the African elite, from the nationalist locomotive'.[24] Likewise, the army's suppression of any political activity within the RAR's ranks was intended to prevent nationalists from gaining a foothold within the army.

My interviewees did recall fleeting instances of political activity on the part of a few black soldiers during the mid-to-late 1960s, and these instances were severely punished by the army. TM recounted how on the eve of UDI, the main body of 1RAR was dispatched to Victoria Falls. This was part of a Rhodesian deployment posture designed to deter British intervention.[25] A small RAR group remained in barracks in

---

[20] Interview with TM. [21] Interview with JM.
[22] Stapleton, *African Police and Soldiers*, pp. 171–2. [23] Ibid., pp. 172–3.
[24] West, *Rise of an African Middle Class*, p. 51.
[25] Wood, *So Far and No Further!*, p. 459.

Bulawayo, and some junior soldiers staged a protest expressing their outrage at UDI and its aim of perpetuating minority rule:

> The main [protest] took place [when] some young soldiers – I think the most senior was a corporal – tried to organise a way of reacting [to UDI]. They were apprehended, arrested and detained at Victoria Falls and later were court-martialled. Four of them, who turned out to be the ringleaders, after thorough investigations, were court-martialled, and, I can't remember the exact sentences, but it was I think up to ten years in prison. This appeared a severe punishment and also a deterrent to others who had been sympathising with these youngsters. Other soldiers who had sympathised with them saw the danger and just went quiet. There were no more comments about UDI and what had been said [by Ian Smith] over the radio.[26]

Likewise, DSN, who joined the army in 1967, told me of a black sergeant major who 'used to wear these ZAPU hats, you know those [leopard] skin ZAPU [fur] hats ... He got into trouble, at the end of the day he was cashiered [discharged] from the army'.[27] These harsh punishments could be read to imply that the army hierarchy were worried about the loyalty of African soldiers generally, although Rhodesian government documents from the mid-to-late 1960s demonstrate that it was contented as to the loyalty of 'African members of the police and armed forces'.[28] Instead, the severe reaction of the army hierarchy in these instances was likely intended to act as a 'deterrent', as TM argued, that would forestall any threats to loyalty.

The army's coercive attitude towards any sign of overt political discourse cemented the conception among black soldiers that they should avoid all politics, and that any such acts were a cardinal form of 'impermissible indiscipline'. SM told me, 'the commanders, the whites we had, they didn't want the soldiers to talk about politics. If they hear you talking about politics you'll be in the box [imprisoned] for that ... They were very strict. They didn't want people to talk about it'.[29] WM said, 'as soldiers, we were not allowed to talk about politics. Not within the army'.[30] MSW felt 'we were not allowed to participate in politics'.[31] TM recalled that while political discussion sometimes did occur, it was quickly shut down:

> Sometimes during functions we were allowed to mix with the officers and if some people got too carried away and started talking politics, it had to be stopped. Or, the following day, word would be sent round that there was talk of politics and this was never to be repeated. On both sides – you had blacks who had their own feelings and wanted to vent them out, and the whites who had extreme feelings as well – but the army in general was not interested [and was] apolitical.[32]

[26] Interview with TM.   [27] Interview with DSN.
[28] Stapleton, *African Police and Soldiers*, p. 178.   [29] Interview with SM.
[30] Interview with WM.   [31] Interview with MSW.   [32] Interview with TM.

DC recalled how, during the early 1970s, rumours of political discussion among him and his peers had been reported to army commanders. 'They actually called the CIDs to come and investigate ... to find out what was their political motive and what-what. We told them! "No we are not interested in politics, we have come to do work!" ... they were very paranoid.'[33] This atmosphere of surveillance and censorship had a chilling effect on the political expression of black soldiers. PM recounted he did not dwell on political ideas or participate in political discussion as he 'got that feeling that you'd end up ... losing employment – I need the job [for] my family, if I [were dismissed for political activity] who is going to feed them and that? So then we remained neutral'.[34] The army's policing of politics enshrined a conception within the RAR that political activity was not within the purview of the soldier.

It appears that the army's policing of politics served the Rhodesians' goal, likely aided by how, as argued earlier, the violence of the war entrenched enmity between soldiers and nationalists. As Stapleton argued, it appears that 'there was more nationalist sympathy within the RAR in the late 1950s and early 1960s than during the war years', as soldiers and nationalists who were 'previously occasional if awkward associates, now became wartime enemies'.[35]

Some of my interviewees also stated that they were disinterested in the political process in general. This has been observed of soldiers elsewhere, too, in a small and emergent literature. For instance, during World War II, Wehrmacht soldiers 'wore their ideological indifference like a badge. They repeatedly asserted that they were "non-political", had "never cared about politics", and did "not want to have anything to do with politics"'.[36] Similarly, BM told me that he had only voted 'once up to now', and the reason for this was that he has 'no interest at all' in taking part.[37] DSN said that he 'didn't feel anything [in terms of political allegiance] because I didn't know about politics. [We] didn't want to talk about politics in the army'.[38] As black soldiers were all volunteers, it is highly unlikely that those young men who shared nationalist political consciousness would have enlisted in the army in the first instance.

Furthermore, a general lack of political consciousness among black Rhodesian soldiers is unsurprising given that most could not cast their first ballot until 1979.[39] As HZ told me, this meant that many in the RAR

---

[33] Interview with DC. [34] Interview with PM.
[35] Stapleton, *African Police and Soldiers*, pp. 178–9.
[36] Römer, 'Milieus in the Military', p. 143. [37] Interview with BM.
[38] Interview with DSN.
[39] Few black soldiers met the Rhodesian educational and property criteria required of voters by its racist and unrecognised 1970 constitution, and even if they did meet these

'were not interested in politics, maybe we had not got used to see what is politics, we didn't know anything. So we said, "What is there today is what we follow." This is what we were doing. We never minded of politics'.[40] A disconnect between personal political beliefs and military service was also evidenced by some white enlisted soldiers from ordinary backgrounds, such as the white deserter discussed earlier,[41] and Chris Cocks, a white trooper in the RLI, who in retrospect described how his post-conscription voluntary re-enlistment in 1977 was motivated not by politics, but out of a sense of 'camaraderie' to his fellow soldiers: 'I was vaguely opposed to Ian Smith and his politics, but here I was serving as a trooper in one of his most effective strike units.'[42]

Thus the general apolitical ethos of black troops was not mere happenstance: it was shaped through the army's recruitment practices, which intentionally omitted the middle class and highly educated, and focused upon rural areas where nationalism was less prevalent in the 1960s and early 1970s, and also by the army's use of surveillance and coercion that punished even the most benign forms of political discourse among black soldiers. The increased enmity between black soldiers and the liberation movements as violence intensified created a new dynamic that dissuaded support for the liberation movements among black troops. However, this apolitical stance should not be taken to infer that black soldiers were devoid of political views, and I argue that a specific form of politics was prevalent.

Vested in the State: The Politics of 'Apolitical' Soldiers

Black soldiers squared the circle of fighting in the settler state's army while often also supporting majority rule (or at least not supporting minority rule) by using a particular language of loyalty vested in the country, the government of the day, or often to the RAR or the army itself. This rendered their allegiance superficially apolitical; however, I argue that these beliefs were themselves a subtle form of politicking that allowed black Rhodesian soldiers to distance themselves from the Smith regime and advertise their professionalism to a future majority-rule government.

---

requirements, they could vote for only 8 of 56 seats. 'Africans over the age of 21 who have completed not less than 12 months service' in the army were technically enfranchised by the November 1977 Electoral Amendment Bill (Flood, *Brothers-in-Arms?*, p. 44). However, this was moot, as the first time soldiers could exercise this vote was the April 1979 'Internal Settlement' election, which was the first – and only – poll during the Rhodesian era in which all black adults were entitled to vote (although only for 72 of 100 seats).

[40] Interview with HZ.   [41] Cohen, 'War in Rhodesia', p. 484.
[42] Cocks, *Fireforce*, p. 123.

In her 1980 book *Ethnic Soldiers*, the political scientist Cynthia Enloe asserted that young black men enlisting in the Rhodesian Army towards the end of the 1970s had to be wary, as 'enlisting now becomes an act of political allegiance, and a statement of communal allegiance'.[43] This was the view of many nationalists, but it was not how my interviewees understood their service in the army. It did not imply a party political allegiance or indeed a view on the merits of minority rule, but was instead, in their language, service to the government of the day that persisted irrespective of the party in power.

It is important to be clear that none of my interviewees expressed support for the Smith regime or for minority rule. While this may seem an obvious stance to take in retrospect, considerable historical evidence exists that this was the case during the war too, as discussed later in this chapter.

In fact, the loyalties of colonial troops were rarely contingent upon political allegiance to the regime in power. As Ruth Ginio argued of post–World War II African troops in the French army, soldiering was 'not a political or ideological statement'.[44] Grundy, writing on black soldiers within apartheid South Africa, noted that 'political support for the regime' was 'quite rare'.[45] Bolliger noted that Namibians in apartheid South Africa's external army units 'described their military service as wage employment, and many compared it to any other government job, such as teaching or nursing': 'ideological convictions were largely absent'.[46] Algerian *harkis* who fought on the side of the French COIN forces against the FLN have also argued in retrospect that they fought 'against the terror imposed by the FLN ... but not against Algerian independence'.[47]

Similarly, several long-serving RAR veterans pointed out that, from their enlistment in the late 1950s through to their retirement in the late 1980s, they had served under governments formed by very different parties: the United Federal Party until 1962, the RF until 1979, and thereafter ZANU-PF.[48] Black soldiers' private political sympathies were not vested in the Smith regime. This sentiment was unanimous among

---

[43] Enloe, *Ethnic Soldiers*, p. 195.
[44] Ginio, *The French Army and Its African Soldiers*, p. 83.
[45] Grundy, *Soldiers without Politics*, pp. 28–9.
[46] Bolliger, 'Apartheid's Transnational Soldiers', p. 200; Bolliger, 'Chiefs, Terror, and Propaganda', pp. 125–6.
[47] Crapanzano, *Harkis*, pp. 30–2. As noted earlier, it is unclear whether, when referring to *harkis*, Crapanzano is referring solely to the 55,000 *harki* auxiliaries (*supplétifs*), or is also referring to the 20,000 Algerian regulars and 40,000 Algerian conscripts who served in the colonial French Army.
[48] Interviews with SM, GN, GMH, and TM.

my interviewees. DSN told me, 'we couldn't worship Smith or whoever' else was part of the RF government.[49]

The views of RAR soldiers were vividly illustrated by a chance encounter in 1972. A British Royal Commission was touring Rhodesia 'to ascertain the opinion of the population as a whole' regarding the acceptability of the Anglo-Rhodesian 'settlement' thrashed out by the Conservative government and the RF.[50] The proposals would have essentially enshrined minority rule for decades to come. Thus when the commissioners visited different areas of the country to ask black Rhodesians about their disposition towards the settlement, the response was resoundingly negative. The commissioners chanced upon a group of RAR soldiers in Mashonaland North.[51] Its members:

including senior NCOs, rejected the Proposals (with one exception) largely for reasons related to a feeling of unjust and racially biased treatment by the Government, although they were obviously treated as a privileged group. Even these men, employed in an important security role and evidently imbued with a high degree of regimental morale and efficiency expressed political and social reservations about the Government no less strong than those expressed by other Africans.[52]

The commissioners' report demonstrated the complex political views of RAR soldiers. To continue serving the Rhodesian government of the day was their duty, but that did not mean they approved of its politics or policies. These troops did not fight for *Smith's* government, but rather for *the* government. WM told me that black soldiers may not have liked the political status quo, but they would serve it in part because they felt that they could outlast it: they would 'soldier on until things were right'.[53]

In a further illustration of this dynamic, most RAR members voted for Robert Mugabe in the 1980 election.[54] Stapleton noted that 2RAR had its own polling station in Fort Victoria, which meant that the way its soldiers voted – overwhelmingly for Mugabe – was thus known. The local Special Branch officer felt that many soldiers voted for ZANU-PF not out of

---

[49] Interview with DSN. [50] White, 'Normal Political Activities', p. 322.
[51] Mashonaland North and South were colonial provinces split up after independence. Although in the official report, these soldiers are termed a generic 'African Security Unit', presumably an effort on part of the authors to avoid getting any of the RAR soldiers in trouble for expressing political opinions, Maxey affirms that they were RAR (*Fight for Zimbabwe*, p. 34).
[52] Cmd. 4964, *Rhodesia*, p. 166. This page from the report is widely cited in the secondary literature, although for some reason it is usually abridged. See Wilkinson, 'Insurgency in Rhodesia', p. 14; Stapleton, *African Police and Soldiers*, p. 180; Preston, 'Stalemate and the Termination of Civil War, p. 75; Maxey, *Fight for Zimbabwe*, p. 34; Roberts, 'Towards a History of Rhodesia's Armed Forces'; Beckett, 'Rhodesian Army', p. 174.
[53] Interview with WM. [54] Beckett, 'Rhodesian Army', p. 174.

a 'surge of nationalism', but rather owing to 'pressure from [their] wives, who thought that electing Robert Mugabe's party was the only way to end the long war'.[55]

It is also the case that RAR soldiers simply wished for the end of minority rule. TM told me black soldiers had long wished for a black government.[56] SM said, 'everybody wanted this country to be run by us! Even me, I was in the war [as a Rhodesian soldier], but I wanted this country to be run by us, we all wanted that'.[57] MC, a teacher at the 2RAR barracks in Masvingo and the wife of a soldier, supported ZANU-PF:

because we thought the people from the struggle were going to make life for us better, and we'd mix better. But then it didn't happen that way. We were not fearful at all, we were quite happy, we even voted for them [ZANU-PF] because we were expecting change. 1980 I voted for [Mugabe], but that was the last time I did it [*laughs*]. From there then, I never voted for him again.[58]

Likewise, JC told me 'we all voted for Mugabe'.[59] Support for Mugabe was not, however, unanimous, and some RAR soldiers supported the 'moderate' Abel Muzorewa.[60]

The salient fact here is that black RAR soldiers did not vote for Smith. They did not perceive their soldierly loyalty as to his particular government, but to constituted authority, and within that to the army and the RAR itself. As Jakkie Cilliers argued, 'the primary loyalty of the black soldier lay towards his unit' and this did not preclude support for majority rule, a position that could be contrasted to the 'politically motivated' Auxiliaries, whose loyalties were premised upon 'political and an ethnic representation'.[61] In other words, the apolitical soldierly loyalty of black troops did not constitute a specific political allegiance.

Cilliers locates the stopping point of loyalty in the unit, but I argue that black soldiers nested that loyalty within loyalty to the state itself, which they referred to as the government of the day. This was the state rendered in the abstract as a 'willed-for' entity as discussed earlier: just, meritocratic, and competent, in effect a projection of an idealised version of the RAR itself, instead of the state as it existed – that is, captured by the RF. Black troops asserted that they soldiered for their country, which meant that they would not hesitate to bear arms against those forces that attacked the state, civilians, or their comrades. This was a form of politics in itself, in which black Rhodesian soldiers portrayed support for the incumbent government of the day as axiomatically legitimate, even if they did not approve of that government's politics. Such conceptions of

---

[55] Stapleton, *African Police and Soldiers*, p. 181.   [56] Interview with TM.
[57] Interview with SM.   [58] Interview with MC.   [59] Interview with JC.
[60] Interviews with PM and WR.   [61] Cilliers, *Counter-Insurgency in Rhodesia*, p. 214.

the state have historically been found among other troops recruited from marginalised groups, as noted in Chapter 1.

This conception was widely espoused by my interviewees. DSN told me that the RAR were 'professional soldiers; they weren't politicians', and that RAR soldiers served 'the government of the day'.[62] Similarly, PM said 'being in the army, we were guided by the instruction that a soldier is not a politician. A soldier is not a civilian. When you are a soldier, you are a soldier for the ruling government – party of government – the government which is in power that time, that is your master'.[63] HZ told me, 'we were not looking into what will happen with the top hierarchy; we didn't mind. All what we knew was we are soldiers of the country. That was what we were. Whether [different political factions would triumph during elections], we didn't mind about that'.[64] CD saw the RAR soldier as 'a non-political soldier. We were not into politics. We were told we are apolitical'.[65] GN stated:

> The main point I can bring out to you [is that] I was loyal to both governments [i.e. Rhodesian and Zimbabwean, since] I joined [in] 1963; from then I was so loyal to the government of that time [and] all those other governments who came in the middle until the present government. I was so loyal as well, to [the Mugabe] government, until I left [the army].[66]

Concordant with this view, DSN stated that in retrospect, he and his:

> comrades always go back and say, 'Rhodesian soldiers were loyal to any government.' Because they *served*. Some served the Southern Rhodesian government, some served the Rhodesian government, some served the Zimbabwe-Rhodesian government, and they still serve the ZANU government. That is loyalty. They are not politicians. They don't side; they just follow the government of the day.[67]

DSN's succinct description of this dynamic encapsulated the sense of my interviewees that they were apolitical because they rendered service to governments headed by Smith and Mugabe alike.

By highlighting that their soldierly loyalty was to the army/state and thus to the country, these soldiers were not, at least superficially, making a bold or totally original claim. As we have seen, black RNR soldiers during World War I and black RAR troops during World War II espoused similar loyalties. However, in the context of the liberation war, these claims to serve the country had a particular salience because they in effect replaced the nation, the cause of the liberation movements, with abstractions of their own that allowed them a crucial range of manoeuvrability.

---

[62] Interview with DSN.   [63] Interview with PM.   [64] Interview with HZ.
[65] Interview with CD.   [66] Interview with GN.   [67] Interview with DSN.

It is possible that my interviewees magnified the prevalence of apolitical norms among black soldiers in retrospect. As the historian Luise White argued, oral testimonies have 'already been selected, culled, and ordered for a very specific reading'.[68] Rendering themselves apolitical, soldiers carried an implicit exculpatory message: they cannot be held responsible for the actions or policies of the Rhodesian government, and they were merely professional and apolitical soldiers, as found everywhere, carrying out their lawful duties in a time of war. For instance, GM told me, 'there is no country who hasn't got protection [from its military] ... I was one of those who provided protection'.[69] This framing can be interpreted as functioning as a pre-emptive rebuttal to the tenets of the all-pervasive 'Patriotic History' discourse of the present, and in particular accusations of collaboration with the Smith regime, or of being a sell-out. In this context, the wartime history of my interviewees cannot be divorced from the taboo surrounding colonial service – one ZANU(PF) has repeatedly stoked for political purposes, especially after 2000.

My interviewees' narratives also intimate that their work as soldiers was not exceptional and that their vocation was the moral equivalent of that of any other person employed by the Rhodesian state, be they a railwayman, livestock-dip attendant, or civil servant. These narratives of moral equivalency can be seen as a pre-emptive riposte to accusations from ZANU(PF) supporters of having fought for the wrong side, for if one places oneself on the side of the government of the day, rendered as omnipresent and impartial, one cannot have fought for any particular side, let alone the wrong one. The subtext of RAR soldiers labelling themselves as apolitical and professional is also important. It stakes a clear claim that they were not excessive in their use of violence, nor were they responsible for atrocities, and nor did they fight for their own ethnic group or political faction. This discourse serves to distance them from those members of other RSF units that were widely portrayed as involved in atrocities, extrajudicial violence and executions, and political dirty tricks, such as the CIO, Selous Scouts, and BSAP Special Branch.

However, while there are clear incentives for black veterans to highlight the apolitical nature of their service and loyalties to the army, there is clear and plentiful historical evidence to show that black soldiers' wartime loyalties were indeed grounded in this apolitical ethos. As discussed earlier, at the institutional level, this included the army's British-derived ethos, its practices of recruitment that omitted middle-class urban and educated recruits, and its surveillance and policing of soldiers' politics. Within the RAR, black soldiers felt loyalty to their comrades and their

[68] White, 'Telling More', p. 21.   [69] Interview with GN.

The Politics of 'Apolitical' Soldiers 203

unit, bonds enhanced by the intensification of the war. During the war, black soldiers did not express statements of political allegiance to the Smith regime – quite the opposite, as indicated by their testimony to the Pearce Commission and their voting record in 1980.

Furthermore, the claim to be fighting for the government of the day and not the white regime was one soldiers made publicly during the war. For instance, in 1977, a journalist from *The Times* noted that black soldiers had little interest in the politics of Muzorewa, Sithole, and Chirau, rival 'moderate' nationalist leaders within Rhodesia, and an RAR sergeant explained this. 'You cannot work for a nationalist leader and be a soldier at the same time. We are just here to fight for whichever government is in power.'[70] In 1979, the 1RAR regimental sergeant major, WOI Julius Manunure, a soldier of twenty-six years' service, veteran of Malaya, and the most senior enlisted man in the army, stated to a journalist from the *New York Times*, 'I'm not fighting for whites, I'm fighting for my country.'[71] Thus, although my interviewees may have emphasised the apolitical character of their army service in retrospect so as to make their past as palatable as possible in the postcolonial period, it is clear that RAR soldiers were apolitical in important respects during the war too.

In the latter stages of the war, some black soldiers were troubled by their post-independence prospects. As we have seen, they were denounced by nationalists, and black soldiers and their families had been targeted in the rural areas, and ZANU-PF made explicit threats to punish black soldiers after the war too. In November 1976, an Associated Press correspondent said: 'The big question hanging over these new black officers is . . . what their future will be when an African government takes over. Will they be regarded as traitors to the nationalist cause for fighting in a white man's army?'[72]

A *New York Times* journalist, interviewing an RAR soldier in March 1977, wrote: '"Our future is very bleak" said the [RAR] soldier . . . he told of the fears aroused among blacks in the Government forces by the threats of the black guerrilla leaders . . . Robert Mugabe, among others, has pledged to punish blacks working for the white minority if the guerrilla forces gain power.'[73]

In November 1978:

ZANU deputy secretary, Eddison Zvobgo issued a threat that blacks working with the interim government would be 'priority military targets' if they did not cease to do so immediately. Zvobgo threatened: 'You are liable to be arrested or shot on

---

[70] Ashford, 'The Blacks Who Fight for the White Regime in Salisbury'.
[71] Burns, 'How Blacks View Their Larger Role in Rhodesia's Army'.
[72] Associated Press, RR7647A 'Rhodesia War or Diplomacy?', *Roving Report Rhodesia*, 26 November 1976.
[73] Burns, 'Fear Rules Rhodesian Blacks'.

sight; there is no hiding place in Zimbabwe'. Included among the people named were the three black members on the Executive Council, members of the Ministerial Council, black MPs, soldiers and policemen. A second list of 'traitors, puppets and collaborators' was promised at the end of December.[74]

Unsurprisingly, these threats made some black soldiers fearful. By shrewdly framing their service as to the government of the day, they signalled to an incoming nationalist government that their loyalty was transferable to whichever party took power. This profession of apolitical loyalty functioned as a form of political claim-making. By foregrounding their professionalism and combat experience, rather than wartime allegiance, RAR soldiers were claiming a stake in a post-independence future and its envisaged technocratic security institutions.

This strategy was successful, for, as we shall see, black soldiers were all retained in the ZNA after independence. British plans for peace had, since at least 1977, been premised upon the 'RAR battalions as the core of the new ZNA', and stressed the disbandment of the 'unacceptable' white units.[75] It seems that, during the war, for many nationalists the RAR also came to represent the acceptable face of the Rhodesian Army. While this is difficult to assess in retrospect, we do have some insight on the thoughts of senior liberation movement figures from the archives: during the February 1978 talks in Malta, the commander of ZIPRA, 'Alfred Nikita' Mangena, was asked by Field Marshal Lord Carver, the Anglo-American's envisaged transitional governor:

> Whether Mangena thought that the existing battalions of the existing Rhodesian African Rifles could be classified as 'acceptable elements' of the Rhodesian Defence Forces for integration in the ZNA? Mangena said he thought they could be, as far as ZIPRA was concerned, there would be less problem with them than the police support units [paramilitary Rhodesian police units renowned for their brutal treatment of civilians]. The important thing he said was getting rid of the territorials and other all-white units.[76]

It seems the liberation movements made a political judgement premised upon their own assessment that the RAR was a professional force, unlike the white units and the auxiliaries.

During subsequent Anglo-American and Patriotic Front talks in Dar-es-Salaam two months later, Mugabe initially demanded that the prospective UN Force's first function be 'to restrict to barracks, disarm and dismantle all units of the Rhodesian Army and Air Force', but in response

---

[74] Wood, *War Diaries of Andre Dennison*, p. 289.
[75] Whitaker, *'New Model' Armies of Africa?*, p. 226.
[76] US Dept. of State Cable, London, 'RHODESIA: ZAPU MILITARY ATTITUDES TOWARDS CARVER PLAN', 2 February 1978, 1978LONDON01858_d.

to US Secretary of State Cyrus Vance's questioning of this, affirmed that in fact some 'acceptable elements' of the RSF *could* be entrusted with security responsibilities in conjunction with the PF and the UN Force.[77] Carver responded:

That the acceptable elements of the RSF would be the current three battalions of the Rhodesian African Rifles which would be merged with 'four of five infantry battalions from your force [i.e. ZANLA and ZIPRA] [and also] asked whether the PF accepted that on transition day PF commanders would come under the authority of the resident commissioner in order to take the necessary steps to carry out agreements on the ceasefire and ZNA. Mugabe responded that this was acceptable as long as all issues are worked out in advance of transition.[78]

Thus it seems there was a willingness from early 1978 onwards on the part of the ZANU and ZAPU leadership, including both Mugabe and Nkomo, that the RAR would form a core part of the ZNA.

I will return to the acceptability of the RAR and its role in the integration of the ZNA shortly. Beforehand, I discuss why this acceptability did not apply to the army's white units, whose loyalties were largely rooted in political support for minority rule, making them not only unacceptable for integration into the ZNA, but which also meant their morale withered as majority rule neared.

Contrasting Loyalties

In Shakespeare's *Henry V*, the Irishman Captain Macmorris of the king's army, itself drawn from across four kingdoms, exclaims, 'What is my nation? Who talks of my nation?'[79] This centuries-old observation coveys that within a multi-ethnic army, there can be competing understandings of the nation, which nation is being fought for, and why. As we have seen, black soldiers held that they had fought for their country and for an abstract state, and not for the whites or the regime. There is a clear difference here with what many white Rhodesians said they were fighting for.

Black RAR soldiers fought loyally and efficiently throughout the war while white units increasingly suffered from desertions and low morale. This was because black soldiers fought for the government of the day and envisaged their futures in Zimbabwe, whereas many white soldiers fought for minority rule, and when its prospects seemed bleak, they swiftly left the country. This suggests that the 'push' and 'pull' factors, which were

---

[77] US Dept. of State Cable, Pretoria, 'RHODESIA: ANGLO-AMERICAN/PF MEETING AFTERNOON APRIL 15', 16 April 1978, 1978SECTO04074_d.
[78] Ibid.
[79] Shakespeare, *The Life of Henry the Fifth*, III.II.1250–3. This passage first came to my attention in the writings of the historian Ciarán McDonnell.

not prevalent among black soldiers as discussed in Chapter 5, were highly applicable to many whites.

For instance, recall that for most black soldiers, the 'pull' factors of a safe haven and a sympathetic network to receive any deserters did not exist. In contrast, as WM told me, whites often had countries that they could flee to (or indeed return to), and 'most of the Europeans didn't like this war; they would desert'.[80] Some of my white interviewees affirmed that by the end of the war, desertions were commonplace among RLI soldiers, many of whom 'gapped it' to South Africa.[81] This mirrored how thousands of white civilians 'gapped it' as the pace of the war gathered speed: 42,873 *officially* emigrated between 1975 and 1979, with many more likely unrecorded.[82] As Brownell argued, transience was the defining characteristic of the white population:

> From 1955 to 1979, a total of 255,692 immigrants arrived in Rhodesia, but over the same period 246,047 emigrants left ... a rate of turnover [that] is especially noteworthy when compared against the total white population, which during this same period averaged only 228,583 ... This would be the percentage equivalent of the entire cities of Birmingham, Leeds, Liverpool, and Manchester being completely replaced by new people every year in the UK.[83]

Despite white Rhodesia's favoured myth of Pioneer-era settler-farmers' rugged individualism, the white population did not reflect this image: fully 71 per cent lived in the four major cities and only 3.2 per cent were engaged in agriculture;[84] the majority of whites were post–World War II arrivals, and less than a third were born in Rhodesia.[85]

As Luise White argued, the memoirs of some white servicemen give a sense that many were fighting to retain a privileged colonial lifestyle rather than for the nation or state of Rhodesia.[86] Very little patriotism was evidenced, 'and even less sense of loyalty to a specific place'.[87] It is perhaps unsurprising that the loyalties of many whites to the Rhodesian state were fleeting.

As the war intensified in the late 1970s, the loyalty of black soldiers was vested in their country, where they envisaged staying, whereas for many whites, their loyalty was solely to a Rhodesian colonial way of life. Much

---

[80] Interview with WM.
[81] Interview with anonymous white veterans, Bulawayo, 2017, 2018.
[82] Brownell, *Collapse of Rhodesia*, chapter 4, pp. 75, 87–9, and 125; Moorcraft, *Short Thousand Years*, p. 2; L. White, *Unpopular Sovereignty*, p. 194.
[83] Brownell, *Collapse of Rhodesia*, pp. 72–3.
[84] Stedman, 'End of the Zimbabwean Civil War', p. 129.
[85] Caute, *Under the Skin*, p. 56.
[86] White, 'Civic Virtue, Young Men, and the Family', p. 120.
[87] White, *Unpopular Sovereignty*, p. 204.

of the received narrative of the war has elided this factor: Preston, for instance, argued that 'though fighting for a supposedly alien regime, African troops proved just as loyal as Europeans'.[88]

In fact, not only did black soldiers make clear that they did not fight for the RF regime and instead they fought for the government of the day, but they also served the state far better than their white counterparts. A huge number of the purportedly 'loyal Europeans' evaded the draft: 'half the eligible 3,000 men evaded conscription in 1973, and 6,500 evaded it in 1976'.[89] As the CIO director Ken Flower told the Cabinet in 1976, many white soldiers who had completed their contracted service were emigrating, denuding the TF of soldiers.[90] The TF units were chronically undermanned: in 1977, the Rhodesian Army possessed, on paper, twenty-six TF companies, but this nominal force 'represented only 11 full companies of 100 men each', and 58 per cent of these were 'well below strength'.[91] In August 1977, the anticipated intake of National Service troops for the next year had to be revised downward by 27 per cent, and the supply of TF servicemen aged eighteen to thirty-eight had 'almost been exhausted'.[92] As the war heated up, Rhodesia's white citizen army evaporated.

Manpower problems plagued the small white regular component of the army too. As Chris Cocks, a white RLI NCO, argued, 'by the mid-seventies the RLI was forced, because of the shortage of volunteers, to accept conscripts, and by 1976 there were more conscripts in the RLI than regulars'.[93] The army made up some of this shortfall by recruiting white foreign soldiers, largely from the Anglosphere, who numbered some 1,500 at their peak according to Henrik Ellert, a former Special Branch officer.[94] In contrast to the undermanned white regular infantry companies, forced to resort to conscription, the RAR was always fully manned, and indeed had a large surplus of applicants even during the war's denouement, as noted earlier.

This combination of manpower shortages and the intensification of the war caused the morale and combat effectiveness of white units to plummet. As Cocks recounted, his operational tour of 1978 was difficult, 'because there were so few of us, which allowed no respite from the

[88] Preston, 'Stalemate and the Termination of Civil War', p. 75.
[89] White, 'Civic Virtue, Young Men, and the Family', p. 107.
[90] PKF, A3, Memorandum from CIO Director, 'Morale and Leadership in the Security Forces', 20 December 1976, p. 2.
[91] PKF, WC(S) (77) 7, OCC/1/1, 'OCC Memorandum on Sterile Zones and Food Control', 16 February 1977, p. 3.
[92] PKF, WC(S) (77) War Council Minutes, 25th Meeting, 3 August 1977.
[93] Cocks, *Fireforce*, chapter 15. [94] Ellert, *Rhodesian Front War*, p. 129.

waves of daily [Fireforce] call-outs'. Doubts had set in. A year later, he wrote that prior to deployment he:

began experiencing bouts of real naked fear ... I was terrified ... the strain had begun to tell on all of us. In 1976 we [RLI troops] had been enthusiastic when the siren sounded [to deploy on Fireforce] – it was great to get out and see some action ... but things had changed. We didn't have enough helicopters nor enough troops to cope with the overwhelming tide of incoming guerrillas.[95]

Within twelve months, doubts had turned to fear and despair. The heavy casualties the RLI suffered after 1975 may account for this: from 1964 to 1974, fourteen RLI soldiers were killed in action; in the four years after 1975, seventy were killed in action.[96] Although this number was comparable to other regular units – fifty-seven soldiers from 1RAR were killed in action from 1975 to 1979, and fifty-four from 2RAR[97] – the RLI was a small unit drawn from the tiny white population, which was itself highly conscious of these losses. By 1979, white Rhodesian casualties were 'proportionately more than ten times those suffered by the Americans in Vietnam'.[98]

By the end of the war, the RAR, now four times the size of the RLI, was providing most of the regular army's firepower. My interviewees felt that the RLI, once an elite unit they aspired to emulate (and a unit far better resourced than the RAR, as noted earlier, which may explain this early military disparity), had become lacklustre.

For instance, BM remarked that when he joined the RAR in 1968, 'the best [battalion] was the RLI, then the RAR was second ... but [later] we were number one during the war'.[99] WM commented that by the end of the war, the 'RLI mostly were national servicemen, [and had] very few [long-serving] regulars like sergeants and warrant officers', who are vital to any professional army. He believed that its conscripts were not comparable in quality to regular troops.[100]

Similar opinions were also heard from other sources. An RLI commanding officer, reflecting on the war in 1989, said that his troops 'developed bad habits if left on Fireforce duties too long – they forgot bush skills, the need for stealth, became lazy from operating only in daytime, and developed a "kill or be killed" nature not conducive to "hearts and minds" efforts. The RAR soldiers adapted much better to changing roles without loss of skill'.[101]

[95] Cocks, *Fireforce*, pp. 197, 239.
[96] 'Roll of Honour', *The Cheetah: Regimental Journal of the Rhodesian Light Infantry* (October 1980), pp. 57–9.
[97] Binda, *Masodja*, pp. 405–6.   [98] Downie, 'Rhodesia', p. 345.
[99] Interview with BM.   [100] Interview with WM.
[101] Melson, *Fighting for Time*, pp. 139–40.

Luise White said that Rhodesian Army studies had determined that 'by every possible measure 1RAR was the most effective unit in the Rhodesian Army. They had the best performance in operational areas: the most kills and the fewest unit deaths'.[102]

By late 1977, Major Andre Dennison, an experienced British special forces veteran commanding A Company, 2RAR, was disparaging of the performance of the RLI.[103] A Rhodesian Army intelligence Research Section study in the late 1970s came to the conclusion that the RAR 'were better Fire Force troops than' the RLI.[104] Charles Melson quoted an internal Rhodesian Army report from 1978 which said that 'If the RLI are the Incredibles [the RLI regimental nickname], RAR must be the Phenomenals.'[105] In July 1979, a white RAR officer noted of a joint Fireforce deployment that there was 'a definite lack of interest on part of the RLI, a factor which is becoming the norm these days for what was once the "Incredibles"'.[106]

The performance of white soldiers had thus dramatically declined by the end of the war. I argue that this was because most whites' loyalties were not to the state, but simply to settler-colonial rule, whereas black soldiers continued to fight loyally for the government of the day, because – as discussed in Chapter 7 – they intended to stay in Zimbabwe after the war, unlike many whites. The ultimate expression of this was found in how black soldiers came to fight on behalf of Robert Mugabe's new government and, in doing so, claimed that they saved the country from civil war, as Chapter 7 addresses.

Conclusion

This chapter has argued that black soldiers conceived of themselves as apolitical, a product in part of the army's practices in recruitment and its policing of black troops' politics. However, the apolitical ethos of black soldiers was also constructed by them and functioned to distance them from overt allegiance to a political faction. None of my interviewees supported the Smith regime or minority rule, and they privately supported majority rule. They stressed that they distinguished between their soldierly loyalties and their private, personal political preferences. This explains why, even though the RAR fought loyally against ZANLA

---

[102] White, *Fighting and Writing*, p. 128.
[103] Wood, *War Diaries of Andre Dennison*, p. 212.
[104] Cilliers, *Counter-Insurgency in Rhodesia*, p. 227. See also Melson, *Fighting for Time*, p. 107, which is likely a citation of the same study.
[105] Melson, *Fighting for Time*, p. 140.
[106] Wood, *War Diaries of Andre Dennison*, p. 343.

throughout the war, it seems that many, perhaps most, RAR soldiers voted for Robert Mugabe in 1980.

Furthermore, being apolitical was in itself a political claim. It foregrounded the soldiering skills and experience of RAR troops and sought to stake out their post-independence future as part of the army. This was in marked contrast to white soldiers, whose morale and combat performance plummeted by the late 1970s. These divergent paths were rooted in how black soldiers envisaged themselves staying in Zimbabwe and conceived of their loyalty as pledged to the country, whereas whites were, in the main, loyal to the Smith regime and colonial privilege. For this reason, during the latter stages of the war, when fighting was at its most intense, black soldiers displayed more loyalty to the Rhodesian Army than white soldiers did – a striking colonial paradox.

Black soldiers' apolitical status was recognised by the liberation movements. This had important implications for their post-colonial future, as both the liberation movements and international powers came to perceive the RAR as the acceptable face of the RSF and earmarked them for inclusion after independence. As Chapter 7 shows, this apolitical status thus served to ensure the safety and future careers of RAR soldiers in Zimbabwe.

7 A New 'Government of the Day' Dawns
The Loyalties of 'Formers' in Zimbabwe, 1980–1981

At independence in Zimbabwe, ZANU(PF) took power and opted not only to reconcile with its erstwhile enemies in the RAR, but also to retain them in the new ZNA. This was highly unusual. In the aftermath of many wars of decolonisation, the fate of those who had fought for the colonial army was dire. In Algeria, Guinea-Bissau, and Vietnam, thousands of ex-colonial troops and auxiliaries were tortured and massacred.[1] Although a limited, ad hoc integration of former Portuguese colonial soldiers occurred after Angola achieved independence in 1974, Zimbabwe's decision to retain the RAR in situ was unprecedented. This chapter argues that the loyalties particular to regular black soldiers ensured that they were retained.

Certainly, they were experienced and expert soldiers, and the new government's desire to retain them was, in part, motivated by its desire to possess a professional army. However, I argue that the Mugabe government's prime motive was to retain the RAR's military capabilities, which it relied upon to control conflicts between the liberation armies in the tumultuous post-independence period. It felt that it could rely on the old RAR as its soldiers' regimental loyalties explicitly renounced any form of ethnopolitical allegiance, meaning they posed no threat to ZANU(PF) control over the government.

My interviewees recalled much uncertainty and fear as to their future during the ceasefire period and how they enthusiastically embraced what they perceived as the hand of reconciliation on the part of ZANU(PF). They recalled this gratitude as tempered by a realistic appraisal of why ZANU(PF) had opted to retain them, for, as we have seen, its propaganda had long called for reprisals against Rhodesian troops. Black Rhodesian soldiers were, after independence, colloquially referred to as 'formers' (former Rhodesian troops), and my interviewees felt they had been retained for three principal reasons.

---

[1] Coelho, 'African Troops in the Portuguese Colonial Army', p. 149; Horne, *Savage War of Peace*, p. 538; Alexander et al., 'The "War without a Name"', p. 4; Crapanzano, *Harkis*, p. 30; Scheipers, 'Irregular Auxiliaries after 1945', pp. 25–6; Evans, 'Reprisal Violence', p. 97; Webb, 'Foreword', p. xv; Burns, Novick, and Ward, 'Weight of Memory'.

Firstly, they were a potent military force that the ZANU(PF) government could use to counter a ZIPRA rebellion, a capability its own ZANLA guerrilla forces could not offer. Secondly, they felt that the RAR's long-demonstrated loyalty to the 'government of the day' assured the new government that its orders would be obeyed. Lastly, the RAR were widely deemed the acceptable face of the Rhodesian Army, a unit that could be included in the ZNA, whereas unacceptable units such as the auxiliaries could not. As discussed earlier, they possessed a certain cachet as professionals who used violence solely in pursuit of their war aims, in contrast to other units, whose use of violence was widely condemned as political or conducted with personal gain in mind.

As noted in Chapter 3, the military efficacy and soldierly loyalties of black Rhodesian troops were mutually constitutive, and my interviewees' narratives convey a belief that the new government recognised that the loyalties of the formers were particular to regular soldiers. To reiterate, their professional capabilities were themselves a potent form of loyalty: black Rhodesian soldiers fought well and fought hard because they felt a deep allegiance to their comrades in the first instance. Thereafter, their regimental loyalty foregrounded their deep-rooted connection to their battalion, and only thereafter the wider army. Over the course of the war, these soldierly loyalties were explicitly rendered as apolitical, which, as discussed in Chapter 6, was a product of both the RAR's military culture and the army's political censorship and surveillance, but also itself a subtle form of politicking on the part of black Rhodesian troops. It clearly signalled that their allegiance was not to the racist RF regime, but to their comrades at the micro level and the army itself at the macro level, and that this apolitical loyalty could happily endure under a new government.

In the second part of this chapter, I discuss how the formers played a decisive role in quelling inter-liberation army fighting in the Assembly Points (APs) and the ZNA battalions that were being integrated during 1980 and early 1981. In my interviewees' accounts, the RAR did not hesitate to follow the orders of the 'government of the day', vindicating the oft-professed apolitical character of their soldierly loyalties. They felt that their performance further assured the retention of the formers in the first decade after independence. Finally, I discuss the nostalgic reminisces of these veterans and how the hindsight of the post-2000 crisis years has impacted their narratives.

Loyalties in the Moment of Transition

The war ended with the ceasefire agreed at Lancaster House on 21 December 1979. The ceasefire was, in the main, adhered to. Most members of the RAR returned to barracks and awaited the elections and, thereafter, independence, which arrived on 18 April 1980. Although in retrospect, it seems obvious that ZANU(PF) would win the poll, there was much contemporary uncertainty over who would triumph. In accordance with the Lancaster House Agreement, the liberation forces directed many of their fighters to one of sixteen APs set up around the country.[2] The ZANLA, ZIPRA, and Rhodesian commanders were dubious of the merit of the rather paltry Commonwealth Monitoring Force (CMF) sent to oversee the election, and of its prospects for ensuring the ceasefire held.[3] There was a general air of insecurity, as liberation fighters of both armies had rejected or remained suspicious of the ceasefire and 'refused to come in to APs, or made sorties outside them, and regularly cached arms and ammunition' in anticipation of further attacks by their wartime enemies.[4] Black Rhodesian soldiers possessed mixed views of guerrillas during this time, which spanned fear of renewed violence through to a belief that their own military victory had been forestalled. However, my interviewees recalled quickly coming to realise that they had a vital role in the new order, one in which their soldierly loyalties assured their future.

In 1980, black Rhodesian soldiers were in limbo: the war was over, but the nature of the peace and its implications for them could not be fully ascertained. Some recalled being happy the war had ended, as they were tired of the long conflict:

Well, I felt ready [for the end of the war], because I was a bit tired of staying away from my family.[5]

I was feeling happy. For a change, yeah![6]

We were happy about it, because the villages on the rural area, they were staying in this bad situation.[7]

We were happy because we thought, 'Ah, there'll be no more war.' Everybody was happy. Because everybody didn't like war. Also I was very happy – I thought maybe things will be better. Now, now I don't see it [*laughs*].[8]

However, this elation was tempered by the fact that black soldiers did not know whether they would be persecuted after independence. As Miles

---

[2] Tendi, *Army and Politics*, p. 134.
[3] Rice, *Commonwealth Initiative in Zimbabwe*, p. 60.
[4] Alexander et al., *Violence and Memory*, p. 181.   [5] Interview with DSN.
[6] Interview with GM.   [7] Interview with GMH.   [8] Interview with MK.

Tendi wrote, many 'expected to be lynched as "sell-outs" or to suffer other forms of grievous retribution'.[9]

A number of my interviewees remembered their fear at this key juncture. WM explained in a laconic, matter-of-fact, tone: 'we thought after independence we were going to be shot, because we were fighting our own kinspeople'.[10] His words succinctly summarised the source of many soldiers' anxieties. GN told me: 'That fear always was there. We'll never know what is coming next, since we were entering a new era. So we were thinking what is going to happen with us?'[11] MN remembered:

Ah it was so dangerous. Because that time, when we were getting the information [from ZANU propaganda broadcasts on Radio Maputo] of saying 'All the Rhodesian soldiers are going to be killed'... Yes, we were afraid. But with myself, I only said, 'Ah, I haven't got a home. I haven't got money [to flee abroad].' That was my own decision. Where would I go? [If] I go to the reserve, they will kill me. So, [for] the best, I better stay [in the army]. If they don't chase me, I will stay. And they didn't chase me and I stayed.[12]

Likewise, DT recalled how fleeing would only be a last resort:

Yeah, we were feeling [it was] very dangerous because they [the guerrilla forces] were saying that 'those people [Rhodesian soldiers] we're going to crush them', yes, so we were very afraid... we couldn't do anything, because where can I go? This is my country... It was only just to look if they started doing that [reprisals against soldiers], then take my family and go [abroad].[13]

Given the widespread targeting of Rhodesian soldiers and their families during the war, reciprocal violence seemed eminently plausible.

Black Rhodesian soldiers tempered this fear with accounts of their own combat prowess, and some even maintained that they had hoped the war would continue as their military efficacy would assure their safety. DSN stated that he had not been afraid as 'we knew that we could thrash them [the guerrilla forces in any potential conflict]. They were too young for us'.[14] Likewise, WR stressed that 'we used to win the battle, but we lost the war [*laughs*]. I don't ever recall them ever overrunning an RAR platoon, company, or section during the war. Every time they met us they ran. So yes, we won the battles.'[15] These statements conveyed the prevalent belief among black Rhodesian soldiers in their military superiority. DSN recalled that this sentiment left some soldiers frustrated with the ceasefire. They felt that they were winning the war and were dismayed at having to 'surrender': 'when we got [to the] end [of the war], many [soldiers] got angry. They said, "[General] Walls is a coward; he's not

[9] Tendi, *Army and Politics*, p. 165. [10] Interview with WM. [11] Interview with GN.
[12] Interview with MN. [13] Interview with DT. [14] Interview with DSN.
[15] Interview with WR.

worried [as he is not] fighting" [on the front line]. That was African soldiers. They said, "We are fighting but how can he surrender to these terrorists?".'[16]

As the ceasefire continued to hold, the black troops of the RAR began to feel that their post-war status would be protected by the agreements made at Lancaster House, a view spread in rumour and the messages coming from commanders. BM, an RAR Company sergeant major, told me that he had heard a rumour that the ZANLA commander Josiah Tongogara had 'told everybody [at Lancaster House], "Once we get back home we are going to be combined operation together – ZANLA forces, ZIPRA forces, RAR forces who want to stay with the government – they can stay together"'.[17] He reassured his worried soldiers that the RAR had a useful future role to play owing to its skills and experience:

[Some RAR] were worried [about persecution]; some they would say we were going to be abandoned, but we were already [saying to those who were scared,] 'Don't worry,' as the British [said at Lancaster House] – '*You* are going to be the leader of these younger people [i.e. of the guerrilla veterans integrating into the ZNA] that doesn't know [conventional soldiering]. You fought a war' ... That's why we didn't become afraid or worried.[18]

He recalled telling his soldiers that the RAR had fought in World War II and Malaya too, and that this long experience gave it a credible claim to form a part of the new army.

BM told me that their officers had stressed that their loyalties to the 'government of the day' would not change after independence: 'The officers they used to tell us, "When you join [the RAR, you become part of an apolitical regiment, and the] RAR doesn't change under what comes [after independence]. Although if the guerrilla wins, don't think that you are going to be chased from the army, no. You are loyal to the government."'[19]

MSW said, 'when independence was close, we were told, "don't panic; everything is going to be controlled"'.[20] Likewise, Martin Rupiya discussed how in one unit (likely the Selous Scouts):

The [black] RSM [the most senior enlisted soldier in a regiment] asserted publicly that he had been following orders and supporting the Government of the day since enlisting in 1956 and would weather the diatribe of retribution and continue to do the same. As a result, nearly ninety per cent of the African members of the unit elected to stay.[21]

The specific understanding of loyalty developed over a long period thus gave credibility to the statements of these officers.

---

[16] Interview with DSN. [17] Interview with BM. [18] Ibid. [19] Interview with BM.
[20] Interview with MSW. [21] Rupiya, 'Demobilization and Integration'.

The experience of many black soldiers during the ceasefire period was in the end uneventful, as the RAR returned to barracks for the first time in fifteen years, a sharp change of pace to such a long time on operations.[22]

For instance, two weeks after the ceasefire, a journalist from *The Times* described how the security situation in Bindura was calm and 'black troops from the RAR' were spending their time 'cutting the grass and weeding the camp flowerbeds'.[23] Other members of 1RAR and 2RAR undertook extensive training on the Somabula Plain with their newly acquired infantry-fighting vehicles, with a view to becoming the then-envisaged mechanised infantry battalions of the ZNA.[24]

These routines did not, however, apply to all. Some of my interviewees continued in an operational role, which involved liaising with the liberation forces in the APs, as the CMF wished to avoid a security vacuum once they withdrew after the election.[25] Significantly, most Rhodesian units dispatched to AP liaison tasks were from the RAR and integrated units such as Grey's Scouts, whereas the white 'Praetorian Guard' of the RLI and RhSAS were engaged on decidedly political tasks, including running an 'illicit Fireforce' used to 'confront guerrillas', which was a blatant contravention of the ceasefire,[26] and rehearsing elaborate plans for a putative white coup that was aborted only at the last minute.[27] This meant that black Rhodesian soldiers were often at the forefront of breaking the ice with their erstwhile enemies in the liberation forces.

Meeting a recent adversary face to face could be nerve-wracking. DSN told me, 'well, you know, at first it was scary because at first they [the guerrillas] came in APs with their guns. So we couldn't know, didn't know what might happen there – maybe a shootout might take place'.[28] BM told me how he assisted the CMF to monitor AP Mike, which was

---

[22] As noted earlier, 1RAR CO Lt Col. Shute wrote in 1976 that by then RAR soldiers 'had been continually on operations ... for ten years', having first taken casualties in the war a decade before ('Editorial', *Nwoho* (April 1978), p. 8). The demands on black soldiers only increased after 1976 as the war escalated.

[23] Ashford, 'Flexible Approach Brings Success in Rhodesian Ceasefire'.

[24] Rhodesian Army Association, 'Rhodesian Armoured Car Regiment Uncovered'.

[25] Moorcraft and McLaughlin, *Rhodesian War*, p. 175; Tendi, 'Soldiers contra Diplomats', p. 947.

[26] Ginifer, *Managing Arms in Peace Processes*, p. 40.

[27] For more on the purported white Rhodesian coup, see Cole, *Elite*, pp. 413–20; Tendi, 'Soldiers contra Diplomats', p. 946; Alao, *Mugabe and the Politics of Security*, p. 39; Petter-Bowyer, *Winds of Destruction*, p. 384; Anglin, 'Zimbabwe', pp. 677–8; Rice, *Commonwealth Initiative*, pp. 103, 178; Binda, *Equus Men*, pp. 211–13; Moorcraft, 'Rhodesia's War of Independence', pp. 11–17; Wood, *War Diaries of Andre Dennison*, p. 372.

[28] Interview with DSN.

a 'serious trouble spot' that saw 'gun battles in which civilians, police and guerrillas were killed' during early 1980.²⁹

> Yes [we were fearful that things could go wrong], but they [the guerrillas] didn't do anything, or to fight with us, or to fight by themselves, no. But we used to be, if we hear a sound of gunfire, we used to be going with the officers from [the CMF] with a platoon [of] RAR people, yes. Then we went and talked to them – 'Why are you firing?' They said 'Ah, no, we are happy' [the firing had been celebratory]. They [the CMF] challenged them, to do that – 'We don't allow'.³⁰

The provocative actions of white RSF members sometimes created tensions too. WR told me how he had organised a game of football for the assembled forces at AP Hotel near Chiredzi. When a plane carrying a doctor on his rounds came in to land, it 'buzzed' the AP in an aggressive, intimidating show of force:

> The pilot – typical Rhodesian-type pilot, full of nonsense – he says, 'I'd like to fly over the camp.' He asks permission, so the commander says, 'Okay, but if they shoot you down, it's your fault.' But I'd like you to picture this – twenty-two people on a football field. I was there as well, and this plane went [*makes whoosh sound and indicates a steep diving motion*].³¹

The pilot made this low pass in a manner intentionally reminiscent of its devastating wartime role as part of the Fireforce. Unsurprisingly, this instantly provoked panic among the guerrilla fighters: 'And out of twenty-two people there was a tussle around the ball, about four or five people around it, and next minute they all disappeared. And all you heard was the ball bouncing on the field. That's how much they hated aircraft.'³²

Such provocations by white Rhodesians were not unusual in the transition, as Norma Kriger argued.³³ For WR, such incidents provoked introspection, and he sought to get to know his wartime adversary better:

> The one guy, I spoke to him, I said, 'When the helicopters came [during the war as part of the Fireforce], how did you feel?' and he took off his shirt and he literally had a wound, a scar, on his whole back. So I said, 'What happened? Was it napalm or something?' He says, 'No. I was trying to dodge the helicopter. I was trying to get into the tree, not around the tree.' That's how he scraped himself, with the fear.³⁴

These early interactions helped liberation forces members and RAR soldiers who were wary of one another to establish a bond through exploring the suffering and strife of the war years.

---

²⁹ Alexander, 'Dissident Perspectives', pp. 152–3. ³⁰ Interview with BM.
³¹ Interview with WR. ³² Ibid. ³³ Kriger, *Guerrilla Veterans*, p. 105.
³⁴ Interview with WR.

The deployment of Rhodesian soldiers in the APs created other forms of mutuality by reassuring the liberation forces, massed in confined spaces, that the RhAF would not bomb 'their vulnerable positions in support of a white coup after the elections'.[35] WR, an RAR officer from the small Coloured community as discussed earlier, told me he felt the real purpose of his small, lightly armed 2RAR unit deploying to AP Hotel was not to act as a military deterrent to would-be ceasefire breakers, but instead to act as collateral to provide reassurance to the liberation forces:

The whole AP was still totally armed. You know, you go [there as] ten men, which was your cook, two drivers, a medic, a few riflemen. I don't know who planned that, but we took a chance. The guys in the AP at the time, they were about 3,000–4,000 ... We were just 10 [*laughs*] put in the centre of the camp. It was scary, I promise you. You drove up to the camp and all they had was just a tree boom across the road. And guys were fully armed, so you had to drive up to this and, *gee*, I promise you it was scary! ... and I don't think there was ever an incident [between the RAR and guerrillas]. I think we were more security, that there would not be an attack on the AP – which I think was being planned – but it gave the combatants a piece of mind to say, 'Oh, they wouldn't attack with [their own soldiers in the AP].' But they [the Rhodesians] would have taken us [out] – I think we were having the only tents [in the AP], we'd be the first target of the [Rhodesian] aeroplanes![36]

As WR explained, he established a good rapport with ZANLA, but remained preoccupied with security concerns. He recounted one incident which he considered his 'worst experience of the war', worth quoting at length:

I don't know exactly how long we stayed at [AP Hotel] but one night I had a really horrific experience. Two guys burst into my little tent in the centre of the camp, and I don't know whether it was drug-drunk or alcohol-drunk, local brew, but they wanted to kill me. They said they missed me during the war, 'So we're going to kill you.' The guy actually cocked his AK rifle and, unfortunately, I had just finished cleaning my pistol [rendering it unusable until reassembled], which I usually put under my pillow. And my FN [rifle] was in the corner. So I decided this guy having a cocked weapon, if I went for my weapon, he'd shoot me. So I tried to talk them down, the two of them – the one guy sort of, after talking to them, speaking in their language, Shona, they eventually, the other guy dragged him out and said what is the use of killing me now. As soon as they left my tent, I went in to the coordinator's tent and said, 'Listen, I've just been nearly killed.' He said, 'By who?' Luckily they were not far from my camp; they were still making their way to where they were sleeping and I identified them, and I said, 'To show you that I'm telling the truth, cock his rifle; he's got a round up his AK.' He cocked the rifle and the round ejected, so that proved it. You know, they physically beat this guy to death in front of my eyes. So that was it. As I say, I don't

---

[35] Gregory, 'Zimbabwe Election', p. 29. [36] Interview with WR.

A Marriage of Convenience

know how we could've been asked to do such a task, in a 3,000[-strong AP]. We were fighting each other but a day before; next minute you're in their camp, trying to make sure they got fed and all that.[37]

As WR's vivid recollection relays, this period was extremely unusual. Combatants who had been fierce enemies were suddenly thrown together and had to improvise cooperation and forge a bond across the wartime divide. While the prospect was intimidating, it was testament to the bravery of all involved that, in the main, it was a success.

WR's shock at the severe ZANLA punishment is also demonstrative of the gap in understanding. He was used to a juridical disciplinary system, as discussed earlier, yet ZANLA's coercive mode of punishment was not novel or distinctive to the APs: as Gerald Mazarire argued, such harsh punishment was routinely meted out in ZANLA camps in exile.[38]

My interviewees recalled their duties in the APs as challenging and frightening. But they also felt it was their duty to attempt to implement the Lancaster House Agreement and to continue to follow orders as a professional force, in stark contrast to some of the white units who turned to provocation. The more they interacted with the liberation forces, the more they felt that they would not be persecuted and that they could find a new role in a Zimbabwean military.

GN told me, 'our fears cooled down because we were mixing a little bit, a little bit, a little bit' with the liberation forces.[39] During this period, black soldiers' anxieties were also eased by news of a concord reached between the wartime factions as to their future, as discussed later in this chapter. For my interviewees, their confidence in the new government was sealed by the striking of agreements between the RSF top brass and ZANU(PF) leaders after the ceasefire, as well as a series of extraordinary summits that occurred between members of the liberation movements and Rhodesian troops.

'That's Why They Were Loving RAR': A Marriage of Convenience

The post-war path of black Rhodesian soldiers bore some similarities to ex-colonial troops in Angola. The post-1974 MPLA government took political power while still facing military competition from rival liberation factions. In that context, it adopted 'an attitude of expediency' towards former colonial troops, integrating many into its army.[40] The utility of these former colonial troops as skilled soldiers overrode political

---

[37] Ibid. [38] Mazarire, 'Discipline and Punishment in ZANLA', pp. 571–91.
[39] Interview with GN. [40] Oliveira, 'Saved by the Civil War', pp. 137–8.

objections to their colonial affiliations, as the MPLA sorely needed experienced soldiers who could be depended upon and who did not pose a political threat. I argue that this was also the case in Zimbabwe, as the militarily insecure new government deemed the formers both militarily useful and politically unthreatening.

After Mugabe's decisive election victory, it was clear ZANU(PF) would wield power. The writ of the new government, however, was finite. As the war had merely been frozen by an externally brokered political settlement rather than fought to a conclusive military outcome, further violence was a distinct possibility. There was obvious potential for a flare-up between ZANLA and ZIPRA, which 'had fought for independence but also battled each other' during the war.[41] The ZANU(PF) politburo was mindful (or paranoid) of the potential competition for power from ZAPU, which had also prosecuted the war to its conclusion only to see its prospects for power slip away in a worse than anticipated electoral performance.[42]

This was a devastating shock to ZAPU's leadership, yet it remained potent militarily, and 'ZIPRA's capacity for conventional warfare was also a source of friction ... the possibility that the clearly surprised and disappointed ZAPU would use these forces, which were still based largely outside the country, to obtain victory by other means was a source of concern.'[43] It was widely thought that ZIPRA's armoured brigade would very likely rout ZANLA guerrillas if such a conflict arose, as ZANLA possessed few conventional warfare capabilities, glaringly lacking armour, artillery, or an air force.[44]

Within Zimbabwe, the only force powerful enough to challenge ZIPRA was the old Rhodesian Army units, and therefore it was imperative for Mugabe to retain them. Building upon earlier understandings reached at Geneva and Malta, discussed in Chapter 6, it was understood among the antagonists that the acceptable RAR would be integrated into the ZNA in some form. During the ceasefire, a concord was struck between ZANU(PF) and most of the top Rhodesian securocrats and commanders who, in return for retaining their positions in the new dispensation, agreed to back the new government and integrate their forces.[45]

---

[41] Kriger, *Guerrilla Veterans*, p. 4.
[42] Ndlovu-Gatsheni, 'Post-colonial State and Matabeleland', pp. 121–2.
[43] Alexander et al., *Violence and Memory*, p. 181.
[44] Alao, *Mugabe and the Politics of Security*, p. 38.
[45] Tendi, 'Soldiers contra Diplomats', p. 947; Wiseman and Taylor, *From Rhodesia to Zimbabwe*, p. 41; Jaster, 'Front-Line States and the Rhodesian Peace Settlement', p. 18; Stedman, 'End of the Zimbabwean Civil War', pp. 158–9; Moorcraft and McLaughlin, *Rhodesian War*, p. 178. The chronology of these events is contested, as Kriger has noted (*Guerrilla Veterans*, p. 63).

A Marriage of Convenience 221

The apocrypha attributed to Talleyrand that 'treason is merely a matter of dates' rang true, for some key elements of the RSF hierarchy came to embrace Mugabe's new dispensation, such as CIO chief Ken Flower. The RAR members, who had in wartime been chastised as sell-outs by the liberation movements, and had been threatened with post-war reprisals and targeted by ZANLA cadres in their home areas, were suddenly recast as soldiers of Zimbabwe.

As we saw in the previous section, shortly after the ceasefire, news that the RAR would be integrated, not persecuted, percolated down to the RAR rank and file from their officers. They greeted the news enthusiastically. HZ, for example, recalled:

What made us not be afraid of our future service is we had a delegation of former [Rhodesian] army soldiers and ZIPRA and ZANLA who represented us at a conference in KGVI [barracks in Harare], saying what will happen ... So we knew nothing was going to happen [to us and] we were only going to be integrated into the ZNA ... I know here in 2RAR we had representatives who went. We had all given [instructions to the 2RAR representatives], we said, 'Yes, we want to be integrated.' Because we knew [that the war was over, as] already the guerrillas were inside [Zimbabwe]. So we said, 'We are pleased, provided we are not hurt' ... [Attending the meeting at KGVI] was the ZIPRA and ZANLA [commanders] plus the former army commanders. People like Masuku, General Walls, Nkomo, Nhongo – security top hierarchy.[46]

SM attended a further, extraordinary meeting hosted by the newly elected prime minister at Inkomo Barracks near Harare. He recalled this summit as a sincere attempt to clear the air, with an emphasis on reconciliation. It was explicitly stressed that victor's justice would not be pursued against Rhodesian troops, so long as they pledged their loyalty to Zimbabwe:

Battalion commanders were all there, all the officers ... Every unit commander was there from the Rhodesian army and the guerrillas too ... It was [quite strange] ... [Mugabe] said himself, 'nobody is going to be discharged, nobody is going to be chased away, everybody is going to be a soldier and become one [together] ... there will be no regiment that is for whites only or blacks only. We are all going to be one together ... All Zimbabwean soldiers ... All the names which we called ourselves in the war: it's finished, we were all Zimbabwe army. There's no ZIPRA, no ZANLA, no 1RAR, no 2RAR, whatever ... They were all one unit, which is the Zimbabwe National Army ...' I think he wanted to make people united. [Mugabe] didn't chase anybody, any whites, he didn't say, 'You have to go or you have to leave'; he said we want to be together. He even pointed to Peter Walls [and said] you are going to be the army commander of this country. We were there when he said that.[47]

---

[46] Interview with HZ. [47] Interview with SM.

For my interviewees, these summits sealed what would become a symbiotic pact between the formers and the new ZANU(PF) government. As MSW told me, black Rhodesian soldiers greeted this news with much relief:

> [The liberation forces] said we were going to look after these opposition [Rhodesian] soldiers, they didn't say something bad. Although we were panicking [at first, bad things] didn't happen ... since we had these [CMF observers from overseas, and then afterwards] BMATT. We were working hand in hand, so with the three armies all together – ZIPRA-ZANLA-former Rhodesians – we make one fighting unit. So we didn't have problems with all of those things.[48]

Publicly, the new alliance between ZANU(PF) and the formers was portrayed as part of a broader magnanimous act of reconciliation.[49]

Mugabe's stately rhetoric at public events – 'I urge you, whether you are black or white, to join me in a new pledge to forget our grim past, forgive others and forget' – suggested a sincere, conciliatory motive.[50] Specifically in regard to the military, in his televised inaugural address to the nation in March 1980, he stated: 'The need for peace demands that our forces be integrated as soon as possible, so we can emerge with a single national army. Accordingly, I shall authorize General Walls, working in conjunction with the ZANLA and ZIPRA commanders, to preside over the integration process.'[51]

Yet Mugabe's desire to integrate the old Rhodesian Army was far from reconciliatory in its motivation: it was, to a large extent, an expedient measure to safeguard ZANU(PF)'s rule against any potential attack from ZIPRA – and a prelude to crushing ZAPU as a political opponent. Despite the public proclamations of reconciliation and togetherness, ZANU(PF) felt they were the legitimate inheritors of the state owing to their own wartime sacrifices, as evidenced by its refusal to contest the election as the Patriotic Front coalition. Tellingly, Mugabe reserved the title of minister of defence for himself during the first two years of independence, in addition to his prime ministerial office, and removed the vital police intelligence remit from Nkomo's Home Affairs ministership, neutering his portfolio.[52] As Kriger argued, ZANU(PF) never seriously considered bona fide power-sharing with ZAPU, and talk of 'reconciliation' generally was merely a euphemism for the subordination of rivals into ZANU(PF)-dominated hierarchies.[53]

---

[48] Interview with MSW.   [49] Carver, 'Zimbabwe', p. 70.
[50] Tendi, *Making History in Mugabe's Zimbabwe*, p. 109.
[51] R. Mugabe, 'Address to the Nation by the Prime Minister Elect', Zimbabwe Ministry of Information, Immigration and Tourism, Record No. 1, 4 March 1980.
[52] Whitaker, *'New Model' Armies of Africa?*, pp. 235–7; Kriger, *Guerrilla Veterans*, p. 63; Gregory, 'Zimbabwe Election', p. 36.
[53] Kriger, *Guerrilla Veterans*, p. 21.

Furthermore, ZANU(PF) had, since its own internecine struggles of the mid-1970s, sought to ensure that the 'party had the right to command the gun', so that politicians retained complete control over the military. ZANU(PF)'s Central Committee made clear this relationship was to be perpetuated once in government.[54] Thus ZANU(PF) required an army that was subordinate to the party and contained no alternative political loyalties, and 'Mugabe sought to exercise firm civilian oversight' over the ZNA, given that it represented 'a potential powder keg'.[55]

The RAR was, in this context, highly useful. It not only claimed an apolitical professional ethos, but it also lacked a political hinterland, for association with Rhodesian rule rendered the formers politically unviable. As Zibani Maudeni argued, after independence, the formers had no political base, and few of the new Zimbabwean political elite sympathised with them as they had not been in the colonial forces themselves, unlike in other instances of decolonisation where former loyalists had acceded to power, such as in Kenya or Uganda.[56] Formers were thus dependent upon the government's good graces to maintain their positions. Even within the military, the formers did not have a powerbase. As we have seen, they had been prevented by Rhodesian racist policies from acquiring senior military ranks, and so lacked the commensurate authority and influence that would have existed if there had been, for instance, black battalion commanders or senior staff officers.

Some of my interviewees recalled being well aware of their military value to the new government. DSN remarked: 'ZANLA, they were no regular soldiers. ZIPRA had a standing army. So ZANLA were only guerrillas. So this is where Mugabe was afraid, for him to let the guerrillas take over, that's why he wanted to keep the Rhodesian Army.'[57] Black soldiers also felt that the RAR's long-standing apolitical stance played a key role in this marriage of convenience. As BM told me, it was not simply the fact that the RAR had a strong combat record and military capacity, but also that it was 'loyal to the government of the day', and for BM, 'that's why [the ZANU(PF) government] they were loving RAR'.[58]

As argued in Chapter 1, during wars of decolonisation, regular soldiers differed fundamentally from irregulars in that their allegiance was not premised upon ethnopolitical factors, and they possessed formidable military capabilities. In this vein, the new Zimbabwean government made a clear distinction between regular black soldiers and their irregular counterparts in the Auxiliaries and paramilitary Guard Force.

[54] Tendi, 'Ideology, Civilian Authority and the Zimbabwean Military', p. 836.
[55] Tendi, *Army and Politics*, p. 156.
[56] Maudeni, 'Why the African Renaissance Is Likely to Fail', p. 202.
[57] Interview with DSN.   [58] Interview with BM.

These unacceptable units were deemed politically aligned to the RF or one of the 'internal' African parties, or to have committed widespread abuses, and were summarily disbanded. The government justified their disbandment by stating that they had been 'established for political purposes', were 'associated with atrocities during the war', and had not been 'intended to be permanent forces'. Mugabe disdainfully called them 'irregular features'.[59] As Alao argued, the 'ruling party's dislike' for these units 'was public knowledge' given their partisan and 'unprofessional' character, and this led to their swift disbandment.[60] The RLI and Selous Scouts, whose creation and wartime practices were so intricately connected to the RF's desire to perpetuate minority rule, were also deemed unacceptable units, and their disbandment was announced to much public fanfare.[61] The contrast with the treatment of the RAR was striking.

Aside from their apolitical status, black soldiers were also retained for their skills and experience. The decision to retain the British-derived doctrine of the Rhodesian Army was made by Mugabe in light of a British offer to turn its CMF into a British Military Advisory and Training Team (BMATT).[62] This had a significant benefit for the formers, as they were experts in this doctrine, unlike the liberation forces.

Furthermore, as Tendi argued, the former ZANLA commander Lt Gen. Rex Nhongo, who played the most important role in the creation of the ZNA, had particular 'regard for expertise and professionalism', and 'black Rhodesian soldiers had a professional ethos, as understood by Nhongo, and they became an important contributory element to the making of the ZNA'.[63] The formers were thus in a prime position to act as trainers and mentors to ex-guerrillas in the ZNA, and the ZNA's large size also mandated many more officer positions, which the formers were ideally placed to fill.

My interviewees recalled that the new government's reliance upon formers reassured those who were still nervous as to their safety. DT told me he felt contented 'only when I realised [former guerrillas] didn't know anything [about conventional soldiering, and we were to teach]

---

[59] Dzineza, *Disarmament*, pp. 84–5; Kriger, *Guerrilla Veterans*, p. 70.

[60] Alao, 'Metamorphosis of the "Unorthodox"', p. 107.

[61] Certainly the wartime strength of these units was depleted by independence: most of the RLI (which, as argued earlier, had a high proportion of foreigners in its ranks) left at independence, and in the case of the Selous Scouts, most of its members were subtly re-badged as RAR before the integration process. The supposed disbandment of these units was in fact merely a political gesture, and it would be more accurate to say that they were simply reconstituted as the ZNA's elite units. The Selous Scouts provided the foundation of the Paragroup, and the RLI of One Commando, and for several years after independence key command and training positions continued to be held by ex-Rhodesian officers. For more see Howard, 'Allies of Expedience', pp. 139–57.

[62] Tendi, *Army and Politics*, p. 156.   [63] Ibid., pp. 164–6.

A Marriage of Convenience 225

them everything. All courses – weapons, training, everything, signallers, we were teaching them'.[64] DSN told me if ZANLA's guerrilla fighters alone 'had taken over [the ZNA] it was going to be chaos. Because they knew nothing about soldiering, so that's why he intended to keep Rhodesian forces'.[65] GM recalled that the decision to integrate the army meant he now had faith in the viability of reconciliation, for it had been orchestrated and agreed to by the top military commanders, meaning 'we didn't fear that [we would be persecuted] ourselves. We know everything was going to be under control'.[66]

Conversely, the loyalties of most white soldiers were, as we have seen, not to the state, and they did not greet the integration of the ZNA enthusiastically. Many were hostile to the ceasefire and integration process, with persistent racism and non-cooperation the hallmark of their participation.[67] By independence, white morale had fallen through the floor. As Martin Rupiya argued, 'reasons for whites to bear arms disappeared' and many fled the country.[68] Many of the whites from units outside the RAR that stayed in the ZNA, Kriger argued, were characterised by BMATT as 'messing up' and 'doing nothing', but stayed until they could qualify for their pensions.[69]

In contrast, the white officers in the RAR remained in situ. As Whitaker noted, there was a group of white officers, referred to by BMATT as the Young Turks, 'who were dedicated to making it work', and who 'committed themselves to the future of the Zimbabwean regime'.[70] Tendi noted that two white officers, 'Colonels Dudley Coventry and Lionel Dyck', in particular, 'forged strong bonds with [Lt Gen. Rex] Nhongo because they were first-rate conventional soldiers committed to the attainment of an effective ZNA'.[71] A BMATT member recalled to Kriger that white 'RAR officers said they were staying on to look after their guys'.[72] This further served to reassure the formers as to their post-independence prospects.

In sum, the formers were not persecuted as they had feared, instead continuing their careers in a ZNA that retained British doctrine, meaning their skills and experience were valued and of great utility. The RAR were retained by Mugabe because they met three key criteria. Firstly, they were an acceptable unit as they were considered devoid of political allegiance

---

[64] Interview with DT.   [65] Interview with DSN.   [66] Interview with GM.
[67] Rice, *Commonwealth Initiative*, pp. 171–2.
[68] Rupiya, 'Demobilization and Integration', p. 33. See also Kriger, *Guerrilla Veterans* p. 124; Jackson, 'Civil War Roots', p. 383.
[69] Kriger, *Guerrilla Veterans*, p. 130.
[70] Whitaker, 'New Model' Armies of Africa?, pp. 257, 314.
[71] Tendi, *Army and Politics*, p. 163.   [72] Kriger, *Guerrilla Veterans*, p. 105.

and did not have a reputation for abuses, unlike other Rhodesian units. Secondly, they could be counted on to serve the 'government of the day' owing to their lack of a political base and their reputation for professionalism. Thirdly, they were a potent military force that offered a counter to ZIPRA's well-trained conventional units, a capability ZANLA cadres did not offer. Their retention proved crucial during the conflicts of 1980 and early 1981.

Postcolonial Enforcers: The Old RAR Fight for Mugabe's Government

The utility of the RAR in the political calculations of the ZANU(PF) government can be seen in its treatment and uses in the early years of independence. Unlike ZIPRA and ZANLA cadres, the RAR was not initially integrated into the new ZNA battalions, and its battalions remained stand-alone units until December 1981.[73] During this two-year interregnum, the only material change for the RAR was that they were officially renamed: 1RAR became 11 Infantry Battalion ZNA, for instance.[74] The security situation in 1980 was unstable, with many armed guerrillas traversing between the APs and the countryside, and firefights between guerrillas and the police.[75] Wartime tension between ZANLA and ZIPRA members also simmered. In June 1980, a journalist observed that fighting between the rival armies 'remains a possibility', and that the need for ZNA integration was pressing.[76]

The ZNA's integration did not proceed smoothly. Partly this was for political reasons, as immediately after independence ZANU(PF) commenced a process of overtly politicising the ZNA, seeking 'to make itself and its guerrillas the base of the nation and the state', and excluding ZIPRA in violent and humiliating ways.[77] Additionally, both liberation armies had kept some of their best units in exile as an insurance policy against the Rhodesians, and each other, in case the Lancaster House Agreement did not hold. This meant that BMATT could not know the true size of the force to be integrated, and its plans had to be continually altered as new units were slowly declared.[78]

Furthermore, Mugabe's decision to guarantee all former combatants who wished to become soldiers a place in the ZNA meant it grew to be one of the largest armies in Africa, eventually integrating more than 60,000 personnel, which a war-torn country of 7 million neither needed

[73] Ibid., p. 109.   [74] Interview with GN; Binda, *Masodja*, p. 389.
[75] Alexander, 'Dissident Perspectives', pp. 152–3.
[76] Ashford, 'Mr Mugabe's Balancing Feat on the Political Tightrope'.
[77] Kriger, *Guerrilla Veterans*, pp. 74–7.   [78] Ibid., p. 116.

nor could afford.[79] The integration process alone cost Z$378 million, a quarter of the government's annual budget.[80] London had not adequately resourced the BMATT to train this number of soldiers. It was only 127 strong by late 1980, and at its peak in August 1981 numbered only 161, meaning its trainers were spread very thinly.[81] The BMATT was faced with competing demands and constraints that included, inter alia, Mugabe's demand for swift integration, its own meagre resources, the unprecedented task of integrating wartime antagonists and concurrently training them, uncertainty over the size of the army it was to train, and a lack of military direction from the Joint High Command. In response it simply improvised a plan in May 1980, named Operation Sausage Machine.

This plan consisted of an attempt to focus the BMATT's scant resources on the key command levels where it felt the most difference could be made, rather than training rank-and-file soldiers.[82] Operation Sausage Machine involved a month of training, conducted by BMATT and the 'formers', for those ZANLA and ZIPRA who had been selected to be officers and NCOs in ZNA. Thereafter these new commanders would join the rank-and-file of the nascent integrated battalions, comprised equally of ZIPRA and ZANLA personnel, and were to 'lead them through a four-week basic training period that would involve minimal British participation'.[83]

This was too little time to turn recruits into professional soldiers in even the most favourable circumstances. As Whitaker argued, 'training guerrillas to become conventional soldiers was a time-consuming task made exponentially more complicated by the need to integrate the force'.[84] The results of Operation Sausage Machine were inevitably poor. In April 1981, BMATT reported that 'even after a year of training, the ZNA was still an embryonic organization that could fall apart at the slightest inter-factional provocation': much more time was needed to complete integration.[85]

From the outset of the integration process, many of the new battalions fragmented, and the formers were required to enforce the writ of the government. In June 1980, an RAR battalion was used 'to put down a mutiny' among ZANLA troops within the first battalion to be integrated, after which 400 former guerrillas were discharged from the ZNA.[86] These discharged troops, some of whom had 'formed part of

---

[79] Ibid., pp. 109–11, 131.   [80] Evans, 'Making an African Army', p. 235.
[81] Whitaker, 'New Model' Armies of Africa?, pp. 247, 270.
[82] Jackson, 'Military Integration from Rhodesia to Zimbabwe', p. 56; Whitaker, 'New Model' Armies of Africa?, pp. 255–9, 264–9.
[83] Whitaker, 'New Model' Armies of Africa?, pp. 244–6.   [84] Ibid., p. 281.   [85] Ibid.
[86] Evans, 'Making an African Army', p. 236; Whitaker, 'New Model' Armies of Africa?, p. 251.

the honour guard during Zimbabwe's independence celebration' two months previously, represented a third of the 1,200 ex-guerrillas thus far integrated,[87] indicating the seriousness of the fledgling ZNA's problems. In September 1980, BMATT, worried about the potential for ZANLA-ZIPRA conflict, considered the RAR 'the only disciplined force' in the ZNA that the government could rely on to restore order.[88]

That same month – June 1980 – Mugabe stated to the press that the old RAR were not yet integrated and that 'a delegation from the old RAR recently asked him why they were not included in the integration exercise'.[89] As Whitaker noted, the delegation comprised black former-RAR officers, who 'petitioned Mugabe directly for the integration of their battalions into the new ZNA units. However their request went unanswered and they remained a separate force'.[90]

The reasons for the RAR not being integrated was very likely the government's concern at the security situation. The BMATT commander and deputy commander at the time later told Kriger that the 'regular army' was kept intact as 'Mugabe recognised' that they 'might be needed'.[91] Luise White argued that there was 'speculation that Mugabe wanted to leave the RAR alone; some said he wanted to make them into a "Praetorian guard"'.[92] This was an exaggeration, as the Praetorians famously intervened directly in Roman politics, whereas although the old RAR were used instrumentally by the ZANU(PF) government to put down challenges to its authority, they did not perceive of themselves as political actors in this manner and, as we have seen, couched their loyalty as simply to the 'government of the day'.

In November 1980 and February 1981, a series of serious battles occurred among cadres awaiting ZNA integration, in which hundreds of guerrillas and civilians died.[93] The proximate cause was that thousands of ZIPRA and ZANLA had been moved to two large camps in late 1980 on the recommendation of BMATT, as they could no longer remain in the ill-equipped APs, which had only been intended as a temporary contingency.[94] These were situated in Entumbane in the Bulawayo suburbs, which housed approximately 5,200 from both factions, and Chitungwiza, a huge dormitory town thirty kilometres outside Harare, which housed approximately 6,900.[95] Co-locating these antagonists, who

---

[87] Ashford, 'Creation of Zimbabwe Army Held Up'.
[88] Whitaker, *'New Model' Armies of Africa?*, p. 261.
[89] Ibid.; Cleary, 'Pretoria Accused of Recruiting Former Rhodesian Auxiliaries'.
[90] Whitaker, *'New Model' Armies of Africa?*, p. 261.
[91] Kriger, *Guerrilla Veterans*, p. 109.
[92] White, 'Whoever Saw a Country with Four Armies?', p. 622.   [93] Ibid., p. 623.
[94] Tendi, *Army and Politics*, p. 186; Alexander, 'Dissident Perspectives', p. 153.
[95] Kriger, *Guerrilla Veterans*, pp. 87–8.

had easy access to weapons and alcohol and who could easily move outside of their temporary camps in close proximity to each other, and to often politically hostile civilians, created a tinderbox.

Within the APs and the camps at Entumbane and Chitungwiza, sporadic episodes of factional violence created a tense atmosphere filled with rumour and mutual suspicion.[96] During the preceding months, ZANU(PF) politicians had visited the APs seeking to exploit wartime tensions for their own political gain, and just before the November 1980 violence broke out at Entumbane, Enos Nkala gave an excoriating speech calling for one-party rule.[97] This inflammatory rhetoric likely sparked the battle which came to be known as Entumbane I.

During this incident, the old RAR's involvement was limited, as its orders were only to fire if fired upon, and after its companies had conspicuously readied themselves to assault both groups of belligerents, the fighters laid down their arms and agreed to a ceasefire, bringing the battle to a close. To monitor adherence to the ceasefire and the surrender of heavy arms, the Beer Hall that overlooked the ZANLA and ZIPRA camps was reinforced with bunkers and mortar emplacements and was thereafter occupied by rotating companies from the old 1RAR acting 'as a peacekeeping force' (see Figure 7.1).[98] After the clashes, ZANLA moved 500 more guerrillas into Entumbane and both factions smuggled in heavy weaponry in anticipation of further fighting (see Figure 7.3).[99]

In February 1981, several more serious conflicts occurred, of which the largest was again in Entumbane, commonly referred to as the Battle of Bulawayo or Entumbane II, in which hundreds died, including many civilians.[100] In the preceding months ZANU(PF) had made several moves against ZAPU politicians, most notably demoting Joshua Nkomo in the Cabinet, and many ZIPRA troops believed they were being marginalised and humiliated by the government. The fighting commenced in Entumbane on the evening of 11 February. It was attributed to several trivial causes, including a 'barroom brawl', a 'quarrel over food', and 'a fistfight' within Entumbane, and incidents of inter-liberation army violence during the previous three days at the nearby Glenville Camp and Connemara Barracks outside Gweru.[101] As Alexander argued, after the initial spark, fighting 'escalated rapidly, revealing a certain amount of preparedness on both sides, as well as the pervasiveness of fear and tension'.[102]

---

[96] Ibid., pp. 117–19.   [97] Tendi, *Army and Politics*, p. 186.
[98] Kriger, *Guerrilla Veterans*, p. 251; Binda, *Masodja*, p. 384.
[99] Alexander, 'Dissident Perspectives', pp. 154–5.
[100] White, 'Whoever Saw a Country with Four Armies?'; Binda, *Masodja*, pp. 384–5.
[101] Alexander, 'Dissident Perspectives', p. 154; Ashford, 'Spark That Set the Tribes Alight'; Kriger, *Guerrilla Veterans*, p. 120; Binda, *Masodja*, pp. 384–5.
[102] Alexander, 'Dissident Perspectives', p. 154.

Figure 7.1 A Coy, 1RAR convoy of Mine Protected Combat Vehicles (MPCVs), 1981. RAR troops manning the locally designed and manufactured MPCV, an infantry fighting vehicle that entered service in 1979 but that did not see active service until after Zimbabwe's independence (Photograph courtesy of John Wynne Hopkins)

My interviewees' perspectives of these clashes offer a fascinating new perspective of these battles, as their account has not been heard. They espoused that their involvement in the fighting demonstrated in no uncertain terms the nature of what I have termed their professional loyalties, and the enduring power of what I refer to as their regimental loyalty in the face of interethnic conflict. In the recollections of the formers, their performance during these battles cemented the new government's embrace of them and assured their careers in the ZNA. Their vivid accounts of the battles also offer an important corrective to prevailing partisan accounts of Entumbane II in particular.

After the shooting commenced at Entumbane, a convoy of ZIPRA BTR-152 armoured cars set off from Esigodini, forty kilometres south-east of Bulawayo, and, as WR told me, drove along 'the Beitbridge Road and they tried to come up to engage the ZANLA forces in Entumbane'.[103] DSN told me that if this ZIPRA armour had reached Entumbane, 'they were going to wipe ZANLA off the map' because ZANLA's 'weapons were too light' to counter ZIPRA's armour.[104] The BTR-152s were intercepted as they

[103] Interview with WR. [104] Interview with DSN.

Figure 7.2 The Beer Hall at Entumbane, referred to by the RAR as 'The Alamo' (Photograph courtesy of John Wynne Hopkins)

entered the city and destroyed by high-explosive anti-tank rounds fired by the old Rhodesian Armoured Car Regiment, supported by the old 1RAR. GM described to me how the aftermath was grisly: 'people were shot at inside there [and were] burning and others who were stuck on the walls of these tanks', and lamented that these deaths had been caused by what he saw as needless fighting.[105]

In Entumbane, the fighting was fierce and lasted through the night. C Company of the old 1RAR, commanded by Lionel Dyck and assisted by Support Company, manned the Beer Hall and bore the brunt of the fighting. It was targeted by both ZANLA and ZIPRA, taking fire from heavy machine guns, mortars, and rockets, with several assaults mounted to try and take the Beer Hall.[106]

For my interviewees, it was an abrupt return to war after almost a year of relative peace. BM told me the fighting 'was dangerous' and that he personally was targeted with lots of small-arms and 'bazooka' [RPG-7] fire.[107] JC, who also fought during the battle, told me how, during an attempt to resupply the Beer Hall, his vehicle was struck by machine gun fire and, fearing for his life, he returned lethal fire.[108] BM described the battle as

[105] Interview with GM. [106] Interview with Lionel Dyck. [107] Interview with BM.
[108] Interview with JC.

Figure 7.3 RAR troops with captured Chinese-origin 75mm recoilless rifles, and with mounted 106 RCLs. Top: an RAR RCL team at Entumbane with captured Chinese-origin 75mm recoilless rifles (1981). Bottom: RAR troops with the 106 RCLs loaned to the Rhodesian Army by Pretoria during the war. The RCLS were part of the considerable amount of hardware discreetly returned to South Africa in 1980 (Photographs courtesy of John Wynne Hopkins).

Figure 7.4 Soldiers from 3 Pl A Coy 1RAR pictured in 1981 (Photographs courtesy of John Wynne Hopkins)

dominated by the RAR: 'we were given the order to go and destroy them. Ah, we destroyed them *straight*. We started at 8 'o'clock in the evening. Then the following morning, 7 o'clock, we were finished'.[109] According to the *New York Times*, a ceasefire was only agreed to in the morning by the ZANLA forces because the ZIPRA elements 'who had already taken a mortar barrage from the RAR, were still covered by the guns of their mutual enemy'.[110]

BM noted that, unlike Entumbane I, the old RAR's orders gave them wide latitude to use force, which resulted in many deaths 'because they told us "anybody who has got an AK[-47] – shoot [them]. But if he surrenders, don't shoot"'. The instruction to use lethal force came not from Mugabe but from Nkomo: 'those who returned fire to us, we were told to kill them, by Joshua Nkomo. He told us, he give us the order'.[111] For BM, the RAR's use of lethal force, and the ensuing large number of casualties, was legitimated by the direct orders of a minister of the 'government of the day'. Nkomo told journalists the day after the fighting ended that the old RAR 'had being doing their duty as they were ordered'.[112]

[109] Interview with BM. [110] Lelyveld, 'Grim Benefit in Zimbabwe'.
[111] Interview with BM. [112] Taylor, 'Tension in Bulawayo'.

My interviewees felt that their performance demonstrated their military capabilities and that their experience and training were qualitatively better than that of the guerrilla units. BM derided the lack of professionalism of many of the ex-guerrillas and felt that this had caused unnecessary loss of life, 'because some they were not well trained, they were people from school just given an AK, you see? That's why they fought each other. They didn't know that with a rifle you have got some rules'.[113] This was a clear iteration of, as argued earlier, how RAR soldiers abided by a moral conception of the use of force which held that soldiers should only use violence in a proper, professional manner: when given orders, and solely against military targets. BM's contemptuous rendering of the ex-guerrillas suggested that the formers still held most ex-guerrillas in contempt. As CD recalled, 'we had never dreamed of this in the Rhodesian time, soldiers fighting soldiers. What's this? We were taken aback'.[114] CD's conception demonstrates that he expected former guerrillas to have shed their old allegiances once they joined the integration process and suggests that RAR troops were not widely aware of the difficulties and inadequacies of Operation Sausage Machine, which had not been resourced adequately to inculcate the kind of soldierly loyalties familiar to the RAR.

In this vein, the divisions among the liberation armies were remembered as senseless by RAR soldiers, who contrasted these political divisions to the unity of the RAR. HZ, who fought during Entumbane II as part of Support Company, told me of his sadness at seeing the fighting flare up. He saw the bodies of ex-guerrillas: 'Buried in trenches by their own friends. They fought against each other because they could not understand each other. They were fighting to say, "You are a ZIPRA"; "You are a ZANLA" – against their political motivation. But we were not like that to say – you're Ndebele, Shona, what-what. No, we didn't have that.'[115]

Here HZ juxtaposed the ex-RAR's regimental loyalties, which overcame interethnic discrimination, as we have seen, with the political enmities between ZIPRA and ZANLA. HZ implied that, had the newly integrated battalions also been exposed to an extended process of military socialisation, which foregrounded the unit as the epicentre of 'regimental loyalty' as per the RAR, then such a breakdown would likely have not occurred.

Whitaker argued that the old RAR 'soldiers who saved the regime were representing the old Rhodesian Army and showcasing their professionalism (as compared to the ex-guerrillas)'.[116] However, my interviewees instead iterated that their actions primarily showcased their professional

---

[113] Interview with BM. [114] Interview with CD. [115] Interview with HZ.
[116] Whitaker, 'New Model' Armies of Africa?, p. 278.

loyalties in the first instance, and thereafter their regimental loyalty to the RAR itself, rather than to the wider Rhodesian Army. They expressed pride in what they claimed as a victory over the guerrillas and attributed it to their greater military capacity. For instance, suppression of the fighting during Entumbane II was, for BM, the sole work of the RAR, rather than other elements of the old RSF. As he told me, 'the people who stopped that war in Entumbane, its RAR', as although [the air force] 'sent those jets [Hawker-Hunters] they didn't drop any bombs. We have finished them with the rifles'.[117] Here BM is referring to how the air forces' Hawker-Hunter jets did not drop any munitions and simply 'buzzed' the ex-guerrillas,[118] which for him signified that the old RAR had defeated the ex-guerrilla forces alone by virtue of its professionalism.

Binda's account also lauded the role of the old 1RAR, who he described as killing '400 of the enemy without incurring a single fatal casualty – an astounding achievement given the odds against them'.[119] As argued earlier, the triumphalism of such accounts must be interpreted critically. It should be recalled that, after Entumbane I, the Beer Hall had intentionally been chosen as the site of the old 1RAR's 'peacekeepers' because it dominated the ground and it had been fortified with bunkers and preplaced mortars. Its surrounds had been well reconnoitred by the old 1RAR companies that rotated through in the interim, and Dyck's C Company within the Beer Hall also had use of their MPCV infantry fighting vehicles, which were equipped with medium machine guns (see Figure 7.2).

Undoubtedly the old RAR fought both bravely and well. Their professionalism and military efficacy have also been outlined in great detail in previous chapters. Lastly, they were indeed heavily outnumbered. However, just as with accounts of the liberation war, ex-Rhodesian assessments of the RAR's military prowess during Entumbane II fail to account for the decisive military advantages it possessed. Thus RAR soldiers' narratives of their soldierly prowess should be critically interpreted, for like much of the scholarship on the liberation war, the wider military context is not adequately discussed. This is not to claim that this lack of context is a deliberate omission, but instead to argue that triumphalist accounts of Entumbane II themselves function as a particular form of claim-making.

Furthermore, for my interviewees, their assertion of the criticality of their role at this juncture did not solely rest upon their decisive intervention at Entumbane. Their accounts also emphasised that other units comprised of black formers also played an important role in maintaining

[117] Interview with BM. [118] Taylor, 'Tension in Bulawayo', p. 4.
[119] Binda, *Masodja*, p. 389.

order during the transition in other, largely unheralded, conflicts that occurred at the same time. Although Entumbane II saw the fiercest fighting, the conflicts of February 1981 occurred countrywide which, as WM told me, the formers paid rapt attention to, as 'news would move like wildfire because we had [army] radios so whatever was happening anywhere you could hear it'.[120] Outside of Entumbane, conflict occurred at Chitungwiza south-east of Harare, Gwaai River Mine in Matabeleland North, and – as WM told me – there were 'three disturbances in fact' at Connemara Barracks north of Gweru (see Figure 7.5).[121]

WR, then an officer in A Company of the old 2RAR, told me he was 'called to help bring order back to Connemara [Barracks]', as ZIPRA had 'captured the armoury' and were firing upon ZANLA.[122] At Connemara ZIPRA troops got to the armoury 'first and "hunted down" their ZANLA Comrades'.[123] The *New York Times* described the fighting as 'so one-sided as to be classifiable as a massacre of Mr Mugabe's followers, as many as 50 of whom may have been killed'.[124] When WR's platoon, equipped with newly acquired MPCV infantry fighting vehicles, arrived, '[ZIPRA fighters] were sort of monitoring us, and when we approached our assembly area, the whole company ready to attack them, they gave up, stopped fighting'.[125]

DSN, an officer in Grey's Scouts, perceived the battles in purely military terms, rather than accounting for the wider political context of ZANU(PF) seeking to dominate those it perceived as aligned to ZAPU, telling me that he took his troop to Chitungwiza 'to suppress this mutiny'. He informed me of the context prior to his arrival: ZIPRA and ZANLA were housed in adjacent camps, and at night 'would shoot each other' as they 'were only demarcated by a road'. After several nights, 'at last the ZIPRAs assaulted the ZANLAs; that is when they had to call us'. He recalled that when his troop of dragoons arrived on horseback, both groups 'surrendered because we could chase them with horses, then they would drop their guns'.[126] For DSN, the formers success was attributable to their military capabilities.

Accounts such as these were told to make the case that the intervention of the formers saved the country from civil war and thus served to underline the military value of the RAR and other black Rhodesian soldiers to the new government and to the nation. DSN told me that 'it was going to be a civil war; it was going to be like Angola'. BM said, 'we are the ones who put the peace [and if the old RAR were not there] it was a problem'.[127] WR and GM both told me they suspected that the locations of the conflicts

[120] Interview with WM.   [121] Ibid.   [122] Interview with WR.
[123] Alexander, 'Dissident Perspectives', p. 155.
[124] Lelyveld, 'Grim Benefit in Zimbabwe', p. A9.   [125] Interview with WR.
[126] Interview with DSN.   [127] Interviews with DSN and BM.

Figure 7.5 RAR soldiers with a captured T34 at Brady Airfield in 1981 (Photograph courtesy of John Wynne Hopkins). The Rhodesian Army acquired eight Polish-built T-54/55s as a gift from South Africa in 1979. The tanks, supplied by Libya and intended for Idi Amin's regime in Uganda, were confiscated from a freighter that had docked in Durban. They did not see active service during the war.

evidenced a plan by elements of ZIPRA to capture the strategic Bulawayo-Harare road so as to enable other ZIPRA forces, including mechanised units, to rapidly enter the country and destroy ZANLA.[128]

These claims of a putative ZIPRA plot reflected wider narratives of the supposed strategic significance of these conflicts, which were prevalent at the time. These were stoked not least by the ZANU(PF) government, with Mugabe asserting there were '"very sinister undertones, a definite organised pattern" to the conflict'.[129] Others also spoke of the potential for civil war. For instance, one unnamed African diplomat told *The Guardian*, 'without the loyalty of several old units of the Rhodesian Army such as the RAR, Mr Mugabe would by now be fighting a civil war'.[130] These narratives were amplified in the international press. As early as September 1980, newspaper headlines had asserted 'Civil War

---

[128] Interviews with WR, GM.   [129] Alexander, 'Dissident Perspectives', p. 155.
[130] MacManus, 'Zimbabwe Averts Civil War'.

Figure 7.6 An RAR WOII poses with a T-54/55 from E Sqn RhAC in 1981 (Photograph courtesy of John Wynne Hopkins). The Rhodesian Army acquired eight Polish-built T-54/55s as a gift from South Africa in 1979. The tanks, supplied by Libya and intended for Idi Amin's regime in Uganda, were confiscated from a freighter that had docked in Durban. They did not see active service during the war.

Imminent in Zimbabwe',[131] and this rhetoric was rehashed after Entumbane II, with *The Guardian* claiming 'Civil War Averted', and the *New York Times* saying that the 'threat of civil war appeared to be receding'.[132] Later interpretations have also made similar claims, such as Luise White's 2007 account which argued that 'in 1981 Zimbabwe was a state shored up by soldiers of the old regime'.[133]

I argue that the civil war narrative is exaggerated and deterministic. Even in the immediate aftermath of Entumbane II, civil war narratives were criticised as over-egged.[134] Senior ZAPU/ZIPRA figures had never endorsed the fighting: 'ZAPU leaders denied a pattern and stressed the tensions which had reigned amongst guerrillas since the first Entumbane conflict.'[135] As we have seen, Joshua Nkomo himself directly ordered to the old RAR to engage ZIPRA fighters during Entumbane II, while

[131] Ashford, 'Civil War Imminent Headline Stirs Up Anger'.
[132] Borrell, 'Civil War Averted'; Lelyveld; 'Zimbabwe Quells Mutiny'.
[133] White, 'Battle of Bulawayo', p. 631.
[134] Ashford, 'Spark That Set the Tribes Alight'.
[135] Alexander, 'Dissident Perspectives', p. 155.

leading ZIPRA figures had made 'sky shouts' during the fighting in an attempt to put a stop to it. Furthermore, the purported strategic rationale for the location of the conflicts was incidental, as they largely occurred in ex-Rhodesian Army barracks, which the settler-colonial authorities had deliberately sited in strategic locations many decades previously.

This is not to denude these conflicts of significance, but it is more apt to deem them as 'momentous mutinies' that 'acutely threatened independent Zimbabwe's domestic stability', as Tendi argued, rather than necessarily a prelude to civil war.[136] My interviewees' assumption of credit for forestalling a civil war reflects their decisive intervention as well as the legitimacy it afforded them in the eyes of the government and as protectors of the peace of the new nation. Their actions during these conflicts were widely lauded, in stark contrast to wartime and post-2000 renderings of them as sell-outs' and so became, in their telling, their finest hour.

Regardless of the true strategic significance of the interventions by the formers, my interviewees recalled that Entumbane II gave tangible effect to their loyalty to the 'government of the day'. HZ told me, 'it was us defending the whole country, defending Mugabe – not ourselves'.[137] This was an extraordinary change in fortune, as just five months previously black RAR officers had worried that their not being integrated meant that 'they were being left behind'.[138]

For my interviewees, their performance during Entumbane II had convinced the government to retain them. As WM told me, 'the former army was called in to quench the violence, so that's when we started to earn respect from the prime minister, because if we did not intervene I think his ZANLAs would have been wiped out because the ZIPRAs were well trained as opposed to the ZANLAs. So that was another incident that earned us respect'.[139] Likewise, HZ told me:

If we [RAR] were not there [to fight for the government], what was going to happen? [Lionel] Dyck was the one who was commanding there, they [guerrilla forces] didn't know how to command, they didn't know anything. But because we knew how to fight, or if the battle is like that you fight it this way, so they kept us until we taught them.[140]

My interviewees' narratives reflect the government pronouncements of the time. For instance, the minister for state security (now the current president of Zimbabwe), Emmerson Mnangagwa, 'went out of his way to compliment the [old RAR] troops who for so long were his enemy' at a press conference, and said it was 'appropriate to single out for special praise' their 'sense of

---

[136] Tendi, *Army and Politics*, pp. 165–6.   [137] Interview with HZ.
[138] Whitaker, *'New Model' Armies of Africa?*, p. 261.   [139] Interview with WM.
[140] Interview with HZ.

duty'.[141] It is clear that the soldierly loyalties of the 'formers' served to ingratiate them with the government, sealing the 'marriage of convenience'.

My interviewee's narratives also emphasised that, despite many of them having experienced lethal violence over many years during the liberation war, the scale of casualties during Entumbane II was truly shocking to them. WR told me, 'Entumbane was a real-a real fistfight between the two. You know, bodies were kept in the rail wagons, they couldn't even fit them in the mortuary.'[142] BM told me that the dead bodies 'filled up the carriages of the train' wagons.[143] Both WR and BM claimed that the real death toll of Entumbane II was much higher than the official number of 300.[144] It is quite possible they are correct, as the government went to considerable effort to cover up the scale of the violence, seizing and destroying journalists' footage of the events at the airports in Harare and Bulawayo.[145] Later in 1981, Mugabe suppressed the findings of his own official enquiry into Entumbane II,[146] and its report has never been made public, with the government claiming in both 2000 and 2019 that it had been 'lost'.[147]

In sum, the conflicts that took place in APs, barracks, and integrated ZNA units in late 1980 and early 1981 were key events, allowing the formers to demonstrate their loyalties as soldiers who fought for the 'government of the day'. DSN summed this up when I asked him why the formers had fought for the new government, and he replied matter-of-factly, 'ah, they were professional soldiers; taking orders is their job'.[148] My interviewees also perceived their combat performance, particularly during Entumbane II, as demonstrative of their efficacy vis-à-vis the ex-guerrilla forces. They felt this had accorded them great respect and cemented their retention in the ZNA. This was a marriage of convenience which, like many such relationships, would not last.

Postlude: 'Formers' in the ZNA and 'Nostalgia' for Rhodesia

The conflicts between ZIPRA and ZANLA in the first years of independence demonstrated the fragility of the post-war security situation. ZANU(PF)-ZAPU relations plunged to a new low.[149] ZANU(PF)'s plan

---

[141] Ross, 'Mugabe Moves to End Factional Violence'.   [142] Interview with WR.
[143] Interview with BM.
[144] 'In Zimbabwe, 2 Rival Factions Count the Dead'; Catholic Commission for Justice, Peace in Zimbabwe, *Breaking the Silence*, p. 7; Binda, *Masodja*, p. 389.
[145] Ross, 'Size of Toll in Zimbabwe Raises Fear of New Battle'; Taylor, 'Tension in Bulawayo'.
[146] Alexander, 'Dissident Perspectives', p. 155; CCJP, *Report on the 1980s Disturbances*, p. 43.
[147] Mabuza, 'Dumbutshena, Chihambakwe Reports "Have Been Lost"'.
[148] Interview with DSN.   [149] Alexander, 'Dissident Perspectives', p. 155.

to dominate the ZNA at the expense of ZAPU, already in motion, was accelerated by Entumbane II.[150] Integration was officially completed in August 1981 – that is, the moment ZIPRA's fighters in the APs had been disarmed, demobilised, and placed within new military structures – and thereafter the government moved decisively to destroy ZAPU's power.[151]

The ZNA began a systematic purge. In September, 2,763 men were involuntarily demobilized, of whom 2,432 were ex-ZIPRA.[152] In February, the government made its move against ZAPU proper, using a supposed ZAPU coup plot as pretext.[153] Nkomo was dismissed from the government and senior ZIPRA figures were imprisoned for years on trumped-up charges, including treason. Ex-ZIPRA officers in the army were arrested, harassed, tortured, imprisoned, and summarily discharged.[154] Many, seeing the writing on the wall, simply left the army. In 1983, the predominantly ZANLA Fifth Brigade was unleashed in Matabeleland and targeted supporters of ZAPU in a campaign that left at least 10,000 dead.

As Whitaker argued, within the first three years of independence, ZANU(PF) succeeded in politicising the upper echelons of the ZNA.[155] While many neo-Rhodesian accounts have stridently criticised this process, it can be seen as a replication of the overt politicisation of the Rhodesian Army that the RF itself undertook two decades previously, as discussed earlier.

This placed the 'formers' in an ambiguous position. Although they were never fully trusted, they were valued for their military skills, particularly by Lt Gen. Nhongo, who, as Tendi argued, 'admired the Rhodesian Army's operational effectiveness during the liberation war'. Nhongo ensured that black Rhodesian soldiers were treated fairly, although he 'did not favour them'.[156] Nhongo was singled out for praise in this regard by my interviewees, who admired his commitment to professionalism and felt that he was important in their retention.[157]

A post-1981 history of formers in the ZNA is beyond the remit of this book. However, I briefly outline their trajectory here. In December 1981, the old RAR battalions were finally disbanded and integrated into the ZNA, although 'even then' its individual companies 'were kept together as far as possible'.[158] The dissolution of the old RAR battalions decisively ended my interviewees' 'regimental loyalties' and also rendered the RAR's distinctive military culture extinct.

[150] See Tendi, *Army and Politics*, pp. 175–9; Evans, 'Making an African Army', pp. 238–9; Alao, 'Metamorphosis of the Unorthodox'.
[151] Kriger, *Guerrilla Veterans*, p. 70.
[152] Whitaker, *'New Model' Armies of Africa?*, p. 302.   [153] Yap, 'Sites of Struggle', p. 18.
[154] Alexander, 'Dissident Perspectives', pp. 155–6; Kriger, *Guerrilla Veterans*, pp. 135–7.
[155] Whitaker, *'New Model' Armies of Africa?*, p. 322.
[156] Tendi, *Army and Politics*, pp. 164–6.   [157] Interview with DSN.
[158] Kriger, *Guerrilla Veterans*, p. 109.

Figure 7.7 A former RAR soldier pictured as a captain of the ZNA Paragroup, undated but likely mid-1980s (Photograph of interviewee's original by author)

Black Rhodesian soldiers went from comprising 85 per cent of a small regular Rhodesian Army in 1980 to just 5 per cent of the enormous ZNA in August 1981.[159] Nonetheless, the training and experience of the formers placed them in good stead. All of my interviewees who wished to become officers did so. At least two formers commanded the old RAR battalions they had once served in as privates, including the late Moses Pongweni, formerly a bugler in the RAR band.[160] Into the 1990s, the ZNA's two best regiments, the Paragroup and One Commando, contained many ex-RAR men.[161] As Tendi argued, Dyck's role at Entumbane II was the start of a long relationship between him and Lt Gen. Nhongo.[162] This had important implications for some formers, as Dyck could recommend them for promotions and postings, often to his

[159] For figures see ibid., p. 131. [160] Interview with WM.
[161] Interviews with SM and GM. [162] Tendi, *Army and Politics*, p. 188.

Paragroup.[163] As DSN told me, Dyck often forcefully removed those he deemed not professional from his units, stating that 'we don't want any political soldiers here'.[164] In this telling, the old apolitical ethos of the RAR persisted within some elite ZNA units, in contrast to other ZNA battalions which were widely deemed as politicised and militarily inefficacious.

However, there were limits to the government's embrace of the formers, which my interviewees perceived as directly related to their utility and their status. DSN told me that 'after [Mugabe] had us train his men and they became regulars, he started to neglect us, you know? For instance he said that all the Rhodesian Army soldiers, especially officers, they're at their ceiling now. They want to promote these other officers [from ZANLA]'.[165] WR told me that 'all promotions were based on being [acceptable to or aligned with] ZANU(PF)'.[166] DC told me how he felt systemic corruption, factionalism, and mismanagement became prevalent. He contrasted the professional Rhodesian Army with the politicised ZNA by way of metaphor: 'we were mixing water and oil. And you can't do that easily'.[167]

My interviewees lamented the politicisation of the ZNA and held that this had a deleterious impact upon its military capabilities. For them, aside from within the elite units, the 'professional' ethos of the old army had not survived integration.[168] This politicisation imposed constraints upon even well-connected formers. As Kriger argued:

> Despite the Parachute Battalion being like a praetorian guard, despite the hot-line that Colonel Dyck had to Army Commander Rex Nhongo, and despite his loyalty, his prospects of promotion, because he was white, were nil. Ex-RAR Africans became commanders of the Parachute Battalion and of One Commando, but promotion to colonel was also the limit for Africans who had served in the Rhodesian army. The absence of improvement in privates' salaries and low prospects for promotion, despite their superior training and their demonstrated loyalty, soon drove most ex-RAR Africans out of the army, though they stayed longer than the whites.[169]

Kriger's depiction, drawn from interviews with former BMATT commanders, is complicated in two ways by my interviewees' accounts. Firstly, although they were rare exceptions, at least two formers managed to break the ceiling of the rank of colonel and were promoted to brigadier.[170] Secondly, only two of my interviewees left the army

---

[163] Interview with Lionel Dyck. [164] Interview with DSN. [165] Ibid.
[166] Interview with WR. [167] Interview with DC.
[168] Interviews with CD, BM, GMH, DSN, JM, and HZ.
[169] Kriger, *Guerrilla Veterans*, p. 138.
[170] Interviewees anonymised by author; see also Evans, 'Making an African Army', p. 247.

voluntarily in frustration at the creeping politicisation.[171] The remainder continued serving until the late 1980s, largely because they felt they were too old to change careers, that their lives as officers were relatively comfortable, that they were accruing pensionable service, and that their prospects outside the ZNA as a former would have been quite difficult.[172]

In 1989, formers without high-level connections were compulsorily retired. This process was systematic, and my interviewees recalled a batch of signals sent to ZNA units informing 'formers' of this process. BM told me, 'we were written letters, signals: "Those who are going to retire from this date are: Name, Name, Name." *Finished.* Everybody [who was a "former"] was out'.[173] HZ told me, 'all former army people were forced to resign and there was nothing we could do, we just accept it'.[174] WM told me, 'it was a forced retirement. I didn't want to leave at the time. But the former army soldiers were served with a one-year notice'.[175]

The notices indicated that the marriage of convenience had served its purpose for ZANU(PF). My interviewees felt that they had been used instrumentally and, now that their purpose had been fulfilled, they were simply let go, their positions – generally as middle-ranking officers – to be taken up by those aligned to the party. BM told me that 'we were forced to retire, you see ... they wanted to promote their own people'.[176] HZ told me, 'they kept us until we taught them [conventional soldiering]. Then in 1989 that's when they thought, "Ah, now we are now okay; let's say some of them will leave"'.[177] WM said, 'the motive was now to root us [formers] out. All the vacancies which we were holding would go to the friends, the ex-guerrillas'.[178]

It is likely that the decision to retire the formers was also influenced by the government's reassessment of its security needs. Indeed, in the eighteen months prior to the retirement of the formers, the perceived threat from ZANU(PF)'s two principal antagonists had markedly lessened. HZ told me that he felt the December 1987 Unity Accord with ZAPU meant that the government no longer feared an internal military or political threat, unlike in the early 1980s, which influenced the decision.[179] In February 1989, the end of Botha's rule of apartheid South Africa saw the commencement of a period of political reform that reduced the threat from south of the Limpopo.[180]

These factors likely influenced the government to decide that the need for the formers was less acute than it had been previously. It is also

---

[171] Interviewees anonymised by author.
[172] Interviews with TM, WM, SM, GM, and GN.   [173] Interview with DC.
[174] Interview with HZ.   [175] Interview with WM.   [176] Interview with BM.
[177] Interview with HZ.   [178] Interview with WM.   [179] Interview with HZ.
[180] Chitiyo and Rupiya, 'Tracking Zimbabwe's Political History', p. 355.

possible that their professionalism, which had previously made them so valuable to ZANU(PF) when its rule was under threat, now rendered them a liability in a more politicised army.

Some of my interviewees were bitter at their forced retirement. DC said that 'we were not retired respectfully ... it was actually saying, "we don't want people from the old army"'.[181] BM told me that he felt he could have continued, as 'when I [left] the army I was forty years of age, instead of the [compulsory retirement age of] fifty' that his contract stated.[182] HZ told me that the government 'did not want to make it open that "We don't want you former army soldiers," so they said, "You all now have pensionable service, so you've got to leave"'.[183]

That most formers had accrued sufficient service to entitle them to a full pension lessened this blow. WM told me that while he 'served the one year's termination of contract, others immediately after receiving it put in their resignation – or retirement, as such – because we had already served over twenty years' pensionable service'.[184] MN told me that while some formers were bitter, in actuality they were not treated badly, and 'it depends how you look at things!'.[185] Although they were pushed out of the army, most formers had accrued full pensions, which continue to be paid today as guaranteed by the Lancaster House Agreement.[186]

In comparison to other post-liberation war contexts in which thousands of ex-colonial troops were tortured and massacred, in Zimbabwe, the formers were not abused or persecuted. While, as we have seen, there were powerful instrumental reasons for the new government to embrace them, they were treated quite fairly in general.

The positive experiences of many former black RAR soldiers was, however, blunted by Zimbabwe's post-2000 crisis. The pensions formers received were hugely devalued (as were those of all pensioners), and like many Zimbabweans, they faced a precipitous decline in living standards and challenging economic circumstances.[187] GMH told me:

The pension, hey, this government of ours – we've had five months now, go to the bank, no money [during this period there were serious shortages of currency in Zimbabwe]. Why? [They were told] 'Go and swap'? [i.e. barter for goods] You can't go and swap every time [as a pensioner]. Ah pension, it's very hard. All Zimbabwean pensioners I'm telling you they are suffering.[188]

---

[181] Interview with DC. [182] Interview with BM. [183] Interview with HZ.
[184] Interview with WM. [185] Interview with MN.
[186] Secretary of State for Foreign and Commonwealth Affairs, *Southern Rhodesia: Report of the Constitutional Conference, Lancaster House, London September–December 1979* (London, HMSO, 1980), Section H, 'Pension Rights of Public Officers'.
[187] Raftopoulos, 'Crisis in Zimbabwe', pp. 201–32. [188] Interview with GMH.

MN told me, 'things started changing because of the economy ... the present moment it is becoming a little bit hard to survive'.[189] My interviewees have struggled to make ends meet, compounding their sense of injustice at being forcibly retired at the end of the 1980s. They are locked out of patronage networks available to their old ZNA peers who are connected to ZANU(PF).[190]

Some veterans' recollections evinced a lingering nostalgia for the settler era, contrasting its relative material plenty to post-crisis Zimbabwe. In particular, they highlighted the ease with which, as soldiers, they and their families had been able to access medical care and education.[191] Many expressed their frustration with the prevalence of systemic corruption and drew explicit links between the politicisation of the ZNA and the onset of the economic malaise.[192]

Crisis-era Zimbabwe was also sometimes contrasted with what they described as a competent and non-corrupt Rhodesian government. CD, for instance, told me: 'Corruption, that has destroyed it all. I believe it's everywhere now. If they [the government] had run things without corruption or nepotism whatever, if they'd run it the Rhodesian way, I think this country could be richer than any other country [in the region].'[193]

DSN told me:

Rhodesia was better than Zimbabwe. Far much better than what we are seeing here – no money, nothing. This is painful. People who lived in Rhodesia like us, find the situation abnormal. But not these youngsters who just grow up and see things like this. They say, 'Ah, it's alright,' which is very painful for us ... You know, the problem with these politicians is taking these farms.

The reference to taking farms alluded to the Fast Track resettlement programme of the post-2000 period, in which the government seized predominantly white-owned farms with the largest given to the well connected, which was often associated with the start of Zimbabwe's political and economic crisis.

DSN asserted that previously 'there was plenty of food, plenty of jobs, plenty of farms, everything was there', but since the crisis devastated the agricultural sector, 'now Zambia is feeding us, once we were feeding Zambia' and 'that's why Mugabe when [he] said, "we messed it", for sure he was speaking the truth. There was a mess, they messed up everything'.[194] In a similar narrative mode, GMH told me, 'that's why

---

[189] Interview with MN.
[190] Interviews with MSW, GM, GMH, MS, DC, SJM, and DT.
[191] Interviews with JM, DC, DSN, MK, and BM.   [192] Interview with GMH.
[193] Interview with CD.   [194] Interview with DSN.

we say Mugabe make a fuck up of the country ... What do you know about how to rule the country? What they know is to steal, that's all'.[195]

The narratives of the former RAR call to mind Jacob Dlamini's monograph *Native Nostalgia*, wherein he interprets the nostalgic reminiscences of life under apartheid as articulated in retrospect by residents of the Katlehong township:

[I]t is both illuminating and unsettling to hear ordinary South Africans cast their memories of the past in such a nostalgic frame ... What does it mean for a black South African to remember life under apartheid with fondness? What does it mean to say that black life under apartheid was not all doom and gloom and that there was a lot of which black South Africans could be, and indeed were, proud? Only lazy thinkers would take these questions to mean support for apartheid. They do not.[196]

The narratives of black Rhodesian veterans are comparably nostalgic. As we have seen, they had no allegiance to the RF or minority rule. Their nostalgic recollections are instead rooted in their memories of a period in which they and their families had material security and opportunities for social mobility, which have dramatically withered in the past two decades.

As Dlamini argued, we must acknowledge that 'the irony about nostalgia is that, for all its fixation with the past, it is essentially about the present. It is about present anxieties refracted through the prism of the past'.[197] These veterans' narratives of the Rhodesian period are inextricably linked with post-crisis life in Zimbabwe. It is apposite to understand the nostalgic memories of black Rhodesian veterans as those of a small group – soldiers – who were exceptionally well provisioned for and afforded a special status by the Rhodesian state, in contrast to the rest of the black population. Their nostalgic reminiscences of colonial life are rooted in this experience. The obvious contrast between their relative material plenty as soldiers and their post-crisis struggles has informed their nostalgic recollections.[198]

These veterans, like the residents of Katlehong, also recall the non-material aspects of their time as Rhodesian soldiers with pride and fondness. This is unsurprising, as they were elite soldiers, and members of a fine regiment with a proud history that demonstrated a high level of

---

[195] Interview with GMH. [196] Dlamini, *Native Nostalgia*, pp. 6, 13. [197] Ibid., p. 16.
[198] Nostalgia for the comparative prosperity of the Rhodesian era has become a recurring narrative in some Zimbabwean online discussion forums too. Images of urban areas, public spaces, government services, and enterprises from the Rhodesian period are often juxtaposed with the dilapidation of post-crisis Zimbabwe. Such posts are often made by those born long after independence. These posts do not imply any sort of endorsement of the Smith regime or Rhodesian racism, but instead are intended to demonstrate the malign impact of the Mugabe regime and ZANU(PF) upon Zimbabwe's economy.

military performance throughout the war. The RAR's 'military culture' held a large significance in their lives. Again, this does not imply endorsement of minority rule.

My interviewees nuanced their nostalgia. Many tempered their wistful recollections of the Rhodesian era by simultaneously noting its pervasive racism, the lack of opportunities for social mobility outside of the military, and the violent realities of the war.[199] Neatly summarising these complex sentiments held by many of my interviewees, DSN recalled his time as a Rhodesian soldier during the colonial period as 'the good old bad old days'.[200]

In sum, the nostalgic recollections of black Rhodesian veterans are melancholic. They do not constitute an endorsement of minority rule, but instead hold ZANU(PF) responsible for ruining the ZNA and the wider economy, and point to what they perceive as the strong and non-corrupt economy during the Rhodesian period. This hurt is compounded by the fact that these veterans feel that they were instrumentally used and then discarded by Mugabe and his party.

Conclusion

Contrary to black Rhodesian soldiers' fears of persecution, after independence, they were retained en bloc by their former enemies in the new government. My interviewees believed that their soldierly loyalties were crucial to their retention, particularly their mutually constitutive professionalism, which underwrote both their military skill and their fierce bond towards their comrades. Furthermore, their regimental loyalties emphasised that their allegiance was not political in character and that they were loyal to the 'government of the day'. These attributes made the old RAR ideal for Mugabe's government, which could depend upon it to crush ZIPRA. During the conflicts of 1980–1, my interviewees felt that their military performance demonstrated their loyalty to the 'government of the day' and their military skills and thus cemented their place in the ZNA.

After the dissolution of the old RAR, my interviewees were treated fairly in the ZNA, and many became officers. Although they lamented what they saw as the politicisation of the ZNA and felt the professionalism of the RAR had been eroded, many were still disappointed to be compulsorily retired in 1989. The post-2000 crisis in Zimbabwe and the struggles of these veterans in retirement has caused their perceptions of the Rhodesian period to become tinged with nostalgia.

[199] Interviews with CD, DC, and HZ.   [200] Interview with DSN.

Conclusion
The Loyalties of Professionals

This book has contributed to a new understanding of the loyalties of black Rhodesian soldiers during the era spanning the terminal years of the Federation of Rhodesia and Nyasaland, Zimbabwe's war of liberation, and the tumultuous first two years of independence from 1980. That these black soldiers fought for white-minority rule in Rhodesia appears, superficially, both paradoxical and extraordinary, and it has led to their characterisation as supporters of the RF, mercenaries, or 'sell-outs' in neo-Rhodesian and nationalist literatures.

Drawing upon extensive interviews with black former Rhodesian soldiers, I have argued that their soldierly loyalties were, however, quite differently constructed. These loyalties were based upon the soldiers' 'professionalism' and 'regimental loyalty', powerful forms of identity deeply rooted in practices and institutional cultures. Incorporating the work of Siniša Malešević, I have analysed these solidarities as applying to both micro (professional) and macro (regimental loyalty) levels.[1]

In building upon Malešević's scholarship, I have sought to add a new dimension to the canonical scholarly literature on soldierly loyalty that has focused almost exclusively upon Western forces in the post–World War II era, reflecting its origins in a post-1945 academy whose authors and audience were preoccupied with the war in Europe or with Western armies. I have sought to broaden these understandings of soldierly loyalties through exploring the particular context in which black Rhodesian soldiers fought, and in doing so, I have contended that the content of their soldierly loyalties was distinctive.

The 'new school' of academic work on African colonial soldiers, which has sought to complicate and reframe previous portrayals of their service, has also been incorporated. Its insights have largely applied to troops who fought in the late nineteenth and mid-twentieth centuries and who are long dead, and these insights have thus typically been drawn from archival sources.

[1] Malešević, *Sociology of War and Violence*.

While the 'new school' has provided a good understanding of why African colonial soldiers enlisted in the first instance, and outlined their operational histories and conditions of service, their loyalties during wartime are less well understood. Consequently, I have followed in the footsteps of a more recent strand within this literature – the work of Timothy Stapleton, Lennart Bolliger, and Kaushik Roy – which has utilised the oral histories of colonial veterans themselves.[2]

These three scholars have argued that colonial soldiers' initial motivations to enlist in the army were distinct from the factors that sustained their loyalties during wartime. That they have emphasised this cleavage is no accident, for the oral testimony of colonial veterans offers invaluable insights into soldierly loyalties in wartime that are not readily apparent from documentary or secondary sources.

This book has, in a similar vein, drawn extensively upon the accounts of black Rhodesian Army veterans, predominantly those who served in the RAR, a regular army regiment comprised of black soldiers and white officers (with a small number of black officers commissioned after 1977), which was the largest and most militarily important regiment by the end of the war. Their oral history testimonies offer an invaluable corrective to much of the literature on these troops, which distorts, marginalises, or simply ignores them. Perhaps more importantly, their stories afford a new insight into how the soldierly loyalties of black Rhodesian troops were unique.

The salience of the cleavage between the initial motivation to enlist and wartime loyalty among regular soldiers, such as those of the RAR, is crucial. It highlights the importance of extensive periods of training and socialisation that occurred within the 'total institution' of the military, which served to differentiate soldiers from other types of combatants who were allied with settler or colonial powers, who did not inhabit a regimental milieu.

As David Anderson and Daniel Branch's work has argued, the 'loyalists' who fought for the colonial powers at the 'end of empire' played a novel and important wartime role, and were raised with expeditious haste and in great number to fight against nationalists. These 'loyalists' were predominantly paramilitaries, typically auxiliaries or militiamen, whose allegiances were premised upon ethnic, political, material, or regional factors, and whose military training was poor. Anderson and Branch's framework is a watershed historiographical moment, reframing and properly contextualising the solidarities and motives of these 'loyalists'.[3]

---

[2] Bolliger, *Apartheid's African Soldiers*; Roy, 'Military Loyalty in the Colonial Context'; Stapleton, *African Police and Soldiers in Colonial Zimbabwe*.
[3] Anderson and Branch, 'Allies at the End of Empire'.

Conclusion: The Loyalties of Professionals

I have drawn upon Anderson and Branch's approach and sought to develop it further, arguing that among the assorted 'allies at the end of empire', regular colonial troops possessed loyalties that were distinct from those of irregular 'loyalists', in large part because they belonged to military institutions in which training and comradely obligation were central to their soldierly identity, and their wider loyalties were vested in their regiment and the army rather than the regime. Furthermore, despite their small number relative to the multitudinous irregulars, regular soldiers were often the most militarily important of those forces that fought on the colonial side.

Utilising an array of historical evidence, I have shown that black Rhodesian soldiers were particularly notable for their combat efficacy and steadfastness: they endured gruelling, prolonged, and continuous operational COIN deployments on the front line, and the service of many of my interviewees spanned more than a decade of the liberation war. The question then arises as to why and how such strong bonds of loyalty took root among these troops.

I have addressed this through exploring micro- and macro-level soldierly loyalties as they were made and practised within the Rhodesian Army, showing that they took forms that reflected this particular historical context. The macro-level loyalties of black Rhodesian soldiers differed markedly to the assumptions of much of the military history written on this topic, which adheres to a Western normative conception of loyalty that assumes the primacy of patriotic, religious, or ideological factors at the macro level. In the accounts of black Rhodesian soldiers, these elements were not of importance. An alternative understanding is necessary.

Malešević has critiqued the assumption that war itself begets macro-level solidarities, arguing that instead they 'require a great deal of long-term institutional work. In-group solidarity is not something that "just happens" and naturally occurs in times of war'.[4] I have developed this insight to offer an alternative conception of black Rhodesian soldiers' macro-level loyalties, which I have termed their 'regimental loyalties'. I have argued that these were not vested in a political or patriotic loyalty to the Rhodesian settler regime or minority rule. Instead, they were vested in the first instance in their own battalion, and only thereafter to the wider institution of the Rhodesian Army as a whole, which served as a proxy for an idealised 'state'. These loyalties were honed over time, particularly in the unique environment of the RAR and its distinctive military culture. The RAR mimicked the pageantry and symbolic power of the British regimental system, utilising conspicuously 'invented traditions' in order

---

[4] Malešević, *Sociology of War and Violence*, p. 179.

to create a sense of 'group homogeneity' among its troops. It also functioned as a quintessentially Goffmanite 'total institution': the RAR was not only black soldiers' employer, but its cantonments were also where they resided, socialised, and raised their families. Through this institution, RAR soldiers told of a greater sense of loyalty to the army and state, one that stood in for a regime, an ideology, or a sense of patriotism.

We can see evidence of this macro-level loyalty in soldiers' explanations of their recruitment, which contradicted those offered by the Rhodesian state. After the end of the Federation of Rhodesia and Nyasaland, the Rhodesian state sought to mould 'traditions' of regional and familial recruitment. However, the accounts of my interviewees refuted the existence of preferential treatment for any one ethnic group.

Despite frequent assertions in the literature of a supposed Karanga dominance of the RAR, my interviewees' accounts demonstrated that although there existed a preponderance of recruits from Masvingo, and, to a lesser extent, from particular families, black Rhodesian soldiers hailed from throughout the country and enlisted for reasons beyond ethnicity and regional affiliation. In their accounts, the unit itself became the object of allegiance, and my interviewees emphasised that the RAR's military culture forbade preferential treatment for particular ethnolinguistic groups. Thus the 'regimental loyalties' of these soldiers worked against ethnic disputes and bolstered a sense of in-group belonging to an institution.

My interviewees often described relationships with this institution in kinship terms, a sense of a regimental family that extended to barracks life. Regular soldiers in other contexts have been termed 'social isolates' who live life 'behind the wire' away from mainstream society, which itself solidifies loyalty to the unit. Black Rhodesian troops were no exception, as they lived within military cantonments with their families and their children attended army schools. In my interviewees' accounts, their unit was the vector of their loyalty to the state, and thus the ideals and ethos of the army were of great importance, in contrast to the political ideology of the ruling party, which was of marginal concern. This conception of a macro loyalty to the army (and so the 'state'), rather than the regime, has also been demonstrated in recent literature on other groups of marginalised soldiers in other contexts, particularly Arab and Druze soldiers in the IDF in work by Rhoda Kanaaneh and Alon Peled, respectively.[5]

While macro-level solidarities were undoubtedly important, during combat they were superseded in importance by micro-level loyalties. I have characterised the micro-level loyalties of RAR soldiers as

---

[5] See Kanaaneh, *Surrounded*; Peled, *Question of Loyalty*.

'professional', once again emphasising the institutional context, but here extending it to daily practices and relations in wartime. A wider scholarly literature on the solidarities of soldiers, predominantly the work of military historians and sociologists, and in particular Anthony King, has argued that micro-level loyalties are of paramount importance to conventional soldiers, and has identified training as an important element in creating these loyalties.[6] Unlike the irregular combatants typical of the 'loyalist' literature, black Rhodesian soldiers underwent prolonged periods of training, in particular an arduous initial period which functioned as a process of induction into the 'total institution' of the Rhodesian Army. My interviewees described it as a trial by fire, recalling their induction into this military culture as overwhelming and challenging, and revealing that this process of metamorphosis altered their previous civilian identity to that of the regular soldier.

This intense period of training of course foregrounded discipline, physical strength, and stamina, and military skills such as marksmanship, as key aspects of a soldierly identity. But, importantly, it also emphasised the fundamental importance of acting as a collective and instilled the notion that soldiers must be mutually reliant. Inherent to black Rhodesian soldiers' micro-level loyalties were these two prongs of what I have termed 'professionalism': martial competence and solidarity. These factors were mutually reinforcing, and the 'professional' ethos emphasised that soldiers' obligation to their comrades was just as important as their military proficiencies.

The RAR's making of a particular idea of 'professionalism' was in clear contradistinction to the systematic and widespread racism of wider Rhodesian society: in practice, it constructed an alternative to it, one that was crucial to black soldiers' loyalty. As discussed later in this conclusion, 'professionalism' in the RAR implicitly encompassed respect and comradeship across race, despite the institutional racism of the army and wider society.

As King and many others have argued, in regular armies, a distinctive in-group solidarity is created between comrades, in which reciprocal bonds of obligation bind them together. Establishing a fierce soldierly kinship between troops ensured that they fought, in the first instance, for their peers. Adherence to the tenets of 'professionalism' meant that black Rhodesian soldiers strove for high standards of performance, and also that they, by their own volition, faced danger on the battlefield so as not to let their comrades down. Their 'professional' loyalties thus created a virtuous cycle wherein troops sought to perform as best they could,

[6] King, *Combat Soldier*.

which in turn further motivated their peers to aspire to the same standards.

During Zimbabwe's war of liberation, this type of loyalty was unique to black Rhodesian soldiers and distinguished them from other combatants, such as the SFA. Such 'professional' loyalties flowered within the RAR in particular as it was possessed of a distinctive military culture, which mitigated wider Rhodesian racism and allowed a constrained form of professional meritocracy to take root, in stark contrast to wider Rhodesian society.

These soldiers were not automatons and did not simply conform to the army's strict disciplinary system, or to the dictates of this 'total institution': micro-level loyalties had to be made and remade in practice continuously, at times through coercive means which were carefully legitimated in military terms. The military culture of the RAR implicitly recognised this. I argue that its officers tacitly condoned incidences of 'permissible indiscipline', which I have defined as those acts which, while technically rule-breaking, were not inimical to the unit's military efficacy, such as using marijuana or brawling in town. For 'impermissible' acts, the army's quasi-juridical processes were recalled by my interviewees as largely just and proportionate. In their accounts, they emphasised that military law served in the main to punish criminal acts, rather than acting as a source of combat motivation. This distinguished the RAR from other colonial army units which, as scholars such as Bolliger have observed, were reliant upon coercion to force marginalised soldiers to fight for them.[7]

I have argued that, after the end of the Federation, Rhodesia's requirement for volunteer 'professional' black soldiers and its need to retain them resulted in RF ministers and senior army officers lobbying for improved pay and conditions to maintain the 'social contract', but this met strong, continual opposition from politicians and officials wedded to the RF's racist policies. Thus a stuttering, gradual process of reform occurred in the army. Using my interviewees' testimony and official archival sources I have demonstrated that despite this reform, deep inequity persisted within the Rhodesian Army, and in particular the disparities in pay and accommodation between black and white soldiers were pronounced. Furthermore, I have argued that the army's limited reform initiatives were crippled by senior Rhodesian officers and ministers, notably Lt Gen. Peter Walls, who sought to frustrate the advancement of black soldiers. This discrimination belies wartime Rhodesian propaganda and post-war neo-Rhodesian narratives, which have asserted that black and

---

[7] Bolliger, *Apartheid's African Soldiers*, chapter 5.

white Rhodesian soldiers fought as equal partners in the supposed war against 'communism'.

Within the RAR, the overt institutional racism of the army was somewhat mitigated by the unit's distinctive military culture, which emphasised relationships between black and white soldiers premised upon mutual respect, and relatively meritocratic processes determined the career trajectories and promotion prospects of black soldiers. Although my interviewees loathed the entrenched inequities that remained in place across the army as a whole, I have argued that – contrary to an argument commonly asserted in the literature – the Rhodesian Army's systematic racism was not corrosive to their loyalties. For my interviewees, the prejudice they faced within the army in terms of pay and other material provisions was less severe than that experienced in civilian life.

They also recalled strong interracial relationships, both on and off duty, which were highly rare in civilian Rhodesian society. My interviewees recalled life in the RAR as harmonious and asserted that its military culture enabled strong battlefield performance. I have argued that this further bolstered the 'regimental loyalties' of black soldiers, who took much pride in the RAR and felt a deep sense of loyalty to its traditions. Furthermore, in their accounts, my interviewees recalled the RAR as not merely an employer, but also an extended regimental family, particularly during the intense latter phase of the war when off-duty black soldiers and their families were widely targeted in rural areas.

In the accounts of black Rhodesian soldiers, the army's slow process of reform from the mid-1970s created a widely shared belief that the army was becoming more equitable. Despite the fanfare over the commissioning of black officers and integration of most army units, the impact of these reforms was in fact minimal. Although they occurred too late in the war to have any kind of determinative military impact, these reforms bolstered the 'social contract' between black soldiers and the army and signified that they were of vital military importance, epitomised above all by the commissioning of black officers. Although many of my interviewees benefitted from these reforms, their real significance was symbolic, as they creating a sense among black Rhodesian soldiers that their service enabled reform to the racism of the wider army and Rhodesian society.

Training and barracks life was crucial to the making of the RAR's micro- and macro-level loyalties. So was the battlefield. I have argued that black troops' unique experience of the war, and especially their involvement in combat against the liberation forces, further cemented their particular soldierly loyalties. Through historical comparison to other comparable wars of decolonisation or COIN, I have demonstrated that there were very few incidents of desertion, mutiny, or refusal to fight on the part of black Rhodesian soldiers, and that the 'fragging' of officers did not occur. In seeking to explain this, I have drawn upon an emergent scholarly literature, particularly the work of Holger Albrecht and Kevin Koehler, that has looked at the 'push' factors that cause disaffection in the first instance, and the 'pull' factors that turn disaffection into disloyalty, discussed later in this conclusion.[8] I have argued that such factors were not prevalent among black Rhodesian soldiers.

Of the 'pull' factors, I have argued that the most salient was black soldiers' experience of combat. In contrast to other instances of conflict where poor battlefield performance causes desertions, my interviewees argued that they had militarily triumphed in their battles with the liberation forces, and this fed into a sense that they were winning the war, which benefitted their morale greatly. In contrast to other colonial armies during wars of decolonisation, where losses in combat, ineffective commanders, or poor provision of weaponry and supplies saw loyalties become strained and disloyal behaviour become commonplace, my interviewees recalled a fulsome sense that they were militarily better than their opponents. This conception reflected the tactical day-to-day experiences of black soldiers, who were among the Rhodesian Army's elite infantry and possessed considerable advantages over the liberation forces in terms of air support, training, equipment, and experience, rather than the overall strategic reality of the war. This should not, however, detract from the potency of the sentiment: black soldiers' belief that they were winning the war fed into the low levels of desertion and other forms of disloyalty. Furthermore, the 'professional' ethos of the RAR – its sense of skill and military efficacy inculcated through training, co-constitutive of mutual obligation among comrades – was bolstered by its combat experiences, and not only by its successes. When the RAR performed poorly, the army demonstrated the institutional capacity to learn from its mistakes and implement corrective measures, largely through refining processes of training.

A second key 'push' factor is a sense of moral grievance, identified by Albrecht and Koehler as a sense that the conduct of a war was unjust. This factor was also not applicable to black Rhodesian soldiers. In the accounts of my interviewees, they characterised their actions in terms of protecting civilians from guerrilla violence as the war escalated, and hence as morally justified. As with their conception of the military trajectory of the war, this did not reflect the overall picture: many elements of the Rhodesian forces committed atrocities and used gross levels of violence indiscriminately. However, my interviewees held that the RAR was rarely involved in such acts; this was in contrast to units such as the Selous Scouts, the Special

[8] Albrecht and Koehler, 'Going on the Run'.

Branch, and the auxiliaries which have been widely cited as such in the literature. My interviewees argued that part and parcel of 'professionalism' was exercising restraint in the use of lethal force and that their discipline in this regard fundamentally distinguished them from other combatants.

Related, the escalation of the war also led to a surge in guerrilla violence targeting soldiers and their families in the rural areas, which compounded the contempt my interviewees felt for the methods used by some guerrillas and reinforced their sense of themselves as 'moral' actors. This violence also served to reinforce black soldiers' 'regimental loyalties' because, in response to this threat, a large expansion occurred in the number of military families living in or adjacent to the military cantonments. The RAR's metaphorical 'regimental family' became ever more incarnate as the war progressed. These measures also meant that the 'pull' factor of a kinship network, or network of sympathisers to which soldiers might desert, as has been observed in other conflict contexts, did not exist within Rhodesia. Violence against black soldiers and their kin reached such a level of intensity that, by the end of the war, RAR troops were almost as much at risk off duty in the rural areas as they were on active service. This further instilled a belief among my interviewees that they were 'moral' and 'masculine' actors, as they held that their use of violence occurred on the battlefield and was directed towards a recognised wartime enemy, a characterisation they juxtaposed with the guerrillas, particularly ZANLA, who they deemed as amoral and illegitimate for using violence in a wanton fashion and against non-military targets.

In their accounts, my interviewees also emphasised that their loyalties were 'apolitical' in the sense that their loyalty was to the institution of the army and the state, and hence to 'the government of the day', whoever that might be. Such claims have an obvious vindicatory subtext in the context in which I carried out the interviews. In post-crisis Zimbabwe, ZANU(PF) has regularly characterised former allegiance to the colonial state as treasonous. I have argued, however, that historical evidence demonstrates that black soldiers conceived of their service during the war in this 'apolitical' manner too. Such a claim could not be made by all parts of the Rhodesian Army.

While the Rhodesian Army was nominally apolitical owing to its mimicking of the institutional culture of the British Army, I have argued that, after UDI, the higher echelons of the army became markedly politicised, personified by the clear support for minority rule of the most important Rhodesian military officer of the war, Lt Gen. Peter Walls. The army instituted a draconian system of political surveillance and censorship which policed the political expression of black soldiers while turning a blind eye to white troops' oft-stated support for the RF. This instilled a norm within the RAR that, for black soldiers, 'politics' had to be avoided. The army deliberately sought to deter potential recruits with nationalist sympathies from joining the army, or simply prohibited them from joining if they applied. With the exception of those soldiers recruited as teachers and medics, well-educated recruits or those from the black middle class were treated with suspicion or outright hostility. This further entrenched the 'apolitical' ethos of the RAR.

The Rhodesian Army was keen to prevent the expression of political views among its black soldiers. However black soldiers themselves played the most important role in the construction of the 'apolitical' ethos because, by embracing it, they portrayed themselves as beyond political, factional, or ethnic allegiance. This served to distance themselves from other combatants whose loyalties and use of violence were premised upon ethno-political power imperatives, such as the auxiliaries allied to the 'internal' parties, traits that were fundamentally incompatible with the 'professional' soldierly identity as it was elaborated within the RAR. The 'apolitical', professional loyalties of RAR soldiers came to have an exculpatory value: their service in the Rhodesian Army had become highly contentious during the war of liberation, and they were widely chastised as 'sell-outs' and collaborators in nationalist propaganda. Black soldiers rejected this portrayal, seeing themselves both during and after the war as serving their country and the 'government of the day', regardless of its political orientation. My interviewees robustly rejected the notion that they had fought for the Smith regime or minority rule. This 'apolitical' ethos also squared the circle of their personal political sympathies, which, as I have shown, were overwhelmingly in favour of majority rule, and their service in the Rhodesian Army. It also distinguished them from white soldiers, whose loyalties were often fundamentally political in nature and shattered as the end of minority rule neared.

As the war reached its intense latter stages, black soldiers' positioning of themselves as 'apolitical' allowed them to become the 'acceptable' face of the Rhodesian Army in the eyes of nationalist leaders. They were thus able to render their 'professionalism' and 'regimental loyalties' as an asset readily available to an incoming nationalist government. This would serve to ensure their post-war safety from reprisals and ongoing military careers after independence.

The clearest demonstration of this 'apolitical' ethos was, for my interviewees, their loyalty to the newly elected ZANU(PF) government in the unstable first years of independence. In their accounts, they argued that the fledgling Zimbabwean government would have been drawn into a conflict with ZIPRA – one that it could not win – had they not remained loyal to the state during the 1980–1 conflicts. My interviewees' claims of

Conclusion: The Loyalties of Professionals

their instrumental importance in Zimbabwe narrowly avoiding a civil war can be viewed sceptically as a bid for legitimacy. It is unsurprising that they emphasised their role as the guardians of post-independence peace, as this role appeared to be an unambiguous good, in contrast to their wartime service, which remains contentious to some. In this context, the claims of the 'formers' to have forestalled a civil war can be read as an attempt to garner increased legitimacy in contemporary Zimbabwe.

This book's interpretation of black Rhodesian soldiers' loyalties has thus sought to fuse the 'new school' of African military history with insights as to why soldiers fight drawn from military sociology, history, and politics. In emphasising the 'professional' and 'regimental' loyalties of these soldiers, it has sought to explain and contextualise their wartime service. This constitutes a novel historical contribution both for what it reveals of the military side of the war, and in its refutation of the dominant, politicised narratives of the service of black soldiers as espoused by 'Patriotic History' and 'neo-Rhodesian' narratives.

In conclusion, the loyalties of black Rhodesian soldiers were unique, forged in a very particular colonial context. Their solidarities were forged in the army of a settler-colonial state that waged a destructive war against nationalist forces instead of decolonising, but the accounts of black troops themselves refute the idea that their allegiance was to the settler regime or minority rule. Instead, their loyalties were formed in and by a military institution. They fought, in the first instance, out of a sense of 'professionalism', which emphasised mutual dependence upon their comrades and the normative expectation of a high level of martial performance.

The salience of 'professionalism' to the micro-level loyalties of black Rhodesian soldiers distinguishes them from other types of combatants allied with the settler state in Zimbabwe's war of liberation, and also from colonial forces during other wars of decolonisation. It is highly likely that more work on the loyalties regular troops in colonial (or other comparable) contexts will further enhance the still Western-dominated scholarly literature on why soldiers fight during wartime and of what their loyalties are made.

Furthermore, I have argued that the 'professionalism' of black Rhodesian soldiers was undergirded by their 'regimental loyalty', in which their macro-level solidarities were vested through the regiment to the army and an idea of the state. That this was forged in such seemingly paradoxical circumstances has a clear resonance in more recent contexts where troops from marginalised groups have fought for regimes whose policies and practices oppress them. Given that we know remarkably little about how the military cultures of such regiments begets these dynamics of loyalty, further research on such units in existence in the present may well shed further light on how the loyalties of professionals are forged in such circumstances.

Bibliography

Interviewees

BM, 2017, Bulawayo, Zimbabwe. Rhodesian African Rifles. Twenty-one years of service. Retired as a ZNA Warrant Officer Class II.

CD, 2017, Bulawayo, Zimbabwe. Rhodesian African Rifles. Seventeen years of service. Retired as a ZNA Staff Sergeant.

DC, 2018, Mutare, Zimbabwe. Rhodesian Army Education Corps. Twenty-four years of service. Retired as a ZNA Warrant Officer Class I.

DSN, 2017, Bulawayo, Zimbabwe. Rhodesian African Rifles and Grey's Scouts. Twenty-nine years of service. Retired as a ZNA Lieutenant Colonel.

DT, 2017, Matabeleland North, Zimbabwe. Rhodesian Army Corps of Signals. Twenty years of service. Retired as a ZNA Sergeant.

GM, 2017, Harare, Zimbabwe. Rhodesian African Rifles. Twenty-nine years of service. Retired as a ZNA Warrant Officer Class I.

GMH, 2018, Harare, Zimbabwe. Rhodesian African Rifles. Thirty-two years of service. Retired as a ZNA Major.

GN, 2017, Matabeleland South, Zimbabwe. Rhodesian African Rifles. Twenty-one years of service. Retired as a ZNA Major.

HZ, 2018, Masvingo, Zimbabwe. Rhodesian African Rifles. Twenty-two years of service. Retired as a ZNA Warrant Officer Class II.

JC, 2018, Masvingo, Zimbabwe. Rhodesian African Rifles. Twenty-eight years of service. Retired as a ZNA Captain.

JM, 2017, Bulawayo, Zimbabwe. Rhodesian African Rifles. Eleven years of service. Left the ZNA as a Corporal.

Lionel Dyck, Western Cape, South Africa, 2018. Rhodesian African Rifles. Twenty-six years of service. Left the ZNA as a Colonel.

MC, 2018, Mutare, Zimbabwe. Civilian teacher employed to teach at military schools from 1966 until 1980: firstly Inkomo Barracks and New Sarum in Salisbury, and thereafter the Rhodesian African Rifles school in Masvingo. Continued teaching the children of ZNA servicemen until 1990.

MK, 2017, Bulawayo, Zimbabwe. Rhodesian Army Corps of Engineers. Twenty-four years of service. Retired as a ZNA Warrant Officer Class II.

MN, 2017, Matabeleland North, Zimbabwe. Rhodesian Army Corps of Signals. Thirty years of service. Retired as a ZNA Warrant Officer Class I.

MS, 2018, Mutare, Zimbabwe. Wife of a now-deceased Rhodesian African Rifles soldier who retired from the ZNA after nineteen years of service.

MSW, 2017, Bulawayo, Zimbabwe. Rhodesian African Rifles. Seventeen years of service. Left the ZNA as a Captain.
PM, 2017, Harare, Zimbabwe. Rhodesian African Rifles. Twenty-one years of service. Retired as an RAR Warrant Officer Class II.
SJM, 2017, Bulawayo, Zimbabwe. Rhodesian Army Services Corps. Ten years of service. Left the Rhodesian Army as a Private.
SM, 2016, Midlands Province, Zimbabwe. Rhodesian African Rifles and Selous Scouts. Thirty-one years of service. Retired as a ZNA Captain.
TM, 2016, Gweru, Zimbabwe. Rhodesian Army Education Corps. Twenty-eight years of service. Retired as a ZNA Major.
WM, 2016, Midlands Province, Zimbabwe. Rhodesian African Rifles. Twenty-five years of service. Retired as a ZNA Captain.
WR, 2017, Gweru, Zimbabwe. Rhodesian African Rifles. Thirteen years of service. Retired as a ZNA Lieutenant Colonel.

Archival Sources

Assegai: The Magazine of the Rhodesian Army, October 1979.
Catholic Commission for Justice and Peace in Zimbabwe. *Report on the 1980s Disturbances in Matabeleland and the Midlands*, 1997.
The Cheetah: Regimental Journal of the Rhodesian Light Infantry, October 1980.
Cmd. R. R. 17. *Annual Reports of the Secretary for Defence, the Chief of the General Staff, and the Chief of the Air Staff for the Year Ended 31st December 1969* (Salisbury: Government Printer, 1970).
Cmd. 4964. *Rhodesia: Report of the Commission on Rhodesian Opinion under the Chairmanship of the Right Honourable Lord Pearce* (London: Her Majesty's Stationery Office, 1972).
Ian Smith Papers, Cory Library for Historical Research, Rhodes University, Makhanda, South Africa.
Mugabe, R. 'Address to the Nation by the Prime Minister Elect', Zimbabwe Ministry of Information, Immigration and Tourism, Record No. 1, 4 March 1980.
Nwoho: The Rhodesian African Rifles Regimental Magazine, April 1976.
Nwoho: The Rhodesian African Rifles Regimental Magazine, October 1976.
Nwoho: The Rhodesian African Rifles Regimental Magazine, October 1977.
Nwoho: The Rhodesian African Rifles Regimental Magazine, April 1978.
Papers of Ken Flower, Bodleian Library, Oxford.
Rhodesian Army Archive, British Empire and Common Museum, Bristol. Scans from this now closed archive were kindly provided by Yagil Henkin.
Secretary of State for Foreign and Commonwealth Affairs, *Southern Rhodesia: Report of the Constitutional Conference, Lancaster House, London September–December 1979* (London: Her Majesty's Stationery Office, 1980).

Newspapers

Ashford, N. 'The Blacks Who Fight for the White Regime in Salisbury', *The Times*, 21 December 1977, p. 12.
Ashford, N. 'Civil War Imminent Headline Stirs Up Anger', *The Times*, 17 October 1980, p. 7.

Ashford, N. 'Creation of Zimbabwe Army Held Up', *The Times*, 7 June 1980, pp. 1, 4.
Ashford, N. 'Flexible Approach Brings Success in Rhodesian Ceasefire', *The Times*, 8 January 1980, p. 4.
Ashford, N. 'Mr Mugabe's Balancing Feat on the Political Tightrope', *The Times*, 12 June 1980, p. 8.
Ashford, N. 'The Spark That Set the Tribes Alight', *The Times*, 24 February 1981, p. 12.
Barber, T. 'Russia Is Once Again Rewriting History', *The Financial Times*, 5 January 2020.
Borrell, J. 'Civil War Averted As Rebellion Is Crushed', *The Guardian*, 14 February 1981, p. 6.
Borrell, J. 'Mugabe Sends in Jets to Stop Guerrilla Clashes as 18 Die', *The Guardian*, 11 November 1980, p. 1.
Borrell, J. 'Mugabe Sets Old Enemy on Rebels', *The Guardian*, 13 February 1981, p. 1.
Burns, J. 'Fear Rules Rhodesian Blacks', *New York Times*, 27 March 1977, p. 1.
Burns, J. 'How Blacks View Their Larger Role in Rhodesia's Army', *New York Times*, 4 January 1979, Section A, p. 2.
Burns, J. 'In Rhodesia, Connections and Attitudes Are Keys to Covering the War', *New York Times*, 22 April 1978, p. 4.
Burns, J. 'Killing of Black Troops Adds to Rifts in Rhodesia', *New York Times*, 24 August 1979, p. A2.
Burns, J. 'Reporter's Notebook: Fear Rules Rhodesian Blacks', *New York Times*, 27 March 1977, p. 1.
Burns, J. 'Rhodesia Fearful of a Descent into Chaos', *New York Times*, 4 February 1979, p. E3.
Cleary, F. 'Pretoria Accused of Recruiting Former Rhodesian Auxiliaries', *The Times*, 19 September 1980, p. 7.
Hiltzik, M. 'White Ex-soldier's Book Opens Old Wounds in Black-Ruled Zimbabwe', *Los Angeles Times*, 29 July 1989.
'In Zimbabwe, 2 Rival Factions Count the Dead', *New York Times*, 16 February 1981, p. 1.
Kawadza, S. 'ZNA Sticks to Its Guns on Training', *Herald*, 15 May 2018. www.herald.co.zw/zna-sticks-to-its-guns-on-training [Accessed April 2020].
Knipe, M. 'Is Mr Smith Trying to Split the African Tribes?', *The Times*, 26 August 1976, p. 12.
Lelyveld, J. 'Grim Benefit in Zimbabwe', *New York Times*, 18 February 1981, p. A9.
Lelyveld, J. 'Zimbabwe Quells Mutiny; War Fear Eases', *New York Times*, 14 February 1981, p. 3.
MacManus, J. 'Zimbabwe Averts Civil War', *The Guardian*, 22 February 1981, p. 1.
Manzongo, J. 'Wafa Wafa: Only for the Brave', *Herald*, 10 October 2012. www.herald.co.zw/wafa-wafa-only-for-the-brave [Accessed April 2020].
Manzongo, J. 'Zimbabwe Army Commandos Graduation: Pictures', *Bulawayo 24 News*, 16 June 2017. https://bulawayo24.com/index-id-news-sc-local-byo-112301.html [Accessed April 2020].

Reynolds, C. 'Army Crash Course for Africans', *Rhodesia Herald*, 22 October 1977.
'Rhodesia Revising Laws on Blacks', *New York Times*, 15 June 1976, p. 7.
Ross, J. 'Mugabe Moves to End Factional Violence by Disarming Ex-guerrillas', *Washington Post*, 18 February 1981.
Ross, J. 'Size of Toll in Zimbabwe Raises Fear of New Battle', *Washington Post*, 16 February 1981.
Taylor, S. 'Tension in Bulawayo Will Be a Key Test of Mr Nkomo's Ability to Control ZIPRA', *The Times*, 14 February 1980, p. 4.
van der Vat, D. 'Lt Gen Peter Walls Obituary: Commander of the White Rhodesians Who Resisted Black Rule', *The Guardian*, 28 July 2010.

Bibliography

Abbott, P. & Botham, P. *Modern African Wars: Rhodesia 1965–80* (London: Bloomsbury, 2011).
Alao, A. 'The Metamorphosis of the "Unorthodox": The Integration and Early Development of the Zimbabwe National Army'. In N. Bhebe & T. Ranger (eds.) *Soldiers in Zimbabwe's Liberation War* (Oxford: James Currey, 1995), pp. 104–17.
Alao, A. *Mugabe and the Politics of Security in Zimbabwe* (Montreal: McGill-Queen's University Press, 2012).
Albrecht, H. & Koehler, K. 'Going on the Run: What Drives Military Desertion in Civil War?', *Security Studies*, 27, 2 (2018), pp. 179–203.
Alexander, J. 'Dissident Perspectives on Zimbabwe's Post-independence War', *Africa*, 68, 2 (1998), pp. 151–82.
Alexander, J. 'Loyalty and Liberation: The Political Life of Zephaniah Moyo', *Journal of Eastern African Studies*, 11, 1 (2017), pp. 166–87.
Alexander, J. *The Unsettled Land: State-Making & the Politics of Land in Zimbabwe, 1893–2003* (Oxford: James Currey, 2006).
Alexander, J. & McGregor, J. 'Adelante! Military Imaginaries, the Cold War, and Southern Africa's Liberation Armies', *Comparative Studies in Society and History*, 62, 3 (2020), pp. 619–50.
Alexander, J. & McGregor, J. 'War Stories: Guerrilla Narratives of Zimbabwe's Liberation War', *History Workshop Journal*, 57, 1 (2004), pp. 79–100.
Alexander, J., McGregor, J. & Ranger, T. *Violence and Memory: One Hundred Years in the 'Dark Forests' of Matabeleland, Zimbabwe* (Oxford: James Currey, 2000).
Alexander, M., Evans, M. & Keiger, J. 'The "War without a Name", the French Army and the Algerians: Recovering Experiences, Images and Testimonies'. In M. Evans & J. Keiger (eds.) *The Algerian War and the French Army, 1954–62: Experiences, Images, Testimonies* (Basingstoke: Palgrave Macmillan, 2002).
Anderson, D. *Histories of the Hanged: The Dirty War in Kenya and the End of Empire* (New York: W. W. Norton & Company, 2005).
Anderson, D. 'Making the Loyalist Bargain: Surrender, Amnesty and Impunity in Kenya's Decolonization, 1952–63', *International History Review*, 39, 1 (2017), pp. 48–70.

Anderson, D. & Branch, D. 'Allies at the End of Empire: Loyalists, Nationalists and the Cold War, 1945–76', *International History Review*, 39, 1 (2017), pp. 1–13.

Andreski, S. *Military Organization and Society* (Berkeley: University of California Press, 1968).

Anglin, D. 'Review: Counter-insurgency in Rhodesia by J. K. Cilliers', *Journal of Developing Areas*, 20, 2 (1986), pp. 253–5.

Anglin, D. 'Zimbabwe: Retrospect and Prospect', *International Journal*, 35, 4 (1980), pp. 663–700.

Anti-Apartheid Movement. *Fireforce Exposed: The Rhodesian Security Forces and Their Role in Defending White Supremacy* (London: Anti-Apartheid Movement, 1979).

Arbuckle, T. 'Rhodesian Bush War Strategies and Tactics: An Assessment', *RUSI Journal*, 124, 4 (1979), pp. 27–33.

Arrighi, G. 'The Political Economy of Rhodesia', *New Left Review*, 39 (1966), pp. 35–65.

Associated Press, RR7647A 'Rhodesia War or Diplomacy?' *Roving Report Rhodesia*, 26 November 1976.

Atlas, P. M. & Licklider, R. 'Conflict among Former Allies after Civil War Settlement: Sudan, Zimbabwe, Chad, and Lebanon', *Journal of Peace Research*, 36, 1 (1999), pp. 35–54.

Baker, D. G. 'Time Suspended: The Quenet Report and White Racial Dominance in Rhodesia', *Zambezia*, 7, 2 (1979), pp. 243–53.

Bannister, R. 'How Are We to Write Our Music History? Perspectives on the Historiography of Military Music', *Musicology Australia*, 25, 1 (2002), pp. 1–21.

Banton, M. 'Destroy? Migrate? Conceal? British Strategies for the Disposal of Sensitive Records of Colonial Administrations at Independence', *Journal of Imperial and Commonwealth History*, 40, 2 (2012), pp. 321–35.

Barkawi, T. *Soldiers of Empire: Indian and British Armies in World War II* (Cambridge: Cambridge University Press, 2017).

Baxter, P. *Selous Scouts: Counter-insurgency Specialists* (Warwick: Helion, 2012).

Beach, D. 'Ndebele Raiders and Shona Power', *Journal of African History*, 15, 4 (1974), pp. 633–51.

Beach, D. 'The Politics of Collaboration: Southern Mashonaland, 1896–7'. University of Rhodesia, Department of History, Seminar No. 9 (1969).

Bearman, P. 'Desertion As Localism: Army Unit Solidarity and Group Norms in the US Civil War', *Social Forces*, 70, 2 (1991), pp. 321–42.

Beckett, I. 'The Rhodesian Army: Counter-insurgency, 1972–1979'. In I. Beckett & J. Pimlott (eds.) *Counter-insurgency: Lessons from History* (Barnsley: Pen & Sword, 2011).

Ben-Ari, E. & Levy, Y. 'Getting Access to the Field: Insider/Outsider Perspectives'. In J. Soeters, P. Shields & S. Rietjens (eds.) *Routledge Handbook of Research Methods in Military Studies* (Abingdon: Routledge, 2014).

Bhebe, N. *The ZAPU and ZANU: Guerrilla Warfare and the Evangelical Lutheran Church in Zimbabwe* (Gweru: Mambo Press, 1999).

Bhebe, N. & Ranger, T. 'Introduction'. In N. Bhebe & T. Ranger (eds.) *Soldiers in Zimbabwe's Liberation War* (Oxford: James Currey, 1995).

Bhebe, N. & Ranger, T. *Society in Zimbabwe's Liberation War*, Vol. 2 (Oxford: James Currey, 1996).
Binda, A. *The Equus Men: Rhodesia's Mounted Infantry: The Grey's Scouts 1896–1980* (Warwick: Helion, 2016).
Binda, A. *Masodja: The History of the Rhodesian African Rifles and Its Forerunner the Rhodesia Native Regiment* (Johannesburg: 30° South, 2007).
Bolliger, L. 'Apartheid's African Soldiers: A History of Black Namibian and Angolan Members of South Africa's Former Security Forces, 1975 to the Present' (Doctoral Thesis, University of Oxford, 2019).
Bolliger, L. *Apartheid's Black Soldiers: Un-national Wars and Militaries in Southern Africa* (Athens: Ohio University Press, 2022).
Bolliger, L. 'Apartheid's Transnational Soldiers: The Case of Black Namibian Soldiers in South Africa's Former Security Forces', *Journal of Southern African Studies*, 43, 1 (2017), pp. 195–214.
Bolliger, L. 'Chiefs, Terror, and Propaganda: The Motivations of Namibian Loyalists to Fight in South Africa's Security Forces, 1975–1989', *South African Historical Journal*, 70, 1 (2018), pp. 124–51.
Bonello, J. 'The Development of Early Settler Identity in Southern Rhodesia: 1890–1914', *International Journal of African Historical Studies*, 43, 2 (2010), pp. 341–67.
Borovik, A. *The Hidden War: A Russian Journalist's Account of the Soviet War in Afghanistan* (New York: Grove Press, 2001).
Branch, D. 'The Enemy Within: Loyalists and the War against Mau Mau in Kenya', *Journal of African History*, 48, 2 (2007), pp. 291–315.
Brent, W. *Rhodesian Air Force: A Brief History* (Kwambonambi: Free World, 1987).
Brickhill, J. 'Daring to Storm the Heavens: The Military Strategy of ZAPU 1976 to 1979'. In N. Bhebe & T. Ranger (eds.) *Soldiers in Zimbabwe's Liberation War* (Oxford: James Currey, 1995).
Brownell, J. *The Collapse of Rhodesia: Population Demographics and the Politics of Race* (London: I. B. Tauris, 2010).
Bührer, T. 'Muslim *Askaris* in the Colonial Troops of German East Africa, 1889–1918'. In X. Bougarel, R. Branche & C. Drieu (eds.) *Combatants of Muslim Origin in European Armies in the Twentieth Century: Far from Jihad* (London: Bloomsbury, 2017).
Burns, L., Novick, K. & Ward, G. *The Vietnam War*. Episode 10, 'The Weight of Memory' (PBS Television, 2017).
Carver, R. 'Zimbabwe: Drawing a Line through the Past', *Journal of African Law*, 37, 1 (1993), pp. 69–81.
Castro, C. 'Anthropological Methods and the Study of the Military: The Brazilian Experience'. In H. Carreiras & C. Castro (eds.) *Qualitative Methods in Military Studies: Research Experiences and Challenges* (Abingdon: Routledge, 2012).
Catholic Commission for Justice, Peace in Zimbabwe, *Breaking the Silence, Building True Peace: A Report on the Disturbances in Matabeleland and the Midlands, 1980 to 1988* (Harare: Legal Resources Foundation, 1997).
Caute, D. *Under the Skin: The Death of White Rhodesia* (London: Penguin, 1983).

Chennells, A. 'Rhodesian Discourse, Rhodesian Novels and the Zimbabwe Liberation War'. In N. Bhebe & T. Ranger (eds.) *Society in Zimbabwe's Liberation War* (Oxford: James Currey, 1996).

Chinodya, S. *Harvest of Thorns* (London: Heinemann, 1991).

Chitiyo, K. & Rupiya, M. 'Tracking Zimbabwe's Political History: The Zimbabwe Defence Force from 1980–2005'. In M. Rupiya (ed.) *Evolutions and Revolutions: A Contemporary History of Militaries in Southern Africa* (Pretoria: Institute of Security Studies, 2005).

Cilliers, J. *Counter-Insurgency in Rhodesia* (London: Croom Helm, 1985).

Clark, S. *Soviet Military Power in a Changing World* (Abingdon: Routledge, 1991).

Cockerham, W. 'Attitudes towards Combat among US Army Paratroopers', *Journal of Political and Military Sociology*, 6, 4 (1978), p. 4.

Cocks, C. *Fireforce: One Man's War in the Rhodesian Light Infantry* (Johannesburg: 30° South Publishers, 2011).

Coelho, J. 'African Troops in the Portuguese Colonial Army, 1961–1974: Angola, Guinea-Bissau and Mozambique', *Portuguese Studies Review*, 10, 1 (2002), pp. 129–50.

Cohen, B. 'The War in Rhodesia: A Dissenter's View', *African Affairs*, 76, 305 (1977), pp. 483–94.

Cole, B. *The Elite: The Story of the Rhodesian Special Air Service* (Durban: Three Knights Press, 1985).

Cooper, F. 'Conflict and Connection: Rethinking Colonial African History', *American Historical Review*, 99, 5 (1994), pp. 1516–45.

Cox, E. & Seatter, E. (2018) 'Rhodesia Nostalgia "Screams Out Extreme Hatred", Say Zimbabweans', *Ricochet Magazine*, November. https://ricochet.media/en/2409/rhodesia-nostalgia-screams-out-extreme-hatred-say-zimbabweans [Accessed October 2019].

Crapanzano, V. *The Harkis: The Wound That Never Heals* (Chicago, IL: University of Chicago Press, 2011).

Dabengwa, D. 'ZIPRA in the Zimbabwe War of National Liberation'. In N. Bhebe & T. Ranger (eds.) *Soldiers in Zimbabwe's Liberation War*, Vol. 1 (Oxford: James Currey, 1995).

Davis, S. *The ANC's War against Apartheid: Umkhonto We Sizwe and the Liberation of South Africa* (Bloomington: Indiana University Press, 2018).

de Meneses, F. & McNamara, R. 'The Last Throw of the Dice: Portugal, Rhodesia and South Africa, 1970–74', *Portuguese Studies*, 28, 2 (2012), pp. 201–15.

de Meneses, F. & McNamara, R. 'The Origins of Exercise ALCORA, 1960–71', *International History Review*, 35, 5 (2013), pp. 1113–34.

de Meneses, F. & McNamara, R. *The White Redoubt, the Great Powers and the Struggle for Southern Africa, 1960–1980* (Basingstoke: Palgrave Macmillan, 2018).

Dlamini, J. *Askari: A Story of Collaboration and Betrayal in the Anti-Apartheid Struggle* (London: Hurst, 2014).

Dlamini, J. *Native Nostalgia* (Auckland Park: Jacana Media, 2009).

Dorman, S. *Understanding Zimbabwe: From Liberation to Authoritarianism* (London: Hurst, 2016).

Downie, N. *Frontline Rhodesia* ('TV Eye', Granada Television [ITV], 1978).
Downie, N. 'Rhodesia: A Study in Military Incompetence', *Defence*, 10, 5 (1979), pp. 342–5.
Dwyer, M. *Soldiers in Revolt: Army Mutinies in Africa* (Oxford: Oxford University Press, 2017).
Dzineza, G. A. 'Disarmament, Demobilization, Reintegration, Repatriation and Resettlement (DDRRR) in Zimbabwe, Namibia and South Africa' (Doctoral Thesis, University of the Witwatersrand, 2006).
Echenberg, M. *Colonial Conscripts: The Tirailleurs Sénégalais in French West Africa, 1857–1960* (Oxford: James Currey, 1991).
Editorial Notes, 'The Rhodesian African Rifles', *Africa*, 43, 171 (1944), pp. 51–2.
Ehrenreich, F. 'National Security'. In H. Nelson (ed.) *Zimbabwe: A Country Study* (Washington, DC: Foreign Area Studies, American University, 1983).
Ellert, H. *The Rhodesian Front War: Counter-insurgency and Guerrilla War in Rhodesia, 1962–1980* (Gweru: Mambo Press, 1989).
Ellis, S. 'The Historical Significance of South Africa's Third Force', *Journal of Southern African Studies*, 24, 2 (1998), pp. 261–99.
Enloe, C. *Ethnic Soldiers: State Security in Divided Societies* (Athens: University of Georgia Press, 1980).
Evans, Martin. 'Reprisal Violence and the Harkis in French Algeria, 1962', *International History Review*, 39, 1 (2017), pp. 89–106.
Evans, Michael. *Fighting against Chimurenga: An Analysis of Counter-Insurgency in Rhodesia, 1972–9*, 37 (Harare: Historical Association of Zimbabwe, 1981).
Evans, Michael. 'Making an African Army: The Case of Zimbabwe, 1980–87'. In N. Etherington (ed.) *Peace, Politics and Violence in the New South Africa* (London: Zell, 1992).
Evans, Michael. 'The Wretched of the Empire: Politics, Ideology and Counterinsurgency in Rhodesia, 1965–80', *Small Wars & Insurgencies*, 18, 2 (2007), pp. 175–95.
Ferdi, S. *Un Enfant Dans La Guerre* (Paris: Seuil, 1981).
Fieldhouse, D. *The Colonial Empires: A Comparative Survey from the Eighteenth Century* (London: Weidenfeld & Nicolson, 1966).
Finer, S. *The Man on Horseback: The Role of the Military in Politics* (London: Pall Mall, 1962).
Flood, Z. 'Brothers-in-Arms? White and Black Soldiers in the Rhodesian Army' (BA Thesis, Oxford University, 2005).
Flower, K. *Serving Secretly: An Intelligence Chief on Record. Rhodesia into Zimbabwe, 1964 to 1981* (London: John Murray, 1987).
Frederikse, J. *None but Ourselves: Masses vs. Media in the Making of Zimbabwe* (London: Heinemann, 1983).
Freund, B. *The Making of Contemporary Africa: The Development of African Society since 1800* (London: Macmillan, 1984).
Gann, L. 'The Development of Southern Rhodesia's Military System, 1890–1953'. In *National Archives of Rhodesia, Occasional Papers, No. I* (Salisbury: Government Printer, 1965).
Gann, L. *A History of Southern Rhodesia* (London: Chatto & Windus, 1965).

Garnham, N. 'Military Desertion and Deserters in Eighteenth-Century Ireland', *Eighteenth-Century Ireland*, 20 (2005), pp. 91–103.

Gates, J. 'The "New" Military Professionalism', *Armed Forces & Society*, 11, 3 (1985), pp. 427–36.

Geertz, C. *The Interpretation of Cultures: Selected Essays by Clifford Geertz* (New York: Basic Books, 1973).

Gibbs, P., Phillips, H. & Russell, N. *Blue and Old Gold: The History of the British South Africa Police, 1890–1980* (Johannesburg: 30° South, 2009).

Gilbert, A. 'Why Men Deserted from the Eighteenth-Century British Army', *Armed Forces & Society*, 6, 4 (1980), pp. 553–67.

Gill, L. 'Creating Citizens, Making Men: The Military and Masculinity in Bolivia', *Cultural Anthropology*, 12, 4 (1997), pp. 527–50.

Ginifer, J. *Managing Arms in Peace Processes. Vol. 9: Rhodesia-Zimbabwe* (New York: United Nations, 1995).

Ginio, R. 'Blood for Equality: African Soldiers' Struggles for Rights after World War II', *Tocqueville Review*, 40, 1 (2019), pp. 81–101.

Ginio, R. *The French Army and Its African Soldiers: The Years of Decolonisation* (Lincoln: University of Nebraska Press, 2017).

Glass, C. *The Deserters: A Hidden History of World War II* (London: Penguin, 2013).

Godwin, P. *Mukiwa: A White Boy in Africa* (New York: Harper Collins, 1996).

Godwin, P. & Hancock, I. *'Rhodesians Never Die': The Impact of War and Political Change on White Rhodesia, c.1970–1980* (Oxford: Oxford University Press, 1993).

Goffman, E. *Asylums: Essays on the Social Situation of Mental Patients and Other Inmates* (New York: Anchor, 1961).

Good, K. 'Settler Colonialism in Rhodesia', *African Affairs*, 73, 290 (1974), pp. 10–36.

Gortzak, Y. 'Using Indigenous Forces in Counterinsurgency Operations: The French in Algeria, 1954–1962', *Journal of Strategic Studies*, 32, 2 (2009), pp. 307–33.

Gregory, M. 'The Zimbabwe Election: The Political and Military Implications', *Journal of Southern African Studies*, 7, 1 (1980), pp. 17–37.

Grundy, K. *Soldiers without Politics: Blacks in the South African Armed Forces* (Berkeley: University of California Press, 1983).

Hack, K. 'Everyone Lived in Fear: Malaya and the British Way of Counterinsurgency', *Small Wars & Insurgencies*, 23, 4–5 (2012), pp. 671–99.

Harold-Barry, D. 'One Country, Two Nations: No Dialogue'. In D. Harold-Barry (ed.) *Zimbabwe: The Past Is the Future* (Harare: Weaver, 2004).

Harries-Jenkins, G. & Van Doorn, J. 'Armed Forces and the Social Order: A Pluralist Approach', *Current Sociology*, 22, 1–3 (1974), pp. 1–33.

Harris, A. 'Writing Home: Inscriptions of Whiteness/Descriptions of Belonging in White Zimbabwean Memoir-Autobiography'. In R. Muponde & R. Primorac (eds.) *Versions of Zimbabwe: New Approaches to Literature and Culture* (Harare: Weaver, 2005).

Harris, S. *Rock of the Marne: The American Soldiers Who Turned the Tide against the Kaiser in World War I* (New York: Penguin Random House, 2015).

Harrison, M. 'Resource Mobilization for World War II: The U.S.A., U.K., U.S.S.R., and Germany, 1938–1945', *Economic History Review*, 41, 2 (1988), pp. 171–92.

Hart, E. 'British Regimental Marches: Their History and Romance', *Musical Quarterly*, 4, 4 (1918), pp. 579–86.

Higate, P. (ed.) *Military Masculinities: Identity and the State* (London: Praeger, 2003).

Hopkins, J. 'Organisation of an RAR Battalion'. https://johnwynnehopkins.wordpress.com/2014/04/13/organisation-of-an-rar-battalion [Accessed June 2020].

Horne, A. *A Savage War of Peace: Algeria 1954–1962* (Basingstoke: Macmillan, 2012).

Horne, G. *From the Barrel of a Gun: The United States and the War against Zimbabwe, 1965–1980* (Chapel Hill: University of North Carolina Press, 2001).

Horne, J. 'Masculinity in Politics and War in the Age of Nation-States and World Wars, 1850–1950'. In S. Dudink, K. Hagemann & J. Tosh (eds.) *Masculinities in Politics and War: Gendering Modern History* (Manchester: Manchester University Press, 2004).

Hove, M. 'War Legacy: A Reflection on the Effects of the Rhodesian Security Forces (RSF) in South Eastern Zimbabwe during Zimbabwe's War of Liberation 1976–1980', *Journal of African Studies and Development*, 4, 8 (2012), pp. 193–206.

Hughes, D. *Whiteness in Zimbabwe: Race, Landscape, and the Problem of Belonging* (Basingstoke: Palgrave Macmillan, 2010).

Huntington, S. *The Soldier and the State: The Theory and Politics of Civil–Military Relations* (Cambridge, MA: Harvard University Press, 1981).

Hutchings, K. 'Making Sense of Masculinity and War', *Men and Masculinities*, 10, 4 (2008), pp. 389–404.

Hynes, S. *The Soldiers' Tale: Bearing Witness to a Modern War* (London: Penguin, 1998).

International Institute for Strategic Studies. *Strategic Survey: Southern Africa*, 78, 1 (1977).

Jackson, P. 'The Civil War Roots of Military Domination in Zimbabwe: The Integration Process Following the Rhodesian War and the Road to ZANLA Dominance'. *Civil Wars*, 13, 4 (2011), pp. 371–95.

Jackson, P. 'Military Integration from Rhodesia to Zimbabwe'. In R. Licklider (ed.) *New Armies from Old: Merging Competing Military Forces after Civil Wars* (Washington, DC: Georgetown University Press, 2014).

Janowitz, M. *Military Conflict: Institutional Analysis of War & Peace* (London: Sage, 1975).

Janowitz, M. *The Professional Soldier: A Social and Political Portrait* (New York: Free Press, 1960).

Jaster, R. 'The Front-Line States and the Rhodesian Peace Settlement', *International Institute for Strategic Studies Adelphi Papers*, 23 (1980), pp. 8–19.

Jeffery, K. 'An English Barrack in the Oriental Seas'? India in the Aftermath of the First World War', *Modern Asian Studies*, 15, 3 (1981), pp. 369–86.

Jeffery, K. 'The Irish Military Tradition and the British Empire'. In K. Jeffery (ed.) *An Irish Empire? Aspects of Ireland and the British Empire* (Manchester: Manchester University Press, 1996).

Johnson, R. *True to Their Salt: Indigenous Personnel in Western Armed Forces* (London: Hurst, 2017).

Jones, T. 'The British Army, and Counter-guerrilla Warfare in Transition, 1944–1952', *Small Wars & Insurgencies*, 7, 3 (1996), pp. 255–66.

Kalyvas, S. *The Logic of Violence in Civil War* (Cambridge: Cambridge University Press, 2006).

Kanaaneh, R. *Surrounded: Palestinian Soldiers in the Israeli Military* (Stanford, CA: Stanford University Press, 2008).

Kay, R. P. 'The Geopolitics of Dependent Development in Central Africa: Race, Class and the Reciprocal Blockade', *Commonwealth & Comparative Politics*, 49, 3 (2011), pp. 379–426.

Keegan, J. *The Face of Battle: A Study of Agincourt, Waterloo and the Somme* (London: Random House, 2011).

Kellett, A. *Combat Motivation: The Behaviour of Soldiers in Battle* (Boston, MA: Springer, 1982).

Kennedy, D. *Islands of White: Settler Society and Culture in Kenya and Southern Rhodesia, 1890–1939* (Durham, NC: Duke University Press, 1987).

Kennes, E. & Larmer, M. *The Katangese Gendarmes and War in Central Africa: Fighting Their Way Home* (Bloomington: Indiana University Press, 2016).

Kenrick, D. *Decolonisation, Identity and Nation in Rhodesia, 1964–1979: A Race against Time* (Basingstoke: Palgrave Macmillan, 2019).

Kenrick, D. 'The Past Is Our Country: History and the Rhodesiana Society c.1953–1970', Paper given at Newcastle University, November 2014, p. 7. www.societies.ncl.ac.uk/pgfnewcastle/files/2014/11/The-Past-is-Our-Country-History-and-the-Rhodesiana-Society-c.-1953-1970.pdf [Accessed March 2020].

Kesby, M. 'Arenas for Control, Terrains of Gender Contestation: Guerrilla Struggle and Counter-insurgency Warfare in Zimbabwe 1972–1980', *Journal of Southern African Studies*, 22, 4 (1996), pp. 561–84.

Killingray, D. & Plaut, M. *Fighting for Britain: African Soldiers in the Second World War* (London: Boydell & Brewer, 2012).

Killingray, D. 'The Idea of a British Imperial African Army', *Journal of African History*, 20, 3 (1979), pp. 421–36.

King, A. *The Combat Soldier: Infantry Tactics and Cohesion in the Twentieth and Twenty-First Centuries* (Oxford: Oxford University Press, 2013).

King, A. 'The Existence of Group Cohesion in the Armed Forces: A Response to Guy Siebold', *Armed Forces & Society*, 33, 4 (2007), pp. 638–45.

King, A. 'The Word of Command: Communication and Cohesion in the Military', *Armed Forces & Society*, 32, 4 (2006), p. 493.

Kirke, C. 'Insider Anthropology: Theoretical and Empirical Issues for the Researcher'. In H. Carreiras & C. Castro (eds.) *Qualitative Methods in Military Studies: Research Experiences and Challenges* (Abingdon: Routledge, 2012).

Kirke, C. 'Seeing through the Stereotype: British Army Culture. An Insider Anthropology'. In G. Kümmel, G. Caforio & C. Dandeker (eds.) *Armed*

Forces, Soldiers and Civil–Military Relations: Essays in Honor of Jürgen Kuhlman (Wiesbaden: VS Verlag für Sozialwissenschaften, 2009).

Koehler, K., Ohl, D. & Albrecht, H. 'From Disaffection to Desertion: How Networks Facilitate Military Insubordination in Civil Conflict', *Comparative Politics*, 48, 4 (2016), pp. 439–57.

Kössler, R. 'Facing a Fragmented Past: Memory, Culture and Politics in Namibia', *Journal of Southern African Studies*, 33, 2 (2007), pp. 361–82.

Krebs, R. *Fighting for Rights: Military Service and the Politics of Citizenship* (Ithaca, NY: Cornell University Press, 2006).

Kriger, N. 'From Patriotic Memories to "Patriotic History" in Zimbabwe, 1990–2005', *Third World Quarterly*, 27, 6 (2006), pp. 1151–69.

Kriger, N. *Guerrilla Veterans in Post-war Zimbabwe: Symbolic and Violent Politics, 1980–1987* (Cambridge: Cambridge University Press, 2003).

Kriger, N. 'War Veterans: Continuities between the Past and the Present', *African Studies Quarterly*, 7, 2 (2003), pp. 139–52.

Kriger, N. 'Zimbabwe: Political Constructions of War Veterans', *Review of African Political Economy*, 30, 96 (2003), pp. 323–8.

Kriger, N. *Zimbabwe's Guerrilla War: Peasant Voices* (Cambridge: Cambridge University Press, 1991).

Kruijt, D. 'Research on Latin America's Soldiers Generals, Sergeants and Guerrilla Comandantes'. In H. Carreiras & C. Castro (eds.) *Qualitative Methods in Military Studies: Research Experiences and Challenges* (Abingdon: Routledge, 2012).

Lan, D. *Guns and Rain: Guerrillas and Spirit Mediums in Zimbabwe* (Berkeley: University of California Press, 1985).

Larsen, L. 'Notions of Nation in Nairobi's Nyayo-Era Monuments', *African Studies*, 70, 2 (2011), pp. 264–83.

Law, K. *Gendering the Settler State: White Women, Race, Liberalism and Empire in Rhodesia, 1950–1980* (Abingdon: Routledge, 2015).

Ledwidge, F. *Losing Small Wars: British Military Failure in Iraq and Afghanistan* (New Haven, CT: Yale University Press, 2011).

Lepre, G. *Fragging: Why US Soldiers Assaulted Their Officers in Vietnam* (Lubbock: Texas Tech University Press, 2011).

Liebenberg, I. 'Evolving Experiences: Auto-ethnography and Military Sociology. A South African Immersion'. In H. Carreiras & C. Castro (eds.) *Qualitative Methods in Military Studies: Research Experiences and Challenges* (Abingdon: Routledge, 2012).

Lindgren, B. 'The Internal Dynamics of Ethnicity: Clan Names, Origins and Castes in Southern Zimbabwe', *Africa: Journal of the International African Institute*, 74, 2 (2004), pp. 173–93.

Lohman, C. & MacPherson, R. *Rhodesia: Tactical Victory, Strategic Defeat* (US Marine Corps Command and Staff College, US Marine Corps Development and Education Command, 1983).

Lonn, E. *Desertion during the Civil War* (Lincoln: University of Nebraska Press, 1998).

Lovering, T. 'Authority and Identity: Malawian Soldiers in Britain's Colonial Army, 1891–1964' (Doctoral Thesis, University of Stirling, 2002).

Lowry, D. 'The Impact of Anti-communism on White Rhodesian Political Culture, ca. 1920s–1980', *Cold War History*, 7, 2 (2007), pp. 169–94.

Mabuza, S. 'Dumbutshena, Chihambakwe Reports "Have Been Lost": NPRC Chairman', ZimLive.com, 19 April 2019. www.zimlive.com/2019/04/19/dumbutshena-chihambakwe-reports-have-been-lost-nprc-chairman [Accessed June 2020].

MacQueen, N. 'Portugal: Decolonization without Agency'. In M. Thomas & A. Thompson (eds.) *The Oxford Handbook of the Ends of Empire* (Oxford: Oxford University Press, 2018).

Malešević, S. *The Sociology of War and Violence* (Cambridge: Cambridge University Press, 2010).

Maley, A. & Hawkins, D. 'The Southern Military Tradition: Sociodemographic Factors, Cultural Legacy, and US Army Enlistments', *Armed Forces & Society*, 44, 2 (2018), pp. 195–218.

Maringira, G. 'Politics, Privileges, and Loyalty in the Zimbabwe National Army', *African Studies Review*, 60, 2 (2017), pp. 93–113.

Marriott, A. 'Manufactured Tradition? The Victoria Cross', *Post-medieval Archaeology*, 54, 1 (2020), pp. 1–16.

Martin, D. & Johnson, P. *The Struggle for Zimbabwe: The Chimurenga War* (London: Faber & Faber, 1981).

Martin, M. & Turner, P. 'Why African-Americans Loathe "Uncle Tom"'. In *Character* (NPR, 2008). www.npr.org/templates/story/story.php?storyId=93059468 [Accessed March 2020].

Martinez, I. 'The History of the Use of Bacteriological and Chemical Agents during Zimbabwe's Liberation War of 1965–80 by Rhodesian Forces', *Third World Quarterly*, 23, 6 (2002), pp. 1159–79.

Matthews, R. 'From Rhodesia to Zimbabwe: Prerequisites of a Settlement', *International Journal*, 45, 2 (1990), pp. 292–333.

Maudeni, Z. 'Why the African Renaissance Is Likely to Fail: The Case of Zimbabwe', *Journal of Contemporary African Studies*, 22, 2 (2004), pp. 189–202.

Maxey, K. *The Fight for Zimbabwe: The Armed Conflict in Southern Rhodesia since UDI* (London: Rex Collings, 1975).

Mazarire, G. 'Discipline and Punishment in ZANLA: 1964–1979', *Journal of Southern African Studies*, 37, 3 (2011), pp. 571–91.

Mazarire, G. 'Rescuing Zimbabwe's "Other" Liberation Archives'. In C. Saunders (ed.) *Documenting Liberation Struggles in Southern Africa: Select Papers from the Nordic Africa Documentation Project Workshop, 26–27 November 2009, Pretoria, South Africa* (Uppsala: Nordic Africa Institute, 2010).

McGrath, J. *The Other End of the Spear: The Tooth-to-Tail Ratio (T3R) in Modern Military Operations* (Fort Leavenworth, KS: US Army Command and General Staff College, 2007).

McGregor, J. 'Containing Violence: Poisoning and Guerrilla/Civilian Relations in Memories of Zimbabwe's Liberation War'. In K. Rogers, S. Leydesdorff & G. Dawson (eds.) *Trauma and Life Stories: International Perspectives* (Abingdon: Routledge, 1999).

McLauchlin, T. 'Desertion and Collective Action in Civil Wars', *International Studies Quarterly*, 59, 4 (2015), pp. 669–79.
McLaughlin, P. 'The Legacy of Conquest: African Military Manpower in Southern Rhodesia During the First World War'. In M. Page (ed.) *Africa and the First World War* (Basingstoke: Palgrave Macmillan, 1987).
McLaughlin, P. *Ragtime Soldiers: The Rhodesian Experience in the First World War* (Bulawayo: Books of Zimbabwe, 1980).
McLaughlin, P. 'The Thin White Line: Rhodesia's Armed Forces since the Second World War', *Zambezia*, 6, 2 (1978), pp. 175–86.
McLaughlin, P. 'Victims As Defenders: African Troops in the Rhodesian Defence System 1890–1980', *Small Wars & Insurgencies*, 2, 2 (1991), pp. 240–75.
Melson, C. *Fighting for Time: Rhodesia's Military and Zimbabwe's Independence* (Havertown: Casemate, 2021).
Melson, C. 'Top Secret War: Rhodesian Special Operations', *Small Wars & Insurgencies*, 16, 1 (2005), pp. 57–82.
Metsola, L. 'The Struggle Continues? The Spectre of Liberation, Memory Politics and "War Veterans" in Namibia', *Development and Change*, 41, 4 (2010), pp. 589–613.
Mhanda, W. *Dzino: Memories of a Freedom Fighter* (Harare: Weaver Press, 2011).
Mills, G. 'BMATT and Military Integration in Southern Africa', *South African Defence Review*, 2 (1992), pp. 1–10.
Mills G. & Wilson, G. 'Who Dares Loses?', *RUSI Journal*, 152, 6 (2007), pp. 22–31.
Minter, W. & Schmidt, E. 'When Sanctions Worked: The Case of Rhodesia Reexamined', *African Affairs*, 87, 347 (1988), pp. 207–37.
Mlambo, A. 'From the Second World War to UDI, 1945–1960'. In B. Raftopoulos & A. Mlambo (eds.) *Becoming Zimbabwe: A History from the Pre-colonial Period to 2008* (Harare: Weaver, 2008).
Moorcraft, P. 'Rhodesia's War of Independence', *History Today*, 40 (1990), pp. 11–17.
Moorcraft, P. *A Short Thousand Years: The End of Rhodesia's Rebellion* (Salisbury: Galaxie Press, 1979).
Moorcraft, P. & McLaughlin, P. *The Rhodesian War: A Military History* (Barnsley: Pen & Sword, 2010).
Moore, B. 'In-Depth Interviewing'. In J. Soeters, P. Shields & S. Rietjens (eds.), *Routledge Handbook of Research Methods in Military Studies* (Abingdon: Routledge, 2014).
Moyd, M. *Violent Intermediaries: African Soldiers, Conquest, and Everyday Colonialism in German East Africa* (Athens: Ohio University Press, 2014).
Mtisi, J., Nyakudya, M. & Barnes, T. 'War in Rhodesia, 1965–1980'. In B. Raftopoulos & A. Mlambo (eds.) *Becoming Zimbabwe: A History from the Pre-colonial Period to 2008* (Harare: Weaver Press, 2008).
Munochiveyi, M. '"We Do Not Want to Be Ruled by Foreigners": Oral Histories of Nationalism in Colonial Zimbabwe', *Historian*, 73, 1 (2011), pp. 65–87.
Mutambara, A. *The Rebel in Me: A ZANLA Guerrilla Commander in the Rhodesian Bush War, 1974–1980* (Warwick: Helion and Company, 2014).

Mutangadura, T. C. 'A Study of the Problems Encountered by Retiring Regular African Members of the Rhodesian Army Seeking Civilian Employment and the Educational and Training Implications Involved in Re-settlement' (Dissertation, University of Rhodesia, 1977).

Ndlovu-Gatsheni, S. J. 'The Death of the Subject with a Capital "S" and the Perils of Belonging: A Study of the Construction of Ethnocracy in Zimbabwe', *Critical Arts*, 26, 4 (2012), pp. 525–46.

Ndlovu-Gatsheni, S. J. 'Mapping Cultural and Colonial Encounters'. In B. Raftopoulos & A. Mlambo (eds.) *Becoming Zimbabwe: A History from the Pre-colonial Period to 2008* (Harare: Weaver Press, 2008).

Ndlovu-Gatsheni, S. J. 'The Post-colonial state and Matabeleland: Regional Perceptions of Civil-Military Relations, 1980–2002', *African Journal on Conflict Resolution*, 3, 1 (2003), pp. 99–134.

Ndlovu-Gatsheni, S. J. & Willems, W. 'Making Sense of Cultural Nationalism and the Politics of Commemoration under the Third Chimurenga in Zimbabwe', *Journal of Southern African Studies*, 35, 4 (2009), pp. 945–65.

Nhongo-Simbanegavi, J. (2000) *For Better or Worse? Women and ZANLA in Zimbabwe's Liberation Struggle* (Harare: Weaver Press, 2000).

Ninh, B. *The Sorrow of War* (New York: Pantheon, 1990).

Nissimi, H. 'Illusions of World Power in Kenya: Strategy, Decolonization, and the British Base, 1946–1961', *International History Review*, 23, 4 (2001), pp. 824–46.

O'Brien, K. *The South African Intelligence Services: From Apartheid to Democracy, 1948–2005* (Abingdon: Routledge, 2011).

O'Brien, K. 'Special Forces for Counter Revolutionary Warfare: The South African Case', *Small Wars & Insurgencies*, 12, 2 (2001), pp. 79–109.

Oliveira, P. 'Saved by the Civil War: African "Loyalists" in the Portuguese Armed Forces and Angola's Transition to Independence', *International History Review*, 39, 1 (2017), pp. 126–42.

Orwell, G. 'Marrakech', *New Writing*, 3 (1939).

Owen, C. *The Rhodesian African Rifles* (London: Leo Cooper, 1970).

Page, M. *The King's African Rifles: A History* (Barnsley: Pen and Sword, 2011).

Pandya, P. *Mao Tse-tung and Chimurenga: An Investigation into ZANU's Strategies* (Johannesburg: Skotaville, 1988).

Parsons, T. *The 1964 Army Mutinies and the Making of Modern East Africa* (London: Praeger, 2003).

Parsons, T. 'African Participation in the British Empire'. In S. Hawkins & P. D. Morgan (eds.) *Black Experience and the Empire* (Oxford: Oxford University Press, 2006).

Parsons, T. *The African Rank-and-File: Social Implications of Colonial Military Service in the King's African Rifles, 1902–1964* (London: Heinemann, 1999).

Parsons, T. 'The Lanet Incident, 2–25 January 1964: Military Unrest and National Amnesia in Kenya'. *International Journal of African Historical Studies*, 40, 1 (2007), pp. 51–70.

Passerini, L. *Fascism in Popular Memory: The Cultural Experience of the Turin Working Class* (Cambridge: Cambridge University Press, 1987).

Peled, A. *A Question of Loyalty: Military Manpower Policy in Multiethnic States* (Ithaca, NY: Cornell University Press, 1998).
Percox, D. 'Circumstances Short of Global War: British Defence, Colonial Internal Security, and Decolonisation in Kenya, 1945–65' (Doctoral Thesis, University of Nottingham, 2001).
Petter-Bowyer, P. *Winds of Destruction: The Autobiography of a Rhodesian Combat Pilot* (Johannesburg: 30° South Publishers, 2005).
Phimister, I. 'Zimbabwe: The Combined and Contradictory Inheritance of Struggle against Colonialism', *Workshop on the South African Agrarian Question* (1987).
Pilossof, R. 'The Unbearable Whiteness of Being: Land, Race and Belonging in the Memoirs of White Zimbabweans', *South African Historical Journal*, 61, 3 (2009), pp. 621–38.
Popplewell, R. '"Lacking Intelligence": Some Reflections on Recent Approaches to British Counter-insurgency, 1900–1960', *Intelligence and National Security*, 10, 2 (1995), pp. 336–52.
Preston, M. 'Stalemate and the Termination of Civil War: Rhodesia Reassessed', *Journal of Peace Research*, 41, 1 (2004), pp. 65–83.
Primorac, R. 'Rhodesians Never Die? The Zimbabwean Crisis and the Revival of Rhodesian Discourse'. In J. McGregor & R. Primorac (eds.) *Zimbabwe's New Diaspora: Displacement and the Cultural Politics of Survival* (Oxford: Berghahn Books, 2010).
Raftopoulos, B. 'The Crisis in Zimbabwe, 1998–2008'. In B. Raftopoulos & A. Mlambo (eds.) *Becoming Zimbabwe: A History from the Pre-colonial Period to 2008* (Harare: Weaver, 2009).
Raftopoulos, B. *The Hard Road to Reform* (Harare: Weaver, 2013).
Ranger, T. 'The Invention of Tradition in Colonial Africa'. In E. Hobsbawm & T. Ranger (eds.) *The Invention of Tradition* (Cambridge: Cambridge University Press, 1983).
Ranger, T. 'Nationalist Historiography, Patriotic History and the History of the Nation: The Struggle Over the Past in Zimbabwe', *Journal of Southern African Studies*, 30, 2 (2004), pp. 215–34.
Ranger, T. 'Review: Counter-insurgency in Rhodesia by J. K. Cilliers', *African Affairs*, 84, 336 (1985), pp. 474–5.
Ranger, T. *Revolt in Southern Rhodesia, 1896–7: A Study in African Resistance* (London: Heinemann, 1967).
Reese, R. 'Motivations to Serve: The Soviet Soldier in the Second World War', *Journal of Slavic Military Studies*, 20, 2 (2007), pp. 263–82.
Reid, R. *Warfare in African History* (Cambridge: Cambridge University Press, 2012).
Reid-Daly, R. & Stiff, P. *Selous Scouts: Top Secret War* (Durban: Galago, 1982).
Reno, W. *Warfare in Independent Africa* (Cambridge: Cambridge University Press, 2011).
Rhodesian Army Association, 'Rhodesian Armoured Car Regiment Uncovered'. http://rhodesianforces.org/RhodesianArmouredCarRegt.htm [Accessed June 2020].

Rice, S. 'The Commonwealth Initiative in Zimbabwe, 1979–1980: Implications for International Peacekeeping' (Doctoral Thesis, University of Oxford, 1990).

Riseman, N. 'The Rise of Indigenous Military History', *History Compass*, 12, 12 (2014), pp. 901–11.

Roberts, R. S. 'Towards a History of Rhodesia's Armed Forces', *Rhodesian History (Journal of the Central Africa Historical Association)*, 5 (1974), pp. 103–10.

Römer, F. 'Milieus in the Military: Soldierly Ethos, Nationalism and Conformism among Workers in the Wehrmacht', *Journal of Contemporary History*, 48, 1 (2013), pp. 125–49.

Rotberg, R. *The Founder: Cecil Rhodes and the Pursuit of Power* (Oxford: Oxford University Press, 1988).

Roy, J. *The Battle of Dienbienphu* (New York: Harper & Row, 1965).

Roy, K. 'Military Loyalty in the Colonial Context: A Case Study of the Indian Army during World War II', *Journal of Military History*, 73, 2 (2009), pp. 497–529.

Rupiya, M. 'Demobilization and Integration: Operation Merger and the Zimbabwe National Defence Forces, 1980–1987'. In J. Cilliers (ed.) *Dismissed: Demobilisation and Reintegration of Former Combatants in Africa* (Johannesburg: Institute for Defence Policy, 1995).

Sachikonye, L. 'Whither Zimbabwe? Crisis & Democratisation', *Review of African Political Economy*, 29, 91 (2002), pp. 13–20.

Samkange, S. J. T. *Origins of Rhodesia* (New York: Praeger, 1969).

Saunders, C. & Smith, I. 'Southern Africa, 1795–1910'. In A. Porter (ed.) *The Oxford History of the British Empire: Volume III: The Nineteenth Century* (Oxford: Oxford University Press, 1999).

Scarnecchia, T. 'The "Fascist Cycle" in Zimbabwe, 2000–2005', *Journal of Southern African Studies*, 32, 2 (2006), pp. 221–37.

Scarnecchia, T. *The Urban Roots of Democracy and Political Violence in Zimbabwe: Harare and Highfield, 1940–1964* (Rochester, NY: University of Rochester Press, 2008).

Scheipers, S. 'Irregular Auxiliaries after 1945', *International History Review*, 39, 1 (2017), pp. 14–29.

Schubert, J. '2002, Year Zero: History As Anti-politics in the "New Angola"', *Journal of Southern African Studies*, 41, 4 (2015), pp. 835–52.

Segal, D. & Segal, M. 'Change in Military Organization', *Annual Review of Sociology*, 9, 1 (1983), pp. 151–70.

Seirlis, J-K. 'Undoing the United Front? Coloured Soldiers in Rhodesia 1939–1980', *African Studies*, 63, 1 (2004), pp. 73–94.

Selous, F. C. *Sunshine and Storm in Rhodesia* (Bulawayo: Books of Rhodesia, 1968 [1896]).

Sevy, G. *The American Experience in Vietnam: A Reader* (Norman: University of Oklahoma Press, 1989).

Shils, E. & Janowitz, M. 'Cohesion and Disintegration in the Wehrmacht in World War II', *Public Opinion Quarterly*, 12, 2 (1948), pp. 280–315.

Shutt, A. '"The Natives Are Getting Out of Hand": Legislating Manners, Insolence and Contemptuous Behaviour in Southern Rhodesia, c.1910–1963', *Journal of Southern African Studies*, 33, 3 (2007), pp. 653–72.

Sibanda, E. *The Zimbabwe African People's Union, 1961–87: A Political History of Insurgency in Southern Rhodesia* (Asmara: Africa World Press, 2005).
Siebold, G. 'The Essence of Military Group Cohesion', *Armed Forces & Society*, 33, 2 (2007), pp. 286–95.
Simpson, J. & Speake, J. (eds.) *The Oxford Dictionary of Proverbs* (Oxford: Oxford University Press, 2008).
Sinclair, I., Phiri, J. & Bright, S. *Flame* (California Newsreel Productions, San Francisco, 1996).
Slantchev, B. *Military Threats: The Costs of Coercion and the Price of Peace* (Cambridge: Cambridge University Press, 2011).
Soeters, J., Winslow, D. & Weibull, A. 'Military Culture'. In G. Caforio (ed.) *Handbook of the Sociology of the Military* (Boston, MA: Springer, 2006).
Stapleton, T. *African Police and Soldiers in Colonial Zimbabwe, 1923–80* (Rochester, NY: University of Rochester Press, 2011).
Stapleton, T. 'Extra-territorial African Police and Soldiers in Southern Rhodesia (Zimbabwe) 1897–1965', *Scientia Militaria: South African Journal of Military Studies*, 38, 1 (2010), pp. 98–114.
Stapleton, T. *No Insignificant Part: The Rhodesia Native Regiment and the East Africa Campaign of the First World War* (Waterloo: Wilfrid Laurier University Press, 2006).
Stedman, S. 'The End of the Zimbabwean Civil War'. In R. Licklider, *Stopping the Killing: How Civil Wars End* (New York: New York University Press, 1993).
Stewart, M. 'The Rhodesian African Rifles: The Growth and Adaptation of a Multicultural Regiment through the Rhodesian Bush War, 1965–1980' (Master's Thesis, US Army Command and General Staff College, 2011).
Stockwell, S. 'Decolonisation beyond the Public Record Office: Non-official Sources for Studying the End of Empire', *Contemporary Record*, 6, 3 (1992), pp. 557–66.
Telfer, A. & Fulton, R. *Chibaya Moyo, The Rhodesian African Rifles: An Anthology 1939–1980* (Johannesburg: 30° South Publishers, 2015).
Telfer, A. & Fulton, R. *Chibaya Moyo 2, The Rhodesian African Rifles: An Anthology of Anecdotes* (Johannesburg: 30° South Publishers, 2019).
Tendi, B-M. *The Army and Politics in Zimbabwe: Mujuru, the Liberation Fighter and Kingmaker* (Cambridge: Cambridge University Press, 2020).
Tendi, B-M. 'Ideology, Civilian Authority and the Zimbabwean Military', *Journal of Southern African Studies*, 39, 4 (2013), p. 836.
Tendi, B-M. *Making History in Mugabe's Zimbabwe: Politics, Intellectuals, and the Media* (New York: Peter Lang, 2010).
Tendi, B-M. 'Patriotic History and Public Intellectuals Critical of Power', *Journal of Southern African Studies*, 34, 2 (2008), pp. 379–96.
Tendi, B-M. 'Soldiers contra Diplomats: The Rhodesia/Zimbabwe Ceasefire (1979–80) Reconsidered', *Small Wars and Insurgencies*, 26, 6 (2015), pp. 937–56.
Tendi, B-M. 'Transnationalism, Contingency and Loyalty in African Liberation Armies: The Case of ZANU's 1974–1975 Nhari Mutiny', *Journal of Southern African Studies*, 43, 1 (2017), pp. 143–59.

Thomas, C. & Doron, R. 'Out of Africa: The Challenges, Evolution, and Opportunities of African Military History', *Journal of African Military History*, 1, 1–2 (2017), pp. 3–23.

Thompson, P. S. '"Loyalty's Fair Reward": The Natal Native Horse in the Zulu Rebellion of 1906', *South African Historical Journal*, 66, 4 (2014), pp. 656–76.

Thompson, P. S. *The Voice of the Past: Oral History* (Oxford: Oxford University Press, 2000 [1988]).

Tonkin, E. *Narrating Our Pasts: The Social Construction of Oral History* (Cambridge: Cambridge University Press, 1992).

Tungamirai, J. 'Recruitment to ZANLA: Building Up a War Machine'. In N. Bhebe & T. Ranger (eds.) *Soldiers in Zimbabwe's Liberation War* (Oxford: James Currey, 1995).

Ucko, D. 'The Malayan Emergency: The Legacy and Relevance of a Counter-insurgency Success Story', *Defence Studies*, 10, 1–2 (2010), pp. 13–39.

Ukpabi, S. C. 'The Changing Role of the Military in Nigeria, 1900–1970', *Africa Spectrum*, 11, 1 (1976), pp. 61–77.

US Army Training and Doctrine Command. *Range and Lethality of U.S. and Soviet Anti-Armor Weapons* (Monroe, VA: US Army Training and Doctrine Command, 1975).

Veracini, L. *Settler Colonialism: A Theoretical Overview* (Basingstoke: Palgrave Macmillan, 2010).

Ware, V. *Military Migrants: Fighting for YOUR Country* (Basingstoke: Palgrave Macmillan, 2012)

Webb, J. 'Foreword'. In A. Wiest (ed.) *Vietnam's Forgotten Army: Heroism and Betrayal in the ARVN* (New York: New York University Press, 2008), p. xv.

Weinrich, A. K. H. 'Strategic Resettlement in Rhodesia', *Journal of Southern African Studies*, 3, 2 (1977), pp. 207–29.

Weitzer, R. 'In Search of Regime Security: Zimbabwe since Independence', *Journal of Modern African Studies*, 22, 4 (1984), pp. 529–57.

Werbner, R. *Memory and the Postcolony: African Anthropology and the Critique of Power* (London: Zed, 1998).

West, M. *The Rise of an African Middle Class: Colonial Zimbabwe 1898–1965* (Bloomington: Indiana University Press, 2002).

Wheeler, D. L. 'African Elements in Portugal's Armies in Africa (1961–1974)', *Armed Forces & Society*, 2, 2 (1976), pp. 233–50.

Whitaker, B. 'The "New Model" Armies of Africa? The British Military Advisory and Training Team and the Creation of the Zimbabwe National Army' (Doctoral Thesis, Texas A&M University, 2014).

White, L. 'Animals, Prey, and Enemies: Hunting and Killing in an African Counter-insurgency', *Journal of Contemporary African Studies*, 34, 1 (2016), pp. 7–21.

White, L. *The Assassination of Herbert Chitepo: Texts and Politics in Zimbabwe* (Bloomington: Indiana University Press, 2003).

White, L. 'Civic Virtue, Young Men, and the Family: Conscription in Rhodesia, 1974–1980', *International Journal of African Historical Studies*, 37, 1 (2004), pp. 103–21.

White, L. *Fighting and Writing: The Rhodesian Army at War and Postwar* (Durham, NC, Duke University Press, 2021).
White, L. '"Heading for the Gun": Skills and Sophistication in an African Guerrilla War', *Comparative Studies in Society and History*, 51, 2 (2009), pp. 236–59.
White, L. '"Normal Political Activities": Rhodesia, the Pearce Commission, and the African National Council', *Journal of African History*, 52, 3 (2011), pp. 321–40.
White, L. 'Telling More: Lies, Secrets, and History', *History and Theory*, 39, 4 (2000), pp. 11–22.
White, L. *Unpopular Sovereignty: Rhodesian Independence and African Decolonization* (Chicago, IL: University of Chicago Press, 2015).
White, L. '"Whoever Saw a Country with Four Armies?" The Battle of Bulawayo Revisited', *Journal of Southern African Studies*, 33, 3 (2007), pp. 619–31.
White, L. & Larmer, M. 'Introduction: Mobile Soldiers and the Un-national Liberation of Southern Africa', *Journal of Southern African Studies*, 40, 6 (2014), pp. 1271–4.
Wiest, A. *Vietnam's Forgotten Army: Heroism and Betrayal in the ARVN* (New York: New York University Press, 2008).
Wilkinson, A. R. 'Insurgency in Rhodesia 1957–73: An Account and Assessment. The Pearce Commission and Aftermath', *International Institute for Strategic Studies Adelphi Papers*, 13, 100 (1973), pp. 14–18.
Windrow, M. *The Last Valley: Dien Bien Phu and the French Defeat in Vietnam* (Cambridge MA, Da Capo Press, 2004).
Wiseman, H. & Taylor, A. *From Rhodesia to Zimbabwe: The Politics of Transition* (New York: Pergamon, 1982).
Wood, J. R. T. 'Countering the Chimurenga: The Rhodesian Counterinsurgency Campaign'. In D. Marston & C. Malkasian (eds.) *Counterinsurgency in Modern Warfare* (Oxford: Osprey, 2010).
Wood, J. R. T. 'Counter-punching on the Mudzi: D Company, 1st Rhodesian African Rifles, on Operation "Mardon" 1 November 1976', *Small Wars & Insurgencies*, 9, 2 (1998), pp. 64–82.
Wood, J. R. T. 'Fire Force: Helicopter Warfare in Rhodesia: 1962–1980' (1996). www.jrtwood.com/articleFfireforce.asp [Accessed June 2020].
Wood, J. R. T. *So Far and No Further! Rhodesia's Bid for Independence during the Retreat from Empire 1959–1965* (Bloomington, IN: Trafford, 2005).
Wood, J. R. T. *The War Diaries of Andre Dennison* (Durban: Ashanti, 1989).
Woodfork, J. 'Senegalese Soldiers in the Second World War: Loyalty and Identity Politics in the French Colonial Army' (Doctoral Thesis, University of Michigan, 2001).
Yap, K. 'Sites of Struggle: The Reorientation of Political Values in the Matabeleland Conflict, Zimbabwe 1980–1987', *African Sociological Review*, 6, 1 (2002), pp. 17–45.
Young, C. 'The End of the Post-colonial State in Africa? Reflections on Changing African Political Dynamics', *African Affairs*, 103, 410 (2004), pp. 23–49.

ZANU(PF). *Traitors Do Much Damage to National Goals* (Harare, ZANU PF Information and Publicity Department, 2004).
ZANU(PF). *Zimbabwe News*, 10, 5 (1978).
Zvobgo, E. 'For Black Zimbabwean Traitors This Is a Time of Crisis and Decision', *ZANU PF Information & Publicity Department*, 13 November 1978.

Index

1RAR, 14, 129, 139, 153, 216, 226, 229, 231
  A Company, 104, 106, 161
  C Company, 231
  D Company, 161, 173
  E Company, 107, 146
  Support Company, 169, 231, 234
2RAR, 119, 153, 160, 216
  A Company, 95, 135, 159, 169, 173, 236
  B Company, 115, 172
  C Company, 169
  Support Company, 106
3RAR, 120

Algerian War of Independence, 8, 28, 152, 153
AP Hotel, 217, 218
Apolitical ethos, 189
Apolitical identity, 38
Archives
  National Archives of Zimbabwe, 40
  Rhodesian Army Archive, 40
  Rhodesian government destruction, 39
Askari Platoon, 56
Assembly Points (APs), 212
Auxiliaries, 47–48

Basic training, 90
Battle of Bulawayo, 229
Beer Hall, 229
British Army
  Influence on RAR, 23
British Military Advisory and Training Team (BMATT), 224, 227
British South Africa Police (BSAP), 52, 54, 96
Burma, 5, 56, 69, 71

Central African Federation, 59
Chitungwiza, 228, 236
CIO, 81

CMF, 216
Colours, Regimental, 75
Commonwealth Monitoring Force (CMF), 135, 213
Counter-insurgency (COIN), 78

Desertion, 148
Discipline, 94
  Impermissible indiscipline, 97
  Permissible indiscipline, 95, 97
Disloyalty, 145
Drill, 90, 102

Entumbane, 228, 230

Federation of Rhodesia and Nyasaland, 59
Fifth Brigade, 241
Fireforce, 167
First Matabele War, 52
Flower, Ken, 119, 130, 221
Food, 115
Fort Victoria, 52, 66
Forward Air Fields, 167
French colonial army, 134, 146, 148
French colonial units, 18, 101, 111
Frontline Rhodesia documentary, 164

Grey's Scouts, 81, 135, 216, 236
Guard Force, 223
Guinea-Bissau, 211
Gutu, 66
Gwaai River Mine, 236
Gweru, 229, 236

Heliborne operations, 60

Indian Army, 34
Invented traditions, 62, 73
Israeli Defence Force, 36, 37

Jameson Raid, 52

281

282   Index

Karanga, 64, 67
Kenya
   Mau Mau conflict, 28
King's African Rifles (KAR), 145

Lancaster House, 213, 245
Llewellin Barracks, 100, 186
Loyalists, 28

MAG, 159
Malaya, 71, 77, 215
Malayan Emergency, 59, 69
Martial masculinity, 96, 175
'Martial races', 18
Masvingo, 52, 66, 69
Matabeleland Native Police, 53
Methuen Barracks, 71
Military culture, 89
Military socialisation, 192
Mnangagwa, Emmerson, 239
MPLA, 219
Mugabe, Robert, 1, 10, 221, 222
Music, military, 74, 76
Mutiny, 145

National Service, 207
Nhongo, Rex, 224, 225, 241, 243
Nkomo, Joshua, 233

Officers, 130
   Commissioning of black officers, 133
   'White African' officers, 135
Operation Sausage Machine, 227
Oral histories, 42

Parachuting, 104, 168
Parades, 74
Patriotic History, 8
Patriotism, 37
Platoon warrant officer (PWO), 138
Pongweni, Moses, 242
Portuguese
   Colonial war/liberation war, 28
   Colonial army, 211
Professionalism, 19, 101
   Engendering loyalty, 35
   Ethos, 22
   Theory, 22, 28, 29

Quenet Report, 128, 133

Racism, 110
   Integration of army units, 124
   Pay, 112
   Segregation, 123
Regimental loyalty, 19, 73

Rhodesia Native Regiment (RNR), 55
Rhodesian African Rifles (RAR)
   During World War II, 56
   Expansion of, 78
Rhodesian Air Force (RhAF), 165, 218
Rhodesian Armoured Car Regiment, 231
Rhodesian Army
   (Independent) Company, 126
   Recruitment criteria, 74, 88
   Strength, 84
Rhodesian Army Corps of Signals, 106, 114
Rhodesian Army Education Corps, 92, 114
Rhodesian Corps of Engineers, 80
Rhodesian Corps of Signals, 80
Rhodesian Front (RF), 77
Rhodesian Light Infantry (RLI), 78, 79, 121, 135, 197, 207, 216, 224
Rhodesian Special Air Service (RhSAS), 78, 122, 216
Rule, Kim, 139

Second Matabele War, 53
Security Force Auxiliaries (SFA), 107, 200, 223
Sellouts, 10
Selous Scouts, 81, 224
Settler colonies
   Propensity for warfare, 32
Social contract, 33
Soldierly identity, 86
South African Army, 37
Suez Canal, 59

Territorial Force (TF), 82, 135, 207
Tirailleurs Sénégalais, 146
Total institutions, 87, 99
Tracking, 158
Traditions (invented), 25
Training, 102

Unilateral Declaration of Independence (UDI), 121, 193

Vietnam, 146, 153, 211

Wafa Wafa, 124, 157
Walls, Peter, 59, 113, 121, 130, 214, 221

Zimbabwe African National Union ZANU(PF), 211, 213, 220
Zimbabwe African National Liberation Army (ZANLA), 1, 162, 212, 225
Zimbabwe National Army (ZNA), 204, 211
Zimbabwe People's Revolutionary Army (ZIPRA), 1, 162, 212, 220

African Studies Series

1. *City Politics: A Study of Leopoldville, 1962–63*, J.S. La Fontaine
2. *Studies in Rural Capitalism in West Africa*, Polly Hill
3. *Land Policy in Buganda*, Henry W. West
4. *The Nigerian Military: A Sociological Analysis of Authority and Revolt, 1960–67*, Robin Luckham
5. *The Ghanaian Factory Worker: Industrial Man in Africa*, Margaret Peil
6. *Labour in the South African Gold Mines*, Francis Wilson
7. *The Price of Liberty: Personality and Politics in Colonial Nigeria*, Kenneth W. J. Post and George D. Jenkins
8. *Subsistence to Commercial Farming in Present-Day Buganda: An Economic and Anthropological Survey*, Audrey I. Richards, Fort Sturrock, and Jean M. Fortt (eds.)
9. *Dependence and Opportunity: Political Change in Ahafo*, John Dunn and A. F. Robertson
10. *African Railwaymen: Solidarity and Opposition in an East African Labour Force*, R. D. Grillo
11. *Islam and Tribal Art in West Africa*, René A. Bravmann
12. *Modern and Traditional Elites in the Politics of Lagos*, P. D. Cole
13. *Asante in the Nineteenth Century: The Structure and Evaluation of a Political Order*, Ivor Wilks
14. *Culture, Tradition and Society in the West African Novel*, Emmanuel Obiechina
15. *Saints and Politicians*, Donal B. Cruise O'Brien
16. *The Lions of Dagbon: Political Change in Northern Ghana*, Martin Staniland
17. *Politics of Decolonization: Kenya Europeans and the Land Issue 1960–1965*, Gary B. Wasserman
18. *Muslim Brotherhoods in the Nineteenth-Century Africa*, B. G. Martin
19. *Warfare in the Sokoto Caliphate: Historical and Sociological Perspectives*, Joseph P. Smaldone
20. *Liberia and Sierra Leone: An Essay in Comparative Politics*, Christopher Clapham
21. *Adam Kok's Griquas: A Study in the Development of Stratification in South Africa*, Robert Ross
22. *Class, Power and Ideology in Ghana: The Railwaymen of Sekondi*, Richard Jeffries
23. *West African States: Failure and Promise*, John Dunn (ed.)
24. *Afrikaaners of the Kalahari: White Minority in a Black State*, Margo Russell and Martin Russell

25. *A Modern History of Tanganyika*, John Iliffe
26. *A History of African Christianity 1950–1975*, Adrian Hastings
27. *Slaves, Peasants and Capitalists in Southern Angola, 1840–1926*, W. G. Clarence-Smith
28. *The Hidden Hippopotamus: Reappraised in African History: The Early Colonial Experience in Western Zambia*, GywnPrins
29. *Families Divided: The Impact of Migrant Labour in Lesotho*, Colin Murray
30. *Slavery, Colonialism and Economic Growth in Dahomey, 1640–1960*, Patrick Manning
31. *Kings, Commoners and Concessionaries: The Evolution of Dissolution of the Nineteenth-Century Swazi State*, Philip Bonner
32. *Oral Poetry and Somali Nationalism: The Case of Sayid Mahammad 'Abdille Hasan*, Said S. Samatar
33. *The Political Economy of Pondoland 1860–1930*, William Beinart
34. *Volkskapitalisme: Class, Capitals and Ideology in the Development of Afrikaner Nationalism, 1934–1948*, Dan O'Meara
35. *The Settler Economies: Studies in the Economic History of Kenya and Rhodesia 1900–1963*, Paul Mosely
36. *Transformations in Slavery: A History of Slavery in Africa, 1st edition*, Paul Lovejoy
37. *Amilcar Cabral: Revolutionary Leadership and People's War*, Patrick Chabal
38. *Essays on the Political Economy of Rural Africa*, Robert H. Bates
39. *Ijeshas and Nigerians: The Incorporation of a Yoruba Kingdom, 1890s–1970s*, J. D. Y. Peel
40. *Black People and the South African War, 1899–1902*, Peter Warwick
41. *A History of Niger 1850–1960*, Finn Fuglestad
42. *Industrialisation and Trade Union Organization in South Africa, 1924–1955*, Stephen Ellis
43. *The Rising of the Red Shawls: A Revolt in Madagascar 1895–1899*, Stephen Ellis
44. *Slavery in Dutch South Africa*, Nigel Worden
45. *Law, Custom and Social Order: The Colonial Experience in Malawi and Zambia*, Martin Chanock
46. *Salt of the Desert Sun: A History of Salt Production and Trade in the Central Sudan*, Paul E. Lovejoy
47. *Marrying Well: Marriage, Status and Social Change among the Educated Elite in Colonial Lagos*, Kristin Mann
48. *Language and Colonial Power: The Appropriation of Swahili in the Former Belgian Congo, 1880–1938*, Johannes Fabian

49. *The Shell Money of the Slave Trade*, Jan Hogendorn and Marion Johnson
50. *Political Domination in Africa*, Patrick Chabal
51. *The Southern Marches of Imperial Ethiopia: Essays in History and Social Anthropology*, Donald Donham and Wendy James
52. *Islam and Urban Labor in Northern Nigeria: The Making of a Muslim Working Class*, Paul M. Lubeck
53. *Horn and Crescent: Cultural Change and Traditional Islam on the East African Coast, 800–1900*, Randall L. Pouwels
54. *Capital and Labour on the Kimberley Diamond Fields, 1871–1890*, Robert Vicat Turrell
55. *National and Class Conflict in the Horn of Africa*, John Markakis
56. *Democracy and Prebendal Politics in Nigeria: The Rise and Fall of the Second Republic*, Richard A. Joseph
57. *Entrepreneurs and Parasites: The Struggle for Indigenous Capitalism in Zaire*, Janet MacGaffey
58. *The African Poor: A History*, John Iliffe
59. *Palm Oil and Protest: An Economic History of the Ngwa Region, South-Eastern Nigeria, 1800–1980*, Susan M. Martin
60. *France and Islam in West Africa, 1860–1960*, Christopher Harrison
61. *Transformation and Continuity in Revolutionary Ethiopia*, Christopher Clapham
62. *Prelude to the Mahdiyya: Peasants and Traders in the Shendi Region, 1821–1885*, Anders Bjorkelo
63. *Wa and the Wala: Islam and Polity in Northwestern Ghana*, Ivor Wilks
64. *H.C. Bankole-Bright and Politics in Colonial Sierra Leone, 1919–1958*, Akintola Wyse
65. *Contemporary West African States*, Donal Cruise O'Brien, John Dunn, and Richard Rathbone (eds.)
66. *The Oromo of Ethiopia: A History, 1570–1860*, Mohammed Hassen
67. *Slavery and African Life: Occidental, Oriental, and African Slave Trades*, Patrick Manning
68. *Abraham Esau's War: A Black South African War in the Cape, 1899–1902*, Bill Nasson
69. *The Politics of Harmony: Land Dispute Strategies in Swaziland*, Laurel L. Rose
70. *Zimbabwe's Guerrilla War: Peasant Voices*, Norma J. Kriger
71. *Ethiopia: Power and Protest: Peasant Revolts in the Twentieth-Century*, Gebru Tareke
72. *White Supremacy and Black Resistance in Pre-Industrial South Africa: The Making of the Colonial Order in the Eastern Cape, 1770–1865*, Clifton C. Crais

73. *The Elusive Granary: Herder, Farmer, and State in Northern Kenya*, Peter D. Little
74. *The Kanyok of Zaire: An Institutional and Ideological History to 1895*, John C. Yoder
75. *Pragmatism in the Age of Jihad: The Precolonial State of Bundu*, Michael A. Gomez
76. *Slow Death for Slavery: The Course of Abolition in Northern Nigeria, 1897–1936*, Paul E. Lovejoy and Jan S. Hogendorn
77. *West African Slavery and Atlantic Commerce: The Senegal River Valley, 1700–1860*, James F. Searing
78. *A South African Kingdom: The Pursuit of Security in the Nineteenth-Century Lesotho*, Elizabeth A. Elredge
79. *State and Society in Pre-colonial Asante*, T. C. McCaskie
80. *Islamic Society and State Power in Senegal: Disciples and Citizens in Fatick*, Leonardo A. Villalon
81. *Ethnic Pride and Racial Prejudice in Victorian Cape Town: Group Identity and Social Practice*, Vivian Bickford-Smith
82. *The Eritrean Struggle for Independence: Domination, Resistance and Nationalism, 1941–1993*, Ruth Iyob
83. *Corruption and State Politics in Sierra Leone*, William Reno
84. *The Culture of Politics in Modern Kenya*, Angelique Haugerud
85. *Africans: The History of a Continent, 1st edition*, John Iliffe
86. *From Slave Trade to 'Legitimate' Commerce: The Commercial Transition in Nineteenth-Century West Africa*, Robin Law (ed.)
87. *Leisure and Society in Colonial Brazzaville*, Phyllis Martin
88. *Kingship and State: The Buganda Dynasty*, Christopher Wrigley
89. *Decolonialization and African Life: The Labour Question in French and British Africa*, Frederick Cooper
90. *Misreading the African Landscape: Society and Ecology in an African Forest-Savannah Mosaic*, James Fairhead, and Melissa Leach
91. *Peasant Revolution in Ethiopia: The Tigray People's Liberation Front, 1975–1991*, John Young
92. *Senegambia and the Atlantic Slave Trade*, Boubacar Barry
93. *Commerce and Economic Change in West Africa: The Oil Trade in the Nineteenth Century*, Martin Lynn
94. *Slavery and French Colonial Rule in West Africa: Senegal, Guinea and Mali*, Martin A. Klein
95. *East African Doctors: A History of the Modern Profession*, John Iliffe
96. *Middlemen of the Cameroons Rivers: The Duala and Their Hinterland, c.1600–1960*, Ralph Derrick, Ralph A. Austen, and Jonathan Derrick

97. *Masters and Servants on the Cape Eastern Frontier, 1760–1803*, Susan Newton-King
98. *Status and Respectability in the Cape Colony, 1750–1870: A Tragedy of Manners*, Robert Ross
99. *Slaves, Freedmen and Indentured Laborers in Colonial Mauritius*, Richard B. Allen
100. *Transformations in Slavery: A History of Slavery in Africa*, 2nd edition, Paul E. Lovejoy
101. *The Peasant Cotton Revolution in West Africa: Cote d'Ivoire, 1880–1995*, Thomas J. Bassett
102. *Re-imagining Rwanda: Conflict, Survival and Disinformation in the Late Twentieth Century*, Johan Pottier
103. *The Politics of Evil: Magic, State Power and the Political Imagination in South Africa*, Clifton Crais
104. *Transforming Mozambique: The Politics of Privatization, 1975–2000*, M. Anne Pitcher
105. *Guerrilla Veterans in Post-War Zimbabwe: Symbolic and Violent Politics, 1980–1987*, Norma J. Kriger
106. *An Economic History of Imperial Madagascar, 1750–1895: The Rise and Fall of an Island Empire*, Gwyn Campbell
107. *Honour in African History*, John Iliffe
108. *Africans: A History of a Continent*, 2nd edition, John Iliffe
109. *Guns, Race, and Power in Colonial South Africa*, William Kelleher Storey
110. *Islam and Social Change in French West Africa: History of an Emancipatory Community*, Sean Hanretta
111. *Defeating Mau Mau, Creating Kenya: Counterinsurgency, Civil War and Decolonization*, Daniel Branch
112. *Christianity and Genocide in Rwanda*, Timothy Longman
113. *From Africa to Brazil: Culture, Identity, and an African Slave Trade, 1600–1830*, Walter Hawthorne
114. *Africa in the Time of Cholera: A History of Pandemics from 1817 to the Present*, Myron Echenberg
115. *A History of Race in Muslim West Africa, 1600–1960*, Bruce S. Hall
116. *Witchcraft and Colonial Rule in Kenya, 1900–1955*, Katherine Luongo
117. *Transformations in Slavery: A History of Slavery in Africa*, 3rd edition, Paul E. Lovejoy
118. *The Rise of the Trans-Atlantic Slave Trade in Western Africa, 1300–1589*, Toby Green
119. *Party Politics and Economic Reform in Africa's Democracies*, M. Anne Pitcher

120. *Smugglers and Saints of the Sahara: Regional Connectivity in the Twentieth Century*, Judith Scheele
121. *Cross-Cultural Exchange in the Atlantic World: Angola and Brazil during the Era of the Slave Trade*, Roquinaldo Ferreira
122. *Ethnic Patriotism and the East African Revival*, Derek Peterson
123. *Black Morocco: A History of Slavery and Islam*, Chouki El Hamel
124. *An African Slaving Port and the Atlantic World: Benguela and Its Hinterland*, Mariana Candido
125. *Making Citizens in Africa: Ethnicity, Gender, and National Identity in Ethiopia*, Lahra Smith
126. *Slavery and Emancipation in Islamic East Africa: From Honor to Respectability*, Elisabeth McMahon
127. *A History of African Motherhood: The Case of Uganda, 700–1900*, Rhiannon Stephens
128. *The Borders of Race in Colonial South Africa: The Kat River Settlement, 1829–1856*, Robert Ross
129. *From Empires to NGOs in the West African Sahel: The Road to Nongovernmentality*, Gregory Mann
130. *Dictators and Democracy in African Development: The Political Economy of Good Governance in Nigeria*, A. Carl LeVan
131. *Water, Civilization and Power in Sudan: The Political Economy of Military-Islamist State Building*, Harry Verhoeven
132. *The Fruits of Freedom in British Togoland: Literacy, Politics and Nationalism, 1914–2014*, Kate Skinner
133. *Political Thought and the Public Sphere in Tanzania: Freedom, Democracy and Citizenship in the Era of Decolonization*, Emma Hunter
134. *Political Identity and Conflict in Central Angola, 1975–2002*, Justin Pearce
135. *From Slavery to Aid: Politics, Labour, and Ecology in the Nigerian Sahel, 1800–2000*, Benedetta Rossi
136. *National Liberation in Postcolonial Southern Africa: A Historical Ethnography of SWAPO's Exile Camps*, Christian A. Williams
137. *Africans: A History of a Continent*, 3rd edition, John Iliffe
138. *Colonial Buganda and the End of Empire: Political Thought and Historical Imagination in Africa*, Jonathon L. Earle
139. *The Struggle over State Power in Zimbabwe: Law and Politics since 1950*, George Karekwaivanane
140. *Transforming Sudan: Decolonisation, Economic Development and State Formation*, Alden Young
141. *Colonizing Consent: Rape and Governance in South Africa's Eastern Cape*, Elizabeth Thornberry

142. *The Value of Disorder: Autonomy, Prosperity and Plunder in the Chadian Sahara*, Julien Brachet and Judith Scheele
143. *The Politics of Poverty: Policy-Making and Development in Rural Tanzania*, Felicitas Becker
144. *Boundaries, Communities, and State-Making in West Africa: The Centrality of the Margins*, Paul Nugent
145. *Politics and Violence in Burundi: The Language of Truth in an Emerging State*, Aidan Russell
146. *Power and the Presidency in Kenya: The Jomo Kenyatta Years*, Anaïs Angelo
147. *East Africa after Liberation: Conflict, Security and the State since the 1980s*, Jonathan Fisher
148. *Sultan, Caliph, and the Renewer of the Faith: Ahmad Lobbo, the Tārīkh al-fattāsh and the Making of an Islamic State in West Africa*, Mauro Nobili
149. *Shaping the African Savannah: From Capitalist Frontier to Arid Eden in Namibia*, Michael Bollig
150. *France's Wars in Chad: Military Intervention and Decolonization in Africa*, Nathaniel K. Powell
151. *Islam, Ethnicity, and Conflict in Ethiopia: The Bale Insurgency, 1963–1970*, Terje Østebø
152. *The Path to Genocide in Rwanda: Security, Opportunity, and Authority in an Ethnocratic State*, Omar Shahabudin McDoom
153. *Development, (Dual) Citizenship and Its Discontents in Africa: The Political Economy of Belonging to Liberia*, Robtel Neajai Pailey
154. *Salafism and Political Order in Africa*, Sebastian Elischer
155. *Performing Power in Zimbabwe: Politics, Law and the Courts since 2000*, Susanne Verheul
156. *Revolutionary State-Making in Dar es Salaam: African Liberation and the Global Cold War, 1961–1974*, George Roberts
157. *Race and Diplomacy in Zimbabwe: The Cold War and Decolonization, 1960–1984*, Timothy Lewis Scarnecchia
158. *Conflicts of Colonialism: The Rule of Law, French Soudan, and Faama Mademba Sèye*, Richard L. Roberts
159. *Invoking the Invisible in the Sahara: Islam, Spiritual Mediation, and Social Change*, Erin Pettigrew
160. *Wealth, Land, and Property in Angola: A History of Dispossession, Slavery and Inequality*, Mariana P. Candido
161. *Trajectories of Authoritarianism in Rwanda: Elusive Control before the Genocide*, Marie-Eve Desrosiers
162. *Plunder for Profit: A Socio-environmental History of Tobacco Farming in Southern Rhodesia and Zimbabwe*, Elijah Doro

163. *Navigating Local Transitional Justice: Agency at Work in Post-Conflict Sierra Leone*, Laura S. Martin
164. *Arming Black Consciousness: The Azanian Black Nationalist Tradition and South Africa's Armed Struggle*, Toivo Tukongeni Paul Wilson Asheeke
165. *Child Slavery and Guardianship in Colonial Senegal*, Bernard Moitt
166. *African Military Politics in the Sahel: Regional Organizations and International Politics*, Katharina P.W. Döring
167. *Black Soldiers in the Rhodesian Army: Colonialism, Professionalism, and Race*, M. T. Howard